Reimagining (Bio)Medicalization, Pharmaceuticals and Genetics

In recent years medicalization, the process of making something medical, has gained considerable ground and a position in everyday discourse. In this multidisciplinary collection of original essays, the authors expertly consider how issues around medicalization have developed, ways in which it is changing and the potential shapes it will take in the future. They develop a unique argument that medicalization, biomedicalization, pharmaceuticalization and geneticization are related and coevolving processes, present throughout the globe. This is an ideal addition to anthropology, sociology and STS courses about medicine and health.

Susan E. Bell is A. Myrick Freeman Professor of Social Sciences/Professor of Sociology and Chair of the Department of Sociology and Anthropology, Bowdoin College. She is the author of *DES Daughters: Embodied Knowledge and the Transformation of Women's Health Politics* (Temple, 2009) and the guest editor with Alan Radley of a special issue of *health*, "Another Way of Knowing: Art, Disease, and Illness Experience" (2011).

Anne E. Figert is Associate Professor of Sociology at Loyola University Chicago. She is the author of *Women and the Ownership of PMS: The Structuring of a Psychiatric Disorder* (Aldine de Gruyter, 1996) and the co-editor of *Building Community: Social Science in Action* (Pine Forge Pr* *Current Research on Occupations and Professions*, volume 9 (JAI

Titles of Related Interest from Routledge

Health and Human Rights in a Changing World
Edited by Michael Grodin, Daniel Tarantola, George Annas, Sofia Gruskin

The Disability Studies Reader, Fourth Edition
Edited by Lennard J. Davis

Pain and Suffering
Ronald Schleifer

Sex/Gender: Biology in a Social World
Anne Fausto-Sterling

Depression: Integrating Science, Culture, and Humanities
Bradley Lewis

Autism
Stuart Murray

Reimagining (Bio)Medicalization, Pharmaceuticals and Genetics

Old Critiques and New Engagements

Edited by Susan E. Bell
& Anne E. Figert

Routledge
Taylor & Francis Group

NEW YORK AND LONDON

First published 2015
by Routledge
711 Third Avenue, New York, NY 10017

and by Routledge
2 Park Square, Milton Park, Abingdon, Oxon, OX14 4RN

Routledge is an imprint of the Taylor & Francis Group, an informa business

Library of Congress Cataloging in Publication Data
Reimagining (bio)medicalization, pharmaceuticals and genetics : old critiques and new engagements / edited by Susan E. Bell & Anne E. Figert.
    p. ; cm.
    Includes bibliographical references and index.
    I. Bell, Susan E., editor.   II. Figert, Anne E., editor.
    [DNLM: 1. Medicalization.   2. Drug Industry—trends.   3. Drug Therapy—trends.
    4. Genetic Phenomena. WA 31]
    RS380
    338.4'76153—dc23   2014033649

ISBN: 978-1-138-79370-5 (hbk)
ISBN: 978-1-138-79371-2 (pbk)
ISBN: 978-1-315-76092-6 (ebk)

Typeset in Minion Pro
by Keystroke, Station Road, Codsall, Wolverhampton

Printed and bound in the United States of America by Publishers Graphics, LLC on sustainably sourced paper.

Contents

Foreword

Nearly forty years ago when I was in the midst of writing my PhD dissertation, "Identifying Hyperactive Children," as a deviance-labeling study, a colleague of mine suggested I read an article by Irving Kenneth Zola on "Medicine as an Institution of Social Control." This article introduced me to the term "medicalization," creating a huge intellectual a-ha; yes, that's what I'm studying, the medicalization of deviant behavior. This article, published in a modest British sociological journal, changed the analytic focus of my dissertation, reshaped the trajectory of my career, and in significant ways helped to broaden the horizons of medical sociology. This volume, so many decades later, reflects on how issues around medicalization have developed over the years and, perhaps more importantly, examines ways in which it is changing in the present and likely in the future.

As explicated in this volume there are numerous ways medicalization and related concepts are formulated. As a point of departure, in its most basic common-sense form it means "to make medical." A more formal definition sees medicalization as the process by which previously nonmedical problems become defined and treated as medical problems, usually as diseases or disorders. The emphasis in this perspective is on "process" and "definition." Without going into great detail here, I want to present what I see as five major characteristics of medicalization. (1) The definitional issue is key to medicalization, i.e., how a problem is defined is key to what is done about it. (2) There are degrees of medicalization; some problems are fully medicalized, some partly medicalized and others barely medicalized. There can be contestation and disagreement about a problem's medicalized status. (3) Medicalized categories are elastic and can expand or contract. (4) Physician or other medical personnel involvement in medicalization is variable; sometimes medical professionals are essential to medicalization, sometimes they are marginal or even nonexistent. (5) Medicalization is bidirectional, i.e., there can be demedicalization as well as medicalization. In my view, medicalization research does not adjudicate whether or not an entity is "really" a medical problem, but rather how it became to be depicted (and accepted) as a medical problem and with what consequences. While some authors in this volume may contest some of these characteristics, all would probably agree that over the past four decades there has been much more medicalization than demedicalization and this also makes this volume significant and timely.

Some critics often conflate medicalization with overmedicalization and use the term almost as an epithet. They work from the assumption that medicalization is a "bad" thing. But it is easy to come up with examples where medicalization has had positive effects, e.g., epilepsy as a disease not a curse and, most recently, treatments for chronic pain. The authors in this volume avoid this trap, by examining the processes and consequences of medicalization (and its related concepts). Analysts like the ones contributing to this volume consider issues like genetics or race as social scientists would examine any social phenomena. What makes the big difference here are the various conceptual tools they use to render their scholarly examination.

Medicalization as a concept has moved from being a fundamentally sociological idea to one used by a wide range of academic disciplines. I have read studies of medicalization by historians, anthropologists, physicians, bioethicists, economists, literary scholars, media studies researchers, feminist scholars and numerous others. The concept carries analytical weight in a wide range of academic disciplines and has even been found in the news and public media. When I first studied medicalization issues I would need to explain what I meant by the term; by now I find widespread understanding about what the term means and why it is significant to study it. This might result from more writing about medicalization or perhaps from a wider public experience with more medicalized problems in society.

Since around 1990 we have seen a number of changes related to medicalization. We have witnessed an enormous growth in the pharmaceutical industry, especially behavior- and mental health-related drugs, including blockbuster drugs like Viagra and Prozac. Following the Human Genome Project, increased attention has been paid to the impact of genetics on behavior, conditions and even new areas like genetic approaches to ancestry. While the medical profession maintains some of its historic authority, there are new challenges to medical authority from health insurance companies, patients becoming more like consumers and medical industries. While most of medicalization has been manifested in the USA and in Europe, we are beginning to see an increased globalization of medicalized approaches through the multinational drug industry, the export of Western medicine's categories and approaches and the rise of the Internet. In short, one could see important changes in medicalization by the turn of the century.

It is thus not surprising that medicalization studies have begot new conceptual frames such as biomedicalization, pharmaceuticalization and geneticization. These concepts are all related to medicalization in fundamental ways, but take the study of medically related expansion in new and different directions. As a longtime purveyor of medicalization studies, I may have some differences with how these perspectives relate to what we have long called medicalization. But it is quite apparent individually and together these newer approaches expand the purview of analysis deeper into areas of research that include medical technology, scientific research, human genetics, the pharmaceutical industry and into new and important areas like race and ancestry. This volume builds upon medicalization studies, extending the scope, criticizing the limits, extolling newer and independent analytical perspectives. The editors, authors and commentators endeavor to take the next step in medicalization related research.

The editors are to be congratulated for assembling such a multidisciplinary and distinguished group of contributors and encouraging them to look forward into an increasingly globalized world, whatever conceptual framework they adopt. As the title indicates, the goal is reimagining old and new conceptual frameworks. Indeed, one of the most refreshing aspects of this volume is its commitment to looking forward while remaining grounded in the past. This is a most compelling volume and well worthy of our close attention.

Peter Conrad
Brandeis University, July 2014

Acknowledgments

First we would first like to thank the authors of this collection. They have been thoughtful and insightful contributors to our ongoing conversation, often under tight deadlines. We also want to acknowledge our home institutions Bowdoin College and Loyola University Chicago. Cristle Collins Judd, the Dean for Academic Affairs at Bowdoin College, provided funds for a symposium "Big Pharma, Big Medicine and Technoscience: Investigating Intersections in the Twenty-first Century" at Bowdoin in September 2013 that brought many the authors together. Our colleagues and staff in the Department of Sociology and Anthropology at Bowdoin College and the Department of Sociology at Loyola University Chicago provided assistance and support. We especially thank Emily Hricko and Lori Brackett (Bowdoin) for their assistance with the Symposium and Megan Klein and Amanda Counts (Loyola) for research assistance. A very early conversation with Bernice Pescosolido helped to launch our partnership. We have benefited from conversations with Adele Clarke, Steve Epstein, Jonathan Gabe, Kelly Joyce, Laura Mamo, Kelly Moore, Susan Reverby, Judith Wittner, Rhys Williams, Femi Vaughan and our students. We would also like to thank audiences at the American Sociological Association, International Sociological Association and British Sociological Association Medical Sociology group for responses to early versions of our work and the reviewers of the collection for later constructive critiques. Steve Rutter and Margaret Moore at Routledge have supported this project with enthusiasm. We are grateful to Abelardo Morell for giving us permission to use the photograph "Falling Coins #2, 2006" for the cover of the book. We would also like to thank the reviewers for their feedback:

Elizabeth Rowe	Purdue University
James Anderson	Purdue University
Deborah Merrill	Clark University
Alan Horwitz	Rutgers
Joseph Davis	University of Virginia
Stefan Timmermans	University of California, Los Angeles
Kristin Barker	University of New Mexico
Elianne Riska	University of Helsinki
Anne Pollock	Georgia Tech
Joan Busfield	University of Essex

Finally, we thank our families for their continued love and support.

Introduction
Outlining Old Critiques and New Engagements

SUSAN E. BELL AND ANNE E. FIGERT

The discourse of health and disease is everywhere. Advertisements for pharmaceuticals to treat erectile dysfunction, HIV and menstrual suppression or vaccines for human papillomavirus (HPV) and whooping cough circulate on billboards, public transportation and in physicians' offices. Science and medical news contains daily stories of whether or not caesarean sections cause epigenetic changes and the record growing profit of international pharmaceutical companies. Google News has a link on its home page for Health in which we can learn about health issues around the world 24/7. People post health and medicine studies to Facebook, Twitter and other social media. In July 2014, the "What's New" section of the US Centers for Disease Control and Prevention Website features a story about an outbreak of Ebola in Guinea, Liberia and Sierra Leone in West Africa. There seems to be a pill, medical treatment, shot or vaccine for almost everything ranging from asthma to zygomycosis. In short, we are more aware and talk more about our own bodily conditions and those of people around the world than ever before.

In the 1970s, social scientists developed the concept of medicalization to capture this expanding discourse of health and disease. "Medicalization" refers to the process of defining problems in terms of illnesses or disorders and treating them with medical interventions (Zola 1972). Whether it is hyperactivity or Attention Deficit Hyperactivity Disorder (ADHD) (Conrad 1976), Premenstrual Syndrome (PMS) (Figert 1996) or shyness (Lane 2007), medicine has a diagnosis and offers treatment for these conditions. Medicalization has been a hugely successful concept for sociologists. In their executive summary of a special issue of the *Journal of Health and Social Behavior* celebrating 50 Years of Medical Sociology, Katherine Rosich and Janet Hankin write that medicalization is one of the key and enduring concepts that sociologists have contributed to understanding health and healthcare (Rosich and Hankin 2010:S1). Scholars from related disciplines and professions (including physicians) now use the term consistently to refer to the process of making something medical. In many ways, medicalization has joined the list of sociological terms such as "bureaucracy" (Weber 1946), "social stigma" (Durkheim 1982[1895]; Goffman 1963), "strength of weak ties" (Granovetter 1973) and "cultural capital" (Bourdieu 1986) that have migrated into the public vernacular.

1

In the past decade, scholars in sociology, anthropology, history, Science and Technology Studies (STS) and others have been reviewing the capacity of the concept of medicalization to explain complex and often contradictory global interactions among medicine, the pharmaceutical industry and fields of science and technology. Three "-izations" appear to be the most visible additions to the concept of medicalization: pharmaceuticalization, geneticization and biomedicalization.[1] At issue in each "-ization" is what (if anything) the new concept adds. For example in a study of the relationship between medicalization and genetics in mental illness, homosexuality and susceptibility to chemical exposures, Shostak, Conrad and Horwitz (2008:S310) conclude that "genetic information does not always lead to geneticization, nor does geneticization inevitably lead to medicalization." Geneticization occurs when differences between individuals are reduced to their DNA codes (Lippman 1991). Both "-izations" are useful because they bring different processes into focus. Sometimes the processes overlap, and sometimes they do not.

Similarly, in an early discussion of the role of British newspaper coverage in the social construction of a drug to promote wakefulness, Williams et al. (2008:850) argue that pharmaceuticalization, finding pharmaceutical solutions to problems, "overlaps with but extends far beyond the realms of the medical or the medicalized." Based on their analysis of newspaper coverage about the wakefulness drug Modafinil (brand name Provigil), they conclude that "(t)o the extent, indeed, that press concerns about the potential uptake of this drug cluster around or centre on its actual or potential non-medical uses and abuses, then what we see here is the articulation or amplification of a series of cultural anxieties about the pharmaceuticalisation rather than the medicalisation of alertness, sleepiness and everyday/night life" (Williams et al. 2008:851). In their view, pharmaceuticalization captures a distinctly different process in this case of expanding pharmaceutical use than does medicalization, and thus this "-ization" is a necessary additional conceptual tool.

The third "-ization" – biomedicalization – was proposed to remedy the limitations of medicalization to capture the complex and multidirectional processes of a new era in medicine, that of late modernity and technoscience (Clarke et al. 2003). In this formulation, medicalization and biomedicalization are useful for explaining processes in different eras. The emphasis of this "-ization" is on the demand of different eras for different conceptual tools. Like the other "-izations," the processes that biomedicalization describes exceed the capacity of medicalization. Yet eras are "fuzzily bounded and bleed into one another" and thus older processes are usually "available somewhere" (Clarke et al. 2010:108) and where they are available, medicalization is the right tool for the job of understanding them.

To put it simply, medicalization is a capacious concept but it may not fully capture the global dynamics of biomedicalization, the pharmaceutical industry and technologies of genetics in medicine. In this book, we and the contributing authors consider the utility of additional concepts – biomedicalization, pharmaceuticalization and geneticization – along with medicalization, for explaining these global interactions.

Each of us began to study medicalization in the 1980s (Bell 1986, 1990; Figert 1996, 2011). More recently we have participated in the review of medicalization's capacity to make sense of what is going on today. We first joined forces to rethink this "-ization" when we were invited to write a chapter about medicalization and gender (Bell and Figert 2010). In the chapter we argued that by "continually expanding the concept of medicalization we risk losing its power to capture the processes and consequences of defining problems in medical terms and using medical interventions to treat them. At the same time, without the nuance provided by concepts such as biomedicalization, pharmaceuticalization and geneticization, we also risk losing the ability to capture these very real processes" (Bell and Figert 2010:119). Initially, we outlined an argument for thinking simultaneously about these different concepts and processes. That work led to essays about the intersections between medicalization and expanding use of pharmaceuticals (Bell and Figert 2012a) and the relationship between global clinical pharmaceutical trials and the pharmaceuticalization of public health (Figert and Bell 2014).

In September 2013 we brought together many of the book's authors for a Symposium at Bowdoin College where we adopted the model of papers followed by critical reflective commentaries at the end of each session. The book reflects the discussion that began at the Symposium. We have also added new voices to the conversation by inviting scholars whose research focuses on the global South. In addition, the collection follows through on our efforts to bring multiple fields of knowledge into dialogue: sociologists, anthropologists, science and technology scholars and historians are all brought together in this volume. The present collection is a continuation of our efforts to promote thinking simultaneously with these different "-izations."

The two key papers that proved to be the major impetus for our collaboration have produced a conversation in what we now call "old critiques" and "new engagements" in medical sociology, anthropology and science and technology studies. The first was published in 2003 in the *American Sociological Review* by Adele Clarke and her collaborators at the University of California, San Francisco (Clarke et al. 2003). They wrote that medicalization, as previously defined, insufficiently captured what was going on as a result of tremendous changes in scientific medicine since the 1980s. The concept of biomedicalization might be a more accurate description of the "increasingly complex, multisited, multidirectional processes of medicalization, [processes that are] both extended and reconstituted through the new social forms of highly technoscientific biomedicine" (Clarke et al. 2003:161). Peter Conrad of Brandeis University responded to Clarke et al. in his Leo J. Reeder Award Lecture at the Annual Meetings of the American Sociological Association in 2004, subsequently published in the *Journal of Health and Social Behavior* (2005). Conrad also noted the changes that had occurred in modern medicine (which he calls "the shifting engines") and although he called for a re-examination of medicalization, argued "the definitional center of medicalization remains constant" (Conrad 2005:5). Conrad argued against the need for a new concept. What had changed were shifting engines of medicalization, including many of the processes described by Clarke et al. as biomedicalization such as "biotechnology (especially the pharmaceutical industry and genetics), consumers, and managed care" (Conrad 2005:5). The availability of new pharmaceuticals and the possibility of new genetic treatments increasingly drive new medical categories, and Conrad challenged sociologists to study these emergent engines of medicalization in the twenty-first century:

> This means examining the impact of biotechnological discoveries, the influence of pharmaceutical industry marketing and promotion, the role of consumer demand, the facilitating and constraining aspects of managed care and health insurance, the impact of the Internet, the changing role of the medical profession and physicians, and the pockets of medical and popular resistance to medicalization. This means supplementing our social constructionist studies with political economic perspectives. Medicalization still doesn't occur without social actors doing something to make an entity medical, but the engines that are driving medicalization have changed and we need to refocus our sociological eye as the medicalization train moves into the twenty-first century. (Conrad 2005:11–12)

Most simply the question is: is the addition of "shifting engines" of *medicalization* best suited for describing and understanding science and medicine in the twenty-first century or is a new concept altogether, such as "*biomedicalization*," sometimes required?

Scholars in many disciplines, working in many different national settings, writing in hundreds of publications have been reviewing the capacity of medicalization and biomedicalization (both as terms and as processes) to explain complex and often contradictory global interactions among medicine, the pharmaceutical industry and products of science and technology. The complex interactions between science and technology are conveyed by the word "technoscience."[2] Technoscience is a conjunction of two words that refer to two streams of activity traditionally viewed as separated and separable into "(basic) science" and "(applied) technology." By the mid-1980s the two streams of activity had merged and become almost inseparable. In the late twentieth century, innovations were more and more likely "to be hybrid ones ... generated simultaneously through sciences and technologies and new social forms – most often computer and information technologies and the organizational structures developed to articulate them into the flows of biomedical and related work"

(Clarke et al. 2010:65). Thus, technoscience is a hybrid word that represents a hybrid activity.

If we open up a new set of questions with newer terms and analyses, then we can move sideways to analyze new or evolving social phenomena. Sometimes and in some places, we need to resort to old definitions and old critiques because there are still unanswered questions and particular dynamics that are best explored using these old definitions and critiques. We, and the authors in this book, are wrestling with being comfortable with complexity that the social world creates and presents to us. The old critiques bound up with medicalization theory have a kind of precision, dividing practices, forcefulness and "truth" that rarely occur today. Many of the same issues involve circularity, flexibility, contradictions and multi-sitedness that are not as straightforward or precise and demand new engagements.

Neither Clarke et al. (2003) nor Conrad (2005) specifically used the words "pharmaceuticalization" or "geneticization" in their exchange. But in the past decade scholarship about these other "-izations" has begun to take shape, and scholars have asked whether these new concepts are required. This collection capitalizes on emerging work in the study of medicalization and global health and at the same time contributes to debates by presenting empirical and theoretical papers from sociological, anthropological, historical and STS perspectives. In line with a more global focus, most of the authors locate their analyses within the context of the historical shift to forms of neoliberal governance in the late twentieth century. Moore et al. (2011) provide a guiding definition and perspective about technoscientific knowledge production under neoliberalism.[3] In their work they observe that

> [O]ne common characteristic of neoliberalism at a global level is the new power of owners of large, multinational corporations that benefit from economic policies associated with innovation, trade liberalization, reduced government spending on entitlements and decreased state restrictions on labor, health, and environmental hazards of production. (Moore et al. 2011:507)

In this collection, many of the authors use the concept of neoliberalism to analyze global pharmaceuticals, the creation of gendered and racial categories and the global genomic mapping conducted by both governmental and private corporations. In their analyses, they point out how neoliberal practices and ideologies affect global health and systems of healthcare.

Organization of the Collection

The book's title, *Reimagining (Bio)Medicalization, Pharmaceuticals and Genetics*, lists the themes discussed in each of the sections. The parentheses around the word "biomedicalization" unsettle and draw attention to the conversation begun by Clarke et al. (2003) and Conrad (2005). The book's subtitle, "Old Critiques and New Engagements," points backward to old critiques of medicalization and forward to the possibility of new transnational and interdisciplinary engagements. We designed the organization of the book and the individual contributions to reflect our commitment to a global perspective and to transnationality and interdisciplinarity. The book is divided into three parts: reimaginings of (bio)medicalization, pharmaceuticals and genetics/genomics. The theme of each part is discussed below. We asked chapter authors to draw from their current research and to take into account some or all of the following topics: the global circulation of pharmaceuticals, medicine and technoscience; the global, national and local sites in which these processes or objects circulate; and the intersections and variations from one global site to another. We asked commentators to conclude each part by picking up and extending the discussion in light of old engagements and new critiques.

Part I: Reimaginings: (Bio)Medicalization and Technoscience in the Twenty-First Century

All three chapters in this part start with medicalization, and reimagine it in light of twenty-first century technoscience, illness and disease. The authors ask the following questions: What is medicalization's history and how is it useful today? How are the "-izations" (pharmaceuticalization, biomedicalization, geneticization) defined, and how are scholars in medical sociology, anthropology and science and technology studies employing them? What does it mean to do gender-specific medicine and how does this "medicalize" women's and men's experiences today? Are there race-ethnic specific dimensions of heart disease, cancer and diabetes? What is the relationship between state mandates for inclusion and methodologies for studying race-ethnicity in heart disease, cancer and diabetes?

Bell and Figert define the concepts of medicalization, biomedicalization, pharmaceuticalization and geneticization and they provide an overview of the history of medicalization scholarship. According to Bell and Figert, there is certainly a fair amount of overlap among the "-izations" but they conclude medicalization alone is not adequate for understanding what is going on in the globalizing world of the twenty-first century precisely because it is rooted in modernity and categorical thinking (Bell and Figert 2012a, 2012b). At the same time, they reiterate that the concept of medicalization is worth holding on to because sometimes medicalization is the right tool for the job. It is widely accepted and employed not only among scholars but also among publics. Both the term medicalization and the modern epistemology on which it rests wield cultural authority and can explain how control over phenomena defined medically are produced, accomplished, resisted and transformed. Yet the concept of medicalization simply cannot expand fully enough to encompass and permit sufficiently nuanced and detailed analysis of what is going on today globally. In addition, its connection with modernity and modern processes of control, regulation, knowledge and power make its reach and impact partial. In a world where postmodern forms of knowledge and power circulate, medicalization as a concept is too simple and too narrow for "capturing" the global circulation of pharmaceuticals, genetics and technoscience. The field is at a critical juncture, and this chapter provides a framework for moving forward. Bell and Figert also "move backwards" historically to identify old critiques and highlight how and why we are at this critical juncture and to propose some solutions for moving forward to new engagements.

Ellen Annandale and Anne Hammarström's chapter "A New Biopolitics of Gender and Health? 'Gender-specific Medicine' and Pharmaceuticalization in the Twenty-First Century" shows how gender-specific medicine (GSM) might be considered an example of both biomedicalization and pharmaceuticalization in the context of neoliberalism and recent developments in technoscience. Annandale and Hammarström explore complexity associated with medicalization. They treat biomedicalization, following Clarke et al. (2010), as a localized process that consists of multiple forms of stratification associated with medical goods and procedures that are targeted to different categories of persons, groups and populations. They explore how (bio)medicalization works in a newly developed specialty called "gender-specific medicine" (GSM), one example of such a "targeting" and stratification process. Annandale and Hammarström argue that the rapidly expanding field of GSM has the potential to extend our existing understanding of the relationship between gender and medicalization as well as the recent allied concepts of biomedicalization and pharmaceuticalization. That is, they trace connections between the emerging paradigm of the "gender-specific body" and the practice of the gendered "customization" of pharmaceuticals.

In "Reimagining Race and Ancestry: Biomedicalizing Difference in Post-Genomic Subjects," Janet Shim and her colleagues at the University of California, San Francisco, use biomedicalization and feminist theories to explore changes in scientists' understanding of race in the post-genomic era. They point out that these shifts in doing science are contributing to the conceptualization, use and meaning of race, ethnicity and ancestry. The authors consider how changes in scientific research, such as the introduction of "complexity" as a keyword for understanding and studying disease causation, created a new landscape. The new landscape combines new lines of research enabled by emerging technologies and capacities in genomics, computing and statistics, and transformations in modes of the research enterprise itself. Returning to the themes of this collection, they ask how new engagements of biomedicalization, pharmaceuticalization and genomics target specific categories of persons, groups and populations.

In her commentary Rebecca Herzig steps back to look at tension between feminist critiques of medicalization rooted in conceptions of "we" (the exploited) and "they" (the exploiters) and the multidirectional, multidimensional global dynamics of health and medicine in the twenty-first century. Herzig circles back to "old" feminist questions via "new" tools, techniques and methodologies of biomedicine. As she puts it "what might 'oppression' look like in such a mobile field?" (Herzig 2015:81, Chapter 4, this volume). Looking forward and sideways, Herzig asks how the category of "we" begins to break apart with the queering of "male" and "female" as well as "woman" and "man." What does "suffering" mean in this mobile field, who is the suffering subject, and how do new systems of racial and ethnic categorization (Shim et al. 2015, Chapter 3, this volume) and gender-specific research (Annandale and Hammarström 2015, Chapter 2, this volume) recognize, alleviate, erase and/or exacerbate suffering? The questions she asks about how to keep suffering, domination and subordination in the foreground or center (when these locations seem to disappear as soon as they are seen) as well as her recommendation to add political theory and philosophy to the mix of participants in our reimaginings of biomedicalization, medicalization, pharmaceuticals and genomics, are relevant to the discussions of global pharmaceuticals and genetics/genomics that follow.

Part II: Pharmaceuticals

Scholarly attention has only recently been given to the concept of pharmaceuticalization and its role in people's lives throughout the world. Some of the most interesting and increasingly important questions and topics of research revolve around pharmaceuticals' more prominent role in public health since the mid-twentieth century. This part explores how and why human conditions have been turned into problems requiring either treatment or enhancement with pharmaceuticals and how the process of pharmaceuticalization maps onto global patterns of wealth and poverty. The authors explore the inherent utility of pharmaceuticalization as a concept for understanding the dynamics of drug development, distribution and use historically and today. They also consider whether and how pharmaceuticalization intersects with medicalization and biomedicalization. In this part, the focus is global and international, but each chapter provides evidence that the circulation of pharmaceuticals is heavily influenced by US and global North notions of disease and treatments – in the rise of the concepts of essential drugs and essential medicines (Greene 2015, Chapter 5, this volume), the development of drug donation programs (Samsky 2015, Chapter 6, this volume) and the use of the American Psychiatric Association's *Diagnostic and Statistical Manual of Mental Disorders* (1980) for treatment for mental distress (Cuthbertson 2015, Chapter 7, this volume).

In "Vital Objects: Essential Drugs and Their Critical Legacies," historian of medicine Jeremy Greene explores the global politics of pharmaceutical access that began in the 1970s at the World Health Organization (WHO), with the concept of "essential drugs." In his study of the history and development of global pharmaceuticals, Greene considers the changing role of the state in biomedical therapeutics and policies. How did access to pharmaceuticals – downstream biomedical approaches to disease – become so prominent in global public health, a field long associated with upstream, preventive, non-biomedical health interventions? The turn to pharmaceuticals is a consequence *both* of the overall effectiveness and relevance of medicines for reducing disease and disability *and* of power struggles from different places at different times in international politics, multinational capital formations and transnational networks of consumer advocates, pharmacological experts and consumer activists. In contrast to much of the contemporary scholarship claiming that pharmaceuticalization is a new engine in global health, Greene follows "threads of continuity and contingency that link both past and present" (Greene 2015:90). Greene reminds us that there have been – and still are – global patterns of pharmaceutical underuse as well as of overuse. Accordingly, pharmaceuticalization and the pharmaceuticalization of public health can be better understood through the discourse of essential drugs in the 1970s and essential medicines in the early twenty-first century, as products of linked biological, technical and social changes. These continuities remain obscure if analyses are limited to the past two or three decades. Greene warns that conceptual "izations" can be too easily adopted for understanding global health inequality. Adopting them simplistically risks looking for and finding "inexorable, irreversible, large-scale process without the need to pay attention to actors, context or contingency" (Greene 2015:105).

In "The Drug Swallowers: Scientific Sovereignty and Pharmaceuticalization in Two International Drug Donation Programs," Ari Samsky explores the unintended consequences of widely embracing mass drug administration, both for local communities suffering from tropical disease and for global public health policy. Samsky writes an ethnography about the "gift" of free drugs by two multinational pharmaceutical companies to Tanzanians with onchocerciasis (a blinding parasitic disease transmitted by black flies) treated with Ivermectin and trachoma (a blinding eye infection spread through infected ocular discharge) treated with Zithromax. Samsky's multi-sited ethnography moves between Tanzania and the USA to show the paradoxically conservative nature of the donation programs. He provides details about the underlying dynamics of the program in Tanzania, the USA and the World Health Organization. Providing free treatment for these two diseases for people living in areas where the disease is endemic necessarily leaves out treatment for other diseases and leaves out people with the diseases living in different geographical areas. The programs had social effects as well. The on-the-ground distribution of the pharmaceuticals was carried out and enforced by local inhabitants who levied fines on people who refused to participate in the programs. People who took the drugs referred to themselves in pharmaceuticalized terms as "drug swallowers." In addition to creating new local subjectivities and identities the programs also participated in the pharmaceuticalization of public health.

Courtney Cuthbertson likewise decenters the West in her study "Pharmaceutical Technologies and the Management of Biological Citizens in

Chile." Cuthbertson's case study is informed by and contributes to analysis of the intersections among biomedicalization, pharmaceuticalization and the pharmaceuticalization of public health. She asks how biomedical technologies contribute to the treatment of mental illness and depression in Chile where the use of antidepressants rose by over 470 percent from the early 1990s to the mid-2000s. Using ethnographic data gathered from fieldwork in a mental health clinic in Chile, she documents how the rapid increase of mental health diagnoses in Chilean clinics is linked to the neoliberal policies of using pharmaceutical treatment to control both patients and economic costs to the state. In Chile, patients are in effect obligated to consume and to self-regulate their consumption of antidepressant medications. This approach is based upon standards of diagnosis and treatment enshrined in the American Psychiatric Association's *Diagnostic and Statistical Manual*, 3rd edition (DSM-III 1980), which is best known for its turn to the biomedical model of mental disorders. She shows how medical diagnoses and pharmaceutical decisions made in the clinic are balanced by the perceived psychiatric need of the patient and economic constraints of both the patient and the Chilean healthcare system. These clinical dynamics contribute to the pharmaceuticalization of public health. Cuthbertson revisits Petryna's (2002) concept of "biological citizenship" – when biologically oriented claims for healthcare are made by citizens and recognized by the state. She makes a case for reformulating it in terms of gradations along a continuum from active biological citizenship to passive biological citizenship.

Commentator Matthew Archibald employs the concept of biomedicalization to draw together the chapters in Part II. He steps back from the case studies and places them in the context of institutional and cultural changes related to the global circulation of pharmaceuticals. This focus on the interplay between both structure and culture in the chapters by Greene, Samsky and Cuthbertson is important because "the process of institutional change in biomedicine concerning pharmaceutical technologies is discontinuous and uneven" (Archibald 2015:169, Chapter 8, this volume). As biomedicalization processes shift and change in the twenty-first century, Archibald adroitly highlights the need to focus on the structure/culture interplay as pharmaceuticalization becomes a form of health governance with new forms of power and challenges.

Part III: Genetics/Genomics

This part takes as its starting point the question: Under what conditions is geneticization distinct from medicalization? More broadly, what are the results of the massive economic and technoscientific investment in human genomics research? The chapters in this part highlight the effort to produce a global population science (Bliss 2015, Chapter 9, this volume), the politics of inclusion and exclusion (Benjamin 2015, Chapter 10, this volume) and the study of the effects of gene–environment interaction in genomics (Shostak and Moinester 2015, Chapter 11, this volume).

In "Biomedicalization and the New Science of Race," Catherine Bliss traces how genomic science (in particular, the US-based Human Genome Project) has shaped the global context for DNA research and drive to categorize racial human biodiversity. Bliss is particularly interested in the classification and identification processes of genetics and race. She traces biomedicalization in racial genome projects, health disparities research and gene–environment research. Building her argument on these cases, she concludes that the biomedicalization of race has serious consequences for racial identity processes both for individuals' sense of themselves racially and for the creation of racial and ethnic groups based upon DNA codes. The result is that some groups and individuals are politically disadvantaged by these present developments in biomedicalization, especially around issues of group formation and political advocacy.

Ruha Benjamin further explores the political and structural consequences of genomics for marginalized social groups internationally in "Racial Destiny or Dexterity? The Global Circulation of Genomics as an Empowerment Idiom." Benjamin takes up the question of geneticization by studying the social and political effects of access to tools for genetically based identity in Mexico and India. Do these tools contribute to a new form of genetic determinism or do they contribute to a new form of collective identity for historically marginalized people? What are their implications for global health? Benjamin examines what she refers to as "new-fangled" relations between race and genomics. She shows that new forms of biocitizenship may sediment longstanding inequalities in new and unexpected ways. Benjamin cautions that our newfound ability to intervene upon life in unprecedented ways is not necessarily cause for celebration because it shifts attention from collective social movements to exchanges of genetic information between the biotech industry and individual consumers. "Mexican DNA" and "Indian DNA" are biopolitical imaginaries that strategically calibrate existing social differences, such as race-ethnicity, with genetic groupings. In this political-economic context, tools for group-making inevitably enlist a complex array of scientific and political entrepreneurs. Big Pharma benefits from and has fostered the development of tools for mapping populations – and finding patterns of disease susceptibility and drug response – because the tools have the potential for the development of genomically tailored clinical pharmaceutical trials and genomically tailored medicines.

In "Beyond Geneticization: Regimes of Perceptibility and the Social Determinants of Health," Sara Shostak and Margot Moinester look critically at the debate about the role of the environment in the gene–environment interaction in human health in what they call a post-genomic world. Focusing upon the relatively recent scientific field of the social determinants of health, they argue for moving beyond a geneticization framework and – following

Michelle Murphy (2006) – offer the "regimes of perceptibility" concept as well suited to today's genomic science because it highlights the connections of the science to structural influences. In contrast to the early predictions of the geneticization thesis, the genomic revolution has not resulted in researchers' exclusion of the environment in studies about human health and illness. At the same time, there is no consensus about how the environment should be conceptualized or measured. Shostak and Moinester employ the concept regimes of perceptibility to examine three kinds of environmental exposure – stress, diet and toxics – because it also provides a framework for understanding how "social determinants of health" are made more or less social in nature.

Commentator David Hecht underscores a paradox that runs through each of the chapters in this section: that challenging existing politics and practices of genetic explanations reinforces the very practices and politics the challengers seek to dislodge. In addition, he points out that it is difficult to dislodge current ways of understanding genes, e.g., using the gene as tool for individual identity making versus using it as a tool for group politics. Even when current ways of understanding genes are dislodged and social scientists and scientists attempt to move beyond a gene–environment binary, it remains difficult to translate new understandings into new ways of doing research. As Hecht puts it, adopting the language of complexity that runs through this volume, "arguments derived from genomics can frequently be used to support multiple positions" (Hecht 2015:243, Chapter 12, this volume). And, further, he asks, how do the pictures and stories of genes by experts and publics reflect the historical moments in which we see them, such as in the present era of neoliberalism? Hecht advocates a turn sideways to the humanities as well as the social sciences to understand the "persistent appeal of genes and genetic explanations" and a turn backwards to locate this appeal historically (2015:239).

Using a cartographic metaphor in her epilogue, historian Susan Reverby brings us back to central questions about power, justice and health in a globalized world. Reverby starts with questions about "Power, Politics and Profits" from health activism and scholarship in the 1970s, and proceeds to remap the "biopolitical world" of biomedicine today. As she points out, the old maps rooted in disciplines and associated with modernity were simpler and easier to use. Today, we are often not even working from or using the same maps. In the 1970s, Health/PAC's map was the American Health Empire (Health/PAC 1970). Today's maps have to be global, interdisciplinary and three dimensional. To navigate these new maps, we can use old critiques but these must be accompanied by new engagements. Reverby asks us not to do away with power, politics and profits but to consider what they mean today and how to make and read transnational and global maps based upon them.

In terms of Reverby's felicitous metaphor, this book assembles one group of mapmakers tracing routes in technoscience, genetics and pharmaceuticals, and represents one point in the remapping project. In the 1970s medicalization scholars made a useful map that drew attention to and helped to explain changes in political economy, medicine and culture. Sometimes and in some places it is still a useful map. However, the global discourse of health and disease in genomics, pharmaceuticals and technoscience cannot be mapped with modern tools of medicalization cartography. Taken together, the authors of this collection imagine new routes through new territories as the world of "medicalization" has grown more complex.

Notes

1 We realize there are many "-izations" but others have not yet attracted as much attention or debate either in the scholarly or the popular literatures as these. There are many other "-izations" used by the authors of this collection. In a cursory review of the chapters and commentaries we counted thirty-one additional words ending in "-ization" (thirty-five total if we include medicalization, pharmaceuticalization, geneticization and biomedicalization). Some of the words with the suffix "-ization" are employed in studies of medicine, the pharmaceutical industry and technoscience in the twenty-first century (responsibilitization, technologization, molecularization, racialization), but they have not attracted as much attention or debate either in the scholarly or the popular literatures as have the "-izations" of interest to us. Many of the "-izations" used here are associated with dynamics and conditions of modernity (individualization, privatization, institutionalization, rationalization, routinization, operationalization, centralization, corporatization, optimization and modernization).

2 The *Oxford English Dictionary* definition of the noun "technoscience" is "mutually interacting disciplines, or ... two components of a single discipline; reliance on science for solving technical problems; the application of technological knowledge to solving scientific problems." *OED* online, www.oed.com/view/Entry/256424?redirectedFrom=technoscience#eid (accessed August 6, 2014).

3 According to Moore et al. (2011:508): "[t]he term 'neoliberalism' is used here to describe ideologies and practices that have also varied widely over time and across countries but have a family resemblance on three issues: a tendency to prefer markets over governments as instruments of policy (via privatization or, where regulatory policies are deemed necessary, via regulatory interventions that use marketplace mechanisms such as cap-and-trade systems); to favor trade liberalization over protectionism (with reductions in tariffs, subsidies, floating currencies, and regional and global trade agreements); and to approach poverty from the vantage point of self-responsibility, decentralized public-private partnerships, enterprise development, and other orientations to economic development expected to produce overall increases in the standard of living rather than redistributive change."

References

American Psychiatric Association. 1980. *Diagnostic and Statistical Manual of Mental Disorders*, 3rd edn. Washington, DC: American Psychiatric Association.

Annandale, Ellen and Anne Hammarström. 2015. "A New Biopolitics of Gender and Health? 'Gender-specific Medicine' and Pharmaceuticalization in the Twenty-First Century." Pp. 41–55 in *Reimagining (Bio)Medicalization, Pharmaceuticals and Genetics: Old Critiques and New Engagements*, edited by Susan E. Bell and Anne E. Figert. New York: Routledge.

Archibald, Matthew E. 2015. "Commentary and Reflections: The Ongoing Construction of Pharmaceutical Regimes." Pp. 160–72 in *Reimagining (Bio)Medicalization, Pharmaceuticals and Genetics: Old Critiques and New Engagements*, edited by Susan E. Bell and Anne E. Figert. New York: Routledge.

Bell, Susan E. 1986. "A New Model of Medical Technology Development: A Case Study of DES." *Research in the Sociology of Health Care* 4:1–32.

Bell, Susan E. 1990. "Sociological Perspectives on the Medicalization of Menopause." *Annals of the New York Academy of Sciences* 592(1):173–8.

Bell, Susan E. and Anne E. Figert. 2010. "Gender and the Medicalization of Health Care." Pp. 107–22 in *Palgrave Handbook of Gender and Healthcare*, edited by E. Kuhlmann and E. Annandale. London: Palgrave Macmillan.

Bell, Susan E. and Anne E. Figert. 2012a. "Medicalization and Pharmaceuticalization at the Intersections: Looking Backward, Sideways and Forward." *Social Science & Medicine* 75: 775–83.

Bell, Susan E. and Anne E. Figert. 2012b. "Starting to Turn Sideways to Move Forward in Medicalization and Pharmaceuticalization Studies: A Response to Williams et. al." *Social Science & Medicine* 75:2131–3.

Benjamin, Ruha. 2015. "Racial Destiny or Dexterity?: The Global Circulation of Genomics as an Empowerment Idiom." Pp. 197–215 in *Reimagining (Bio)Medicalization, Pharmaceuticals and Genetics: Old Critiques and New Engagements*, edited by Susan E. Bell and Anne E. Figert. New York: Routledge.

Bliss, Catherine. 2015. "Biomedicalization and the New Science of Race." Pp. 175–96 in *Reimagining (Bio)Medicalization, Pharmaceuticals and Genetics: Old Critiques and New Engagements*, edited by Susan E. Bell and Anne E. Figert. New York: Routledge.

Bourdieu, Pierre. 1986. "Forms of Capital." Pp. 241–58 in *Handbook of Theory and Research for the Sociology of Education*, edited by John G. Richardson. New York: Greenwood.

Clarke, Adele E., Laura Mamo, Jennifer R. Fishman, Janet K. Shim and Jennifer Ruth Fosket. 2003. "Biomedicalization: Technoscientific Transformations of Health, Illness, and U.S. Biomedicine." *American Sociological Review* 68:161–94.

Clarke, Adele, Laura Mamo, Jennifer Ruth Fosket, Jennifer R. Fishman and Janet K. Shim, eds. 2010. *Biomedicalization: Technoscience, Health and Illness in the U.S.* Durham, NC: Duke University Press.

Conrad, Peter. 1976. *Identifying Hyperactive Children.* Lexington, MA: Lexington Books.

Conrad, Peter. 2005. "The Shifting Engines of Medicalization." *Journal of Health and Social Behavior* 46:3–14.

Cuthbertson, Courtney A. 2015. "Pharmaceutical Technologies and the Management of Biological Citizens in Chile." Pp. 137–59 in *Reimagining (Bio)Medicalization, Pharmaceuticals and Genetics: Old Critiques and New Engagements*, edited by Susan E. Bell and Anne E. Figert. New York: Routledge.

Durkheim, Emile. 1982[1895]. *The Rules of Sociological Method and Selected Texts on Sociology and Its Method.* New York: Free Press.

Figert, Anne E. 1996. *Women and the Ownership of PMS: The Structuring of a Psychiatric Disorder.* Hawthorne, NY: Aldine de Gruyter.

Figert, Anne E. 2011. "The Consumer Turn in Medicalization: Future Directions with Historical Foundations." Pp. 291–307 in *The Handbook of the Sociology of Health, Illness & Healing: Blueprint for the 21st Century*, edited by B. Pescosolido, J. Martin, J. Mcleod and A. Rogers. New York: Springer.

Figert, Anne E. and Susan E. Bell. 2014. "Big Pharma and Big Medicine in the Global Environment." Pp. 476–70 in *Routledge Handbook of Science, Technology and Society*, edited by Daniel Kleinman and Kelly Moore. New York: Routledge.

Goffman, Erving. 1963. *Stigma: Notes on the Management of Spoiled Identity.* Englewood Cliffs, NJ: Prentice Hall.

Granovetter, Mark S. 1973. "The Strength of Weak Ties." *American Journal of Sociology* 78(6): 1360–80.

Greene, Jeremy A. 2015. "Vital Objects: Essential Drugs and Their Critical Legacies." Pp. 89–111 in *Reimagining (Bio)Medicalization, Pharmaceuticals and Genetics: Old Critiques and New Engagements*, edited by Susan E. Bell and Anne E. Figert. New York: Routledge.

Health/PAC. 1970. *The American Health Empire: Power, Politics and Profits.* New York: Random House.

Hecht, David K. 2015. "Commentary and Reflections: The Lure of the Gene." Pp. 239–47 in *Reimagining (Bio)Medicalization, Pharmaceuticals and Genetics: Old Critiques and New Engagements*, edited by Susan E. Bell and Anne E. Figert. New York: Routledge.

Herzig, Rebecca. 2015. "Commentary and Reflections: On Stratification and Complexity." Pp. 79–86 in *Reimagining (Bio)Medicalization, Pharmaceuticals and Genetics: Old Critiques and New Engagements*, edited by Susan E. Bell and Anne E. Figert. New York: Routledge.

Lane, Christopher. 2007. *Shyness: How Normal Behavior Became a Sickness*. New Haven, CT: Yale University Press.

Lippman, Abby. 1991. "Prenatal Genetic Testing and Screening: Constructing Needs and Reinforcing Inequities." *American Journal of Law & Medicine* 17:15–50.

Moore, Kelly, Daniel Lee Kleinman, David Hess and Scott Frickel. 2011. "Science and Neoliberal Globalization: A Political Sociological Approach." *Theory and Society* 40(5):505–32.

Murphy, Michelle. 2006. *Sick Building Syndrome and the Problem of Uncertainty: Environmental Politics, Technoscience, and Women Workers*, 1st edn. Durham, NC: Duke University Press.

Petryna, Adriana. 2002. *Life Exposed: Biological Citizens after Chernobyl*. Princeton, NJ: Princeton University Press.

Rosich, Katherine J. and Janet R. Hankin. 2010. "Executive Summary: What Do We Know? Key Findings from 50 Years of Medical Sociology." *Journal of Health and Social Behavior* 51:S1–S9.

Samsky, Ari. 2015. "The Drug Swallowers: Scientific Sovereignty and Pharmaceuticalization in Two International Drug Donation Programs." Pp. 112–36 in *Reimagining (Bio)Medicalization, Pharmaceuticals and Genetics: Old Critiques and New Engagements*, edited by Susan E. Bell and Anne E. Figert. New York: Routledge.

Shim, Janet K., Katherine Weatherford Darling, Sara L. Ackerman, Sandra Soo-Jin Lee and Robert A. Hiatt. 2015. "Reimagining Race and Ancestry: Biomedicalizing Difference in Post-Genomic Subjects." Pp. 56–78 in *Reimagining (Bio)Medicalization, Pharmaceuticals and Genetics: Old Critiques and New Engagements*, edited by Susan E. Bell and Anne E. Figert. New York: Routledge.

Shostak, Sara, Peter Conrad and Allan V. Horwitz. 2008. "Sequencing and Its Consequences: Path Dependence and the Relationships between Genetics and Medicalization." *American Journal of Sociology* 114.S1:S287–S316.

Shostak, Sara and Margot Moinester. 2015. "Beyond Geneticization: Regimes of Perceptibility and the Social Determinants of Health." Pp. 216–38 in *Reimagining (Bio)Medicalization, Pharmaceuticals and Genetics: Old Critiques and New Engagements*, edited by Susan E. Bell and Anne E. Figert. New York: Routledge.

Weber, Max. 1946. "Bureaucracy." Pp. 196–216 in *From Max Weber*, edited by H. H. Gerth and C. Wright Mills. New York: Oxford.

Williams, Simon J., Clive Seale, Sharon Boden, Pam Lowe and Deborah Lynn Steinberg. 2008. "Waking up to Sleepiness: Modafinil, the Media and the Pharmaceuticalisation of Everyday/Night Life." *Sociology of Health & Illness* 30:839–55.

Zola, Irving. 1972. "Medicine as an Institution of Social Control." *Sociological Review* 20:487–504.

I

Reimaginings: (Bio)Medicalization and Technoscience in the Twenty-First Century

Moving Sideways and Forging Ahead
Reimagining "-Izations" in the Twenty-First Century

SUSAN E. BELL AND ANNE E. FIGERT

In the Introduction to this volume, we write that medicalization is a useful concept that has been highly debated within the social sciences, history and biomedicine itself. Although we do not entirely agree with Rose who suggests "medicalization has become a cliché of critical social analysis" (Rose 2007:700), his call to move "beyond medicalization" resonates with us and others. Medicalization still has utility for social analysts if we take it, following Rose (2007:702) as "the starting point of an analysis, a sign of the need for an analysis, but ... not ... the conclusion of an analysis". We also do not entirely agree with Kleinman (2012) who argues that medicalization is no longer an interesting or useful concept because it applies to a process in which conditions move from one category (e.g., badness) to another (e.g., sickness). At the same time we agree with Kleinman that either/or thinking cannot grasp complex processes leading to and emanating from social suffering and global health inequality. In addition to adding related concepts (biomedicalization, pharmaceuticalization and geneticization) alongside that of medicalization, scholars are more recently using the concept of medicalization in new and different ways such as "ambivalent medicalization" (Crowley-Makota and True 2012) and what might be called "simultaneous medicalization and demedicalization," in which professional groups such as lactation consultants are actively working toward demedicalization and medicalization at the same time (Torres 2014).

The role of the analyst of this phenomenon is to not only critique but to engage with its messy and theoretical/practical areas. As the title of the Introduction to this book suggests (Bell and Figert 2015), we still need to engage older critiques about medicalization processes but with newer studies and new tools. To do so, we embrace the conceptual tools of biomedicalization, pharmaceuticalization, the pharmaceuticalization of public health, and geneticization in order to show that medicalization is a capacious concept but it may not fully capture the global dynamics of biomedicine, the pharmaceutical industry and technologies of genetics in medicine. There is certainly a fair amount of overlap but medicalization alone is not adequate for understanding what is going on in the globalizing world of the twenty-first century precisely because it is rooted in modernity and categorical thinking (Bell and Figert 2012a). These "-izations" are related and coevolving concepts and processes; this becomes especially visible when analyzed within a global context. In this chapter we look back over the past forty years of scholarship on medicalization, turn sideways to other disciplines that contribute to this growing field and look ahead to the next decades. We argue that alone each of the concepts captures distinct processes, that each is related to the others, and that each sometimes but not always overlaps with another. In this chapter, we suggest that instead of throwing out one or all of the "-izations" we can move sideways and forge ahead by examining new ways of thinking: globally, scientifically, socially.

Historicizing Medicalization

Our discussion begins here with the widely accepted definition and description of medicalization from US sociologist Peter Conrad as "*defining a problem in medical terms, usually as an illness or disorder, or using a medical intervention to treat it*" (2005:3; emphasis in original) and as "a process by which nonmedical problems become defined and treated as medical problems, usually in terms of illness and disorders" (2007:4). Historians and anthropologists document how medicalization as a phenomenon (as opposed to an analytic term) has its beginnings in late seventeenth- and early eighteenth-century Western modernization along with the application of scientific knowledge to social life (Lock 2004). This location of medicalization within large-scale social processes such as modernization and positivism and public health programs of the modern state echoes throughout the historical and anthropological literature (Nye 2003; Rosenberg 2006). To simplify, "medicalization" is a *process* associated with modernity, and reflects societal and medical practices designed to control and regulate diseases, illnesses and injuries. Foucault's (1965, 1977[1975]) work on the modern state, the clinical gaze and the embodiment of surveillance and control is often cited in the medicalization literature as a major influence on the scholarship about this process (e.g., Lupton 1997; Nye 2003). According to Foucault, medicalization as a process was co-constructed along with modern capitalism and the state. The process of medicalization exemplifies a modern mechanism of power – a manifestation "of the right of the social body to ensure, maintain, or develop its life" (Foucault 1978:136). The modern state replaced the ancient right to take life with the power to foster life. The power over life evolved in two forms that were "linked together by a whole intermediary cluster of relations" (Foucault 1978:137): disciplining the individual body and optimizing its capabilities and regulating the species body (population). The beginning of what Foucault called "biopower" (Foucault 1978:140) is marked by the "explosion of numerous and diverse techniques for subjugation of bodies and the control of populations." Whether medicalization was "co-constitutive of modernity" (Clarke et al. 2003:164) or "the product as well as the cause of societal faith in medical knowledge and practice" (Ballard and Elston 2005:237), the turn to medicine as an institution of social control was part of a more general process of modernization.[1]

The *concept* of medicalization has its roots in mid- to late twentieth-century scholarship in the humanities and social sciences. Many scholars trace the study of what is now called "medicalization" to the 1960s and the work of anti-psychiatrists such as Szasz (1974[1961]) and Laing (1961). Szasz, Laing and others argued that Western medical professionals had the authority and power to classify and diagnose "normal" everyday feelings and behaviors and transform them into psychiatric illnesses (usually for the economic and professional benefit of psychiatrists and psychologists). Other scholars connect it with the concerns expressed by Illich (1975) in the 1970s about medical imperialism and the ever expanding reach and influence of the institution of medicine as the foundation from which medicalization studies emerged.

The concept of medicalization was introduced into the medical sociology literature in the 1970s to understand and look critically at "the involvement of medicine in the management of society" (Zola 1972:488; see also Pitts 1968 for one of the earliest references as it related to definition and social control of deviance). Medical sociologists began to use the concept of "medicalization" to examine the dynamics of an expanding medical institution and the related processes of professional authority, control and the construction (and active defense) of medical diagnoses (Freidson 1970; Zola 1972). At this time, the connection between the dynamics of medicalization and those of deviance and social control was highlighted with examples such as hyperactivity, sexuality and alcoholism (Conrad and Schneider 1980). Scholars showed how deviance was gradually transformed from a religious and criminal problem into a medical problem that is defined, treated and controlled by the medical establishment.

A substantial portion of the early sociological work on medicalization focused specifically upon the technically competent power and authority of physicians in modern society and in the medical encounter itself. As numerous reviews of the literature point out, in medical sociology, "medicalization" has its roots in Parsons' concept of the sick role (1951). At one level, the sick role refers to individuals and interactions in the medical social control of deviance. However, the sick role is also about the larger social structures in which the interactions are situated – the institution of medicine and physicians' state sanctioned authority to diagnose and treat diseases in people seeking "technically competent" help (Freidson 1970). By virtue of having the authority and professional power in modern society to define and control what is formally recognized as a disorder, sickness or deviance, physicians play an important role in the medicalization process (Freidson 1970; Zola 1972; Illich 1975; Conrad and Schneider 1980).

Early sociological analyses often adopted a modernist framework to examine how the institution of medicine developed and applied a scientific worldview to elements of physical and emotional life. By this we mean a worldview in which policies and practices value and are designed to promote progress, rationalization, standardization, precision, enhanced control over external nature, and mass production and consumption (Bell and Figert 2012a:776). Accordingly, in medicalization theory the concept of "control" was prominent, used to explain consumer demand (to control and improve upon their physical bodies) as well as medical imperialism (to control deviance through surveillance and the rational application of science to everyday life), and the turn to treatment as opposed to incarceration or punishment (Lock 2004). As Irving Zola wrote, medicine was "becoming the new repository of truth, the place where absolute and often final judgments are made by supposedly morally neutral and objective experts. And these judgments are made, not in the name of virtue or legitimacy, but in the name of health … [it] is largely an insidious and often undramatic phenomenon accomplished by 'medicalizing' much of daily living, by making medicine and the labels 'healthy' and 'ill' relevant to an ever increasing part of human existence" (Zola 1972:487).

Throughout the period from the 1970s to the early 1990s medicalization scholars continued to refine the concept by documenting how the jurisdiction of medicine expanded and redefined elements of the life cycle and moral, social and legal problems and turned them into medical matters. In the 1980s, most of the sociologically generated scholarship moved away from an explicit focus on deviance and scholarship in the USA took a social constructionist approach to medicalization in its examination of the construction of diagnostic categories and professional process and social control of behaviors (Conrad 1992).

During the early part of this period, an important turn in the development of medicalization scholarship came about when researchers began to point out that medicalization was not just a process done to people but that people and groups were also active agents in advocating for or against diagnoses or the medicalization or demedicalization of life processes.[2] Using perspectives from both the sociology of professions and the sociology of scientific knowledge, medical sociologists were heavily engaged in documenting cases of medicalization such as in the care of children and of veterans of the Vietnam War (Halpern 1990; Scott 1990). Feminist scholars focused on women's bodies (e.g., Riessman 1983; Bell 1987b) and documented cases of the gendered nature of medicalization. Women's health movements (Boston Women's Health Book Collective 1973) also emphasized the unique ways in which women's bodies were more susceptible to medicalization through processes such as childbirth, PMS and menopause (McCrea 1983; Riessman, 1983; Bell 1987a; Figert 1995). By the 1990s the medicalization analysis of gender moved its focus beyond the reproductive realm for women (Plechner 2000; Riska 2003; Barker 2005) and medicalization scholars began to ask how, why and under what circumstances men's bodies are also medicalized (Loe 2004; Rosenfeld and Faircloth 2006; Conrad 2007).[3]

The 2000s: Putting the Bio- into Medicalization, Pharmaceuticals and Genomics

The rise of gender scholarship, the growth of the institution of medicine and the pharmaceutical industry, and other factors contributed to continued scholarly interest in developing the concept and studying the dynamics of medicalization and its related processes in the 2000s. Scholarship revitalized and refocused our analytic gaze from the power and authority of the medical profession and the documentation of cases of medicalization to consider the active participation of individual patient/consumer/users individually and collectively (Brown and Zavestoski 2004; Crossley 2006), resistance to pharmaceuticals (Figert 2011; Williams, Martin and Gabe 2011), and the use of medical prescription drugs for nonmedical purposes (Williams, Gabe and Davis 2008). It has also explored new "engines" of medicalization including the pharmaceutical industry (Conrad 2005), and the role of technoscience (Clarke et al. 2003).

Scholars from many disciplines are also questioning the adequacy of medicalization as a conceptual tool for understanding these processes. One reason is that physician power and authority is changing – indeed waning – as a result of healthcare reforms, insurance policies and (in the USA and New Zealand) direct-to-consumer advertising (DTCA) of pharmaceuticals (Lock 2004; Rose 2007). Even though the medical profession and physicians remain key players in medicalization they are no longer its major promoters (Conrad 2007:156).

Another significant change is that the pharmaceutical industry has become an important proponent of medicalization by targeting physicians through physician-directed communications and targeting (potential) patients directly and indirectly with advertisements (Abraham 2010a; Padamsee 2011). Medicalization theory assumes that the transformation from deviance as badness to deviance as sickness is associated with less stigma both to the individual and to the group of people affected. Big Pharma has held out advertising as a strategy for not only medicalizing but also destigmatizing conditions such as erectile dysfunction, social anxiety and depression. With greater awareness of certain conditions, comes the promise of normalizing and destigmatizing the effect of the conditions (Phelan 2005). As Payton and Thoits write, medicalization was "thought to reduce the blame and stigma attached to deviant conditions such as mental illness" (2011:56). The dynamics of medicalization involving mental illness both in the USA and in other countries are, however, much more complex than this argument assumes. The results of DTCA in the USA in reducing stigma have been mixed, especially regarding mental illness. Payton and Thoits investigated whether or not the rise of DTCA for depression drugs alters negative public opinion about depression and mental illness more generally and found that DTCA did not change Americans' negative perceptions about mental illness but did promote the greater acceptance of medical interventions for mental illness (2011). Pescosolido et al. (2010) found similar results in that DTCA increased public acceptance about the biomedical causes of mental illness and increased support for biomedical treatments and services but did not increase overall acceptance of people with mental illness. Thus, DTCA garners support for medicalization and treatment of mental illness pharmaceutically but this does not mean that people with mental illness are any less stigmatized in the USA as the recent debates on gun violence and lack of mental healthcare has made clear.

The global dynamics of the medicalization of mental illness are also complicated, uneven and at times contradictory as studies of prescriptions in Chile, Japan and Argentina demonstrate. Cuthbertson documents the use of antidepressants in Chilean mental health Clinics as a form of "pharmaceutical governance" by the state (2015, Chapter 7, this volume). In Chile, even when depression is viewed as a medical illness, it is also viewed both as a threat to individual worker productivity and to the national economy. In this case then the medicalization of depression and its pharmaceutical treatment is taken to mean an entirely different thing than it might in a different country such as in the USA. In the USA depression is individualized but not seen as a threat to the national economy. As Applbaum (2006) suggests, the later introduction of newer antidepressants (selective serotonin reuptake inhibitors or SSRIs) such as Prozac in Japan in the mid- to late 1990s was the result of successful global marketing strategies by pharmaceutical companies and not by the state. In this case the harmonization of clinical research data from global clinical trials was key. Successful marketing depended on and produced organizational changes in Japanese governmental agencies about accepting foreign clinical research data collected under the International Conference for Harmonization (ICH), and the adoption of US-based diagnostic categories in the *Diagnostic and Statistical Manual of Mental Disorders* (DSM) and of the WHO's *International Classification of Diseases* (ICD). By contrast, SSRIs were used in Argentina in 2001 to treat social suffering as a result of the country's economic crisis. As Lakoff writes:

> doctors' prescription of SSRIs was dependent neither on a diagnosis of depression nor on a biological understanding of mental disorder. These drugs found a different means of entering the professionally mediated marketplace: doctors understood and used SSRIs as a treatment not for a lack of serotonin in the brain, but for the suffering caused by the social situation – the sense of insecurity and vulnerability that the economic and political crisis had wrought. (2004:247)

In addition to the waning power of the medical profession and the increasing power of the pharmaceutical industry, global health inequality has sharply increased. Whereas some populations in some areas of the world are (over) medicalized or use too many pharmaceuticals, other populations in other parts of the world are (under)medicalized or have limited access to pharmaceuticals (Biehl 2008). The global expansion of clinical trials clearly reflects this. Some populations in some areas of the world serve as research subjects and other populations in other parts of the world benefit from these trial results (Figert and Bell 2014). To put it bluntly, "some people are more medically made up than others – women more than men, the wealthy differently from the poor, children more than adults, and differently in different countries and regions of the world" (Rose 2007:700). Since the 2000s, scholars working in the fields of biomedicalization, pharmaceuticalization and geneticization have been providing evidence of the need to understand how changes in medicalization, the global flow of pharmaceuticals and the increasing turn to genetics shape global health inequality in the twenty-first century. We address each of these in the next section.

Biomedicalization

Science and medicine changed so substantially in the 1980s that when looking back and trying to analyze it, Adele Clarke and her colleagues (2003) argue that the concept of "medicalization" is no longer fully accurate or adequate to explain the substantive organizational and technological changes in medicine. Clarke et al. (2003) introduced the word "biomedicalization" as a tool for illuminating the complex dynamics and effects of technoscientific innovations ushered in since the mid-1980s. Technoscientific innovations merge "basic" science with "applied" technology. These technoscientific innovations in molecular biology, biotechnologies, genomization and transplant medicine make it possible not only to control but to transform both humans and nonhumans from the "inside out" by producing biomedical solutions for health maintenance, enhancement, and optimization as well as illness (Clarke et al. 2003:162). The concept of "biomedicalization" draws attention to the complexities of this process that also produces new subjectivities as well as new medical subjects. For example, as Sara Shostak demonstrates in her research, screening technologies using molecular biomarkers create new categories of people at risk, new opportunities for biomedical surveillance and intervention, and new forms of self-monitoring and regimens of behavior change (Shostak 2013; Shostak and Moinester 2015, Chapter 11, this volume). Bodies are simultaneously "objects and effects of technoscientific and biomedical discourse" (Mamo and Fosket 2009:927).

The transformation of life beyond the *control* of bodies and behaviors to the *constitution* of new forms of life and new subjectivities is associated with a new, postmodern, era in medicine and society more broadly. These dynamics do not easily fit into a conceptual frame of medicalization as either governmental or medical professional control. Adding the prefix "bio" to "medicalization" to make "biomedicalization" draws attention to the complexities of these dynamics (Clarke et al. 2003, 2010). It is a tool for exploring the mutual constitution of political, economic, cultural, organizational and technoscientific trends and processes and connects large, macrostructural changes with new personal identities and subjectivities.

Whereas the process of medicalization might be best conceived in modern terms of engineering, control and rationalization, the process of biomedicalization can be conceived of in postmodern terms of networks, spirals and complexity. Clarke and her colleagues (2003, 2010) argue that the concept of biomedicalization is capable of explaining these complex, often contradictory processes. Thus, from this point of view biomedicalization may be better suited than medicalization to analyze some but not all of the complexities and global dynamics of pharmaceuticals and new genetic technologies in the twenty-first century.

Scholars interested in health inequalities from the perspective of biomedicalization are exploring how the process "carries within itself the ideological, social, and cultural infrastructures that support and maintain racial and class inequalities" (Clarke et al. 2010:29). For example, in his study of BiDil, the first "race-specific drug" approved by the Food and Administration to treat heart failure, Kahn (2010) traces the complex and contradictory pathway through which BiDil was produced by and in turn exploited the processes of biomedicalization. He concludes that BiDil "is part of a much larger dynamic of reification in which the purported reality of race as genetic is used to obscure the social reality of racism" (Kahn 2010:284).

A significant proportion of scholarship in this field takes a feminist approach to biomedicalization, partly because those who developed the concept are committed to feminist health scholarship. As Mamo and Fosket put it, "female corporeality and subjectivity are understood as constituted in and through (cultural) practices of (techno)science" (2009:927). Although the concept of biomedicalization does not necessarily privilege gender, it takes gender – and gendered bodies – seriously. Biomedicalization scholars argue that gender is not a stable, given status but an outcome of performance, following the arguments made by feminist theorist Judith Butler (1993). Gender is "produced in relations – as an effect of power" (Clarke et al. 2010:27). Gender is also not a privileged status or category, but one produced in intersections with race, class, sexuality, disability and so forth. That is, "in life, in bodies, in practice" these categories are "dynamic, changing, and co-constitutive" and thus cannot be understood separately but must be explored simultaneously (Clarke et al. 2010:30). Biomedicalization has been employed, for example, to examine how gendered subjectivities and forms of embodiment are produced in lesbian practices of assisted reproduction (Mamo 2007, 2010), breast cancer prevention technologies (Fosket 2010), contraception/menstruation (Mamo and Fosket 2009) and pharmaceutical interventions for male impotence (Fishman 2010).

Looking back from the perspective of the 2000s, Jonathan Metzl and Rebecca Herzig (2007:697) described these changes in terms of "an age dominated by complex and often contradictory interactions between medicine, pharmaceutical companies, and culture at large" in the industrialized and post-industrialized world. Understanding both the definition and effects of biomedicalization helps to make sense of how and why more and more conditions are defined and treated medically and pharmaceutically in the twenty-first century.

Pharmaceuticals and Pharmaceuticalization

As indicated above, one of the reasons that medicalization studies have changed dramatically in the past decade is due in part to the increased attention to the role of pharmaceuticals and the pharmaceutical industry ("Big Pharma") in modern life, one "engine of medicalization" (Conrad 2005) that exemplifies complexities involved in biomedicalization (Clarke et al. 2010). The growth of Big Pharma has been striking. Beginning in the 1980s worldwide prescription-drug sales grew dramatically (Busfield 2006). Even during the worldwide economic slowdown, they continue to grow albeit at a slightly slower pace (IMS Institute for Healthcare Informatics 2013). The trends are clear, but figures vary from one source to another. According to the IMS Institute for Healthcare Informatics, the market grew to US$837 billion by 2009 and in 2014, "total global spending on medicines will exceed one trillion U.S. dollars for the first time" (IMS Institute for Healthcare Informatics 2013). Spending on pharmaceuticals is concentrated in the "West" and among these societies, the USA continues to be largest market for pharmaceuticals, making up "about half of the world's prescription-drug sales" (Abraham 2010a:290; Ebeling 2011). An emerging pharmaceutical market in China is soon expected to make it the second largest market for worldwide sales (IMS Institute for Healthcare Informatics 2013). Joan Busfield puts it simply: "the pharmaceutical industry is a major power within the global economy and some national economies" (2006:299).

As many scholars have pointed out, a key engine of this pattern of expansion in the USA was the revision of Food and Drug Administration (FDA) regulations in 1997 that "allowed for a wider usage and promotion of off-label uses of drugs and facilitated direct-to-consumer advertising, especially on television" (Conrad 2005:5). DTCA is responsible for major increases of spending in the USA by pharmaceutical companies. In countries where DTCA is not explicitly allowed, pharmaceutical expansion has been fueled by media briefings (instead of advertisements), printed materials left in physicians' offices or pharmacies, and patient groups and online groups (Busfield 2010; Padamsee 2011).

Although social scientists have studied pharmaceuticals and the pharmaceutical industry for many years, pharmaceuticalization as a unique term was introduced by anthropologists (Nichter 1996[1989]) and taken up and developed by sociologists in the 2000s (Williams et al. 2008). Pharmaceuticalization is "the process by which social, behavioral or bodily conditions are treated, or deemed to be in need of treatment/intervention, with pharmaceuticals by doctors, patients, or both" (Abraham 2010a:290). Pharmaceuticalization occurs both for conditions "previously outside the jurisdiction of medicine" and for established medical conditions already in the medical domain (Abraham 2010b:604). It combines "the biological effect of a chemical on human tissue, . . . the willingness of consumers to adopt the technology as a 'solution' to a problem in their lives, and the corporate interests of drug companies" (Fox and Ward 2008:865). The term was initially developed to explain the expansion of the use of (mostly prescription) medicines to treat social or behavioral problems – that is, the use of pharmaceuticals to control an expanding set of behaviors. In studies of the pharmaceuticalization process, power is often conceived of in modern terms. Analysts explore the ability of the pharmaceutical industry to direct the drug development and approval process against "countervailing powers" (Busfield 2006) or to achieve its goals against "national political culture and interests, litigation, patient activism, the mass media, international organization of regulatory agencies, disciplinary and professional interests and regulatory capture" (Abraham 2007:730).

In response to the dramatic increase in global pharmaceutical sales since the 1980s, scholars have focused much of their attention on the economic and political dimensions of the pharmaceutical industry. From the perspective of Big Pharma, the ideal product "can be patented, is used by a large number of people over lengthy periods, and can be priced quite highly in relation to production costs" (Busfield 2006:302). Such an ideal product is used to treat the chronic health problems faced by populations in richer countries where higher prices are in place rather than the infectious diseases of populations in developing countries where lower prices are in place (Busfield 2006). As noted by the Commission on Health Research for Development in 1990, "approximately 10 percent of global drug research and development is focused on the medical problems that cause 90 percent of global disease burden" (cited in Zacher and Keefe 2008:108). In keeping with this perspective on the ideal product, during a period of deregulation in Europe and the USA between 1995 and 2004, the pharmaceutical industry "expanded its market for drugs that offer little or no therapeutic advance in a sea of declining innovation" (Abraham 2010a:303).

Pharmaceuticalization is creating new maps of global patterns of wealth and poverty and of power and inequality. As previously indicated, overall spending on medicines by pharmaceutical companies is expected to exceed US\$1 trillion in 2014 despite slowing growth and reduced contribution from developed markets due to the expiration of patents and the sustained impact of the economic crisis (IMS Institute for Healthcare Informatics 2013). Big Pharma is beginning to turn its focus to middle- and low-income countries as a strategy for economic growth as markets such as those found in China, India, Brazil, Russia and Turkey are on their way to becoming the second largest geographic segment in spending on medicines – surpassing Germany, France,

Italy, Spain and the UK combined, and approaching US levels. As the concept of a "pharmerging market" indicates, pharmerging markets are in middle- and low-income economies with large populations (Hill and Chui 2009). To make sense of this movement of Big Pharma to these pharmerging markets, we have recommended turning sideways to anthropology and to studies of pharmaceuticalization that begin outside the West (Bell and Figert 2012a, 2012b).

A second dynamic of restructuring and fragmentation in the pharmaceutical industry worldwide accompanied Big Pharma's movement to pharmerging markets. Governments in the global South have developed new policies toward patented and generic drugs and fostered the growth of pharmaceutical industries in India, China and Brazil, challenging Big Pharma's dominance. Thus there has developed a tension between pharmaceutical access as a human right and pharmaceuticals as economic commodities.

This tension comes at a time when there has been a decline in overall drug innovation by Big Pharma (see Light 2010). This is especially relevant given recent attention to the lack of research on antibiotics and the rise of antibiotic-resistant strains of diseases. As recently reported in news outlets, many of the major pharmaceutical companies are no longer investing research dollars in antibiotics because of the poor return on investment. The rise in antibiotic-resistant strains of tuberculosis and other formerly treatable diseases has resulted in resolutions from the World Health Organization in May 2014 and pledges from political leaders from the USA, Germany and the UK to reduce roadblocks and increase funding for antibiotics research.[4]

Ironically, the possibility of drug-resistant strains of diseases is even more alarming given that national governments have been moving away from labor-intensive traditional public health prevention efforts toward public health efforts based on treatment with pharmaceuticals, a move that anthropologists label the "pharmaceuticalization of public health" (Biehl 2006, 2007; Whitmarsh 2008). "The pharmaceuticalization of public health" consists of defining access to pharmaceuticals as the primary public health intervention. As a government policy, it involves a shift away from prevention techniques and practices and clinical care to pharmaceutical intervention and treatment at a community level. Countries have taken on this strategy because it appears to be cheaper and more efficient (Biehl 2006; Whitmarsh 2008). The equation of public health with pharmaceutical access is increasing in international trade, fueled in part by Trade-Related Aspects of Intellectual Property Rights (TRIPS).[5] According to Whitmarsh: "[G]overnment purchase of pharmaceuticals combined with adherence to patent and exclusivity laws is increasingly emphasized in this technique of health intervention among resource-poor countries" (2008:39). Ethnographic studies of the pharmaceuticalization of public health in low-income economies have documented that this practice marginalizes other approaches to public health such as education and labor-intensive testing measures, which may be more effective in the long run (Biehl 2006; Petty and Heimer 2011). Furthermore, it has had an enormous impact on the struggles over the importation of patented drugs versus the use of generics.

Pharmaceuticalization is a dynamic and complex heterogeneous socio-technical process. It includes distinct socioeconomic activities and diverse actors such as clinicians, patients or consumers and regulators that contribute to the long-term and ongoing construction and expansion of the pharmaceutical industry (Williams et al. 2011:721). As we explore elsewhere (Bell and Figert 2012b; Figert and Bell 2014) some people are being helped by pharmaceuticals on a daily basis, and political organizations, especially those concerned with treatment for those with HIV/AIDS, have struggled to make drugs available (see also Smith and Siplon 2006). Others gain access to medications by serving as drug trial subjects. Participation in clinical trials can economically and politically empower and disempower people in low-income countries (Petty and Heimer 2011). Political economic, cultural, organizational and technoscientific trends and processes are mutually constituted, and these processes are "manifest in large, macrostructural changes as well as in new personal identities and subjectivities" (Clarke et al. 2010:85).

Although there is not yet a consensus about the dynamics of pharmaceuticalization or the pharmaceuticalization of public health, scholars generally agree that pharmaceuticalization can occur without medicalization, and vice versa. Coveney, Gabe and Williams (2011:389) state the dominant position among contemporary pharmaceuticalization scholars: "medicalization and pharmaceuticalization do not necessarily implicate each other. Rather, they intersect in contingent and unpredictable ways." It is for this reason that we argue that medicalization and pharmaceuticalization are related yet distinct concepts and processes.

Geneticization and Its Limits

Understanding the connection between people's biology and their health has a long history in the scientific and social scientific communities. Early twentieth-century debates about heritability, eugenics and intelligence all focused upon a modern binary that pit social scientists and ethicists against the scientists and policymakers who believed in genetic determinism (Kevles 1985; Duster 2003). By the mid-twentieth century, discovery of the structure of DNA gave "final proof, it was assumed, of the reality of units of inheritance, the genes" and for those on the nature side of the debate it appeared they had won (Lock 2012:133). The Human Genome Project (HGP) at first appeared to give final proof of genetic determinism. Although many accounts of the HGP locate the project within the US-based laboratories of the National Institutes of Health and the Department of Energy, the larger HGP project ultimately involved a global network of laboratories and scientists. The goal was simple: to create a map of the human genome. However, in mapping the human genome the very idea of the gene became fuzzier and more complex to researchers (Bliss 2015, Chapter 9, this volume; Shostak and Moinester 2015). The consequence was that research on the gene undermined the very idea of genetic determinism and decoupled the firm link between gene structure and phenotype. The HGP opened up a space between genotype and phenotype (Lock 2012:162). This is known as "epigenetics." Its key insight is that "gene expression can be altered by environmental exposures, even without changes in the actual sequences of DNA, and ... these patterns of gene expression and regulation are heritable" (Shostak and Freese 2010:421). In other words, social and historical factors interact with DNA.

The concept of geneticization dates to the early 1990s, at height of genetic determinism science and politics. It was part of and developed from a larger conversation in the social sciences and humanities about the processes through which biological and genetic information was developed and the social consequences of this information. The studies gave critical attention to determinist explanations for human difference (especially race, gender/sex and sexuality). These topics have also been longstanding concerns in Science and Technology Studies (STS) (such as Nelkin and Tancredi 1989; Proctor 1988) and among feminists (Bleier 1984; Fausto-Sterling 1985; Hubbard 1990; Keller 2000) and critical race scholars (Braun et al. 2007; Duster 2003; Reardon 2005; TallBear 2007).

The concept of geneticization has been a crucial framework for many critiques of the HGP. It began with Abby Lippman (1991) who proposed the concept to capture the new way of seeing and solving problems that came along with the HGP. Lippman defined geneticization as:

> an ongoing process by which differences between individuals are reduced to their DNA codes, with most disorders, behaviors and physiological variations defined, at least, as genetic in origin. It refers as well to the process by which interventions employing genetic technologies are adopted to manage problems of health. Through this process, human biology is incorrectly equated with human genetics, implying that the latter acts alone to make us each the organism she or he is. (1991:19)

By reducing differences between individuals to their DNA codes, geneticization individualizes social differences and assigns them to decontextualized segments of DNA. Lippman worried that geneticization would indirectly reinforce "racism, social inequalities, and discrimination of those with disabilities" (Lock 2012:137).

Furthermore, Lippman observed a connection between the processes and outcomes of geneticization and medicalization. In popular discourse, genetic variations such as found in a developing fetus were increasingly defined as problems for which there were medical or technological solutions. For example, at the time she proposed the concept, prenatal testing was the most widely used and familiar genetic activity. Accordingly, as part of the feminist scholarship that had been long concerned about genetic testing on women in the 1980s, Lippman gave initial attention to cultural stories about prenatal diagnosis to exemplify "geneticization." Although there are many ways to tell stories about health and disease, and there is an extensive vocabulary to use in telling them, Lippman observed that "an increasing number of these stories are being told in the same way and with the same language: genetics, genes and genetic techniques" (Lippman 1991:44). In her examination of the structure and content of stories about prenatal testing and diagnosis she found that "the best-selling" ones were about reassurance, choice and control (Lippman 1991:44). According to this type of story, prenatal diagnosis enables women to prevent birthing children with disabilities; children born with disabilities are thus failures. Lippman asked, "why are biological variations that create differences between individuals seen as preventable or avoidable while social conditions that create similar distinctions are likely to be perceived as intractable givens?" (Lippman 1991:45). The discourse of prenatal diagnosis stories contributes to and reflects geneticization.

Within the "social control" models of medicalization theory in the 1980s, genetics was rarely mentioned explicitly but was often implicit within discussions about deviance that located the cause within the body or genetic inheritance. Conrad and Schneider (1980) used specific cases of mental illness, alcoholism, ADHD and crime to explore the many ways in which transforming deviant behaviors into medical problems under medical authority absolved individuals of responsibility and relieved their symptoms. For example, mental illness is not a choice made by individuals. Its cause is located within a person's biological body and thus it is "real" and not "imagined" or "faked." Medicalization also individualizes the illness experience or disease or medicalized diagnosis. Similarly, genetic diagnosis frequently gives legitimacy to a disorder as being "truly" biological, instead of a "catchall diagnostic category" (Lock 2012:146). This is similar to what medicalization does in its legitimation of a disorder as "real" instead of a figment of the sufferer's imagination and in individualizing a genetic body.

Although scholars disagree about the extent to which the processes of geneticization and medicalization overlap, all of them agree that there are important differences between the two processes. Gusterson (2001:252) argues that medicalization "cannot convey the novelty and power" of the processes and a new way of seeing made possible by genetic research. Conrad distinguishes between medicalization, which does not "require specific claims about cause, although the assumption is often biological" and geneticization, which "is very specific about where at least part of the cause lies" (Conrad 2000:329).

The concepts of medicalization and geneticization, however, cannot fully capture the global dynamics of the science of genetics/genomics in the twenty-first century. Both medicalization and geneticization are limited to what they can tell us about the ever-changing world of genetics precisely because they are modern concepts developed to explain modern processes. As we wrote in the beginning of this section, the research that came out of the HGP was instrumental in decentering the gene as a causal agent; it decoupled genetic structure and genetic expression. In other words, just because someone is born with a gene does not mean the gene will be expressed or that if it is expressed that it will be expressed consistently across individuals.

In the course of developing post-HGP research scientists have looked beyond the binary between genes and their environment on a cellular and body level. However, it is much easier to study a carefully constructed and researchable gene than it is to study either (and both) messy and complex epigenetics and society. We agree with Lock that the framework of genetics research is consistent with modernity and epigenetics research is consistent with postmodernity. She writes:

> The molecularized universe has turned out to be so very much more complicated and exciting than most people had imagined. It is a universe entirely in tune with postmodernity. It is a landscape littered with a pastiche of shape-shifters (smart genes, transcription factors, jumping genes and so on), an environment of the unexpected in which boundaries formerly thought to be stable are dissolved. (Lock 2009:162–3)

Geneticization is useful to counteract genetic determinism in its various forms. Geneticization is a blunt concept, however, that cannot grasp complex processes associated with epigenetics (Hedgecoe 2001). Individual users are not deterministic and the science is not deterministic any more and yet there are elements of genetic determinism floating out there in concepts of race and citizenship. Shostak and Moinester (2015) make a strong and convincing argument that it is time for scholars to move beyond the geneticization framework (because it assumes a binary between genes and the environments that humans inhabit) and at the same time scholars should retain its original social justice goals. Following Shostak and Moinester's lead, we look forward to sustained discussions that include the old critiques with new engagements.

Moving Sideways to Forge Ahead

We have reviewed some of the historical grounding and developments of medicalization studies and entry of the concepts of "biomedicalization," "pharmaceuticalization," "the pharmaceuticalization of public health" and "geneticization" into social scientists' intellectual toolkits. We end by making a case for turning sideways, as do the contributors to this volume, to other disciplines such as STS, history and anthropology and other locations beyond the USA and Western Europe for clarity and insights. This focus has allowed scholars to more closely examine political, economic and organizational dynamics of global health inequalities that are less visible in many of the studies by sociologists. For example, whereas sociologists primarily study medicalization, biomedicalization, genetics and pharmaceuticals by focusing upon power, economics and treatments in the global North, anthropologists, STS scholars and, yes, even some sociologists have focused upon the issues of pharmaceuticals in people's lives in low- and middle-income countries throughout the world (see Williams, Gabe and Martin 2012). For example, in the global North, pharmaceuticalization is primarily about expanding social and behavioral diagnostic categories and diagnoses, while in the global South, pharmaceuticalization is primarily about expanding access to medicines and public health (Samsky 2012; Samsky 2015, Chapter 6, this volume) or of expanding test sites for pharmaceutical clinical trials (Petty and Heimer 2011). Geneticization in the global North is seen as something primarily embodied either genetically or in the expression of diseases or illnesses that may or may not be technologically fixed or controlled. Geneticization in the global South may be more about documenting or claiming tribal or racial citizenship through genomic or genetically based group identity (see Bliss 2015; Benjamin 2015, Chapter 10, this volume).

Finally, it is not without irony that we return to Irving Zola's work about medicine as an institution of social control. Much of this chapter has been about the need and necessity to move beyond the social control framework of medicalization. However, Zola wrote in 1972: "the labels health and illness are remarkable 'depoliticizers' of an issue. By locating the source and the treatment of problems in an individual, other levels of intervention are effectively closed" (1972:500). We want to acknowledge that this notion of labels or concepts or defining problems in terms of only one "-ization" frame, be it medicalization, pharmaceuticalization, pharmaceuticalization of public health, geneticization or biomedicalization can foreclose other ways of understanding what the problems are and how to alleviate them. The "-ization" definitions and frameworks also have the tendency of assuming that these are processes that are "done to" or "done on" people. Furthermore, "-ization" frameworks can construct problems of health inequality as "inexorable, irreversible, large scale processes" that are driven either by powerful villains or by anonymous external forces (Greene 2015:105, Chapter 5, this volume). When we argue in the introduction of the book that we do not want to "give up" on the utility of medicalization, we are noting that sometimes medicalization actually does capture what is going on in the world; but it does not and cannot fully capture all of the political, economic and scientific changes that are occurring every day. We imply, by extension, that the other "-izations" can provide useful but nonetheless partial ways of seeing the world. Each has its own limits and promise as we have outlined in this chapter. However, the effects of arguing for just one way of understanding what is going on in the global world today are very similar to what Zola described – narrowing the possibilities and, at least in the case of medical-ization, focusing on individuals for solutions that are large scale and global in nature. We have and continue to argue in favor of moving sideways, of drawing from multiple disciplinary perspectives in history, sociology, anthropology and STS, and of attending to complexity and messiness. By doing so, we can move forward toward a richer understanding of the interrelationships between social processes and individual lives, and toward identifying strategies to reduce global health inequalities.

Acknowledgments

We are grateful to Susan Reverby and the reviewers for their quick and thoughtful critique of an earlier version of this chapter. Funding by Bowdoin College's Dean for Academic Affairs made it possible for a lively group of scholars to spend two and half days together in 2013 at a symposium at Bowdoin College, "Big Pharma, Big Medicine and Technoscience: Investigating Intersections in the Twenty-first Century." Thank you to those scholars for pushing us in fruitful directions. We thank our colleagues at Loyola University Chicago and Bowdoin College for ongoing dialogues about moving sideways and forging ahead.

Notes

1 This chapter draws heavily on Bell and Figert (2012a).
2 Individuals and consumer patient groups have long argued and continue to argue for the inclusion in the medical domain or medicalization of their specific bodies/conditions (Barker 2005; Figert 2011). For example, for those women globally who want to become mothers today, participation in medicine (technology, services and knowledge) can be a strategy to accomplish what they perceive to be in their best interests. Childbearing is a key practice in which evidence repeatedly shows how, why and with what consequences women seek medical assistance to achieve (biological) motherhood. In this case, medicalization is "strategic" and empowering (Inhorn 2006).
3 We note that the earlier studies in the medicalization of deviance had a primary focus on men's bodies but did not take a gendered analysis. Men and male bodies were the focus of a few early medicalization studies in sociology, especially those studies focusing upon deviance and social control. Gender was not initially seen or highlighted as an important aspect of the process of medicalization. Annandale and Riska (2009) argue that "the gendered implications of this development have been insufficiently realized to date" (2009:127). For example, Rosenfeld and Faircloth note that "[i]n medicalization research, as in most social-scientific research, gender seems to mean womanhood" (2006:1). The recent turn to understand how men's bodies are also medicalized also explicitly challenges assumptions rooted in social control theories about medicalization that only underrepresented groups are medicalized (Rosenfeld and Faircloth 2006).
4 See, for example, the article in the *Wall Street Journal* about antibiotic development: www.wallstreetotc.com/antibiotics-call-urgent-attention-drug-market-facing-apocalyptic-scenario/25555/ (accessed July 7, 2014).
5 TRIPS was a 1995 deal brokered by the World Trade Organization to support patents on pharmaceuticals and other forms of intellectual property. TRIPS was revised a few years later to enable governments to break patents for certain pharmaceuticals or "essential medicines" to combat the spread and treatment of diseases, a revision that has been especially important for populations in low- and middle-income economies.

References

Abraham, John. 2007. "Building on Sociological Understandings of the Pharmaceutical Industry or Reinventing the Wheel? Response to Joan Busfield's 'Pills, Power, People.'" *Sociology* 41: 727–36.

Abraham, John. 2010a. "The Sociological Concomitants of the Pharmaceutical Industry and Medications." Pp. 290–308 in *The Handbook of Medical Sociology*, edited by Chloe E. Bird, Peter Conrad, Allen M. Freemont and Stefan Timmermans. Nashville, TN: Vanderbilt University Press.

Abraham, John. 2010b. "Pharmaceuticalization of Society in Context: Theoretical, Empirical, and Health Dimensions." *Sociology* 44:603–22.

Annandale, Ellen and Elianne Riska. 2009. "New Connections: Towards a Gender-Inclusive Approach to Women's and Men's Health." *Current Sociology* 57:123–33.

Applbaum, Kalman. 2006. "Educating for Global Mental Health: The Adoption of SSRIs in Japan." Pp. 85–110 in *Global Pharmaceuticals: Ethics, Markets, Practices*, edited by A. Petryna, A. Lakoff and A. Kleinman. Durham, NC: Duke University Press.

Ballard, Karen and Mary Ann Elston. 2005. "Medicalisation: A Multi-dimensional Concept." *Social Theory & Health* 3:228–41.

Barker, Kristin. 2005. *The Fibromyalgia Story: Medical Authority and Women's Worlds of Pain*. Philadelphia, PA: Temple University Press.

Bell, Susan E. 1987a. "Changing Ideas: The Medicalization of Menopause." *Social Science & Medicine* 24(6):535–42.

Bell, Susan E. 1987b. "Premenstrual Syndrome and the Medicalization of Menopause: A Sociological Perspective." Pp. 151–73 in *The Premenstrual Syndrome: Ethical and Legal Implications in a Biomedical Perspective*, edited by B. Ginsburg and B. Frank Carter. New York: Plenum.

Bell, Susan E. and Anne E. Figert. 2012a. "Medicalization and Pharmaceuticalization at the Intersections: Looking Backward, Sideways and Forward." *Social Science & Medicine* 75: 775–83.

Bell, Susan E. and Anne E. Figert. 2012b. "Starting to Turn Sideways to Move Forward in Medicalization and Pharmaceuticalization Studies: A Response to Williams et. al." *Social Science & Medicine* 75:2131–3.

Bell, Susan E. and Anne E. Figert. 2015. "Introduction: Outlining Old Critiques and New Engagements." Pp. 1–15 in *Reimagining (Bio)Medicalization, Pharmaceuticals and Genetics: Old Critiques and New Engagements*, edited by Susan E. Bell and Anne E. Figert. New York: Routledge.

Benjamin, Ruha. 2015. "Racial Destiny or Dexterity?: The Global Circulation of Genomics as an Empowerment Idiom." Pp. 197–215 in *Reimagining (Bio)Medicalization, Pharmaceuticals and Genetics: Old Critiques and New Engagements*, edited by Susan E. Bell and Anne E. Figert. New York: Routledge.

Biehl, João. 2006. "Pharmaceutical Governance." Pp. 206–39 in *Global Pharmaceuticals: Ethics, Markets, Practices*, edited by A. Petryna, A. Lakoff and A. Kleinman. Durham, NC: Duke University Press.

Biehl, João. 2007. "Pharmaceuticalization: AIDS Treatment and Global Health Politics." *Anthropological Quarterly* 80:1083–126.

Biehl, João. 2008. "Drugs for All: The Future of Global AIDS Treatment." *Medical Anthropology* 27:99–105.

Bleier, Ruth. 1984. *Science and Gender: A Critique of Biology and its Theories on Women*. New York: Pergamon Press.

Bliss, Catherine. 2015. "Biomedicalization and the New Science of Race." Pp. 175–96 in *Reimagining (Bio)Medicalization, Pharmaceuticals and Genetics: Old Critiques and New Engagements*, edited by Susan E. Bell and Anne E. Figert. New York: Routledge.

Boston Women's Health Book Collective. 1973. *Our Bodies, Ourselves*. Boston, MA: Boston Women's Health Book Collective.

Braun, Lundy, Anne Fausto-Sterling, D. Fullwiley, Evelyn M. Hammonds and Alondra Nelson. 2007. "Racial Categories in Medical Practice: How Useful Are They?" *PLoS Medicine* 4:e271.

Brown, Phil and Steven Zavestoski. 2004. "Social Movements in Health: An Introduction." *Sociology of Health & Illness* 26(6):679–94.

Busfield, Joan. 2006. "Pills, Power, People: Sociological Understandings of the Pharmaceutical Industry." *Sociology* 40:297–314.

Busfield, Joan. 2010. "'A Pill for Every Ill': Explaining the Expansion in Medicine Use." *Social Science & Medicine* 70:934–41.

Butler, Judith. 1993. *Bodies that Matter: On the Discursive Limits of "Sex."* New York: Routledge.

Clarke, Adele E., Laura Mamo, Jennifer R. Fishman, Janet K. Shim and Jennifer Ruth Fosket. 2003. "Biomedicalization: Technoscientific Transformations of Health, Illness, and U.S. Biomedicine." *American Sociological Review* 68:161–94.

Clarke, Adele, Laura Mamo, Jennifer Ruth Fosket, Jennifer R. Fishman and Janet K. Shim, eds. 2010. *Biomedicalization: Technoscience, Health, and Illness in the U.S.* Durham, NC: Duke University Press.

Conrad, Peter. 1992. "Medicalization and Social Control." *Annual Review of Sociology* 18:209–32.

Conrad, Peter. 2000. "Medicalization, Genetics, and Human Problems." Pp. 322–33 in *Handbook of Medical Sociology*, edited by C. E. Bird, P. Conrad and A. M. Fremont. Upper Saddle River, NJ: Prentice Hall.

Conrad, Peter. 2005. "The Shifting Engines of Medicalization." *Journal of Health and Social Behavior* 46:3–14.

Conrad, Peter. 2007. *The Medicalization of Society: On the Transformation of Human Conditions into Treatable Disorders.* Baltimore, MD: Johns Hopkins University Press.

Conrad, Peter and Joseph Schneider. 1980. *Deviance and Medicalization: From Badness to Sickness.* St Louis, MO: Mosby.

Coveney, Catherine, Jonathan Gabe and Simon Williams. 2011. "The Sociology of Cognitive Enhancement: Medicalisation and Beyond." *Health Sociology Review* 20 (Sociology of Health and Illness in the UK):381–93.

Crossley, Nick. 2006. *Contesting Psychiatry: Social Movements in Mental Health.* London and New York: Routledge.

Crowley-Matoka, Megan and Gala True. 2012. "No One Wants to be the Candy Man: Ambivalent Medicalization and Clinician Subjectivity in Pain Management." *Cultural Anthropology* 27:689–712.

Cuthbertson, Courtney A. 2015. "Pharmaceutical Technologies and the Management of Biological Citizens in Chile." Pp. 137–59 in *Reimagining (Bio)Medicalization, Pharmaceuticals and Genetics: Old Critiques and New Engagements*, edited by Susan E. Bell and Anne E. Figert. New York: Routledge.

Duster, Troy. 2003. *Backdoor to Eugenics.* New York: Routledge.

Ebeling, Mary. 2011. "Get with the Program!: Pharmaceutical Marketing, Symptom Checklists, and Self-Diagnosis" *Social Science & Medicine* 73:825–32.

Fausto-Sterling, Anne. 1985. *Myths of Gender: Biological Theories about Women and Men.* New York: Basic Books.

Figert, Anne E. 1995. "The Three Faces of PMS: The Scientific, Political and Professional Structuring of a Psychiatric Disorder." *Social Problems* 42(1):56–73.

Figert, Anne E. 2011. "The Consumer Turn in Medicalization: Future Directions with Historical Foundations." Pp. 291–307 in *The Handbook of the Sociology of Health, Illness & Healing: Blueprint for the 21st Century*, edited by B. Pescosolido, J. Martin, J. Mcleod and A. Rogers. New York: Springer.

Figert, Anne E. and Susan E. Bell. 2014. "Big Pharma and Big Medicine in the Global Environment." Pp. 456–70 in *The Routledge Handbook of Science, Technology and Society*, edited by Daniel Kleinman and Kelly Moore. New York: Routledge.

Fishman, Jennifer R. 2010. "The Making of Viagra: The Biomedicalization of Sexual Dysfunction." Pp. 289–306 in *Biomedicalization: Technoscience, Health, and Illness in the U.S.*, edited by A. E. Clarke, L. Mamo, J. R. Fosket, J. R. Fishman and J. K. Shim. Durham, NC, and London: Duke University Press.

Fosket, Jennifer Ruth. 2010. "Breast Cancer Risk as Disease: Biomedicalizing Risk." Pp. 331–52 in *Biomedicalization: Technoscience, Health, and Illness in the U.S.*, edited by A. E. Clarke, L. Mamo, J. R. Fosket, J. R. Fishman and J. K. Shim. Durham, NC, and London: Duke University Press.

Foucault, Michel. 1965. *Madness and Civilization.* New York: Bantam Books.

Foucault, Michel. 1977[1975]. *Discipline and Punish.* New York: Pantheon.

Foucault, Michel. 1978. *History of Sexuality, Vol.1, An Introduction.* New York: Random House.

Fox, Nick J. and Katie J. Ward. 2008. "Pharma in the Bedroom … and the kitchen …: The Pharmaceuticalisation of Daily Life." *Sociology of Health & Illness* 30:856–68.

Freidson, Eliot. 1970. *Profession of Medicine: A Study of the Sociology of Applied Knowledge.* New York: Dodd, Mead & Co.

Greene, Jeremy A. 2015. "Vital Objects: Essential Drugs and Their Critical Legacies." Pp. 89–111 in *Reimagining (Bio)Medicalization, Pharmaceuticals and Genetics: Old Critiques and New Engagements*, edited by Susan E. Bell and Anne E. Figert. New York: Routledge.

Gusterson, Hugh. 2001. "Comment: The Kin in the Gene." *Current Anthropology* 42:251–2.

Halpern, Sydney. 1990. "Medicalization as Professional Process: Postwar Trends in Pediatrics." *Journal of Health and Social Behavior* 31:28–42.

Hedgecoe, Adam. 2001. "Schizophrenia and the Narrative of Enlightened Geneticization." *Social Studies of Science* 31(6):875–911.

Hubbard, Ruth. 1990. *The Politics of Women's Biology*. New Brunswick, NJ: Rutgers University Press.

Hill, Raymond and Mandy Chui. 2009. "The Pharmerging Future." *Pharmaceutical Executive* 29(7):1–8. Accessed October 4, 2014 (www.imshealth.com/imshealth/Global/Content/Document/Intelligence.360%20Documents/The_Pharmerging_Future.pdf).

IMS Institute for Healthcare Informatics. 2013. "The Global Use of Medicines: Outlook through 2017." Report by the IMS Institute for Healthcare Informatics. Parsippany, NJ. Accessed June 14, 2014 (www.imshealth.com/portal/site/imshealth/menuitem.762a961826aad98f53c753c71ad8c22a/?vgnextoid=9f819e464e832410VgnVCM10000076192ca2RCRD&vgnextchannel=a64de5fda6370410VgnVCM10000076192ca2RCRD&vgnextfmt=default).

Illich, Ivan. 1975. *Medical Nemesis*. New York: Pantheon.

Inhorn, Marcia. C. 2006. "Defining Women's Health: A Dozen Messages from More Than 150 Ethnographies." *Medical Anthropology Quarterly* 20:345–78.

Kahn, Jonathan. 2010. "Surrogate Markers and Surrogate Marketing in Biomedicine: The Regulatory Etiology and Commercial Progression of 'Ethnic' Drug Development." Pp. 263–88 in *Biomedicalization: Technoscience, Health and Illness in the U.S.*, edited by A. E. Clarke, L. Mamo, J. R. Fosket, J. R. Fishman and J. K. Shim. Durham, NC, and London: Duke University Press.

Keller, Evelyn Fox. 2000. *The Century of the Gene*. Cambridge, MA: Harvard University Press.

Kevles, Daniel. 1985. *In the Name of Eugenics: Genetics and the Uses of Human Heredity*, No. 95. Cambridge, MA: Harvard University Press.

Kleinman, Arthur. 2012. "Medical Anthropology and Mental Health: Five Questions for the Next Fifty Years." Pp. 178–96 in *Medical Anthropology at the Intersections*, edited by M. C. Inhorn and E. A. Wentzell. Durham, NC: Duke University Press.

Laing, R. D. 1961. *The Self and Others*. London: Tavistock.

Lakoff, Andrew. 2004. "The Anxieties of Globalization: Antidepressant Sales and Economic Crisis in Argentina." *Social Studies of Science* 34:247–69.

Light, Donald, ed. 2010. *The Risks of Prescription Drugs*. New York: Columbia University Press.

Lippman, Abby. 1991. "Prenatal Genetic Testing and Screening: Constructing Needs and Reinforcing Inequities." *American Journal of Law & Medicine* 17:15–50.

Lock, Margaret. 2004. "Medicalization and the Naturalization of Social Control." Pp. 116–24 in *Encyclopedia of Medical Anthropology; Health and Illness in the World's Cultures*, Vol. 1, edited by C. W. Ember and M. Ember. New York: Lower Academic/Plenum Publishers.

Lock, Margaret. 2009. "Demoting the Genetic Body." *Anthropologica* 51:159–72.

Lock, Margaret. 2012. "From Genetics to Postgenomics and the Discovery of the New Social Body." Pp. 129–60 in *Medical Anthropology at the Intersections*, edited by M. C. Inhorn and E. A. Wentzell. Durham, NC: Duke University Press.

Loe, Meika. 2004. *The Rise of Viagra*. New York: New York University Press.

Lupton, Deborah. 1997. "Foucault and the Medicalisation Critique." Pp. 94–110 in *Foucault, Health and Medicine*, edited by A. Peterson and R. Bunton. London and New York: Routledge.

Mamo, Laura. 2007. *Queering Reproduction: Achieving Pregnancy in the Age of Technoscience*. Durham, NC: Duke University Press.

Mamo, Laura. 2010. "Fertility, Inc.: Consumption and Subjectification in U.S. Lesbian Reproductive Practices." Pp. 173–96 in *Biomedicalization: Technoscience, Health, and Illness in the U.S.*, edited by A. E. Clarke, L. Mamo, J. R. Fosket, J. R. Fishman and J. K. Shim. Durham, NC, and London: Duke University Press.

Mamo, Laura and Jennifer Ruth Fosket. 2009. "Scripting the Body: Pharmaceuticals and the (Re)Making of Menstruation." *Signs* 34:926–49.

McCrea, Frances. 1983. "The Politics of Menopause: The 'Discovery' of a Deficiency Disease." *Social Problems* 31:111–23.

Metzl, Jonathan and Rebecca Herzig. 2007. "Medicalisation in the 21st Century: Introduction." *The Lancet* 369:697–8.

Nelkin, Dorothy and Laurence R. Tancredi. 1989. *Dangerous Diagnostics: The Social Power of Biological Information*. New York: Basic Books.

Nichter, Mark. 1996[1989]. "Pharmaceuticals, the Commodification of Health, and the Health Care-Medicine Use Transition." Pp. 265–326 in *Anthropology and International Health: Asian Case Studies, Theory and Practice in Medical Anthropology and International Health*, edited by M. Nichter and M. Nichter. Amsterdam: Gordon & Breach Science Publishers.

Nye, Robert. 2003. "The Evolution of the Concept of Medicalization in the Twentieth Century." *Journal of the History of the Behavioral Sciences* 39(2):115–29.

Padamsee, Tasleem. 2011. "The Pharmaceutical Corporation and the 'Good Work' of Managing Women's Bodies." *Social Science & Medicine* 72(8):1342–50.

Parsons, Talcott. 1951. *The Social System*. Glencoe, IL: The Free Press.

Payton, Andrew R. and Peggy A. Thoits. 2011. "Medicalization, Direct-to-Consumer Advertising, and Mental Illness Stigma." *Society and Mental Health* 1:55–70.

Pescosolido, Bernice A., Jack K. Martin, J. Scott Long, Tait R. Medina, Jo C. Phelan and Bruce G. Link. 2010. "'A Disease Like Any Other?' A Decade of Change in Public Reactions to Schizophrenia, Depression, and Alcohol Dependence." *American Journal of Psychiatry* 167:1321–30.

Petty, Ju Leigh and Carol Heimer. 2011. "Extending the Rails: How Research Reshapes Clinics." *Social Studies of Science* 41:337–60.

Phelan, Jo C. 2005. "Geneticization of Deviant Behavior and Consequences for Stigma: The Case of Mental Illness." *Journal of Health and Social Behavior* 46(December):307–22.

Pitts, Jesse R. 1968. "Social Control." Pp. 381–97 in *International Encyclopedia of the Social Sciences*, Vol. 14, edited by David L. Sills and Robert K. Merton. New York: Macmillan.

Plechner, Deborah. 2000. "Women, Medicine, and Sociology: Thoughts on the Need for a Critical Feminist Perspective." *Research in the Sociology of Health Care* 18:69–94.

Proctor, Robert. 1988. *Racial Hygiene: Medicine under the Nazis*. Cambridge, MA: Harvard University Press.

Reardon, Jenny. 2005. *Race to the Finish: Identity and Governance in an Age of Genomics*. Princeton, NJ: Princeton University Press.

Riessman, Catherine Kohler. 1983. "Women and Medicalization: A New Perspective" *Social Policy* Summer:3–18.

Riska, Eliana. 2003. "Gendering the Medicalization Thesis." *Advances in Gender Research* 7:59–87.

Rose, Nikolas. 2007. "Beyond Medicalisation." *The Lancet* 369:700–2.

Rosenberg, Charles. 2006. "Contested Boundaries: Psychiatry, Disease and Diagnosis." *Perspectives in Biology and Medicine* 49(3):407–24.

Rosenfeld, Dana. and Christopher Faircloth. 2006. *Medicalized Masculinities*. Philadelphia, PA: Temple University Press.

Samsky, Ari. 2012. "'Since We Are Taking the Drugs': Labor and Value in Two International Drug Donation Programs." Pp. 37–51 in *The Value of Transnational Medical Research*, edited by A. H. Kelly and P. W. Geissler. New York: Routledge.

Samsky, Ari. 2015. "The Drug Swallowers: Scientific Sovereignty and Pharmaceuticalization in Two International Drug Donation Programs." Pp. 112–36 in *Reimagining (Bio)Medicalization, Pharmaceuticals and Genetics: Old Critiques and New Engagements*, edited by Susan E. Bell and Anne E. Figert. New York: Routledge.

Scott, Wilbur. 1990. "PTSD in the DSM-III: A Case in the Politics of Diagnosis and Disease." *Social Problems* 37:294–310.

Shostak, Sara. 2013. *Exposed Science: Genes, the Environment, and the Politics of Population Health*. Berkeley, CA: University of California Press.

Shostak, Sara and Jeremy Freese. 2010. "Gene-Environment Interaction and Medical Sociology." Pp. 418–34 in *Handbook of Medical Sociology*, edited by C. Bird, A. Fremont, P. Conrad and S. Timmermans. Nashville, TN: Vanderbilt University Press.

Shostak, Sara and Margot Moinester. 2015. "Beyond Geneticization: Regimes of Perceptibility and the Social Determinants of Health." Pp. 216–38 in *Reimagining (Bio)Medicalization, Pharmaceuticals and Genetics: Old Critiques and New Engagements*, edited by Susan E. Bell and Anne E. Figert. New York: Routledge.

Smith, Raymond A. and Patricia D. Siplon. 2006. *Drugs into Bodies: Global AIDS Treatment Activism*. Westport, CT: Praeger Publishing.

Szasz, Thomas. 1974[1961]. *The Myth of Mental Illness: Foundations of a Theory of Personal Conduct*, rev. edn. New York: HarperCollins.

TallBear, Kimberly. 2007. "Narratives of Race and Indigeneity in the Genographic Project." *Journal of Law, Medicine & Ethics* 35:412–24.

Torres, Jennifer. 2014. "Medicalizing to Demedicalize: Lactation Consultants and the (De) Medicalization of Breastfeeding." *Social Science & Medicine* 100:159–66.

Whitmarsh, Ian. 2008. *Biomedical Ambiguity: Race, Asthma, and the Contested Meaning of Genetic Research in the Caribbean*. Ithaca, NY, and London: Cornell University Press.

Williams, Simon J., Jonathan Gabe and Peter Davis. 2008. "The Sociology of Pharmaceuticals: Progress and Prospects." *Sociology of Health & Illness* 30:813–24.

Williams, Simon J., Paul Martin and Jonathan Gabe. 2011. "The Pharmaceuticalization of Society? A Framework for Analysis." *Sociology of Health & Illness* 33:710–25.

Williams, Simon, Jonathan Gabe and Paul Martin. 2012. "Medicalization and Pharmaceuticalization at the Intersections: A Commentary on Bell and Figert (2012)." *Social Science & Medicine* 75(12):2129–30.

Zacher, Mark W. and Tania J. Keefe. 2008. *The Politics of Global Health Governance: United by Contagion*. New York: Palgrave Macmillan.

Zola, Irving. 1972. "Medicine as an Institution of Social Control." *Sociological Review* 20:487–504.

2

A New Biopolitics of Gender and Health?

"Gender-specific Medicine" and Pharmaceuticalization in the Twenty-First Century

ELLEN ANNANDALE AND ANNE HAMMARSTRÖM

Medicalization, pharmaceuticalization and gender have a long, intertwined and well-documented history stemming back to at least the women's health movement of the 1970s. Although early deliberations on medicalization were framed as "gender-neutral" (Riska 2003, 2010), they occurred around the same time that feminists were criticizing male control of the female body and mind expressly through the technological management of childbirth (e.g., Arms 1975; Ehrenreich and English 1978; Reissman 1983) and prescription of antidepressants to remedy the unhappiness of life in a patriarchal world (Chesler 1972). Interest in the gendered aspects of medicalization has grown exponentially over subsequent years. Four developments are especially noteworthy. *First*, medicalization has been part of the groundswell of interest in men's health as gendered (which began around the mid-1990s), particularly in relation to sexuality and sexual health (see, e.g., Rosenfeld and Faircloth 2006; Fishman 2010). *Second*, attention has shifted away from the medical profession and the expansion of medical social control as key drivers of medicalization toward biotechnology, particularly the pharmaceutical industry and genetics (Conrad 2004, 2007, 2013; Bell and Figert 2012). Thus Clarke and colleagues consider that by around the mid-1980s biotechnology was of such importance to necessitate the replacement of medicalization with *bio*medicalization (Clarke et al. 2010a; Clarke and Shim 2011). They argue that while medicalization processes typically emphasize the *control over* medical phenomena, such as diseases, injuries and bodily malfunctions, biomedicalization processes concern *transformations* of bodies and lives. Gender is pivotal to technoscientific developments in areas such as genomics which turn the body "inside out as decisions once made on the basis of the inspectable surfaces of the body become the province of the (now visible) genome" (Turney and Balmer 2003:412–13). For example, the "'technologization" of vitality in the life sciences is palpable in the molecular vision of the organism within regenerative medicine (Rose 2013), an umbrella concept which refers to the replacing, engineering or regeneration of human cells and tissues. This is highly gendered as more often than not it is women's bodies which are plundered for embryos, oocytes, fetal tissue, menstrual blood and umbilical cord blood (Waldby and Cooper 2010).

As Riska (2010) relates, biomedicalization directs attention to the material body not only as a major site of biomedical discourse but also public discourse. Perforce a *third* and related development is the shift of attention toward consumers (Figert 2011). The activities of individuals and social groups in seeking out medical diagnoses, treatments and bodily enhancements have been conceptualized by some as "medicalization from below" (see Furedi 2006; Conrad 2013). In the USA and New Zealand this has been fostered by the bypassing of medical prescription for drugs, such as Viagra (for erectile problems) and Paxil (for anxiety and "social phobia"), by direct-to-consumer advertising (DTCA) on television, at various venues (such as sports events) and on public transport. More widely "medicalization from below" has been supported by the emergence of online pharmacies (Miah and Rich 2008) and advocacy amongst online support groups – many of whom are supported by the pharmaceutical industry – for a wide range of conditions (Barker 2011; Goldacre 2012). Flanking this is the *fourth* notable development of "pharmaceuticaliza-tion," or "the translation or transformation of human conditions, capabilities and capacities into opportunities for pharmaceutical intervention" (Williams, Martin and Gabe 2011:711; and see also Abraham 2010; Conrad 2013; Greene 2015, Chapter 5, this volume; Samsky 2015, Chapter 6, this volume; Cuthbertson 2015, Chapter 7, this volume). As will be discussed in detail later in the chapter, essentialized biological categories of sex (and race) are a vital part of pharmaceuticalization processes.

Although there has been a tendency until fairly recently to depict medicalization as a product of modernity, an "inexorable juggernaut" (Davis 2010:231) moving in one direction toward increasing medical control, most social science commentators now recognize the process to be far more complex (see Bell and Figert 2012; Conrad 2013). As Clarke puts it, "the localization of biomedical innovation is everywhere tempered and complicated by medical pluralisms, partialisms [the partial and contingent availability of various medicines], and multiple forms and loci of stratification" (2010:389). Hence she and others argue that medicalization is often highly stratified as assorted medical goods and procedures are targeted to different categories of persons, groups and populations. "Gender-specific medicine" (GSM) is one example of such a "targeting" and stratification process. Hence a detailed examination of GSM has the potential to extend our understanding of the relationship between gender and medicalization as well as the more recently developed but allied concepts of biomedicalization and pharmaceuticalization. In what follows we first provide a brief overview of the rise of GSM, its drivers, defining characteristics and connections to (bio)medicalization. We then place GSM in the context of recent developments in technoscience as they concern gender. Specifically we speculate on the connections between the emerging paradigm of the "gender-specific body" (Annandale and Hammarström 2011) and the gendered "customization" of pharmaceuticals.

Gender-specific Medicine

GSM is a rapidly expanding field as observed by the books and legion articles in medical and allied journals delineating and advocating its principles and further development. There are several "gender-specific" healthcare and research centers, such as the Partnership for Gender-specific Medicine at Columbia University New York, the Centre for Gender Medicine at the Karolinska Institutet in Stockholm and European Gender Medicine under the auspices of Charité Universitätsmedizin in Berlin. Additionally, several organizations advocate sex differences research, even though they may not always employ the "gender-specific" lexicon, such as the Organization for the Study of Sex Differences (founded by the Society for the Study of Women's Health Research) in the USA, the Men's Health Forum in the UK and the International Society for Gender Medicine. Journals have grown up, such as *Gender Medicine* and *Biology of Sex Differences,* as well as an increasing number of national and international congresses, such as the International Congress for Gender and Sex Specific Medicine, now in its seventh year.

GSM can be dated from the mid-1990s as a visible movement within medicine. But its multifaceted origins can be traced back several decades. As far as women are concerned, the GSM ethos owes much to the questioning by feminists and others of the historical depiction of the human standard of the body in medical thinking and practice as male (except where reproduction is concerned) and the related call to include women in biomedical research and practice (Annandale and Hammarström 2011). In the USA, protectionist policies and guidelines on the exploitation of vulnerable subjects had emerged in the wake of the tragic consequences of the use in pregnancy of the drugs thalidomide (to treat nausea and morning sickness) and diethylstilbestrol (DES) (to prevent miscarriage) (Bell 2009). Researchers became averse to including women in their studies given the risks to those who become pregnant and potentially vulnerable during drug-related research. This began to change in the early 1990s when a US Government Accounting Office (GAO) report to Congress documented the failures of the National Institutes of Health (NIH) to institute the recommendations of the 1985 Public Health Taskforce on Women's Health Issues which stated that biomedical and behavioral research should be expanded to a focus on conditions and disease unique to or more prevalent amongst women (Auerbach and Figert 1995; Eckman 1998). In the late 1990s, the US Institute of Medicine (IOM) formed the Committee on Understanding the Biology of Sex and Gender Differences which was intended to evaluate the "factors and traits that characterize and differentiate males and females across the life span and that underlie sex differences in health (including

genetic, biochemical, physiological, physical, and behavioral elements)"
(Wizeman and Pardue 2001:2). The subsequent report, *Exploring the Biological
Contributions to Human Health. Does Sex Matter?* (Wizeman and Pardue 2001),
which is cited frequently by authors in support of sex differences research in
health, concluded that "sex, that is, being male or female," matters and should be
considered when designing and analyzing biomedical and health-related
research. This would be facilitated by the evolution of the study of sex differences
"into a mature science" (Wizeman and Pardue 2001:3). These developments had
the effect not only of bringing women and the female body into medical
research, but of bringing them in as *specific* beings distinguishable from men
(and vice versa). This clearly resonates with the GSM mandate to value what is
gender-*specific* in experience. A year after the IOM report, progenitor and major
protagonist, US cardiologist Marianne Legato published the book *Eve's Rib*, with
the rather theatrical subtitle, "The New Science of Gender-specific Medicine
and How It Can Save Your Life" (Legato 2002). Establishing herself as "a
rigorously trained biomedical scientist" (Legato 2002:xi), Legato asserts in the
book that "as we compare men and women, we are finding that in every system
of the body, from the very hairs on our heads to the way our hearts beat, there
are significant unique sex-based differences in human physiology" (Legato
2002:xii).

Somewhat surprisingly given the swift pace of development, very little
attention has been given to GSM to date by the social sciences and humanities
(though see Grace 2007; Cutter 2012). In what follows we briefly explore how
GSM effects this transition from one size fits all (men and women) to male and
female group specificity through the accentuation of *difference and the dominion
of sex* and the production of a *fragmented conception* of the body to produce
what we conceptualize as the "gender-specific body" and "gender-specific ethos"
in medical research and practice (Annandale and Hammarström 2011;
Hammarström and Annandale 2012).

Difference and the Dominion of Sex

Difference is an essential platform for establishing and furthering the enterprise
of GSM. As Schofield has identified more generally, almost without exception
the representation of gender in health research is a "binary one of sex-based
aggregations of numerical contrasts in health indicators" (Schofield 2004:20).
First and foremost, GSM constructs two gender-based constituencies – women's
health and men's health – at the heart of which is a robust binarism between the
bodies and experiences of men and women. However, GSM is not only
comparative, but also internally competitive. At various times and in relation to
legion health problems, women are posed as disadvantaged by comparison to
men, and men are posed as disadvantaged by comparison to women. Thus the
proposition that a gender-specific approach advantages men and women alike
sits uncomfortably alongside calls for the resources to be targeted to men's or

targeted to women's health. As Wadham (2002) has argued in relation to men, though not with direct reference to GSM, research and policy justifies itself by a strategy of comparison and equivalence, that is, by comparing the health of men to the health of women to make the argument that while the resources accorded to each should be equivalent, they are not, a point which can be applied equally to research on women. Thus it is common for the importance of men's or of women's gender-specific health to be shored up by what we call "gap identifying" rhetoric. To take one example, on the website of the UK Men's Health Forum, the "key data" for health professionals are commonly interpreted through the lens of comparative disadvantage with men, for example, framed as "more commonly" and "more likely" to experience the health problem at issue. This then interpolates into a "gap closing" rhetoric which, in turn, helps authorize investment of resources.

Although health differences and disadvantages are posed as fundamentally biological the need to attend to them is often endorsed by reference to the social situations of men and women. Thus the negative impact of patriarchy on women's health as uncovered by feminists and others helps to legitimate a concentration on women's specific health needs, while the so-called "crisis of masculinity" is drawn upon to justify the need to attend to men's specific health matters (Annandale and Hammarström 2011). But ultimately the term *gender* in GSM is a misnomer since, as already remarked upon, the difference that matters for its advocates is fundamentally biological in nature. Although it is not uncommon for the social aspects of gender to be flagged as relevant to the health issue at hand, typically they get nullified in their conflation with biological sex (Annandale and Hammarström 2011). Gender is recast and treated as a natural phenomenon rooted in biology that contributes to important differences in disease expression and treatment (Cutter 2012:21). This is far removed from feminist and wider social science accounts where gender is seen as a social expression which is malleable, variable and carrying the potential to "overrule or even negate biological propensities" (Baunach 2003:332). And, since biological differences typically are depicted as fixed by GSM, this neglects the insights of feminist biologists such as Fausto-Sterling (2012:xiii) and others that living bodies are "dynamic systems that develop and change in response to their social and historical contexts."

A further guiding message of GSM is that differences between males and females are far more extensive than generally appreciated and extend way beyond the reproductive body. Thus Legato writes, "everywhere researchers look for differences between men and women, they find them" in the brain, the gastrointestinal tract, the heart and circulatory system, the immune system, the skeleton, the skin, the lung, in drug metabolism, in sexual dysfunction, in pain (Legato 2002:240; see also Baggio et al. 2013). So, as the term specific in "gender-specific medicine" readily connotes, difference is elemental. Without it "gender-specific medicine" would have no existence.

While the identification of differences is the domain of scientists, the lay public is accorded a motivating role in GSM:

> The push for individuating women from men invariably begins with a demand by the lay public (usually communicated to political groups rather than to the medical establishment) for more attention to women's unique health needs. Once involved, the body politic appropriates money and resources to expand what's known beyond reproductive biology and, as the medical establishment begins to use that money to support investigation, it finds that males and females have striking and completely unexpected differences in every system of the body. (Legato 2004:61)

We have argued previously that the seeds of "gender-specific medicine" take root in the fertile ground of the "human genome era" (Annandale and Hammarström 2011:583). For example, the US Society for Women's Health Research (SWHR) disseminates the message to the interested public that biological sex influences the expression of genetic information from embryonic development through adulthood. Visitors to the Society's website have been encouraged to "support sex differences research" financially and, until recently, to purchase items such as branded bags, t-shirts and drinking mugs carrying the slogan "Sexx matters." This occurs though the process of what Burri and Dumit (2007:3) characterize as the "socialization of biomedicine," as the various institutions of society become involved in medical knowledge production and diffusion. As Burri and Dumit (2007) continue, various markets and interests become involved in the shaping of research and the ways that healthcare and health products are consumed and marketed. Under the auspices of the SWHR, for example, the difference message is promoted in books for the public such as the edited collection, *The Savvy Woman Patient: How and Why Sex Differences Affect Your Health* (Greenberger and Wider 2006). Advertising for the book directs readers, "women and men are different. Unfortunately, doctors, medical researchers, and health care providers have not always recognized how these differences can affect health. The result has been that women sometimes receive inappropriate medical care." This "gender-specific" way of thinking is likely to blossom in the popular imagination as progressively it is normalized by such products like this book and in popular science portrayals of "hardwired" differences in male and female brains such as that of Baron-Cohen (2004; for a critique see Fine 2012). It might then be argued that "gender-specific" has become a brand that can be assumed to resonate with patients and consumers alike. Take, for example, the manufacture and marketing of sex-segregated everyday health-related products, such as over-the-counter vitamins. One of the most well-known companies producing "tailored" multivitamins is Centrum. Centrum Men and Centrum Women are marketed with common properties; for men and women the product "supports energy release and immunity," but also with difference. Thus for men they also "contribute to muscle and heart," while for women they "contribute to hair, skin and nails."

A Fragmented Conception of the Body

Advocates of GSM often direct their energies toward conditions that are deemed to have been neglected for men, neglected for women or which deserve more attention, but in "gender-specific" terms (Annandale and Hammarström 2011). For men this includes those conditions which tend to be ignored because they are "female defined," such as osteoporosis, breast cancer and postnatal depression, and hitherto neglected "male-specific" conditions such as prostate cancer. Since sexuality tends to be seen as a "gate" to men's general health, it receives considerable attention, particularly in relation to "erectile dysfunction" and its health sequelae such as depression and anxiety and to the "neglected" male reproductive system, notably the contested issue of the "andropause" (Annandale and Hammarström 2011). Given the bid to go beyond what is presented as an outmoded view of women which "concentrated only on their breasts and reproductive organs and assumed that everything else was exactly as it was in men" (Legato 2005:59), reproductive health has been less of a focus for women with attention drawn instead to health problems which are experienced by both women and men, but which have not been approached in "gender-specific" terms, such as lung cancer and heart disease. The effect of GSM is therefore to draw attention to health problems experienced both by men and women but in "gender-specific" terms.

Eckman's (1998) argument that the overriding message of the "difference agenda" is that we are missing knowledge about *bits* of women's bodies can be extended to encompass men's bodies; it is the heart, the bones, the breast, the lungs, the colon, the penis which become the focus of attention. Hence the "gender-specific" body is a fragmented body. This extends beyond the molar to the molecular. Thus Legato argues that "gender-specific medicine goes far beyond the archaic idea that the only significant differences between men and women are in their reproductive biology; in fact, those differences embrace the entire organism" (2006:S6) to encompass the "hormones," "chromosomes" and "genes," which are labeled as essentially "gendered" (read linked to biological sex). Here then the older ground of critique of the medicalization of women's bodies referred to at the start of the chapter enters new terrain as the search for gender-specific differences and their treatment extends to more and ever "smaller" entities of the body.

"Gender-specific Medicine," Gendered "Customization" and Big Pharma

As should be apparent from the discussion thus far, the gender-specific approach to disease is a construction rather than an ontological reality (Cutter 2012). This leads us to ask the question, why has it come to the fore at the present historical juncture? We suggest that GSM can fruitfully be interpreted as part of the dissolution of the boundary between the body and politics, commonly discussed though the interpretive lens of "biopolitics" (Lemke 2011). To recap on a discussion we have begun elsewhere, GSM can be pictured as one more step along a historical road upon which women's bodies in particular have been a site of intervention and source of what is now conceptualized as biovalue or the "yield of vitality produced by the biotechnical reformulation of living processes" (Waldby 2002:310). Much of GSM is high-tech in orientation and tertiary-care-based (including lab-based research on the cellular structure of the body). Although "gender-specific" wellness and education services exist and might appear to offer a more "holistic" kind of care that differs from biomedical practice, generally they are individual lifestyle focused, concern medical management of problems such as stress and addiction (and may act as loss leaders to encourage women into more profitable clinical services) (Annandale and Hammarström 2011). Indeed, the "gender-specific body" rests heavily on a construction of gender as a property of individuals, framed as attitudes, components of chosen "lifestyles" and "social roles" (Hammarström and Annandale 2012). This reductionist approach resonates with dominant neoliberal medical and public health discourses which construe health and illness as products of a constellation of personal risk factors and not of state policies or the institutional effects of sexism. New ways of governing conduct have elevated individual decision and choice in health matters. Indeed, as Crawford discusses, "individual responsibility for health has become a model of and a model for the neoliberal restructuring of American society" (2006:419). It therefore does not come as a surprise to find in the USA in particular that the "gender-specific" label increasingly is attached, for example, to rehab programs and to various "lifestyle" products such as "gender-specific blended" nutritional supplements.

Situated in this way GSM embraces what Clarke and colleagues (2010b) conceptualize as "stratified biomedicalization" whereby various bodies and social groups – here women and men – are stratified or divided though the increased customization of technologies, pharmaceuticals and other assorted medical goods. It is part of what Epstein (2007:5) dubs the "repudiation of so-called one-size-fits-all medicine" which, while acknowledging variations in dosage in relation to body size, age and sex, has traditionally involved "the development of mass-market therapies based on the assumption that everyone responds in the same way" (Hedgecoe 2004:10–11). In its place we find a growing emphasis on group specificity. Pharmaceuticals are an important part of this process. As Fisher and Ronald (2010) show, sex and gender differences in drug development and marketing are intimately bound up with gender and politics. As already remarked upon, in the pharmaceutical field and beyond, the male body and male experience have been taken as the "gold standard" for the population as a whole within biomedicine, under the assumption – if it is considered at all – that this can be generalized to females. Drawing attention to male/female differences in cardiovascular disease, GSM specialist Regitz-Zagrosek, a leading GSM advocate based at the aforementioned Center for Gender in Medicine at Charité Universitätsmedizin, calls for "gender-specific research on existing drugs and gender-specific strategies in the development of novel agents" (2006:12). And, indeed, GSM seems to hold out the potential to extend pharmaceutical markets. For example, Kos Pharmaceuticals, which produces the statin Niapsan (niacin), applauded the American Heart Association's recommendation of a reduction in the maintenance of triglyceride levels in women from below 200 mg/dl to below 150 mg/dl, remarking that the new guidelines "could almost triple the number of women who would undoubtedly benefit from . . . our products as treatment options for multiple lipid disorders provide considerable opportunity for Kos" (Business Wire 2004).

Gender-specific organizations often have pharmaceutical companies as "corporate partners." For example, amongst others, the Society for Women's Health Research in the USA lists AstraZeneca, Bayer Healthcare, Eli Lilly and Co. and Pfizer Inc. The pharmaceutical industry, which is continually in search of new markets, has developed alongside the construction of the "gender-specific body" within biomedicine. There has been a proliferation of interest in gender-specific pharmacodynamics (drug actions and effects on the body) and pharmacokinetics (the course of drug absorption, distribution, metabolism and excretion) over the last ten or so years (just a few of the published examples include Gandhi et al. 2004; Tingen et al. 2010; Regitz-Zagrosek 2012; Baggio et al. 2013). Instructively, gender-specifics are still often framed as women's difference from men (rather than men's difference from women, or their differences to each other). For example, Regitz-Zagrosek and Seeland maintain that "significant differences in pharmacokinetics and pharmacodynamics have been established due to lower body surface in women [than in men] but also to differences in drug reabsorption, metabolism by hepatic enzymes, kidney function and excretion" (2012:14). In a table depicting mechanisms of "gender-specific differences" in pharmacokinetics, Baggio and colleagues list far more specifics where women differ from men than vice versa, such as "longer gastric emptying time in women due to slower motility" and "lower lean/fat mass ratio in female" (Baggio et al. 2013:715).

Yet, however it is framed, the emphasis on difference is of particular note in the context of the "rush to personalised medicine" (Hedgecoe 2004:12) by "Big Pharma" following the working draft of the genome from the Human Genome Project at the start of the present century. Known as pharmacogenomics or pharmacogenetics, personalized medicine concerns "genetically determined variability in drug response" (Wolf, Smith and Smith, cited in Hedgecoe 2004:4). Tingen et al. (2010:511), for example, propose that "sex-based medicine is the next step in offering true personalised medicine" founded on customization based on the sex of the patient. But Regitz-Zagrosek and Seeland make clear that even though:

> some people argue that gender-based medicine will become irrelevant if all individual factors can be taken into account ... personalised medicine cannot replace gender-based medicine ... gender remains an independent risk factor ... because of this prominent role of gender, clinical care algorithms must include gender-based assessment. (Regitz-Zagrosek and Seeland 2012:17, 4)

This betrays a present concern that advocates seek to rebuff that GSM is at risk of redundancy if personalized medicine renders diagnosis and treatment even more specialized than the "specificity" of gender (read sex). "Gender-specifics," read biological differences, therefore remain sacrosanct.

As already intimated, undoubtedly there are reasons to move away from a one-size-fits-all (typically male normative) approach to pharmacology and pharmacodynamics. However, this might call less for a gender-*specific* approach and more for "critical gender awareness" (Annandale et al. 2007) which recognizes that we need to be alert to gender because as a social structure it informs the social actions of patient, potential patients and care providers while avoiding the ascription of prima facie difference. The biological markers deemed important to pharmacokinetics such as hormones and body fat are not truly dichotomous variables in the manner described by GSM advocates. Thus as Birke expresses, inappropriate "gendered dichotomies are etched deep into the narratives of biology" (1999:41). What in actuality are continua get divided in a process which Hanson (2000) likens to dividing mercury with a ruler; since the dichotomization is empirically false – the phenomena reconstitute themselves when the ruler is removed – research and practice is distorted. Hence, as already remarked upon, what counts as gender-specific is constructed rather than naturally revealed. Thus as Cutter argues (2012:xii), the "facts" of gender-specific disease "are created in the sense that we bring to our descriptions frames or lens through which we 'see' our world." This "seeing" is highly problematic when men and women do not conform biologically or socially to what GSM might expect.

Earlier in the chapter we drew attention to what Epstein (2003, 2007) calls the "inclusion and difference" paradigm in relation to gender. We saw that the push in the 1980s and 1990s to include members of hitherto unrepresented groups, namely women, has intensified the felt need to take difference into account in medical research. Before we consider this a little further it is instructive to reflect briefly on "race" and the fractious debates over "race-specific" profiling for medical purposes in the USA as a parallel illustration. In much the same way that GSM converts gender into sex, racialized medicine turns race into a genetic category (Kahn 2013). In 2005, the Food and Drug Administration (FDA) approved a new drug for the treatment of heart failure (BiDil) targeted at black Americans. As Epstein (2007:204) asks, should this be applauded for bringing medical attention to the "excluded and the underserved?" Or, does it reflect a limited understanding of "the social and biological production of bodily difference, which may not only harm human health but also inappropriately reinforce ideas about the reality of essential differences between groups?" He ultimately lines up with the critics, contending that racial profiling in medicine leads to the improper treatment of the patient who does not live up to the stereotype of his or her phenotypical "racial group" (see also Bliss 2015, Chapter 9, this volume; Shim et al. 2015, Chapter 3, this volume).

Drugs that get approval for one sex often do not start out as such, but end up that way when clinical trial data show efficacy in one sex or differences in effectiveness or adverse effects emerge in clinical use (Fisher and Ronald 2010). With respect to GSM, Epstein (2007) highlights Zelnorm (Tegaserod), a drug manufactured in 2002 by Novartis for the treatment of irritable bowel syndrome (IBS) (and removed from the market in 2007 due to concerns about adverse cardiovascular effects). Zelnorm was one of the first drugs approved by the FDA for use only in women for a condition which affects both men and women. Unlike BiDil which attracted significant media discussion, Zelnorm went unnoticed, something Epstein puts down to the long-accepted history of the production and use of certain drugs for women-only such as hormones and contraceptives. His concern is that Zelnorm was marketed for women despite the fact that its advantage over placebo was not demonstrated as statistically significant in a male and female population.

Conclusion

Similar to wider recent developments in biomedicine gender-specific pharmacology is part of "prospective technoscience" where thoughts of various futures are mobilized to marshal resources and coordinate activities of the present (Brown and Michael 2003). It remains to be seen whether the "gender-specific" will emerge as a strong market in an environment in which the costs of drug development and marketing have sky-rocketed, though the potential of reducing health service budgets by more cost-effective targeted treatments may have a mobilizing effect. More certain is the wider juggernaut of GSM which promises in some countries in particular to colonize the way that we think about male and female bodies, disease and how it is treated.

With its title this chapter poses the question of whether GSM represents a new biopolitics of gender and health. This evokes the larger question, which frames this volume, of the utility of old critiques and whether new forms of conceptual engagements are necessary. While the "old critiques" of the medicalization of women's bodies remain salient, the relationship between sex/gender and biomedicine has grown in complexity with the inclusion of men's health and the drive to "discover" ever more *specific* parts of the sex-differentiated body. The political resistance to medicalization that accompanied the technologization of childbirth, for example, dissipates in GSM which lends itself far more easily to being cast as a virtuous science serving the needs of men and women alike but in specific and suitably tailored ways. The "gender-specific" concept is already well established as a powerful social trope, which suggests that it has potential to reconfigure how we think "gender and health." By turn this implies that it has already fashioned a new kind of "engagement." Yet it is an engagement driven by biomedicine about which we know relatively little except through the claims of its advocates. For example, while GSM casts patients and potential patients as willing consumers of new "gender-specific" treatments, much more critical attention needs to be given to how they actually relate to the "gender-specific" message or to how thinking "gender-specific" might impact on how men and women relate to their bodies or to the health beliefs that they hold.

Acknowledgments

We would like to thank the Susan Bell and Anne Figert and the participants at the Symposium "Big Pharma, Big Medicine and Technoscience: Investigating Intersections in the Twenty-First Century" for helpful comments on earlier versions of this chapter.

References

Abraham, J. 2010. "Pharmaceuticalization of Society in Context: Theoretical, Empirical and Health Dimensions." *Sociology* 44:603–22.

Annandale, E. and A. Hammarström. 2011. "Constructing the 'Gender-specific Body.'" *Health*, 15:577–93.

Annandale, E., J. Harvey, D. Cavers and M. Dixon-Woods. 2007. "Gender and Access to Healthcare in the UK: A Critical Interpretive Synthesis of the Literature." *Evidence and Policy* 3:463–86.

Arms, S. 1975. *Immaculate Deception*. New York: Simon & Schuster.

Auerbach, J. and A. Figert. 1995. "Women's Health Research: Public Policy and Sociology." *Journal of Health and Social Behavior* Extra Issue:115–31.

Baggio, G., A. Corsini, A. Floreani, S. Giannini and V. Zagonel. 2013. "Gender Medicine: A Task for the New Millennium." *Clinical Chemistry and Laboratory Medicine* 51:713–27.

Baron-Cohen, S. 2004. *The Essential Difference*. London: Penguin.

Barker, K. 2011. "Listening to Lyrica: Contested Illnesses and Pharmaceutical Determinism." *Social Science & Medicine* 73:833–42.

Baunach, D.M. 2003. "Gender, Mortality, and Corporeal Inequality." *Sociological Spectrum* 23: 331–58.

Bell, S. 2009. *DES Daughters*. Philadelphia, PA: Temple University Press.

Bell, S. and A. Figert. 2012. "Medicalization and Pharmaceuticalization at the Intersections: Looking Backward, Sideways and Forward." *Social Science & Medicine* 75:775–83.

Birke, L. 1999. *Feminism and the Biological Body*. Edinburgh: Edinburgh University Press.

Bliss, C. 2015. "Biomedicalization and the New Science of Race." Pp. 175–96 in *Reimagining (Bio)Medicalization, Pharmaceuticals and Genetics: Old Critiques and New Engagements*, edited by Susan E. Bell and Anne E. Figert. New York: Routledge.

Brown, N. and M. Michael. 2003. "A Sociology of Expectations: Retrospecting Prospects and Prospecting Retrospects." *Technology Analysis and Strategic Management* 15:3–18.

Burri, R. V. and J. Dumit. 2007. "Introduction." Pp. 1–14 in *Biomedicine as Culture*, edited by R. V. Burri and J. Dumit. London: Routledge.

Business Wire. 2004. "Kos Pharmaceuticals Applauds New AHA Guidelines of Women and Heart Disease: Acknowledgment for Gender Gap and Increasingly Important Role of HDL-C, or

'Good Cholesterol.'" Accessed October 7, 2014 (www.businesswire.com/news/home/20040204005508/en/Kos-Pharmaceuticals-Applauds-AHA-Guidelines-Women-Heart#.VDRPWUlwZqw).

Chesler, P. 1972. *Women and Madness*. New York: Doubleday.

Clarke, A. 2010. "Epilogue: Thoughts on Biomedicalization in its Transnational Travels." Pp. 380–405 in *Biomedicalization: Technoscience, Health, and Illness in the U.S.*, edited by A. Clarke, L. Mamo, J. R. Fosket, J. R. Fishman and J. K. Shim. Durham, NC, and London: Duke University Press.

Clarke, A., J. Shim, L. Mamo, J. R. Fosket and J. R. Fishman. 2010a. "Biomedicalization: A Theoretical and Substantive Introduction." Pp. 1–44 in *Biomedicalization: Technoscience, Health, and Illness in the U.S.*, edited by A. Clarke, L. Mamo, J. R. Fosket, J. R. Fishman and J. K. Shim. Durham, NC, and London: Duke University Press.

Clarke, A., J. Shim, J. Mamo, J. R. Fosket and J. Fishman. 2010b. "Biomedicalization: Technoscientific Transformations of Health, Illness, and U.S. Biomedicine." Pp. 44–87 in *Biomedicalization: Technoscience, Health, and Illness in the U.S.*, edited by A. Clarke, L. Mamo, J. R. Fosket, J. R. Fishman and J. K. Shim. Durham, NC, and London: Duke University Press.

Clarke, A. and Shim, J. 2011. "Medicalization and Biomedicalization Revisited: Technoscience and Transformations of Health, Illness and American Medicine." Pp.173–99 in *Handbook of the Sociology of Health, Illness and Healing*, edited by B. Pescosolido, J. Martin, J. McLeod and A. Rogers. London: Springer.

Conrad, P. 2004. "The Shifting Engines of Medicalization." *Journal of Health and Social Behavior* 46:3–14.

Conrad, P. 2007. *The Medicalization of Society*. Baltimore, MD: Johns Hopkins University Press.

Conrad, P. 2013. "Medicalization: Changing Contours, Characteristics, and Contexts." Pp. 195–214 in *Medical Sociology on the Move*, edited by W. Cockerham. London: Springer.

Crawford, R. 2006. "Health as Meaningful Social Practice." *Health* 10:401–20.

Cuthbertson, C. A. 2015. "Pharmaceutical Technologies and the Management of Biological Citizens in Chile." Pp. 137–59 in *Reimagining (Bio)Medicalization, Pharmaceuticals and Genetics: Old Critiques and New Engagements*, edited by Susan E. Bell and Anne E. Figert. New York: Routledge.

Cutter, M. A. 2012. *The Ethics of Gender-Specific Disease*. London: Routledge.

Davis, J. 2010. "Medicalization, Social Control and the Relief of Suffering." Pp. 211–41 in *The New Blackwell Companion to Medical Sociology*, edited by W. Cockerham. Oxford: Wiley-Blackwell.

Eckman, A. 1998. "Beyond the 'Yentl Syndrome': Making Women Visible in Post-1990 Women's Health Discourse." Pp. 130–68 in *The Visible Woman*, edited by P. Treichler, L. Cartwright and C. Penley. London: New York University Press.

Ehrenreich, B. and D. English. 1978. *For Her Own Good: Two Centuries of the Experts' Advice to Women*. New York: Anchor Press.

Epstein, S. 2003. "Bodily Differences and Collective Identities: The Politics of Gender and Race in Biomedical Research in the United States." *Body and Society* 10:183–203.

Epstein, S. 2007. *Inclusion: The Politics of Difference in Medical Research*. Chicago, IL: University of Chicago Press.

Fausto-Sterling, A. 2012. *Sex/Gender: Biology in a Social World*. London: Routledge.

Figert, A. 2011. "The Consumer Turn in Medicalization: Future Developments with Historical Foundations." Pp. 291–308 in *The Handbook of the Sociology of Health, Illness and Healing: Blueprint for the Twenty-First Century*, edited by B. Pescosolido, J. Martin, J. McLeod and A. Rogers. New York: Springer.

Fine, C. 2012. "Explaining, or Sustaining, the Status Quo? The Potentially Self-fulfilling Effects of 'Hardwired' Accounts of Sex Differences." *Neuroethics* 5:285–94.

Fisher, J. and L. Ronald. 2010. "Sex, Gender, and Pharmaceutical Politics: From Drug Development to Marketing." *Gender Medicine* 7:357–70.

Fishman, J. R. 2010. "The Making of Viagra." Pp. 289–306 in *Biomedicalization: Technoscience, Health, and Illness in the U.S.*, edited by A. Clarke, L. Mamo, J. R. Fosket, J. R. Fishman and J. K. Shim. Durham, NC, and London: Duke University Press.

Furedi, F. 2006. "The End of Medical Dominance." *Society* 43:14–18.

Gandhi, M., F. Weeka, R. Greenblatt and T. Blaschke. 2004. "Sex Differences in Pharmacokinetics and Pharmacodynamics." *Annual Review of Pharmacology and Toxicology* 44:499–523.

Goldacre, B. 2012. *Bad Pharma*. London: Fourth Estate.

Grace, V. 2007. "Beyond Dualism in the Life Sciences: Implications for a Feminist Critique of Gender-specific Medicine." *Journal of Interdisciplinary Feminist Thought* 2:1–18.

Greenberger, P. and J. Wider, eds. 2006. *The Savvy Woman Patient: How and Why Sex Differences Affect Your Health.* Herndon, VA: Capital Books.

Greene, Jeremy A. 2015. "Vital Objects: Essential Drugs and Their Critical Legacies." Pp. 89–111 in *Reimagining (Bio)Medicalization, Pharmaceuticals and Genetics: Old Critiques and New Engagements*, edited by Susan E. Bell and Anne E. Figert. New York: Routledge.

Hammarström, A. and E. Annandale. 2012. "A Conceptual Muddle: An Empirical Analysis of the Use of 'Sex' and 'Gender' in 'Gender-specific' Journals." *PLoS One* 7:e34193.

Hanson, B. 2000. "The Social Construction of Sex Categories as Problematic to Biomedical Research: Cancer as a Case in Point." Pp. 53–68 in *Health, Illness and the Use of Care*, edited by J. Jacobs Kronenfeld. London: JAI.

Hedgecoe, A. 2004. *The Politics of Personalised Medicine.* Cambridge: Cambridge University Press.

Kahn, J. 2013. *Race in a Bottle: The Story of BiDil and Racialized Medicine in a Post-genomic Age.* Chichester: Columbia University Press.

Legato, M. 2002. *Eve's Rib: The New Science of Gender-specific Medicine and How It Can Save Your Life.* New York: Harmony Books.

Legato, M. 2004. "Gender-specific Medicine: The View from Salzburg." *Gender Medicine* 1: 61–3.

Legato, M. 2005. "Men, Women, and Brains: What's Hardwired, What's Learned, and What's Controversial." *Gender Medicine* 2:59–61.

Legato, M. 2006. "Foreword." *Gender Medicine*, Supplement 1, The 1st World Congress on Gender-specific Medicine: S16.

Lemke, T. 2011. *Bio-Politics.* London: New York University Press.

Miah, A. and E. Rich. 2008. *The Medicalization of Cyberspace.* London: Routledge.

Regitz-Zagrosek, V. 2006. "Therapeutic Implications of the Gender-specific Aspects of Cardiovascular Disease." *Nature Reviews Drug Discovery* 5:425–38.

Regitz-Zagrosek, V., ed. 2012. *Sex and Gender Differences in Pharmacology.* Berlin: Springer-Verlag.

Regitz-Zagrosek, V. and U. Seeland. 2012. "Sex and Gender Differences in Clinical Medicine." Pp. 3–22 in *Sex and Gender Differences in Pharmacology*, edited by V. Regitz-Zagrosek. Berlin: Springer-Verlag.

Reissman, C. K. 1983. "Women and Medicalization: New Perspective." *Social Policy* 14:3–18.

Riska, E. 2003. "Gendering the Medicalization Thesis." *Gender Perspectives on Health and Medicine* 7:59–87.

Riska, E. 2010. "Gender and Medicalization and Biomedicalization Theories." Pp. 147–70 in *Biomedicalization: Technoscience, Health, and Illness in the U.S.*, edited by A. Clarke, L. Mamo, J. R. Fosket, J. R. Fishman and J. K. Shim. Durham, NC, and London: Duke University Press.

Rose, N. 2013. "The Human Sciences in a Biological Age." *Theory, Culture and Society* 30:3–34.

Rosenfeld, D. and C. Faircloth, eds. 2006. *Medicalized Masculinities.* Philadelphia, PA: Temple University Press.

Samsky, A. 2015. "The Drug Swallowers: Scientific Sovereignty and Pharmaceuticalization in Two International Drug Donation Programs." Pp. 112–36 in *Reimagining (Bio)Medicalization, Pharmaceuticals and Genetics: Old Critiques and New Engagements*, edited by Susan E. Bell and Anne E. Figert. New York: Routledge.

Schofield, T. 2004. *Boutique Health? Gender and Equity in Health Policy.* Sydney: The Australian Health Policy Institute.

Shim, J. K., K. Weatherford Darling, S. L. Ackerman, S. Soo-Jin Lee and R. A. Hiatt. 2015. "Reimagining Race and Ancestry: Biomedicalizing Difference in Post-Genomic Subjects." Pp. 56–78 in *Reimagining (Bio)Medicalization, Pharmaceuticals and Genetics: Old Critiques and New Engagements*, edited by Susan E. Bell and Anne E. Figert. New York: Routledge.

Tingen, C., A. Kim, P. Wu and T. Woodruff. 2010. "Sex and Sensitivity: The Continued Need for Sex-based Biomedical Research and Implementation." *Women's Health* 6:511–16.

Turney, J. and B. Balmer. 2003. "The Genetic Body." Pp. 399–415 in *Companion to Medicine in the Twentieth Century*, edited by Roger Cooter and John Pickstone. London: Routledge.

Wadham, B. 2002. "Global Men's Health and the Crises of Western Masculinity." Pp. 69–84 in *A Man's World. Changing Men's Practices in a Globalised World*, edited by B. Pease and K. Pringle. London: Zed Books.

Waldby, C. 2002. "Stem Calls, Tissue Cultures and the Production of Biovalue." *Health* 6: 305–23.

Waldby, C. and M. Cooper. 2010 "From Reproductive Work to Regenerative Labour: The Female Body and the Stem Cell Industry." *Feminist Theory* 11:2–22.

Williams, S., P. Martin and J. Gabe. 2011. "The Pharmaceuticalisation of Society? A Framework for Analysis." *Sociology of Health & Illness* 33:710–25.

Wizeman, T. M. and M. Pardue. 2001. *Exploring the Biological Contributions to Human Health: Does Sex Matter?* Washington, DC: National Academy Press.

3

Reimagining Race and Ancestry
Biomedicalizing Difference in Post-Genomic Subjects

JANET K. SHIM,[1] KATHERINE WEATHERFORD DARLING,
SARA L. ACKERMAN, SANDRA SOO-JIN LEE
AND ROBERT A. HIATT

Introduction: The Values of Inclusion and Interaction

What determines who gets sick and who does not, who dies and who lives? What accounts for the often systematic and stratified patterns of disease distribution across human populations? How do we know – or think we know – where and how to intervene in these patterns of disease and risk, and on whom? In turn, what drives how we shape our healthcare systems, our clinical practices and our public health recommendations? Our answers to these questions have profound impacts on the design of our health programs, the kinds of health-related advice we give to individuals and families, and our conceptions of the distribution of responsibility for promoting and maintaining health and addressing disease. Understandably then, these questions have preoccupied the many scientific disciplines that have contributed to our knowledge of health and illness.

In the twenty-first century, a confluence of unique trends in the landscape of health research has shifted the ways in which these questions are being posed and the approaches taken to answer them. First, "complexity" has emerged as a new keyword in discourses about and research on disease causation. However, the ways in which scientists interpret the notion of causal complexity and put it into practice encompass widely variable ideas, models and frameworks for thinking about environment, genes, biology, social factors and culture. Second, new scientific research technologies and capacities – in genomics, clearly, but also in computing and statistics – enable new and different kinds of questions to be asked and pursued. Finally, there have been significant shifts in scientists' and the public's understandings of the research enterprise, from the growing appeal of inter- and transdisciplinary approaches (that aim for true integration rather than merely side-by-side multidisciplinary efforts), to consortium models of research, to cohorts of participants becoming research platforms for multiple studies. These new modes of research work to codify many different versions and variations of "complexity" (Shim et al. 2014a).

In this landscape, the continued stratification of disease distribution, determinants and interventions is compelling scientists to reconsider race, ethnicity and ancestry, and the ways in which they have been mobilizing particular conceptualizations of these terms as they seek to understand such patterns. In this chapter, we consider how race and ethnicity are being made and remade in the post-genomic era. We argue that reimaginings of race and ethnicity exemplify the continued biomedicalization of human bodies, differences and identities, accomplished through molecular techniques that epitomize the highly technoscientific practices of the biomedical era. Biomedicalization theory points to the power of the molecular gaze to produce the truths of biology and indeed, to constitute life itself (Clarke et al. 2010b); here we underscore its ability to shape how we see ourselves and who we think we are.

To trace these post-genomic transformations of race and ethnicity, from 2010 to 2014 we recruited US-based genome scientists conducting research that fit a number of eligibility criteria: (a) identifiable as gene–environment interaction (GEI) research – that is, studies that try to account for the interactions of genetic with environmental factors; (b) inclusion of at least one non-white population, that is, those who had designed their studies in a way to enable comparisons between racial/ethnic groups; and (c) research on the etiology of heart disease, type 2 diabetes and cancer – all conditions for which there exists wide agreement that they are caused by multiple, interacting genetic, behavioral and environmental determinants. We conducted in-depth, semi-structured interviews with these scientists to gather data on their actual research practices – including how and why specific study designs, samples, variables, measures, measurement tools and analytic procedures are selected and implemented – and how these practices have changed over the course of a study. We also conducted observations and informal interviews at scientific conferences where findings from GEI research are presented. This chapter is based on fifty-four in-depth interviews with thirty-three GEI scientists (twenty-one of these interviews were follow-up interviews conducted approximately one year after the first interview), and over 200 hours of observation and additional informal interviews at nine scientific conferences where findings from GEI research were presented. All interview transcripts, observation field notes and selected verbatim transcriptions of podium presentations and question-and-answer sessions were uploaded to the qualitative data analysis software ATLAS.ti. Initial codes were first generated inductively through a collaborative reading and analysis of a subset of interviews, and then finalized through successive waves of coding into approximately eighty categories and codes. The ATLAS.ti query tool was used to extract data tagged with particular codes and we wrote, circulated and revised memos on these queries.

In addition to the changing landscape of biomedical research in the post-genomic era, two other touchstones serve as points of departure for this project.

The first is Steven Epstein's (2007) *Inclusion*. Epstein traces, from the 1990s onward, a transformative shift in our medical "common sense," from the notion that health research conducted on white, middle-aged men could be broadly generalizable to other human populations, to a new "inclusion-and-difference" paradigm that held that diverse individuals must be included in biomedical research to investigate group differences. As Epstein states, we are now fully in an age of inclusion, in which the regulatory mandate to include underrepresented populations has become both scientific and social common sense.

Indeed, this is something that we have seen among the scientist-participants in our research. They see inclusion in research participation as both a representational and social inequality issue. For example, one of our participants spoke of the motivations for his current study:

> All of the populations that were being studied … were Caucasian. Why? Because it was easy to collect those families … [We] said, "This is ridiculous. We know there are huge health disparities. And no one is making an effort to find out why. We have got to start a study that is going to enroll large numbers of African American men and their families and try and figure this out." And that's what we did … [We] went out and found terrific mostly African American clinicians around the country. Put out a contract. These guys got together. They designed their study. They collected these families from all across the country and were phenomenally successful in enrolling African American families so that we finally have a decent number.

Another researcher summarized: "So right now, I think there's no doubt that there is a sense of trying to spread the biomedical dollars to assess questions and other ethnic groups and populations simply because it exposes a much greater diversity of the problem." Thus our scientists seem to be guided by a moral *and* scientific sensibility that inclusion is necessary to pose questions of significant public health impact, to examine questions of genomic and environmental causation within a broadly representative population, and/or to fulfill an ethical mandate to address health disparities.

A second point of departure for our project is Pamela Sankar's (2008) call to move beyond "the two-race mantra." She argues that it is time to let go of the notion that there are two – and only two – conceptions of race: that it is either biological or social.[2] Relatedly, Catherine Bliss (2012; 2015, Chapter 9, this volume) has also traced the emergence of a new "sociogenomic" paradigm in genomic research that calls for a combination of both social and biological inquiry, a race-conscious genomics that explicitly accounts for the social realities of race.

Again, this call is also something we have heard among our participants. To be sure, given that we recruited those engaged in GEI research, it is no surprise that we would see a commitment to examining disease determinants all along the causal spectrum. But at the scientific conferences where we conducted observations, this was also a widely invoked refrain among researchers. Indeed the mandate to examine the influence of race along both biological and social dimensions was framed as part of the solution to the issue of "missing causality." That is, for complex diseases like heart disease, cancer and diabetes, all of the known contributors to disease still do not fully explain who develops the condition and who does not. Thus a great deal of energy and debate is spent on how to solve the etiological puzzle of complex diseases, in both *genetic* and *environmental* respects. The key intervention that was articulated to locate the "missing causality" was the inclusion of diverse populations in etiologic studies. Our study therefore sought to trace how this diversity of populations – mobilized as an important solution to health research – is being accounted for by investigators of GEI research.

Situating Race in Post-Genomic Science

Our aim is to contribute to an expanding literature on the invocation, uses and constructions of race and population differences in genomic research (e.g., Reardon 2005, 2009; Lee 2006; Abu El-Haj 2007; Fullwiley 2007, 2008, 2011; Braun and Hammonds 2008; Lee et al. 2008; Whitmarsh 2008; Fujimura and Rajagopalan 2011; Montoya 2011; Bliss 2012). One widespread claim in the genomics literature is that the approaches and techniques of human population genetics enable a shift from typological notions of *race* to statistical notions of difference among *populations* – that is, from an understanding of race as defined categories or groups, to one that conceptualizes racial differences as more continuous without discernable boundaries or divisions (e.g., Dobzhansky 1963; Lewontin 1972; Cavalli-Sforza and Bodmer 1999[1974]). However, multiple scholars who have analyzed genomic and post-genomic research practices take serious issue with the claim that "old" ideas about racial categories arrayed in a hierarchy have been eclipsed by a "new" logic of populations whose differences greatly overlap and are much more gradual and continuous.

Gannett (2001) argues that the notion of population has not attenuated scientists' inclination to identify and measure group differences that incorporate cultural meanings of race, or precluded stereotypical and racist interpretations of statistical patterns. Similarly, even when scientists are equipped with statistical software that in theory allows them to identify and define population clusters without an a priori use or conceptualization of race, Fujimura and Rajagopalan (2011) found that researchers still brought together notions of population, race and genetic ancestry in ways that were difficult to disentangle. In fact, Lee (2005) identified an "infrastructure of racialization" in post-genomic research wherein biobanks incorporated racialized labels[3] for groups whose DNA samples they store. In so doing, they privileged the body as the grounds in and from which racial difference can be read and genomics as the official language for reading race.

Multiple ethnographies of specific research projects throughout the Western hemisphere illustrate exactly these points. In Barbados, Whitmarsh (2008) argues that while initially the biological, medical, geographical and socially constructed were all simultaneously seen as defining or diagnostic of race as invoked in asthma research, this capaciousness disappeared once results were found. When scientists had to adjudicate, for example, the representativeness of a population to stand in for other populations, or the generalizability of a set of findings, they then resorted to pragmatic and expedient efforts to measure "race" precisely by admixture, for instance, or by presence of genetic variations. Fullwiley (2007, 2008) found much the same in her ethnography of two medical genetics laboratories in the USA. In these labs, the concomitant comparison of purportedly pure "Old World" reference populations to "New World" admixed populations led scientists to read race in DNA and revive race as biogenetically valid. And similarly, Montoya (2007, 2011) found that in a type 2 diabetes study that enrolled Mexican Americans in a county on the Texas–Mexico border, researchers acknowledged the joint genetic and environmental determinants of diabetes. But because the investigators mobilized ideas about admixture and hereditary susceptibility, they constructed their human subjects largely as genetic carriers of diabetes risk, ceding the social and cultural risk factors such as diet and poverty that are widely understood to affect diabetes incidence.

Finally, Bliss (2011, 2012) found in her study of elite genomic scientists that even while these scientists acknowledged the great heterogeneities within racial groups, they attended to race in research participation as a means to ensure racial equality in research and drug development. In the shift "from practicing colorblind science to race positive inquiry" (2012:67), Bliss found that elite scientists were no longer content to use "race" as a catch-all proxy or black box variable for other potential disease determinants. Instead, they were committed to measuring those previously uninterrogated factors in and of themselves. Bliss argues that within an "anti-racist racialism," researchers strategically incorporate racial populations into genome science with the goals of deconstructing biological race and producing an inclusive genomic science.

Given these emergent and enduring connections between genome science and race, ethnicity and ancestry, we summarize the shifting practices of using self-identified race and ethnicity (SIRE) and ancestry informative markers (AIMs), and scientists' specific concerns about and commitments to the investigation of human and social differences. These results have been reported in full elsewhere (Shim et al. 2014b). We argue that GEI researchers' uses of SIRE and AIMs both construct and reflect particularly individualizing understandings of race and human bodies that echo various processes of biomedicalization (Clarke et al. 2003, 2010b).[4] We suggest that bringing both biomedicalization and feminist theories to bear on these phenomena shows how these compulsions shape, in deeply consequential ways, our understandings of human difference in relative rather than relational terms. That is, human differences are perceived to be characteristics of individuals, arrayed on a continuum and relative to one another, rather than the outcomes of unequal relationships and interactions between socially defined groups. Thus researchers were pre-occupied with technical questions of how to classify and measure genetic variation, and how to standardize such classifications. These concerns underscore how tropes of precision, individualization and the continuity of human variation serve to promote genetic expressions of ancestry and to displace techniques that attend to group-based processes and social relations of power. In contrast, we argue that biomedicalization and feminist theories help to highlight and problematize the individualization and personalization of difference.

SIRE: The Convenience and Imprecision of Standardized Categories

As noted above, SIRE indicates the use of self-identification as a means to determine race and ethnicity. For the vast majority of the scientists we observed and interviewed, SIRE refers to the placement of oneself into one or more of the racial and ethnic categories defined by the US Office of Management and Budget (OMB) and required for use in biomedical research funded by the US National Institutes of Health (NIH). This use of SIRE is seen by our participants as now embedded and entrenched in the social practices of conducting research, as mandated by the NIH. They speak of these categories as "what we have" and what they "have to use" because "all NIH research requires [that]"; they "make that question [of race and ethnicity] fit those requirements" in order to "conform with what we have to report to the NIH." These characterizations of SIRE by the scientists underscore its use as a technique of convenience precisely because its collection is compelled by government funding agencies. One scientist rational-ized, "I think the path of least resistance is to stick with self-identified race ethnicity," and another explained that, "When we're measuring it de novo ... I try to ask it in categories that conform to the NCI [National Cancer Institute, one of the institutes that make up the NIH] reporting requirements. Make it easy on everybody."

Thus, because of its institutionalization into biomedical data collection practices and standardization across research studies, SIRE is largely considered *methodologically* robust and consistent, at least in the USA. However, its *conceptual* and *analytic* utility and the kind of questions it answers about etiology are often seen as inadequate. Thus while the measure may exhibit reliability in a technical sense, it is often not perceived to be valid in a scientific sense (see also Shim 2014). Researchers interviewed for this study therefore describe SIRE as having potential but also potential pitfalls, on a spectrum from necessary and convenient, to limited and questionable. While many justify the use of

SIRE for various reasons, mostly having to do with regulatory requirements and expediency, they also feel compelled to question its adequacy in these very regards.

For example, a major part of the compulsion to use preexisting NIH racial and ethnic categories to "make things easy" is to facilitate combining their study's data with those of others. GEI research typically involves not only many variables and measures (from across the genetic, behavioral and environmental spectrum) but also requires that scientists examine their independent as well as interaction effects. This in turn demands extremely large sample sizes. Thus study samples and data sets that are easily harmonizable – that is, combinable with data from other sources, where variable definitions and measurements can be reconciled – are highly desirable. And using routinized racial and ethnic categories is one clear way our participants structured study samples in order to maximize their potential to be recombined with other data sets. Therefore, as scientific entities, standardized racial and ethnic categories served the goals of convenience for researchers and research staff – rather than, for instance, the convenience of their human subjects in finding categories that align with their own identities. Such upstream standardization works to prevent downstream harmonization problems and thereby facilitates efforts to amass large data sets that are necessary to make claims about the joint and interacting effects of genetic and environmental risks on disease.

On the other hand, while the categories by which scientists measure self-identified race and ethnicity may have been standardized and intended to be used in specific ways, the particular practices surrounding their use often do vary. For example, several of the scientists mentioned the confusion regarding the status of "Hispanic/Latino" as an ethnicity, but not a race.[5] One scientist said explicitly that while they report Hispanic *ethnicity* to the NIH as mandated, when they do data analyses in their study, they consider Hispanic to be another *race*. Multiple researchers also described the dilemmas they face when subjects select multiple categories: "If people report multiple things, then we say African-American trumps everything else. Then Hispanic then trumps everything else that's remaining. And then the Asian trumps everything else that's remaining. That's kind of what I think the standard thing that people do." Another participant recalled:

> We've often gone to try to get more granular self-report information … having lots of different possibilities, having lots of different multi-ethnic designations … What we do is we give them the opportunities, then we look at the numbers [of participants choosing those other designations], and it's so small … that we ended up having to fold them back into the same categorization that we've talked about here that has been used for a long time.

Thus even for those who offer multiple possibilities for self-identification that try to go beyond just picking one box, the numbers of subjects who took advantage of such opportunities were so small as to render those more capacious identifications irrelevant when it came to data analysis. Notably, these scientists on the one hand affirm the right for subjects to self-identify as multiracial, but then on the other hand, need to assign them to only one category in the analysis phase.

As these quotes from our participants illustrate, the technique of using SIRE, while seemingly overdetermined by NIH regulations, actually comes with a number of workarounds that scientists have developed over time and in the face of specific predicaments. But even so, conducting research in a "world of standards" (e.g., Timmermans and Berg 2003; Timmermans and Epstein 2010) tips the scales in favor of reusing and replicating those same standardized categories, though not always and not strictly in the ways that they were intended. The simultaneity of the workarounds scientists have arbitrated alongside the continued implementation of SIRE therefore exemplify what Michelle Murphy calls counter-conduct, or "modes of undoing, remaking, and antagonism that are immanent with and animated by hegemonic formations" (2012:183, n. 3). That is, GEI researchers' alternate practices attempt to contest categorization practices that are seen to be imprecise and to accommodate more meaningful acts of self-identification. Yet scientists undertaking such efforts often find that they must revert back to dominant and conventional racial and ethnic categories because of the convenience that they offer and/or because of the scientific futility (at least in statistical terms) of offering more capacious options for self-identification. Thus acts intended to counter racial and ethnic classification rituals that have become so institutionalized as to be hegemonic end up circling back to those same practices, ultimately reanimating the relevance and circulation of the standardized categories of SIRE.

SIRE thus reflects some of the defining attributes of standards and standardization (Bowker and Star 1999; Lampland and Star 2009; Timmermans and Epstein 2010) in that the racial and ethnic categories with which individuals are asked to identify are more or less made uniform through NIH regulations. And in a nominal way, the practice of self-identification itself has become a standard operating procedure, although as we describe above, the particulars of implementation are by no means widely agreed upon. However, we argue that it is precisely the attributes of standards – and in particular, of the standardized categories themselves – that elicit scientists' ambivalence about the *scientific* utility of study subjects' actual, contingent and complex self-identification, even as they express a commitment to individuals' self-representation and self-determination.

To illustrate this point, we elaborate on our scientist-participants' critiques of SIRE. A central focus of their critique involved their understanding of

SIRE as a crude, imprecise and overly confounded metric of human difference. One scientist noted:

> Race is a convenient label to use for studies because you can get it easily. You can get people to answer these questions. But you know, we don't tend ... to think a lot about that variable, what it means, how it's defined, how it's being used. We just sort of use it blindly ... If we were laboratory scientists and we were developing assays, we wouldn't just use the assay somebody else came up with some other purpose. We would develop our own assays and test them and figure out what the coefficients of variability are and the properties of that assay before we applied them in experiments. And so I think that's what should be done ... with a variable like race is that we should develop metrics for what it is we actually want to learn, think about them very carefully, refine them, validate them, et cetera, and then use them in studies.

By the "blind" use of SIRE – a measure that someone else developed for other purposes that are being used only because it is "easy" – this scientist argues that we actually undermine our ability to "see" the determinants important for disease etiology. This participant also draws upon a comparison to "laboratory science," as an implicitly superior, more accurate form of science, as a means to critique the measure of SIRE. Thus the meanings ascribed to SIRE as a technique are that it is rote, a default, insufficient for the purposes for which it is being used and unscientific in that investigators are using a technique of measurement that they did not themselves develop or validate. While understandable as an attempt to honor racial and ethnic identity, and the act of self-identification itself, SIRE is nonetheless seen as encompassing too much, as being always already, overly confounded and confounding.

In turn, scientists asserted that the nature of the OMB/NIH categories – as a technique that over-lumped and under-specified human individuals – undermined their very commitment to subjects' right to self-identify. One participant told us, from a more general perspective:

> It's been on my mind about how we do clump everybody together ... In general the studies that I have worked on don't have a big enough sample size where we would even be able to get down to that level; but it does make us aware when we are interpreting our data that there is some measurement errors ... It's a mishmash.

Similarly another said, "The group called 'white,'" for example, "comprises people from Europe, people from the Middle East, people from North Africa, I mean, a vast variety of people from different cultures." And another participant had a similar critique of the category of Hispanic/Latino: "Hispanic – they're Native Americans, there's people from Africa. So even when you think about Hispanic, to me that's not a very representative category at all of anybody ... Who are these Hispanics? Are these Mexicans? Are they Dominicans? Puerto Ricans?"

Thus as a representational exercise in "identification," the meanings invested into subjects named by SIRE fall short of signifying and denoting their heterogeneity. Scientists use SIRE as an attempt to respond to the twin calls for inclusion and interaction, and participate in what Bliss (2012) terms the new "sociogenomic" paradigm in genetics, or the call to investigate both social and genetic determinants of disease, particularly (though not exclusively) in research on disease disparities. The capaciousness of self-identification, *in theory*, allows individuals to self-identify as they would wish, according to the meanings of racial difference – from the social, to the cultural, environmental and economic, as well as ancestral or genetic – that have significance for them. However, *in practice*, SIRE relies on an infrastructurally embedded history of categories that are now understood to be unstable and underdetermined, and this in turn undermines its own ability to represent human individuals faithfully.

The scientists we interviewed and observed seem to levy a moral critique here, in that SIRE, as a means to specify human subjects, immorally amalgamates those whose distinctiveness should be recognized, by undermining individuals' rights to identify and name themselves. Such comments about the limits of SIRE demonstrate a tacit recognition of the fraught politics of identity in the USA, and the failure of institutionalized, regulatory categories to reflect the more hybrid, shifting social groups with which people identify. For example, in our study, scientists negotiate a moral imperative to represent human diversity with much greater accuracy and refinement through an appeal to the value of "precision." As one scientist summed up:

> I think that there has been a lot of study to try to figure out how better to measure ethnicity and ancestry. But I don't see that it's fundamentally changed yet anything about the way most people do their work . . . I mean, part of the research question is, what is a good measure? Because there are a lot of different ways of summarizing this information . . . Which gives you the best metric, if there is such a thing? And really, the baseline question is, does genomics add anything to what you already know about people? Does it add anything to what box they checked on the census form? And if the answer's no, then, you know, we can stop . . . [But] it's still a research question at this point, whether it adds anything or not.

Thus this preoccupation with the inadequacy of racial and ethnic standardized categories brings them to a consideration of genetic ancestry and its measurement via ancestry informative markers.

AIMs: An Increasingly Routinized Optic "to Know Who You've Got"

For many of our participants, one way to represent human diversity with greater refinement is the use of AIMs. AIMs are sets of genetic variations for particular DNA sequences that appear in different frequencies in populations from different regions of the world. The use of AIMs compares an individual's polymorphisms at these markers with previously analyzed genomic reference sets from people whose ancestral history is purportedly fairly well known. AIMs are used by scientists to estimate the geographical origins of an individual's ancestors, typically expressed as admixture, or the proportion of one's ancestry that comes from different continental or subcontinental regions.

In theory, then, AIMs represent a technique that greatly simplifies ancestry-related data. By producing a set of numbers – the proportions of genetic ancestry that originate from different geographic regions – AIMs not only distill complex family histories into numbers, but standardize them so that they are comparable and can be incorporated into statistical analyses. However, the scientists we interviewed voiced some range of views about the precise utility of AIMs, their meanings and their potential to augment understandings of race, genetics or disease. First, participants were equivocal in terms of whether AIMs in and of themselves were meaningful as markers of disease risk per se. Thus the use of AIMs to characterize their human subjects did not lead scientists to consider those individuals as differentially susceptible to diseases based upon those ancestry markers.

Instead, AIMs were seen as a useful – and now conventional – means to deal with the frequent problem of population stratification, or genetic differences that require statistical control. Population stratification is the presence of systematic differences in the frequencies of genetic variations between groups, possibly due to differences in the ancestry admixture of those groups. Population stratification has long been a problem for genomic researchers: as they seek to establish that a statistical association between a genetic variant and a disease is, in fact, due to the genetic variant itself, they must control for any systematic differences in the frequency of genetic traits between the populations being compared.[6] As one researcher asked rhetorically:

> Do we need to keep track of ethnic differences as a surrogate for population ancestry? Absolutely. And the reason for that is it is well-known that allele frequencies at many loci vary as you move across different ancient geographic regions … [It's] garbage in, garbage out … you put bad data into a computer program, it doesn't matter how good it is, it will give you bad information out.

According to this participant, the point is to characterize and distinguish populations unto themselves and to ensure that they are statistically comparable – and to correct for it when they are not. Our respondents related that in some instances, AIMs allowed for statistical adjustment for populations of differing genetic structure that would otherwise not be comparable. In other cases, admixture analysis revealed fundamental problems in the comparability of cases and controls that necessitated the use of an alternative control population. In one example, an interviewee told us that systematic differences in the admixture of their cases and controls "threw a huge monkey wrench into a lot of our analyses . . . We couldn't really say anything about the causality." The investigators had to return to the messy and resource-intensive tasks of recruiting more participants to find a control group who was more comparable in terms of admixture. At other times, participants were able to use admixture mapping to select among the study subjects they had recruited only those who were relatively homogeneous, in order to avoid the problem of population stratification altogether.

In the "nightmare that is epidemiology," as one of our participants put it, making credible and defensible causal claims about disease etiology is both an essential, vital goal as well as a constant struggle. In this struggle, AIMs help to hedge against the "nightmare," through their ability to preemptively statistically control for the effects of population stratification, to assess post hoc whether there is a problem and how big it is, and to avoid mistaken assumptions about the comparability of populations that can come from the use of SIRE.

At the other end of the spectrum, a small number of our participants disagreed that AIMs were particularly useful. These quasi-dissenters saw the use of AIMs as sometimes being an empty technical routine, devoid of meaning in some research situations, and instead performed because others (particularly funding agencies and grant and manuscript reviewers) mandated that it be done. One investigator told us:

> Now I think that if you're proposing to do any study that's related to race, if you don't talk about ancestry informative markers, you're not going to get funded. Whether they really make a difference or not, I think that reviewers are thinking it's essential . . . [For one grant] we had to submit it three times to get it funded . . . In the first review, it was, "Why aren't you using ancestry informative markers?" And I said, "Well, we can categorize or classify African American enough [with SIRE] to say African American women are more likely to be diagnosed when they're young and to be diagnosed with aggressive breast cancer. We should be able to categorize people to look at tumor differences in the same way. But to make you happy, we'll put these ancestry informative markers in" . . . A lot of stuff I think becomes kind of like fad and, you know, this is what you've got to do now.

Finally, a middle-road position taken by our participants was that AIMs were useful for their anticipated potential and future value. Conducting admixture analyses using AIMs was described as inexpensive, and even if researchers do not yet have a grasp of how AIMs might be meaningful and for what purposes, there was the prevalent view that such data could yield benefits down the road. For example, one investigator told us that "I kind of sometimes feel like bank it, keep it in the anticipation that one day this will be very useful. And then you can be much more informed and start teasing things apart . . . But [the methods and ability to tease things apart are] not yet there. So we're still just more like banking in hopes, I think." In this situation, collecting specimens that allow for admixture mapping, and producing genetic ancestry estimates now is seen by researchers as providing the *potential* to accurately address the interplay of race and disease in the future. Here, AIMs become a practice in anticipation, preparedness and possibility (Adams, Murphy and Clarke 2009).

AIMs are also seen as an anticipatory practice because of the increasingly multiracial nature of human populations. AIMs help to account for subject bodies that are admixed, in a way that seems particularly (though not exclusively) American. This American particularism is seen in the comparisons made between doing research in the USA, versus in locales with much more homogeneous populations like Finland. As one scientist told us:

> In Finland, which is a very homogeneous population . . . I'm not going to have this problem [of admixture] . . . But in the U.S., come on. We're the mongrels of the world. We are the population that is the admixture of all admixture. Seriously. I mean just my own family. My God, I couldn't tell you what I am. I am the biggest little mutt in the world. I know that I have ancestors from all over Europe, but also my family's been here so long I could not possibly tell you all of our ancestors. It only gets more complex as we move on down the next 20, 30, 40 years.

AIMs offer the opportunity not only to do better science, but also to capture more completely all the heterogeneity and variability that exists within a singular person more completely. They allow scientists, as one participant put it, to "de-mystif[y] the self-identification of race for us . . . and mak[e] sure we understand what the makeup is of the participant we have." Thus the technique of AIMs is seen as a means to represent more comprehensively the ancestral complexity of contemporary individuals *as* individuals.

In so doing, scientists we interviewed and observed anticipate the "American mix" – often refracted through personal stories of admixture in their own families. For example, one participant described a recent talk he had given:

> I showed this picture of my niece and her husband and their . . . three kids. The three kids are between six genomes, right? And of the six genomes . . . two are of European origin, two are of South Asian origin, and two are of African origin . . . There's going to be more and more of this. More families are going to be mixed . . . more and more people whose ancestors within them are going to . . . have ancestry from different portions of the world.

This anticipated future is then one that invests AIMs with an ever-increasing mandatory nature. As one scientist told us: "I think anyone in the future generations and coming up are more mixed race, that you can't capture [with SIRE] . . . I've picked up that message that as we go forward, the demographics of the nation are changing. So we need to anticipate doing [AIMs]." And in the words of another: "There's much less barriers between ... the ethnic groups in our country as there used to be, which as far as I'm concerned is a great thing socially. It does make a geneticist's job harder ... What we then do is look at our mixed families and say, all right, what [AIMs] do we really need to use for them?"

Thus despite their questionable utility as clues to differential disease risks, AIMs comprise an increasingly routinized and institutionalized practice among the scientists in our study. In large part the routinization of AIMs is a product of their signification as a means to deal with the current and future American mix. Indeed, this *future* mixture creates an imperative to studying ancestry and admixture *now*. In this future, human subjects are seen as individual unique recombinations of the genomes of their heterogeneous ancestors, potentially from far-flung places. We therefore argue that AIMs constitute a practice of anticipation (Adams et al. 2009), as well as an investment in collecting data that will be usable and useful in the future. Simultaneously, AIMs were seen as a way to much more precisely represent human diversity: because their use leads to the characterization of proportions of genetic ancestry originating from different continental regions, the multiple ancestries of admixed individuals can be represented with greater refinement. Therefore, AIMs are also seen as a practice of more specific, and therefore more scientifically and socially responsible, representation.

On the Valences of Standards and Precision in Biomedicalization

In this section, we continue to explore how the relative utilities of SIRE and AIMs are refracted through the valences of standardization on the one hand, and precision on the other, and propose some potential consequences of these valences for understandings of human difference and disease. We show that AIMs are understood as more accurate and precise measures of unique ancestral recombinations than SIRE, which are seen as blunt and crude categories that overemphasize the differences between and underrepresent the heterogeneity within them. This juxtaposition of the relative utility of AIMs versus SIRE, we argue, serves to elide important questions about race, ancestry, genes and environment in the distribution of health.

The relative precision of AIMs as compared to SIRE was crystallized in an exchange we observed in the field that took place at a scientific conference. During the question-and-answer portion of a panel, one audience member spoke about her conversations with medical professionals about health disparities between black and white women. Despite the fact that epidemiologically speaking, the magnitude of those disparities varies across US cities, she reported that hospital executives "brush[ed] aside" more fundamental problems with the "financial underpinnings of the health care system" as potentially playing a role in producing such disparities, and instead pointed her to genetic studies that attempt to document biological differences. Panelists then took turns responding to her comment. First, two panelists noted both the difficulties and the need for research on multiple fronts, not just on the genetics of health disparities. The third panelist to respond had this to say:

> This is not a personal criticism, but if we are going to talk among disciplines, the term "Caucasian" is genetically undefined. It is an old, racist term, and where would you classify Afghanis? They are in the middle of Asia. They have light skin. They're not East Asians, they're not Europeans, are they Caucasian? Well, I don't use that term. They are Afghanis. And I think we have to be very careful about use of terms, and the medical literature uses "Caucasian" pervasively, and when I get papers to review from *New England Journal of Medicine* or *JAMA*, they're usually about population genetics, and I have a standard paragraph that goes in virtually every review, that you are using undefined, indefinable terms.

This comment served to contract a larger conversation about racial disparities in health into a discussion of race and ancestry in genomic science, and in turn to questions of how to properly classify people (as with Afghani outliers), and how to properly name them. By characterizing the category of "Caucasian" as illegitimate and racist because it is "genetically undefined," this panelist questioned the integrity of standards and legitimacy of standardized practices and labels. The emphasis on the "old racist" categories themselves narrowed the focus of the discussion, and of the articulation of the problem, to the meaninglessness of racial classifications as they are currently defined and to the lack of standardization in how they are being used. Given that the initial question in the conference panel was framed within the context of the racial politics of healthcare resource allocation, this narrowed focus is a particularly telling move. Its use of a new language of genomics and precision functions to remove from discussion factors like the "financial underpinnings of the health care system" and unequal distribution of healthcare resources.

Extensive sociological scholarship on standards and standardization (see Timmermans and Epstein 2010 for review) has noted how such objects and processes often symbolize the epitome of modernity. The diffusion of standards across centers of production, organizations and, notably, science helps explain why certain ways of seeing and doing things come to be perceived as legitimate and authoritative. But they have another valence as well, in that standards and classificatory systems are seen to homogenize and normalize potentially important differences. SIRE is seen as a twentieth-century standard, consistent with the rise of political identity movements and the emergence of a right to self identification. SIRE's standardized categories, previously deemed to be sufficient for that time being, are now viewed as over-lumped and underspecified. In contrast, AIMs are increasingly conceived as a twenty-first-century advance: enabled by the Human Genome Project, AIMs extract and accurately express each person's combination of ancestral origins. This hyper-precise ability to capture fractional identities (Lee 2013) enables AIMs to better accommodate the anticipated American mix. In the domain of gene-environment interaction research, then, AIMs provides a way to navigate past the stage of niche standardization, an approach to the study and management of, and interventions on, human populations that "eschews both universalism and individualism and instead standardizes at the level of the social group" (Epstein 2007:135). In its place is the capacity to produce precise knowledge of and customize interventions to unique individuals.

This valorization of the new, precise standard of AIMs relative to the old, blunt standards of SIRE among many of our GEI scientist-participants illustrates the ongoing impact of biomedicalizing processes on conceptions of human difference. Clarke and colleagues (2003) noted that two of the constitutive processes of biomedicalization include the technoscientization of biomedicine, and transformations of bodies and identities. The purported precision of AIMs amalgamates both of these processes. On the one hand, the molecular science and techniques – hallmarks of the kinds of technosciences that characterize biomedicalization – that underlie the identification and use of genetic markers that inform us about ancestry are part and parcel of how biomedicine is increasingly technoscientized. On the other hand, these markers contribute to the formation of technoscientific identities, in this case, of identities constructed through the means of genomics. In addition to (or perhaps for some, rather than) seeing themselves as members of racial and ethnic groups, individuals can now look at their ancestry estimates calculated via AIMs and think of themselves as genetic recombinations of multiple ancestors each coming from a particular biogeographical place. Thus individuals' genomes can now be thought of as mosaics of various origins: a stretch of DNA from a distant European ancestor, another from a Native American one and another from an African ancestor. Thus identities are being reimagined through concertedly technoscientific means, enabled through the confluence of biomedicine, information technologies and the life sciences that Clarke and colleagues (2003, 2010a) argue help constitute the crucible of biomedicalization.

Despite our participants' circumspection about the links to be made between AIMs and disease susceptibility, this does not constrain them from thinking about human difference and identities – of knowing "who you've got," as one put it – in increasingly technoscientific and biomedicalized ways. That is, the lack of clear connections between disease and genetic ancestry (though some have been reported and substantiated, they are still relatively rare) seems to have little effect on slowing down this biomedicalization of human difference in the name of precision. Perhaps this indicates how much of biomedicalization is not only about how things are "made medical" in a definitional, diagnostic and/or therapeutic sense (as in medicalization theory), but more generally about how the life sciences and biopolitics[7] are coming to shape our thinking about human bodies and life itself (as in biomedicalization theory). That is, even though AIMs have not been explicitly linked to medical ways of intervening (again, save for a few isolated instances), they nonetheless partake of discourses and practices of precision, personalization, knowledge of the body, characterization of human difference and technoscience that permeate and set the grounds for biomedicalization. Thus AIMs may be thought of as anticipatory (Adams et al. 2009) in a different sense, in that they prepare for and make possible opportunities to be enfolded into more explicitly biomedical practices *in the future*.

Altogether, these reflections underscore some of the underlying impulses and consequences of *both* medicalization and biomedicalization, most pertinently their emphases on the individual, the medical and the ways these participate in processes of devolution. What is striking to us is that the shift in value from thinking about SIRE as encompassing a wide range of social, behavioral and possibly biological determinants of disease, to the accuracy of describing human diversity through AIMs, seems to be emblematic of a larger shift from population health to precision medicine. That is, population health – as expressive of the value of studying disease at the population level in and of itself – is giving way to the idea that prevention, diagnostics and treatment should be more precise and customized to the individual. Although many of our participants profess a commitment to promote health at the population level, the ways in which they now seek to do so seem to be underwritten by logics and techniques of refinement, accuracy and exactness that go beyond the category, the group, the population.

By characterizing SIRE as inexact, crude and ill-defined, GEI scientists undermine the practice of using SIRE as a means to explore the social, cultural, economic and environmental heterogeneity of populations. Its persistent and continued use as only a proxy, and the simultaneous use of AIMs as an obligatory technique that says something about "the American mix" but not about American inequality, enables researchers to avoid the conceptually and methodologically more challenging task of measuring environmental, cultural and social determinants in and of themselves. To elaborate on these arguments, we turn now to reconsidering the value added of thinking with "groups" and about social relations.

Groups and Relations

We suggest that our experience in the field, like the vignette we described at the beginning of the previous section, shows how racial specificity in the name of better representation *and* precision (both of which are hybrid social-political-scientific goals) can all too quickly slide into an effacement of population differences and health disparities. That panelist's preoccupation with classification as "the problem" signals, on the one hand, a sensitivity to the complexity of self-identification for *individuals* and the ways in which their uniqueness cannot be captured by gross categories. However, in shifting away from a focus on healthcare resource distribution, the panelist's comments also served to obscure social processes and practices that affect and produce health and disease that often function and operate on the level of *groups*.

These phenomena speak to the questions of what kinds of differences count, and what difference *difference* makes. Reframing the questions in these ways, then, leads us to consider feminist and intersectionality theories and how they might illuminate our analysis of post-genomic ideas about race, ethnicity and ancestry. The explicit crux of intersectionality theory (and more implicitly, much of feminist theory) is that categories of identity or difference cannot be seen as additive; intersectionality analysis instead attempts to understand social locations, experiences and processes that shape the intersections of multiple axes of inequality. Such social locations are historically, geographically and locally specific, and thus members of a social group, their experiences and the meanings that identity holds for them are deeply heterogeneous.

Feminist and intersectionality theories make important use of the notion of categories and the value of thinking with groups. A central tenet of this scholarship is that socially meaningful human differences like race, gender, class and sexuality are simultaneously identities as well as categories that organize interlocking matrices of power and oppression (Spelman 1988). But intersectionality theory is also interested in interrogating the very nature of categories and categorization themselves, thereby questioning the groups and group attributes commonly used to make sense of human difference. It also clearly defines a research agenda that keeps issues of power and relations of domination and subordination at the center of the analysis. As Lynn Weber cogently argues:

> Race, class, gender, and sexuality are power relationships of dominance and subordination, not merely gradations along a scale of resources – who has more than whom – or differences in cultural preferences or gender roles. They are based in relationships of exploitation of subordinate groups by dominant groups for a greater share of society's valued resources. They change because oppressed groups struggle to gain rights, opportunities, and resources – to gain greater control over their lives against dominant groups who seek to maintain their position of control over the political, ideological, and economic social domains. (2010:91)

Thus while attending to difference can mean attending to identity, it is imperative that it also mean attending to inequality, and therefore, to group processes, dynamics and relations of power.

We can also take a theoretical cue from Michael Omi and Howard Winant's concept of racial formation which they define as the "sociohistorical process by which racial categories are created, inhabited, transformed, and destroyed" (1994:55). According to this approach, the process of racial formation is the ongoing, unfolding outcome of "racial projects" in which human bodies and social structures are represented and organized. Racial projects "connect what race *means* in a particular discursive practice and the ways in which both social structures and everyday experiences are racially organized" (1994:56). Thus processes that seek to represent racial differences are coincident and synergistic with those processes that seek to impose material consequences based on such representations.

Together, these conceptual tools set the theoretical grounds for attending to both the representational practices of *individuals* that scientists in our study feel AIMs do better, as well as the material and institutional consequences that ensue from and circle back into practices organized by categorical boundaries drawn between *groups*. If racial and ethnic categories – that is, racial and ethnic *groups* – are seen as "indefinable" and hopelessly heterogeneous and imprecise, then their displacement by more careful language and more precise genetic distinctions may work to conceal how racial categorizations are embedded within social institutions and processes. As scientific knowledge and practices around human difference shift from race and ethnicity as categories to ancestry as an individual quality, we lose sight of race and ethnicity as socially defined groups in favor of ancestry as a technically defined gradation. Simultaneously, we downplay race and ethnicity as social relations of power that occur *between and among groups*, and instead focus on conceptions of ancestry as an *identity of individuals*. And in so doing, we lose our ability to gain traction on understanding the social, cultural and political institutions that configure power and reproduce racial inequalities in health.

Conclusions: From Inclusion and Integration to the Search for "Real Differences"

To conclude, our scientist-participants see SIRE as a technique that makes meaningful yet erroneous claims about the identities and nature of the human subjects it characterizes, because it represents them as categorizable and standardizable. In contrast, AIMs are seen by many as "just" technique – a necessary methodological step to deal with the problem of population stratification, but not necessarily in and of itself making meaning of human subjects. However, as we argue, the technique of AIMs invests subjects with meanings, as highly unique genetic recombinations of an ever-widening variety of ancestors. Therefore, both technically and symbolically, AIMs centrally concern the meanings of particularly (though not necessarily or exclusively) "American mixtures."

In our interviews and observations of scientists conducting gene–environment interaction research, one refrain seems to be a constant: that the first iteration of the inclusion-and-difference paradigm (Epstein 2007) – in which underrepresented groups were brought into the research fold and dimensions of difference accounted for – does not go far enough. Too often investigators found themselves struggling with the challenges of under-specification and over-lumping, of not knowing how to properly characterize the unique individuals that comprise their samples. The imperative of and faith in precision is giving rise to practices that explicitly and implicitly reimagine race and ancestry and elide important claims that categorical race can mobilize. Using biomedicalization theory to analyze this post-genomic commitment to precision shows how highly technoscientific practices continue to shape conceptions of human difference and transform how we view bodies and identities. Using feminist and intersectional approaches that value thinking about groups and categories reveals the tradeoffs between the relative and the relational, and the political costs of a move to individualism. More specifically, we suggest that GEI research is shifting the terms of the debate from groups to individuals, and from inequalities to identities – or ordered differently, from group-based inequality to individually calculated identity. By concentrating attention to and investments in the measurement and definition of racial and ethnic difference as individual ancestry, GEI research practices can obscure alternate politics and scientific knowledge production about the connections to be made between race and health inequalities.

However, perhaps this need not be an "either-or" narrative, but rather a "both-and" approach. Across all of our participants to date, we have heard the constant, recurrent refrain: what, exactly, are the "real differences" that matter for etiology and health disparities? Their pervasive concern with the "real differences" that shape racial differences in health are grounded in the confluence of trends in health research with which we opened this chapter. First, there is the issue of the value and function of "complexity" as a central motif in discourses about and research on disease causation. While scientists' interpretations of causal complexity may vary, at a general level, there is wide agreement that complex diseases require frameworks for thinking about environment, genes, biology, social factors and culture as conjoint determinants. And second, many scientists – and the public – seem to have bought into an understanding of the research enterprise as one that ought to be inter- and transdisciplinary, integrative and highly collaborative. These trends thus reflect and shape the GEI project in the post-genomic era as an appropriately "both-and" endeavor: a professed commitment to looking at the causal continuum, *both* the molecular *and* the social and everything in between, using new approaches to and modalities of conducting research.

In this regard, then, questions of racial and ethnic difference continue to galvanize, motivate and organize the post-genomic project(s) in ways that, potentially, open up possibilities for conceptualizing interactions between biology and sociality, genes and culture, the interior and exterior environments of the body, and between nature and society. As we, along with many sociologists, anthropologists, science studies scholars and others, have argued, this landscape can also be motivated by – and/or gives the appearance of – desires for demo-cratization, inclusion and better care and health for all. Yet even in the face of such potentials, we must also recognize that biological research has a long history of institutionalizing and promoting highly unequal "common sense" ideas about race and difference. We therefore call for continued interrogation of when, where and how "either-or" or "both-and" positions play out in the interdisciplinary work of GEI research and their implications for scientific understandings of health inequalities.

Acknowledgments

Our thanks go first and foremost to our participants, for the time and attention they took to answer our many questions. We are also grateful for the editorial guidance of Susan Bell and Anne Figert, and for the helpful comments of the anonymous reviewers. Research reported in this publication was supported by the National Human Genome Research Institute's Ethical, Legal, and Social Implications (ELSI) Research Program of the National Institutes of Health under award number R01HG005848. The content is solely the responsibility of the authors and does not necessarily represent the official views of the National Institutes of Health.

Notes

1 Authors are listed in order of contribution to the paper. JKS is the Principal Investigator of the study, and took the lead in conceptualizing and designing the study, participated in and supervised the collection and analysis of data, and drafted the manuscript. KWD and SLA participated in data collection and analysis, and in revisions to manuscript drafts, and are listed in reverse alphabetical order by last name. SSL and RAH are Co-Investigators of the study and participated in the conceptualization and design of the study, in data analysis, and in revisions to manuscript drafts.

2 Sankar (2008) also makes the argument that in thinking about race as biological, it would be a mistake to assume that biological race is equivalent to typological race, that is, that humans are divided into discrete groups that have distinctive biological attributes. Rather, she argues, genomic scientists are being careful to use what she calls "statistical race," the idea that some genetic variations may vary in frequency in one population versus another, but not that some variations are predictably present in one group and absent in another.

3 A biobank is a repository that contains biological samples for research. In Lee's (2005, 2006) research, she found that the kinds of racial labels used varied from those referring to continental origin that also align with, for example, US OMB categories (e.g., African, European), to those that referred to more specific groups (e.g., Chinese, Northern European).

4 Biomedicalization, according to Clarke and colleagues (2003, 2010b), refers to the major transformations of medicine occasioned by technoscientific changes and include five key processes: a new biopolitical economy of health and illness in which knowledges, technologies and capital are increasingly co-constituted; an intensified focus on health, risk and optimization; the technoscientization of biomedical practices; transformations in biomedical knowledge production, distribution and consumption; and transformations of bodies and identities.

5 This both reflects and likely contributes to widespread confusion about the difference between "race" and "ethnicity" in the OMB categories, studies by the Census Bureau to improve the accuracy and reliability of its race and ethnicity data, and concerns that including "Hispanic/Latino" as a race, for example, could both clarify how such individuals and populations think about themselves yet might also decrease the number of Hispanics/Latinos counted by the Census.

6   Many of the kinds of studies that characterize GEI research are designed to compare those with disease (or some other risk attribute) and those without. However, if a disease or risk tends to be more frequent in a subpopulation that is also likely to have other genetic variants in common due to nonrandom mating, then this must be statistically controlled for in order to avoid spurious associations between the disease in question and genetic determinants that may be shared but do not actually contribute to the disease. (This is a genetic version of the more common problem of statistical confounding in research.) Individuals that have similar ancestral origins often exhibit this characteristic of also having multiple genetic variants in common, hence genomic scientists studying such individuals often encounter the problem of population stratification in their research. AIMs are a widely used means to control for population stratification.

7   According to Foucault (1978:143), growing governmental concern with the surveillance and regulation of bodies and populations in the seventeenth century led to the development of expert fields of knowledge, and the refinement of diverse and efficient techniques of human control that coalesced to bring "life and its mechanisms into the realm of explicit calculations and made knowledge-power an agent of transformation of human life." Foucault describes biopower – this power over life – as comprised of a continuum between two poles: a disciplinary power or anatomo-politics, and a regulatory power or biopolitics. Anatomo-politics target "the body as a machine: its disciplining, the optimization of its capabilities, the extortion of its forces, the parallel increase of its usefulness and its docility, its integration into systems of efficient and economic controls" (Foucault 1978:139). Biopolitics focus on populations, on "the species body, the body imbued with the mechanics of life and serving as the basis of the biological processes: propagation, births and mortality, the level of health, life expectancy and longevity" (Foucault 1978:139).

References

Abu El-Haj, Nadia. 2007. "The Genetic Reinscription of Race." *Annual Review of Anthropology* 86:283–300.

Adams, Vincanne, Michelle Murphy and Adele E. Clarke. 2009. "Anticipation: Technoscience, Life, Affect, Temporality." *Subjectivity* 28:246–65.

Bliss, Catherine. 2011. "Racial Taxonomy in Genomics." *Social Science & Medicine* 73(7):1019–27.

Bliss, Catherine. 2012. *Race Decoded: The Genomic Fight for Social Justice*. Stanford, CA: Stanford University Press.

Bliss, Catherine. 2015. "Biomedicalization and the New Science of Race." Pp. 175–96 in *Reimagining (Bio)Medicalization, Pharmaceuticals and Genetics: Old Critiques and New Engagements*, edited by Susan E. Bell and Anne E. Figert. New York: Routledge.

Bowker, Geoffrey C. and Susan Leigh Star. 1999. *Sorting Things Out: Classification and Its Consequences*. Cambridge, MA: MIT Press.

Braun, Lundy and Evelynn Hammonds. 2008. "Race, Population, and Genomics: Africa as Laboratory." *Social Science & Medicine* 67:1580–8.

Cavalli-Sforza, L. Luca and Walter Bodmer. 1999[1974]. *The Genetics of Human Populations*. New York: Dober Publications.

Clarke, Adele E., Laura Mamo, Jennifer Ruth Fosket, Jennifer R. Fishman and Janet K. Shim, eds. 2010a. *Biomedicalization: Technoscience, Health, and Illness in the U.S.* Durham, NC: Duke University Press.

Clarke, Adele E., Janet K. Shim, Laura Mamo, Jennifer Ruth Fosket and Jennifer R. Fishman. 2003. "Biomedicalization: Technoscientific Transformations of Health, Illness, and U.S. Biomedicine." *American Sociological Review* 68(2):161–94.

Clarke, Adele E., Janet K. Shim, Laura Mamo, Jennifer Ruth Fosket and Jennifer R. Fishman. 2010b. "Biomedicalization: A Theoretical and Substantive Introduction." Pp. 1–44 in *Biomedicalization: Technoscience, Health, and Illness in the U.S.*, edited by A. E. Clarke, L. Mamo, J. R. Fosket, J. R. Fishman and J. K. Shim. Durham, NC: Duke University Press.

Dobzhansky, Theodosius. 1963. "A Debateable Account of the Origin of Races." *Scientific American* 208:169–72.

Epstein, Steven. 2007. *Inclusion: The Politics of Difference in Medical Research*. Chicago, IL: University of Chicago Press.

Foucault, Michel. 1978. *The History of Sexuality, Volume I: An Introduction*. Trans. R. Hurley. New York: Vintage Books.

Fujimura, Joan H. and Ramya Rajagopalan. 2011. "Different Differences: The Use of 'Genetic Ancestry' Versus Race in Biomedical Human Genetic Research." *Social Studies of Science* 41(1):5–30.

Fullwiley, Duana. 2007. "The Molecularization of Race: Institutionalizing Human Difference in Pharmacogenetics Practice." *Science as Culture* 16(1):1–30.

Fullwiley, Duana. 2008. "The Biologistical Construction of Race: 'Admixture' Technology and the New Genetic Medicine." *Social Studies of Science* 38(5):695–735.

Fullwiley, Duana. 2011. *The Enculturated Gene: Sickle Cell Health Politics and Biological Difference in West Africa*. Princeton, NJ: Princeton University Press.

Gannett, Lisa. 2001. "Racism and Human Genome Diversity Research: The Ethical Limits of 'Population Thinking.'" *Philosophy of Science* 68:S479–S492.

Lampland, Martha and Susan Leigh Star, eds. 2009. *Standards and Their Stories: How Quantifying, Classifying, and Formalizing Practices Shape Everyday Life*. Ithaca, NY: Cornell University Press.

Lee, Sandra Soo-Jin. 2005. "Racializing Drug Design: Implications of Pharmacogenomics for Health Disparities." *American Journal of Public Health* 95(12):2133–8.

Lee, Sandra Soo-Jin. 2006. "Biobanks of a 'Racial Kind': Mining for Difference in the New Genetics." *Patterns of Prejudice* 40(4–5):443–60.

Lee, Sandra Soo-Jin. 2013. "Race, Risk, and Recreation in Personal Genomics: The Limits of Play." *Medical Anthropology Quarterly* 27(4):550–69.

Lee, Sandra Soo-Jin, Joanna Mountain, Barbara Koenig, Russ Altman, Melissa Brown, Albert Camarillo, Luca Cavalli-Sforza, Mildred Cho, Jennifer Eberhardt, Marcus Feldman, et al. 2008. "The Ethics of Characterizing Difference: Guiding Principles on Using Racial Categories in Human Genetics." *Genome Biology* 9(7):404.

Lewontin, Richard. 1972. "The Apportionment of Human Diversity." *Evolutionary Biology* 6:381–98.

Montoya, Michael J. 2007. "Bioethnic Conscription: Genes, Race, and Mexicana/o Ethnicity in Diabetes Research." *Cultural Anthropology* 22(1):94–128.

Montoya, Michael. 2011. *Making the Mexican Diabetic: Race, Science, and the Genetics of Inequality*. Berkeley, CA: University of California Press.

Murphy, Michelle. 2012. *Seizing the Means of Reproduction: Entanglements of Feminism, Health, and Technoscience*. Durham, NC: Duke University Press.

Omi, Michael and Howard Winant. 1994. *Racial Formation in the United States: From the 1960s to the 1990s*. New York: Routledge.

Reardon, Jenny. 2005. *Race to the Finish: Identity and Governance in an Age of Genomics*. Princeton, NJ: Princeton University Press.

Reardon, Jenny. 2009. "Finding Oprah's Roots, Losing the World: Beyond the Liberal Anti-Racist Genome." Presented at Society for Social Studies of Science, Washington, DC.

Sankar, Pamela. 2008. "Moving beyond the Two-Race Mantra." Pp. 271–84 in *Revisiting Race in a Genomic Age*, edited by B. A. Koenig, S. S.-J. Lee and S. S. Richardson. New Brunswick, NJ: Rutgers University Press.

Shim, Janet K. 2014. *Heart-Sick: The Politics of Risk, Inequality, and Heart Disease*. New York: New York University Press.

Shim, Janet K., Katherine Weatherford Darling, Martine D. Lappe, L. Katherine Thomson, Sandra Soo-Jin Lee, Robert A. Hiatt and Sara L. Ackerman. 2014a. "Homogeneity and Heterogeneity as Situational Properties: Producing – and Moving Beyond? – Race in Post-Genomic Science." *Social Studies of Science* 44(4):579–99.

Shim, Janet K., Sara L. Ackerman, Katherine Weatherford Darling, Robert A. Hiatt and Sandra Soo-Jin Lee. 2014b. "Race and Ancestry in the Age of Inclusion: Technique and Meaning in Post-genomic Science." *Journal of Health and Social Behavior*. Published online before print; doi: 10.1177/0022146514555224. Available at: http://hsb.sagepub.com/content/early/2014/11/05/0022146514555224. Accessed November 9, 2014.

Spelman, Elizabeth. 1988. *Inessential Woman: Problems of Exclusion in Feminist Thought*. Boston, MA: Beacon Press.

Timmermans, Stefan and Marc Berg. 2003. *The Gold Standard: The Challenge of Evidence-Based Medicine*. Philadelphia, PA: Temple University Press.

Timmermans, Stefan and Steven Epstein. 2010. "A World of Standards but Not a Standard World: Toward a Sociology of Standards and Standardization." *Annual Review of Sociology* 36:69–89.

Weber, Lynn. 2010. *Understanding Race, Class, Gender, and Sexuality: A Conceptual Framework*. New York: Oxford University Press.

Whitmarsh, Ian. 2008. *Biomedical Ambiguity: Race, Asthma, and the Contested Meaning of Genetic Research in the Caribbean*. Ithaca, NY: Cornell University Press.

4
Commentary and Reflections: On Stratification and Complexity

REBECCA M. HERZIG

All three of the "new engagements" comprising this section share two assumptions common to much "old" feminist scholarship: namely, that (a) oppression exists and (b) oppression should be challenged. Those assumptions often help to concentrate research in potent ways, Janet Shim and her colleagues point out, by placing and keeping "power and relations of domination and subordination at the center of the analysis" (Shim et al. 2015:73, Chapter 3, this volume). Yet while feminism's emancipatory goals offer researchers compelling motivation and focus, they also present persistent conundrums for analyses of contemporary biomedicine. For within biomedicine, the chapters in Part I take pains to emphasize, relations of power are "messy" enough that hierarchies of domination and subordination are not always clear (Bell and Figert 2015:19, Chapter 1, this volume). Indeed, biomedical processes may be best conceived not in terms of hierarchical ladders but "in terms of networks, spirals, and complexity" (Bell and Figert 2015:26). These diffuse networks are "everywhere tempered and complicated by" pluralisms, partialisms and contingencies (Annandale and Hammarström 2015:42, Chapter 2, this volume, citing Clarke 2010:389). Even the most hegemonic formations are "immanent with and animated by" counter-formations, their own "'modes of undoing'" (Shim et al. 2015:63, citing Murphy 2012:183, n. 3). Far from readily captured and pinned "at the center of analysis," then, power in biomedicine flows and fluxes, forming the very subjects it regulates. Thus, for those of us, like Shim and colleagues, trying to challenge "'relationships of exploitation of subordinate groups by dominant groups'" (Shim et al. 2015:73, citing Weber 2010:91), contemporary biomedicine presents some serious challenges. Who (or what) might accurately be characterized as "'oppressed groups struggl[ing] to gain rights, opportunities, and resources,'" and who instead as "'dominant groups ... seek[ing] to maintain their position of control'" (Shim et al. 2015:73, citing Weber 2010:91)? What might "emancipation" even look like, given that biomedicine constitutes the very bodies and subjects that seek deliverance?

This brief comment cannot address those questions in their broadest strokes, of course.[1] I will not even purport to address them in a more limited, context-specific way. I intend merely to draw attention to the tensions generated by the juxtaposition of "feminist" opposition to exploitative, hierarchical relations of power with analyses of biomedicine's multidirectional, multi-sited, life-altering churn. While it might be argued that the analyst's role is to cut through that frothy churn to grasp the relatively fixed structural mechanisms within, my suggestion here, based on the three chapters in Part I, is that the conceptual tensions produced by feminist analyses of biomedicine cannot be so easily wiped away. Drawing on elements of the three chapters, I try to show that such tensions, far from suggesting the irrelevance of feminist approaches to biomedicine, instead highlight their ongoing generativity.

Early critiques of medicalization, thumbnail histories of the concept invariably recount, tended to position professional physicians as the dominant agents of change. While the broader social control of deviance might well serve governmental as well as professional interests, the medicalization of social deviance typically was routed through the authority of the "technically competent" doctor (Bell and Figert 2015:21; see also Freidson 1970; Zola 1972; Illich 1975; Conrad and Schneider 1980). According to those early critiques, Bell and Figert summarize, physicians gained the "authority and professional power in modern society to define and control what is formally recognized as a disorder, sickness or deviance," in a top-down, exclusionary manner (2015:21). To the extent that medical professionals transformed "'normal' everyday feelings and behaviors" into illnesses, early critiques suggested, it was often for their own "economic and professional benefit" (Bell and Figert 2015:21).

In contrast, more recent scholarship shifts the "analytic gaze" from medical professionals to other "key drivers" of social change (Bell and Figert 2015:23; Annandale and Hammarström 2015:41). The proliferation of pharmaceuticals, commercial genetics and new surgeries and devices is said to distribute processes of legitimation and decision-making once concentrated with doctors. Now patients ("consumers") are actively responsible for their individual health and bodily "enhancement." This ceaseless, increasingly commercialized pursuit suggests phenomena unfolding "from below" as much as through the imposition of narrow professional interests (Annandale and Hammarström 2015:42, citing Conrad 2013; Furedi 2006). As Bell and Figert aptly note, contemporary dynamics "do not easily fit into a conceptual frame of . . . governmental or medical professional control" (2015:25). For the affluent, at least, "life itself" has been transformed into an object of ongoing, personalized intervention (Franklin 2000; Rose 2007).

For feminists in particular, engagement with these developments is often framed by the concept of "biomedicalization," first elaborated by Adele Clarke and her colleagues in a 2003 essay cited in some version by all three chapters in Part I. Worth stressing here is that Clarke and her colleagues employ biomedicalization not merely as a theoretical concept, but as a referent to an actual "historical shift" – a dramatic set of material changes in the organization and practice of contemporary medicine. "Power" and "control" in this new historical context are far from simple. As they describe it, biomedicine today is being reorganized "not only from the top down or the bottom up but *from the inside out*" (Clarke et al. 2003:162; emphasis in original). Causality in this context is equally complex: a "fundamental premise" of biomedicalization is that new technical capabilities, new institutional organizations, new political economies, new bodily identities and new social forms are all mutually and reciprocally constituted (2003:163). Attendant to those tangled co-productions are "new forms of agency, empowerment, confusion, resistance, docility, subjugation, citizenship, subjectivity, and morality" (2003:185).

In the midst of all that multidirectional, ongoing, mutual (re)constitution, what becomes of those old warhorses of feminist theory and praxis: domination and subordination? What might "oppression" look like in such a mobile field? Clarke and her colleagues certainly do not ignore the exclusionary actions of biomedicine, including the specific barriers and privileges framed by "race, class, gender, and other attributes" (2003:170). Borrowing terminology from Ginsburg and Rapp's 1995 discussion of reproduction, they label the reconstituted forms of cooptation and exclusion emerging in contemporary biomedicine "stratified biomedicalization" (2003:170–1, citing Ginsburg and Rapp 1995). It is revealing, however, that most specific examples of "stratified biomedicalization" discussed in Clarke et al.'s essay do not address the sorts of *embodied* categories at the heart of so many feminist, antiracist, queer and disability rights critiques of biomedicine. Examples instead tend to concern individual confrontations with financial gatekeeping, such as "stratifying fee-for-service options for those who can afford them" (2003:171). Relationships between bodily difference, social stratification and disparities in health and mortality thus remain unspecified.

Enter the three chapters that comprise Part I, each of which, in its own way, tackles problems of difference, bodies and power headfirst. The burgeoning field of gender-specific medicine (GSM), Annandale and Hammarström begin, might be considered part of a broader "'repudiation of so-called one-size-fits-all medicine'" that sociologist Steven Epstein terms "'the inclusion-and-difference' paradigm" (Annandale and Hammarström 2015:48, citing Epstein 2007:5). Characterized by the assumption that "social identities correspond to relatively distinct kinds of bodies – female bodies, Asian bodies, elderly Hispanic male bodies, and so on," the paradigm further presumes that knowledge about these allegedly distinct forms of embodiment cannot be transferred – or, at least, that one may not presume that knowledge gleaned from the study of one set of bodies might be applied to another (Epstein 2007:2). In other words, it rejects a "standard" or "universal" human subject. The inclusion-and-difference paradigm, codified in the USA in new federal laws, politics and guidelines, insists that "expert knowledge about human health is dangerously flawed" and "health research practices are fundamentally unjust" unless specific populations are adequately represented in biomedical studies (Epstein 2007:4). Yet where the advent of "race-specific" drugs and diagnoses has provoked widespread criticism of racial profiling, Annandale and Hammarström point out, GSM has remained remarkably free of critical scrutiny. In this regard, GSM might be seen as a particularly insidious form of "stratified biomedicalization," as conceptualized by Clarke et al. (Annandale and Hammarström 2015:48).

As Bell and Figert remind us, a major intervention of early feminist work on medicalization was to challenge the image of medicalization as a top-down process, in which patients are merely the passive recipients of physicians' elastic diagnoses and treatments (2015:22). Gendered analyses of medicalization instead highlighted patients as active, if unequal, participants. In Annandale and Hammarström's new engagement, however, the lines of stratification are clear and largely unidirectional. They describe, for instance, several ways in which "the wider juggernaut of GSM" acts to "colonize the way that we think about … male and female bodies" (2015:51), including locking those bodies in a binary frame that is not merely comparative but competitive (2015:51). They further argue that the effects of biomedical innovation are unequally distributed, and the benefits unequally reaped: as they put it, "it is women's bodies which are plundered" for use in biomedicine, "women's" bodies that provide "embryos, oocytes, fetal tissue, menstrual blood and umbilical cord blood" (2015:42, citing Waldby and Cooper 2010; see also Waldby and Cooper 2014).

If GSM has such non- (if not *anti-*) feminist effects, what accounts for its growing popularity? What brings gender-specific medicine "to the fore at the present historical juncture" (Annandale and Hammarström 2015:47–8)? Although vocal proponents of GSM describe the "lay public" as driving the field's growth by demanding attention to "'women's unique health needs'" (Annandale and Hammarström 2015:46, citing Legato 2004:61), Annandale and Hammarström demur. They instead propose that the discourse of gender specificity is blossoming because it "resonates with dominant neoliberal medical and public health discourses" (2015:48). The appeal of gender-specific medicine is tied to "new ways" – i.e., neoliberal ways – "of governing conduct" (2015:48). Particularly in the USA, the advent of gender-specific lifestyle products, such as nutritional supplements, should "not come as a surprise," given the more general "'neoliberal restructuring of American society'" (2015:48, citing Crawford 2006).[2]

Here we see the uneasy relations between what I have been calling a "feminist" concern with domination and exploitation (or "plunder") and analyses of biomedicalization. To be sure, the rise of gender-specific marketing strategies, gender-specific research on existing drugs and other targeting strategies reflect the growing political economic influence of healthcare. Particularly in the USA (which, as Bell and Figert (2015:27) remind us, continues to account for half of the world's prescription drug sales), technoscientific changes in the life sciences have profoundly reshaped economic activity (Rajan 2006). And, to be sure, gender-specific research protocols and target marketing easily might be considered types of "stratification." But the concept of "stratified biomedicalization" on its own does not offer much in terms of delineating the processes or mechanisms of stratification. (Medicalization, recall, tended to attribute causal efficacy to identifiable physicians and their professional guilds.) What laws, policies, guidelines and institutional procedures anchor the "neoliberal political agenda" given causal force here? What are its mechanisms? Who are its chief proponents? What, precisely, does that agenda – one generally associated with the increasing mobility of capital – have to gain by promoting a vision of binary, competitive biological sexual difference, over one of sexual fluidity and mutability?

A key virtue of the biomedicalization framework, I would argue, is that it encourages further reflection on the technoscientific production and legitimation of "real" suffering (Herzig 2005, 2015). Particularly given the tirelessly "women"-centric rhetoric of GSM's proponents, it seems fruitful to define not merely how particular practices of "gender-specific medicine" subordinate or devalue some bodies to the benefit of others' ongoing dominance, but how GSM redefines the parameters of suffering, "colonization" and "plunder." Perhaps the primary beneficiaries of GSM turn out not to be "men" or "women" per se, but cisgender people (individuals whose self-understanding conforms to the sex attributed to them at birth) more generally, at the expense of transgendered people. Following Epstein's analysis of social movements, we might further hypothesize that the growing trans-health movement will alter the landscape of GSM, by queering biomedical definitions of "male" and "female" (2007:256). Similarly, I wonder whether it is accurate to say that "women's bodies" are being "exploited," or rather that some bodies – disproportionately young, poor and of color – are being constituted as "female" (and "human") in potent new ways, to the benefit of bodies constituted as older, more affluent and whiter. Whose "suffering" is recognized and alleviated, exactly, and whose is erased and/or exacerbated?

Indeed, a crucial effect of the ongoing extension of medical authority is to route verification of suffering – including suffering from sexual, gendered racial oppression – through the tools, techniques and methodologies of biomedicine. As Shim et al. in "Reimagining Race and Ancestry" (2015) so expertly show in their account of the steady replacement of self-identified race and ethnicity with ancestry informative markers (AIMs), the "biomedicalizing" of difference in this case may serve to downplay race and ethnicity relations "*between and among groups*" in favor of a concept of ancestry as an individually held, "technically defined gradation" (Shim et al. 2015:74, emphasis in original). While the motives in both expert and lay practices here may well be "just" – an effort to "represent human diversity with . . . greater accuracy and refinement" (Shim et al. 2015:65), in practice AIMs may well elide or strategically obscure inequalities systematically produced by structural forces.

Given Shim et al.'s attention to how "tropes of precision, individualization, and the continuity of human variation" promote expressions of relative genetic admixture rather than relational, group-based processes (Shim et al. 2015:61), I found myself wondering if the same problematization of the individualization of difference might be performed for the *diseases* these gene–environment researchers (and, in turn, these social scientists) have elected to study. The lethal diseases named and framed here – heart disease, cancer and diabetes – all bear the imprint of "seriousness" in affluent, industrialized contexts; as a result, they attract both substantial federal and commercial funding and elevated social status for the researchers who engage them. Might the sort of curiously self-referential, anticipatory investment in AIMs that Shim and her colleagues noted in these scientists unfold differently for researchers in sites imbued with less moral gravitas – dermatological research, say, or commercial ancestry testing? How do the dynamics and relations of power within and across fields of scientific research – commercial versus academic, medical versus cosmetic, human versus veterinary, serious diseases versus "lifestyle" indications – refract charged questions of racial and ethnic difference?

Put another way, scientific and public concern with "the 'real differences' that matter for etiology and health disparities" (Shim et al. 2015:75) not only serve to establish specific notions of human difference (here, "ancestry informative markers" rather than "self-identified race and ethnicity"), but also specific notions of "real" or consequential disparities: a sorting, tacit or explicit, of the differences that matter from those that do not. As Bell and Figert point out, the act of expanding analytical attention from health and illness in the affluent industrialized North to the "political, economic, and organizational dynamics of global health inequalities" immediately shifts discussions of power and privilege (2015:34). Even the analytical lenses we choose limit other ways of understanding what "problems are and how to alleviate them" (2015:34).

As long as transnational practices of science and medicine remain "discursive battlefield[s] in which contested futures of stratification compete" (Montoya 2011:43), the feminist imperative to place domination and subordination at the center of analysis will remain a clarifying flare in the haze. But, as these three chapters show, feminist analyses of (and opposition to) persistent structural inequality often sit uneasily alongside Foucaultian framings of biopolitics. How do "stratifications" develop and persist in mobile, productive fields of power? The answers remain unclear. Perhaps, then, in the turn "sideways" heralded by Bell and Figert, we might draw still further on political theory and philosophy – looking for fresh juxtapositions to unsettle future analytical work.

Notes

1   In their general form, these questions are common among those who admire Foucault's insights into the operations of modern power yet seek more robust accounts of political agency and resistance. For early reflection on these themes, see Butler (1997) and Brown (1997).

2   Addressing a similar "why GSM now?" question in his award-winning book, *Inclusion*, Epstein attributes the relative lack of dissent over sex profiling in medicine, in part, to "ideological divides" within the women's health movement (2007:248). Whereas "communities of color" and "social movements organized on behalf of multiracialism" shared a "historical suspicion of clinical research" which helps explain ongoing skepticism about the use of race in biomedical research (2007:256), Epstein sees no similar unity in gendered social movements. Instead, a broad, professionalized and corporatized women's health movement has sought to distinguish itself from earlier feminist, anti-medicalization movements: advocates today now often seek "to extend scientific scrutiny" of "assertions of biological differences by sex" (2007:247). Gender-specific medicine continues to gain institutional backing and financial support, Epstein argues, because specific social groups advance its progress. "Neoliberalism restructuring" is not the salient agent of change, in Epstein's account.

References

Annandale, Ellen and Anne Hammarström. 2015. "A New Biopolitics of Gender and Health? 'Gender-specific Medicine' and Pharmaceuticalization in the Twenty-First Century." Pp. 41–55 in *Reimagining (Bio)Medicalization, Pharmaceuticals and Genetics: Old Critiques and New Engagements*, edited by Susan E. Bell and Anne E. Figert. New York: Routledge.

Bell, Susan E. and Anne E. Figert. 2015. "Moving Sideways and Forging Ahead: Reimagining '-Izations' in the Twenty-First Century." Pp. 19–40 in *Reimagining (Bio)Medicalization, Pharmaceuticals and Genetics: Old Critiques and New Engagements*, edited by Susan E. Bell and Anne E. Figert. New York: Routledge.

Brown, Wendy. 1997. "The Impossibility of Women's Studies." *differences* 9(3):70–101.

Butler, Judith. 1997. *The Psychic Life of Power: Theories of Subjection*. Stanford, CA: Stanford University Press.

Clarke, Adele. 2010. "Epilogue: Thoughts on Biomedicalization in its Transnational Travels." Pp. 380–405 in *Biomedicalization: Technoscience, Health, and Illness in the U.S.*, edited by Adele Clarke, Laura Mamo, Jennifer R. Fosket, Jennifer R. Fishman and Janet K. Shim. Durham, NC, and London: Duke University Press.

Clarke, Adele E., Janet K. Shim, Laura Mamo, Jennifer Ruth Fosket and Jennifer R. Fishman. 2003. "Biomedicalization: Technoscientific Transformations of Health, Illness, and U.S. Biomedicine." *American Sociological Review* 68(2):161–94.

Conrad, Peter and Joseph Schneider. 1980. *Deviance and Medicalization: From Badness to Sickness*. St Louis, MO: Mosby.

Conrad, P. 2013. "Medicalization: Changing Contours, Characteristics, and Contexts." Pp. 195–214 in *Medical Sociology on the Move*, edited by William Cockerham. London: Springer.

Crawford, R. 2006. "Health as Meaningful Social Practice." *Health* 10:401–20.

Epstein, Steven. 2007. *Inclusion: The Politics of Difference in Medical Research*. Chicago, IL: University of Chicago Press.

Franklin, Sarah. 2000. "Life Itself: Global Nature and the Genetic Imaginary." Pp. 188–227 in *Global Nature, Global Culture*, edited by Sarah Franklin, Celia Lury and Jackie Stacy. London: Sage.

Freidson, Eliot. 1970. *Profession of Medicine: A Study of the Sociology of Applied Knowledge*. New York: Dodd, Mead & Co.

Furedi, Frank. 2006. "The End of Medical Dominance." *Society* 43(6):14–18.

Ginsburg, Faye and Rayna Rapp. 1995. *Conceiving the New World Order: The Global Politics of Reproduction*. Berkeley, CA: University of California Press.

Herzig, Rebecca M. 2005. *Suffering for Science: Reason and Sacrifice in Modern America*. New Brunswick, NJ: Rutgers University Press.

Herzig, Rebecca M. 2015. *Plucked: A History of Hair Removal*. New York: New York University Press.

Illich, Ivan. 1975. *Medical Nemesis*. New York: Pantheon.

Legato, M. 2004. "Gender-specific Medicine: The View from Salzburg." *Gender Medicine* 1:61–3.

Montoya, Michael. 2011. *Making the Mexican Diabetic: Race, Science, and the Genetics of Inequality*. Berkeley, CA: University of California Press.

Murphy, Michelle. 2012. *Seizing the Means of Reproduction: Entanglements of Feminism, Health, and Technoscience*. Durham, NC: Duke University Press.

Rajan, Kaushik Sunder. 2006. *Biocapital: The Constitution of Postgenomic Life*. Durham, NC: Duke University Press.

Rose, Nikolas. 2007. *The Politics of Life Itself: Biomedicine, Power, and Subjectivity in the Twenty-First Century*. Princeton, NJ: Princeton University Press.

Shim, Janet K., Katherine Weatherford Darling, Sara L. Ackerman, Sandra Soo-Jin Lee and Robert A. Hiatt. 2015. "Reimagining Race and Ancestry: Biomedicalizing Difference in Post-Genomic Subjects." Pp. 56–78 in *Reimagining (Bio)Medicalization, Pharmaceuticals and Genetics: Old Critiques and New Engagements*, edited by Susan E. Bell and Anne E. Figert. New York: Routledge.

Waldby, Catherine and Melinda Cooper. 2010. "From Reproductive Work to Regenerative Labour: The Female Body and the Stem Cell Industry." *Feminist Theory* 11:2–22.

Waldby, Catherine and Melinda Cooper. 2014. *Clinical Labor: Tissue Donors and Research Subjects in the Global Bioeconomy*. Durham, NC: Duke University Press.

Weber, Lynn. 2010. *Understanding Race, Class, Gender, and Sexuality: A Conceptual Framework*. New York: Oxford University Press.

Zola, Irving. 1972. "Medicine as an Institution of Social Control." *Sociological Review* 20:487–504.

II
Pharmaceuticals

5

Vital Objects
Essential Drugs and Their Critical Legacies

JEREMY A. GREENE

Expanding access to pharmaceuticals has become one of the most visible planks of twenty-first-century global health efforts. This is evidenced by the moral urgency of antiretroviral rollout to combat the global HIV/AIDS pandemic, the pressing call for new drugs for neglected diseases in the global South like tuberculosis, malaria and trypanosomiasis, and the increasing interest in long-term pharmaceutical delivery systems to address the rising prevalence of chronic disease in both global North and South (Greene 2010).[1] The outsized role prescription drugs now play in international public health is all the more evident when compared to the relatively small role of pharmaceuticals in the framing of international health organizations like the World Health Organization (WHO) in the mid-twentieth century.

The increasing power of pharmacotherapeutics to cure or mitigate disease, from antibiotics to antiretrovirals, has without doubt played an important role in this transformation. Yet the centrality of pharmaceuticals in global health practices today cannot be explained by efficacy alone. Rather, it is as much a consequence of shifts in international politics, multinational capital formations and transnational networks of consumer advocates, pharmacological experts and consumer activists as it is a shift in the overall effectiveness and relevance of medicines. It is perhaps not surprising given these larger scale societal changes that pharmaceutical modalities have come to dominate biomedical imagination over the late twentieth and early twenty-first century. But it is quite important to ask how the field of global public health – which so frequently defines itself as a preventive, upstream alternative to curative, downstream biomedical approaches to disease – has now come to feature pharmaceutical delivery so prominently.

Recent observers of this "pharmaceuticalization of public health," have depicted this historical process as a relatively recent state change from a prior, nonpharmaceutical mode to a present pharmaceutical one, often linked to one or more *fin-du-siècle* crises: globalization, neoliberalization or the new materialism of emerging infectious diseases like HIV/AIDS and multidrug-resistant tuberculosis (Biehl 2007; Nguyen 2010; Williams, Martin and Gabe

2011; Koch 2013). Such accounts – like many "-ization" narratives in the sociology of health and medicine – are accounts of rupture which emphasize change over continuity. From the historian's perspective, however, the critique of the increasing role of pharmaceuticals in global public health is not unique to the twenty-first century, and it is important to pay attention to the threads of continuity and contingency that link both present and past.

This chapter seeks to link recent critiques of the pharmaceuticalization of global public health (Biehl 2007; Nguyen 2010; Koch 2013) with an earlier, analogous critical discourse: the "essential drugs concept," which became a prominent focus of international health politics in the 1970s and 1980s. The essential drugs concept gained global visibility when it became a central tenet of WHO policy under the leadership of Director-General Halfdan Mahler, who warned the 1975 World Health Assembly of an "urgent need to ensure that most *essential drugs* are available at a reasonable price, and to stimulate research and development to produce new drugs adapted to the real health requirements of developing countries" (Mahler 1975).

The essential drugs concept combined two emergent critical discourses regarding the role of biomedicine in public health – the *overuse* of biomedical technologies in the global North and their *underuse* in the global South – in a manner that was highly resonant with changes in the politics of international development and international public health in the 1970s. Critics of pharmaceutical overuse adopted newly available critiques of medicalization – as framed by Ivan Illich (1975), Archie Cochrane (1979) and others – to argue that too many pharmaceuticals were being consumed to combat problems best addressed by preventive, social or economic interventions. Critics of pharmaceutical underuse, in turn, tended to use available critiques of political economy and dependency theory to argue that inequity in the production, distribution, patenting and pricing of pharmaceuticals made a large number of truly effective medicines unavailable to large populations of patients in poor countries unable to afford them. As objects which addressed *both* questions, essential drugs became an ideal test case of Mahler's vision of how "appropriate technologies" should be disseminated through the health systems of the developing world: not too many, not too few, but just enough.

Essential drugs were renamed *essential medicines* at the turn of the twenty-first century, partly to downplay the increasingly negative connotations of the term "drug." And yet while both terms might ostensibly refer to the same concept, the actors, interests and politics that began to crystallize around *essential medicines* in twenty-first-century global health practice constituted a very different formation than those that clustered around *essential drugs* in the 1970s and 1980s. Though one might use the terms essential medicines and essential drugs almost interchangeably, their usage serves to divide historical periods: essential medicines is a twenty-first-century term while essential drugs was largely a twentieth-century term. Viewed in close apposition, these critical engagements old and new offer an opportunity to explore how critiques of the role of pharmaceuticals in public health have grown in resonance and relevance at the same time they have lost their analytic coherence.

Emergence of a Critical Discourse on Global Pharmaceuticals

The concept of essential drugs did not spring fully formed from Halfdan Mahler's office in Geneva in 1975 like Athena from the head of Zeus. In articulating a concept of essential medicines, Mahler implicitly referenced a much older set of concerns within military medicine, colonial medicine and humanitarian intervention that had developed a logistical language of which drugs were essential to the maintenance of public health in out-of-the-way places and which were not: including the "materia medica minimalis" kits developed by the Red Cross to be able to rapidly deploy needed medical care in the setting of a humanitarian crisis (Evatt 1881; Redfield 2008, 2013). In the rapidly changing landscape of international health and development in the 1970s, the introduction of the essential drugs concept into the WHO mission also sat at the intersection of several critical discourses of health, technology and development. These included a series of critical reassessments of modernization theory by bilateral and multilateral aid organizations, critiques of pharmaceutical pricing and provision in the recently independent Southern nations of Sri Lanka, India, Pakistan and Brazil, and a skepticism of the engines of pharmaceutical promotion in the medicalization of everyday life by prominent academics and consumer advocates.[2]

The same surge in pharmaceutical research, development and marketing that made the miracle cures of penicillin, cortisone, chlorpromazine and streptomycin widely available in the early postwar era also pushed forward many less-than-miraculous cures that began to glut markets in both the global North and South.[3] By the early 1960s – most notably in the wake of the global thalidomide disaster – the pharmaceutical industry became the subject of increased public, professional, journalistic and public critique. An ensuing set of regulatory measures intended to protect drug consumers in the USA and northern Europe swiftly reduced the number of brands on the market, and required stringent proofs of efficacy and safety for the marketing of prescription drugs in these nations (Daemmrich 2003). The deployment of effective state-based regulation among nations of the global North, however, would paradoxically work to augment international disparities in drug quality between North and South.

By the mid-1970s, a number of journalists had written popular exposés of the "dumping" of inferior pharmaceuticals (newly unmarketable due to safety and efficacy concerns in the global North) for sale in relatively unprotected markets in the global South (Mintz 1965; Silverman and Lee 1976; Medawar 1979; Melrose 1982). Ironically, those states that had the least ability to regulate the quality of their drug supply spent the highest proportion of their national health budgets importing pharmaceutical products. For example, by 1976, Thailand spent 30.4 percent of its public health budget on drugs, while Bangladesh spent 63.7 percent of its budget on prescription medicines. Disparities between North and South could also be quantified in terms of the sheer number of potentially useless drugs being marketed in the global South compared to the more highly regulated markets of the global North. By the early 1970s, Norway allowed the sale of only 1,000 drug brands, Brazil and Argentina had 24,000 and 17,000 brand name drugs on the market, and the Egyptian market contained a dizzying array of more than 50,000 brands, most of dubious provenance (Kanji et al. 1992).

Many of these journalists and activists who protested the overuse of worthless and wasteful pharmaceuticals in the global South were located in civil society groups in the global North and were influenced by newly available critiques of medicalization, on the one hand, and a growing critique of the powerful role of multinational corporations on the other. Critical works such as Robert Ledogar's (1975) *Hungry for Profits*, and Barnet and Muller's (1976) *Global Reach: The Power of Multinational Corporations* cast Northern-based multi-national companies – Pfizer, Merck and Bristol-Myers among them – as rapacious and unaccountable institutions that squeezed money from the poor health budgets of low-income nations and then applied insidious pressure to any national policies which threatened their profitability.[4] These critiques of waste and *overuse*, however, would clash with another set of critiques of inaccessibility and *underuse*, grounded in the language of political economy and development economics.

The 1970s had also witnessed a period of critical reassessment of development strategies within both United Nations agencies and Bretton Woods institutions such as the World Bank and International Monetary Fund. On some level, the goal of transferring biomedical technologies from North to South had been a part of the larger economic development rhetoric since the end of the Second World War. Yet as Paul Cruickshank (2011) has noted in his recent study of health and international development from 1968 to 1989, the decade of the 1970s witnessed a broadening of the metrics and meanings of development. Following prominent critiques from development economists Gunnar Myrdal (1967) and Dudley Seers (1969), the focus of earlier modernization theorists was critically redesigned to include measures of health and well-being that stretched beyond the gross domestic product (GDP). The result was the approach that World Bank chief Robert McNamara eventually called the "Basic Needs Approach," which included a series of health indicators in its metrics of economic development (Cruickshank 2011).

McNamara and his circle of modernization engineers in the 1970s were influenced by the teleological theories of demographic and epidemiological transitions developed by postwar population scientists (Teitelbaum 1975; Packard 1997). In one particularly widely cited article in the *Milbank Memorial*

Fund Quarterly, Egyptian-born physician and population scientist Abdel Omran traced the historical evolution of the health profile of a given society as a fixed series of stages proceeding from an "age of pestilence and famine" to an "age of receding pandemics" to an "age of degenerative and man-made disease" (Omran 1971:49). While some countries, like Japan, had passed from stage 1 to stage 3 in an "accelerated transition" through rapid Westernization, Omran singled out countries of the global South – such as Ceylon – as being lodged in a "delayed model." Omran's teleology of health and development held out the hope that with proper attention to technology transfer, modernization of the health profiles of the developing world could be "significantly influence[d] by medical technology," especially "imported medical technologies" like modern pharmaceuticals (Omran 1971:510, 522; Weisz and Olshenko-Gryn 2010).

The vital question of access to new medical technologies was not lost on physicians and pharmacologists in recently decolonized countries. Where Omran had singled out Ceylon as an example of a country whose development was being "delayed," Senaka Bibile, founder of the first department of pharmacology on Ceylon was at the same time depicting this dependence on imported pharmaceuticals as a problem that could be solved – through the selection of a short list of essential drugs which could be generically obtained through competitive bidding at a price that would be more feasible for the long-term solvency of a postcolonial healthcare sector.[5] In October of 1970, Bibile was tasked (along with socialist M.P. and fellow physician S. A. Wickremansinghe) "to look into and correct the needless loss of foreign exchange in the import of drugs" (Associated Newspapers of Ceylon 1978:12). The resulting report, published in March 1971 and picked up by the *British Medical Journal* later in the year, argued that benefits of modern pharmacotherapy could only be realized in Ceylon by adopting an aggressive policy prioritizing essential over inessential drugs, generic drugs over brand-name versions, and bringing costs down through competitive bidding, local formulation and rational use (Wickremansinghe and Bibile 1971a, 1971b). In 1972, the governing United Front coalition changed the name of the country from Ceylon to Sri Lanka, and created the State Pharmaceuticals Corporation of Sri Lanka (SPC), which implemented Bibile's plan from 1972 until the collapse of the coalition in 1976.

By that time, a handful of newly independent nations with socialist governments like Sri Lanka had likewise attempted to nationalize their drug industries and create restrictive formularies that would limit their pharmaceutical markets to a small list of generically prescribed essential drugs. But as with Sri Lanka, these unilateral attempts to enact national essential drug policies almost universally succumbed to political and economic pressures attributed to multinational pharmaceutical concerns.[6] Ensuing critiques of North–South inequalities in drug quality and pricing became a visible example of a broader critique of multinational corporations by health ministries of the global South (and sympathetic academics and activists within the global North). Pharmaceuticals became a plank in the international politics of the Non-Aligned Movement when the Fifth Non-Aligned Conference in Colombo (1976) adopted Resolution 25, urging all developing countries to cooperate with international organizations to promote the production, procurement and distribution of pharmaceuticals (UNCTAD 1982).

As I have demonstrated in this section, a highly visible and multi-vocal critique of pharmaceuticals in international health had already developed by the 1970s in the form of the essential drugs concept. As a critical term shared by social scientists, consumer activists and policymakers over a variety of geographies, the essential drugs concept represented a key intersection of critiques of the overuse and underuse of global pharmaceuticals.

Conflicts over Essential Drugs in the 1970s and 1980s

By the late 1970s, the essential drugs concept had become a powerful and morally salient discourse for recently decolonized nations of the global South to call for action *en bloc* in multilateral institutions like the United Nations Conference on Trade and Development (UNCTAD), the United Nations Centre on Transnational Corporations (UNCTC) and the WHO. After broaching the issue with his address to the World Health Assembly in 1975, Mahler tasked the pharmaceutical division of the WHO to form an expert committee that would define an "essential drugs philosophy," create a list of essential drugs and provide technical advice on how such a list could be translated into increased universal access to pharmaceuticals worldwide. The team visited twenty-five countries in four of six WHO regions to interview Ministry of Health officials, doctors, pharmacists and health providers to understand pharmaceutical utilization across all levels of the healthcare systems, and then convened a series of expert panels in Geneva in 1976 and 1977. The committee met to finalize the report in Geneva in October 1977 and circulated the list to regional and national offices for commentary before publication.

The formal definition of essential drugs in the WHO Technical Report 615, "The Selection of Essential Drugs" (1977), privileged prevalent conditions over rare diseases, older drugs of proven efficacy and safety over newer drugs, single agents over combinations and generic names over brand names. As a global reference, the model list of 186 medications was understood to be adaptable by region, country, province, and subdivided by strata of care from primary care clinic to local hospital to tertiary medical center. As a working draft circulated in 1976 noted, the "major objective in the 'essential drug list philosophy' is to reach the greatest number of patients/people with acceptable standards of drug treatment, within the limits set by the resources available, at a certain time or under the actual circumstances" (WHO 1976). Assuming some variance in the burden of disease between temperate and tropical zones, the total number of drugs essential to any one region might range from 50 to 250 active substances (WHO 1976).

Although the first WHO model list of essential drugs was almost exclusively comprised of off-patent medicines that posed little immediate threat to world markets for newer brand-name pharmaceuticals, the list was met with immediate protest by the pharmaceutical industry (Egli 1977). The International Federation of Pharmaceutical Manufacturers Associations (IFPMA) – a consortium of national drug industry lobbyists that set up offices in Geneva and had by the late 1960s been officially recognized as a WHO-affiliated nongovernmental organization (NGO) – responded that the essential drugs concept was "completely unacceptable to the pharmaceutical industry" (SCRIP 1977). As Michael Peretz, the IFPMA's permanent vice-president, later explained, "if WHO was recommending a list of essential drugs it would follow that WHO was implicitly arguing that all other drugs not included in the list were non-essential" (Peretz 1983:132). In a formal statement to Mahler in April 1978, the IFPMA outlined their "serious reservations" that the essential drug concept was both "untenable and patently harmful to medical practice and the public health."[7]

Subsequent diplomacy between the WHO and the IFPMA sought to fine-tune the essential drugs concept in a manner palatable to industry. When published in 1979, the Second Model List of Essential Drugs made two of these restrictions clear: first, that the concept of essential drugs in no way suggested drugs not on the list were inessential, and, second, that the concept of essential drugs would be restricted to the health needs of developing countries (WHO 1979a, 1979b). With these revisions, the IFPMA dropped its direct opposition to the idea and began to steer its member companies to provide a handful of essential drugs for "favorable prices" for the poorest countries: a set of negotiations that would ultimately lead to the development of tiered pricing policies between developed and developing nations.

By the early 1980s, conflict over essential drugs shifted from the practice of list-making to the challenge of implementation (Hey 1978; IFPMA 1978; Reich 1987). The focus of debate now hinged on the structure and function of a newly created WHO Action Program on Essential Drugs, which reported directly to the office of the Director-General and was tasked with building "national capabilities of developing countries in the selection, supply, and proper use of essential drugs to meet their real health needs and in the local production and quality control, wherever feasible, of such drugs" (WHO 1978). The terms of how the essential drugs concept might be implemented would be contested by stakeholders from the WHO, target nations, industry and a newly formed transnational network of consumer advocacy groups focused on pharmaceutical policy, called Health Action International.

Health Action International (HAI) was founded in Geneva in May 1981 in the wake of the successful bid by International Baby Food Action Network

(IBFAN) to pressure the WHO to enact an international code of infant formula marketing.[8] Along with IBFAN, HAI represented a more access-oriented stream of international consumer activism that had become the priority of the International Organization of Consumers' Unions (IOCU) since its presidency and policy headquarters had moved southwards from the Hague to Penang, Malaysia, under the charismatic leadership of Anwar Fazal. In the 1960s the IOCU had largely represented a transatlantic association of consumer-testing organizations in affluent societies (like the American Consumers Union, which produced the consumer products ratings featured in *Consumer Reports*). By the 1970s, its membership included a greater number of consumer organizations in South and Southeast Asia, sub-Saharan Africa and Latin America. This new global geography of membership forced the IOCU to redirect the emphasis of its policy efforts away from the politics of consumer choice (within a world of excessive marketing) to the politics of consumer access (within a paucity of essential commodities) (Hilton 2009).

Fashioning itself as a new model of access-oriented global international consumer activism, HAI included a coalition of consumer advocacy groups from twenty-seven countries and its membership of anthropologists, physicians, pharmacists and organizers was explicitly inclusive across global North and South. Its founding mission concerned the implementation of the essential drugs concept "to further the safe, rational, and economic uses of pharmaceuticals worldwide, to promote the full implementation of WHO's Action Programme on Essential Drugs, and to look for non-drug solutions to the problems created by impure water and poor sanitation and nutrition." HAI defined itself broadly as an "international antibody" against the "ill-treatment of consumers by multinational drug companies" (HAI 1981; Fazal 2006). But as Fazal later clarified, HAI was not merely opposed to the lack of access to essential drugs or medicines, or the all-too-abundant access of inessential medicines, but to the intersection of both of these problems:

> The underlying problem is not that there is not enough to go around, nor that in most developing countries, the conspicuously inessential drugs far outnumber the essential ones. As things stand – in the absence of clean water, good nutrition and basic health delivery systems – to supply even the most valuable of drugs can be like putting the proverbial cart before the proverbial horse. (Fazal 1983:265)

HAI's advocacy and activism walked a fine line between the dialectic of critiquing problems of overuse *and* underuse. To extend Fazal's metaphor, HAI was committed to the provenance of both cart *and* horse. Redefined from the perspective of the global South, Fazal argued, the goal of consumer activists should be a double thrust – both to address nonpharmaceutical solutions to public health problems and, where relevant, to demand access to "the *right pharmaceuticals* at the *right price*" (Fazal 1983:265).

As HAI's transnational alliance of consumer activists squared off against the transnational alliance of industry lobbyists represented by the IFPMA, their competing policy proposals were advanced by sympathetic nation-states within the World Health Assembly. HAI's policies were typically introduced by a coalition of Non-Aligned countries and social-democratic states from northern Europe, while the IFPMA could reliably mobilize France, Germany, the UK and the USA to introduce their policy proposals. For example, at the 1982 World Health Assembly, the HAI agenda for stronger standards on the international marketing of pharmaceuticals was proposed by the Netherlands and supported by Chile, Cuba, Romania, Sudan and Ghana, but was defeated by a coalition led by the USA, Britain, France and Germany. A subsequent HAI push to encourage the "rational use of drugs" at the 1984 World Health Assembly was more success-ful, and involved a team of thirteen lobbyists that coached a series of delegates from northern Europe to demand an international conference on the subject. When this conference opened in Nairobi in November 1985 it began with a somewhat weary appeal from Mahler that the assembly not serve as yet another "international battleground for the pharmaceutical industry and consumers to vent their interests" (Kanji et al. 1992:55).

To summarize, the policy battles over the definition and implementation of essential drugs in the 1970s and early 1980s were forged along geographical as well as ideological divides. As the IFPMA president Max Tiefembacher would pointedly comment, the international pharmaceutical industry saw the essential drugs concept as antithetical to Western definitions of civil rights, adding that "[i]n a totalitarian regime, this may be enforceable, but in a free society this may be neither feasible nor practicable" (Tiefembacher 1979:212). By 1984, conservative think-tanks in the USA such as the American Enterprise Institute and the Heritage Foundation joined the Pharmaceutical Manufacturers of America (PMA) and later the Reagan administration in citing essential medicine implementation as an overextension of the WHO's constitutional role.[9]

As medical anthropologist and HAI activist Anita Hardon recollects, by the 1986 World Health Assembly, the US delegate formally protested the "alarming prospects of politicizing health" and called for a "resolution for reaffirmation" to restrict WHO activities to a conservative reading of the 1946 charter – i.e., to focus on infectious disease surveillance and normative roles regarding international drug nomenclature and not "attempts to regulate commercial products" (Hardon 1992:59). Though this resolution did not pass, the ideological ideas behind it took on further significance when the USA purposively failed to make its financial contribution to the WHO – representing 25 percent of the WHO's regular budget – in 1986 and again in 1987.

By the time the USA reinstated payments in 1988, Hiroshi Nakajima had replaced Halfdan Mahler as Director-General of the WHO and the Action Program on Essential Drugs had been shifted from its prominent position in the Director-General's Office back to a subdivision of the pharmaceuticals sector.

The WHO embarked upon a period of policy drift that presaged increasing concerns about its role in international health and its ability to visibly push forward controversial policy initiatives like the essential drugs concept. The transition from the 1980s to the 1990s would be accompanied by a shift in the balance of global health funding from the WHO to the World Bank; a shift in the sites of reform of pharmaceutical intellectual property from the waning aegis of UNCTC and UNCTAD to the IFPMA and the new and increasingly powerful World Trade Organization (WTO).

Reviving the Critique of Essential Medicines as a Global Health Discourse, 1990s–2000s

The late 1980s and early 1990s were frequently called the "country years" by WHO essential drug program staffers. They describe this as a time in which the visibility of international debate over essential drugs diminished and the WHO medicines program worked methodically in partnership with individual nations to build essential drugs lists and enhance the procurement, distribution, rational use and quality assurance of materials on these lists (Quick et al. 2002; Quick 2003). Scholars such as Ted Brown, Marcos Cueto and Elizabeth Fee (2006) have further characterized these years as a period of marginalization of the WHO in international health agenda-setting, due in part to the decline of its budgetary independence at the same time that the World Bank began to make significant inroads into funding health-related projects. In turn, the re-emergence of the essential drugs critique – now renamed *essential medicines* – as a prominent discourse in global health policy of the late 1990s and 2000s would increasingly be driven by global health actors *outside* of the WHO (Brown, Cueto and Fee 2006; Adams 2010; Anderson 2014).

The new urgency of global access to pharmaceuticals is often attributed to a set of material changes happening at the time: either the emerging epidemiology of the HIV/AIDS pandemic – with devastatingly disproportionate burdens in sub-Saharan Africa, the Caribbean and Southeast Asia – or the development and widespread adoption of novel antiretroviral medications which, deployed in combinations, could transform an AIDS diagnosis from death sentence into a manageable condition. But as a growing group of activists were quick to point out in the late 1990s, access to potentially life-saving pharmaceuticals was determined as much by global intellectual property regimes as by any material difficulty or necessary cost in drug manufacturing. Advocacy groups such as AIDS Coalition to Unleash Power (ACT-UP), Treatment Access Campaign (TAC) and Médecins Sans Frontières (MSF) protested the moral unacceptability of preventable deaths due to the flawed geography of pharmaceutical access. They clamored that by not containing any antiretroviral drugs because of their cost, novelty and patent status the WHO Model Essential Medicines List was at risk of becoming farcical in any country with significant HIV/AIDS burden.

As we have seen, the means of winnowing essential from non-essential medicines had been methodologically and politically challenged since the publication of the first list in 1977. While the selection criteria for the first list of essential drugs invoked commonsensical notions of safety, efficacy, relevance and cost, the exact method for defining the list had been left mostly to the expertise of an elite group of pharmacologists. The formal inclusion of "on the ground" practitioners into the list-making process was not established until 1991 (Howard and Laing 1991). Value-laden and politically charged choices regarding the inclusion or exclusion of palliative medications, cancer chemo-therapeutic agents, drugs for rare diseases and drugs for risk-factor reduction had simmered continuously throughout the program's operation (Reidenberg 2006; Robertson and Hill 2007; Stolk, Willemen and Leufkens 2006). For example, although two oral contraceptives were included on the first draft of the WHO Essential Drugs List, these drugs were still illegal in Ireland and many other Catholic countries by the time of the publication of the second list in 1979. The question of whether contraceptives should be considered essential drugs was a key subtext to the Vatican's *First International Conference on the Ethical and Moral Problems of Pharmacotherapy*, which the WHO Director-General Halfdan Mahler attended (Vatican 1986; SCRIP 1986). The widespread North to South dissemination of contraceptives in the interest of population control – especially following the introduction of the injectable contraceptive Depo-Provera – would become a nidus for postcolonial and feminist critique of the use of pharmaceuticals in international health.[10]

Perhaps the most visibly contentious aspect of the selection of essential medicines, however, was the general exclusion of novel, patent protected medications. Upon observing the publication of the second essential drugs list in 1979, the prominent American clinical pharmacologist Louis Lasagna observed that the list promoted the older (but explosive) anesthetic agent ether in place of newer (non-explosive) but patent-protected anesthetics like halothane, and barred the reportedly new life-saving anti-ulcer drug cimetidine on the basis of its "lack of broad base of experience" (Lasagna 1980:368–9). The list conflated geography with history: old drugs for poor countries, new drugs for rich countries. Lasagna suggested that the essential medicines list would continue to limit the accessibility of promising new drugs from reaching the public sector in the developing world. As John Horton would later allege, extending Lasagna's critique to the beginning of the twenty-first century, much of the original list contained products already "old" in 1977. "One could therefore argue" he continued "that the EDL encourages the provision of outmoded medicines for the people of the developing world, and essentially excludes them from advances in medical science" (Horton 2003:12–13).

Horton's critique – made in support of a 2001 motion for the Royal Society of Tropical Medicine and Hygiene to officially condemn the essential medicines concept – would be answered by Pierre Chirac, a representative of MSF.

Chirac argued that it was the WHO's interpretation of the essential medicines concept – and not the concept itself – that had failed to live up to its "operational, didactic, and symbolic" functions. Declaring itself a "major supporter of the essential drugs concept," MSF was nonetheless "worried that the most recent list is already outdated and does not reflect the essential drug concept as increasingly common medical situations fail to be addressed" (Chirac 2003:11–12; Chirac and Laing 2001; Breckenridge 2003). In distinguishing the ideal (essential drugs concept) from the real (WHO list), MSF presented itself as the new torchbearer of the philosophy of essential medicines.

Médecins Sans Frontières was founded in the 1970s by a group of French physicians frustrated with the limits of formal internationalism in humanitarian relief efforts, principally in complex humanitarian emergencies; subsequent years saw the emergence of local MSF chapters worldwide. Their philosophy of "speed saves lives," and rejection of the priority of national sovereignty and due process of international institutions in situations of humanitarian crisis, would become the archetype for a group of subsequent professional "sans-frontierisme" groups that positioned networks of NGOs, and not the WHO, as a central site for emergent forms of global health (Redfield 2013; Fox 2014). By the late 1990s, MSF had begun to reframe the scale of preventable deaths from global HIV and neglected tropical diseases as a morally urgent crisis, and began a globally prominent "Campaign for Access to Essential Medicines." Receipt of the 1999 Nobel Peace Prize added visibility and further moral weight to the campaign. MSF swiftly progressed from petitioning the WHO Essential Medicines List to include newer medications for HIV/AIDS and trypanosomiasis to leaning on the WTO in the Doha round of the Agreement on Trade-Related Aspects of Intellectual Property Rights (TRIPS) to leverage space for public health patent exemptions for essential medicines to working with specific countries to encourage TRIPS to promote compulsory licensing and parallel importing of generic HIV medications (t'Hoen 2002).[11] Where and when these efforts failed, the transnational organization simply acquired relevant drugs and brought them across national borders on its own, with attendant publicity.

The flexibility and speed with which groups like MSF and the Boston-based Partners in Health could manage logistics for complex regimens for the treatment of HIV and multiple drug-resistant tuberculosis (MDRTB) into collaborating health organizations in resource-poor settings in sub-Saharan Africa, the Caribbean and South America, worked to set the glacial pace of bureaucratic process within international agencies like the WHO and the Joint United Nations Programme on HIVAIDS (UNAIDS) in sharp relief as a pathogenic factor rather than an ameliorating intervention (Farmer 2001; Farmer et al. 2001). If time lost meant further preventable deaths, then the three-year delay between the request to include combination antiretrovirals as essential medications in 1999 and their appearance on the WHO essential medicines list in 2002 was – by these standards – unconscionable (Steiger 2001).

NGO-based forms of lateral delivery circumvented not only the international agency but the role of the nation-state in determining medicines policy, as evidenced by the role of transnational NGOs in funneling antiretrovirals into South Africa during a period marked by Thabo Mbeki's official denial of HIV as the causative agent of AIDS (Fassin 2007). As Mahajan (2010) has argued in the case of India, Nguyen (2010) in the case of Francophone West Africa and Crane (2013) in the rest of sub-Saharan Africa, in the ensuing decade focus on pharmaceutical provision of antiretrovirals through nongovernmental networks has subsequently shifted the population health responsibilities of HIV/AIDS care from the WHO and the nation-state to a loose network of NGOs, American universities and European hospitals.

The rise in prominence of global health NGOs and university programs has supported and been supported by a confluence of individual and institutional philanthropic giving in the early 2000s that increased available funding by orders of magnitude through the sequential establishment of the UN Global Fund to Fight AIDS, Tuberculosis, and Malaria, George W. Bush's President's Emergency Plan for AIDS Relief and the unprecedented generosity of the Bill & Melinda Gates Foundation into the arena of global health (Garrett 2007). All of these philanthropic ventures, and others that followed, hinged on existing or anticipated pharmaceutical solutions to globally neglected diseases which in turn became configured as priority problems within the global health field. Of the fourteen "Grand Challenges in Global Health," which Gates introduced at the World Economic Forum in Davos in January 2003, nine relate directly to improving access to novel or existing pharmaceutical technologies (Varmus et al. 2003).

If the redefinition of the essential medicines concept was central to articulating the new role of NGOs and philanthropies in emergent forms of global health, the term was equally useful to the multinational pharmaceutical industry as it sought to reform its public image from global "robber-baron" back to a more Promethean role. As with MSF and the Gates Foundation, the repurposing of the concept of essential medicines became key to the attempts of pharmaceutical corporations to create new roles for themselves in new structures of global health. In the twenty-first century, several large pharmaceutical firms sought public initiatives in which to demonstrate the industry's capacity to support access to essential medicines as long as the latter was configured in ways that did not threaten pharmaceutical intellectual property. These self-defined programs expressly resisted the notion of essential medicines as a public commons, recasting them instead as private goods that could be donated by altruistically minded corporations (see, for example, Samsky 2015, Chapter 6, this volume). Most prominent among these initiatives, perhaps, was the Accelerating Access Initiative, formed in 2000 by seven large pharmaceutical corporations (Boehringer Ingelheim, Bristol-Myers Squibb, GlaxoSmithKline, Merck, Hoffmann-La Roche, Abbott Laboratories and Gilead Sciences) in cooperation with UNAIDS, the WHO, UNICEF and the World Bank, expressly to strengthen access to antiretroviral medications in Least Developed Countries (LDCs) and sub-Saharan Africa (Sturchio 2006).

The Accelerating Access Initiative was conceptualized as a more systematic and focused extension of earlier forms of pharmacophilanthropy, a defining principle of the globally social-conscious pharmaceutical corporation. The most commonly cited example of pharmacophilanthropy remains the successful and widely celebrated Merck program for the donation of Mectizan (Ivermectin) for African river blindness (Samsky 2015). Mectizan's lack of profitability in human applications could be offset by its extraordinarily profitable veterinary applications, and the program produced both publicity and sense of moral purpose for Merck employees. During the 1980s and early 1990s Merck was commonly depicted as the "white knight" of the pharmaceutical industry as the Mectizan program became attached to the charisma of its leader in the 1990s, Roy Vagelos (Collins 2004).

In turn, the Accelerating Access Initiative proposed a number of company-specific initiatives whereby each corporation could specify the degree and means of access it was willing to grant to resource-poor settings. These initiatives ranged from "sustainable preferential pricing," to donation of drugs at cost, to donation of drugs at loss, to the granting of generic licenses in specific countries, to the declaration (by Hoffmann-La Roche) that it would seek no further patents and offer no protest to generic manufacture of its proprietary medications in LDCs and sub-Saharan Africa.[12] In addition to their impact on the lives of recipients of pharmaceutical aid, these programs could provide a much-needed boost for the public profile of the pharmaceutical industry and the morale of its employees, both of which had suffered from a series of prominent scandals over pharmaceutical marketing and drug safety in the first decade of the twenty-first century (Avorn 2004). Among the many vehicles for converting pharmacophilanthropy to motivational and promotional goals, an outfit called PharmaCorps was celebrated in 2007 for its innovative use of motivational seminars among industry employees to build morale and consciously mobilize them into an army of 450,000 global public relations advocates. A central goal of the PharmaCorps motivational curriculum was to catalog and promote company-specific essential medicines access programs. Pharmaceutical Research and Manufacturers of America (PhRMA) head Billy Tauzin noted in an industry publication that: "Even though our companies improve life for patients here and around the world every day, it is relatively easy for employees to lose sight of the tremendous value our companies deliver to society." He went on to say that "[t]he program is designed to harness employees' pride in what they do and give them the tools they need to start changing the conversation about biopharmaceutical companies and the medicines we make" (cited in Ross 2007).

The intersection of public relations, marketing and the essential medicines concept is not entirely novel to the twenty-first century, but the extent and visibility of this confluence is widening.[13] More recently the unification of these three streams has been harnessed by the Access to Medicines Foundation (ATMF) – a coalition of investors, companies and NGOs largely cobbled together in 2004 by the efforts of Wim Leerveld, an energetic former pharmaceutical marketer who suggested that the extent to which a company invested in access to essential medicines could itself be a marketable trait. Leerveld's group published a report in 2008 that ranked all major multinational pharmaceutical companies by eight criteria of commitment to expanding access to essential medicines (ATMF 2008). GlaxoSmithKline, ranked #1 in the 2008 Access to Medicines Index rankings, has made consistent mention of this in their public relations and in crafting the public persona of their CEO, Andrew Witty (McNeil 2010). Lower-ranked companies such as Merck and Pfizer, in turn, issued statements regarding their plans to position for a better ranking in the second set of Access to Medicines Index rankings which were published in June 2010.[14]

The group has received endorsement from a subset of socially responsible investment firms that seek to differentiate their own financial products by marketing to individual investors the opportunity to invest only in those segments of industry that support essential medicines policies. Bill Gates, for example, cited the initiative as an example of a sustainable market-based solution to problems of pharmaceutical access, noting: "[w]hen I talk to executives from pharmaceutical companies they tell me that they want to do more for neglected diseases, but they at least need to get credit for it. The Access to Medicines Index does exactly that."[15] The fourth Access to Medicines Index rankings are due out in late 2014.

The success of an investor-oriented program such as the Access to Medicines Index – inconceivable as it might have seemed to the framers of the first WHO Model Essential Drugs List – now illustrates the flexibility of the essential medicines concept within increasingly plastic conceptualizations of global health. In the twenty-first century, far from being a litmus test for political identification, the essential medicines concept has taken on somewhat of a moral universality, as a thing that has acquired enough stakeholders and commonsensical status that it is increasingly difficult to argue against and even more difficult to define. The classic dipoles of prior international politics of essential drugs in the 1970s and 1980s – producers vs. consumers, North vs. South, East vs. West – are now softened and entangled in a more diffuse acceptance of the centrality of pharmaceuticals in contemporary global health practices. New conflicts, in turn, break out along new seams: the applicability of global intellectual property law, the feasibility of a patent pool or the ability of a university to determine the licensing of patents built off of its own innovations in LDCs versus middle-income or wealthy nations.

Conclusions: Pharmaceutical Critiques Old and New

At core there remains a kind of moral clarity regarding the importance of naming a set of pharmaceuticals as essential to public health, a project which itself is both necessary and fragile, commonsensical in the general but difficult to define in the particular. Situating the critical discourse of essential drugs in the politics of international development of the 1970s and the 1980s helps to explain why its enduring relevance nonetheless has led to complex and unexpected political formations after its broad resurrection in the late 1990s and early 2000s. Thus reinvigorated, the essential medicines concept has since rejoined clean water, adequate housing and a safe food supply as part of a short list of things necessary for basic humanitarian conditions, and added the "right to medicines" to the broader rights discourse of UN organizations. At the same time, the potential of the essential medicines concept (as initially articulated by consumer advocates within HAI) to uphold pharmaceuticals as a basic necessity rather than a *de facto* commodity is countered by its paradoxical potential (as currently articulated in pharmacophilanthropic programs) to stabilize an otherwise maligned regime of intellectual property instruments.

Placing essential medicines at the center of global health priorities is not without its risks. On the one hand, twenty-first-century critics have noted the risks entailed in reducing the broader goals of global health advocacy to the simple technological challenge of drug delivery (Birn 2005). For medicines to be helpful, and not harmful, they must not merely be available but come wrapped in effective standards of quality and appropriate utilization within durable structures of healthcare delivery. Yet this argument is itself a rewrapping of older critiques. As most careful advocates of the essential drugs concept argued from 1977 onwards (recall the initial manifesto of HAI), access to essential medicines was always only a necessary, not a sufficient condition for the amelioration of disparities in global health.

This narration of how a critical keyword in the politics of international health in the 1970s (the essential drugs concept) was resuscitated and repurposed in the early twenty-first century (as the essential medicines movement) can serve as an instructive case to explore this volume's theme of new engagements with old critiques. The new study of *pharmaceuticalization* which has become increasingly visible in the social sciences of health and medicine in the last decade, however, often has a historical frame that only goes back about a decade or so as well. In the process, accounts of pharmaceuticalization risk overemphasizing the "newness" of the phenomenon, and neglecting the impact of earlier critiques of the role of pharmaceuticals in daily life, critiques which stretch back a half century if not earlier. To take the historical dimension of pharmaceutical studies seriously is to focus on continuity as well as change, to focus on problems of *underuse* as well as *overuse*. Neither of these problems have gone away – and in some areas they have indeed become far more entrenched – in spite of four decades of focused critique by activists and social scientists in health and medicine.

This brief account of an earlier, neglected critique of the role pharmaceuticals of public health – studies of pharmaceuticalization *avant le lettre* – should do more than merely remind us that such analyses existed before the eight-syllable term now used to describe them was coined. First, it is important to understand not only that critiques of the role of pharmaceuticals in global health have been around for a while, but that these critiques came from different places, and were critical of very different aspects of the role of pharmaceuticals in public health. Each critique of pharmaceuticals as a *global* problem came from a particular *local* perspective on how to define the pharmaceutical as a problem: was it overuse or underuse? Too much exposure to potentially harmful chemicals or not enough access to life-saving medicines? The apparent stability of a critical discourse of essential drugs in international health belies a temporary aggregation of many different forms of health advocacy and activism, which could easily disaggregate as well.

Second, although many of the older critiques that gave rise to the essential drugs concept have been resuscitated in the contemporary study of pharmaceuticalization in the twenty-first century, the politics and the geography of this conversation have altered. As historical linguists remind us, the meanings and usages of words are never stable. Terms like "essential drugs" – or, for that matter, terms like medicalization and pharmaceuticalization themselves – gain and lose meanings over time in the hands of different actors. A term initially intended as a critique of the marketing practices of multinational pharmaceutical corporations in one decade can become a marketing tool in its own right a generation later. Following the shifting significance of "essential drugs" from an anti-commercial slogan to a novel form of marketing is not unlike following the shifting meaning of the 1967 Michael McClure poem "Oh Lord Won't You Buy Me a Mercedes Benz." Recorded as a counterculture anthem by Janis Joplin in 1970, the refrain would find new life in a series of memorable advertisements by Mercedes Benz in 1995; selling cars to a group of aging baby boomers who could be counted on to value the irony of an old critique repurposed to novel commercial ends.

To study the history of essential drugs, however, is not merely to observe with ironic distance how once-potent arguments used to claim healthcare as public right have been defanged and used to defend the persistence of logics of healthcare as a private good. To study the new engagements of this old critique is to recognize the importance of *actors* and *context* in the changing politics and economies of how people live (or do not live) with pharmaceuticals or the lack of pharmaceuticals. One of the risks of a term like *pharmaceuticalization* (as with *medicalization*), is that these terms can be gestured at too easily to suggest an inexorable, irreversible, large-scale process without the need to pay attention to actors, context or contingency.

Even when actors are assigned (typically physicians or pharmaceutical marketers) they can collapse all too easily into melodramatic villains with greasepaint mustachios. Even as prominent scholars seek to define terms like pharmaceuticalization as a "value-free" sociological category, the field of social scientists, activists, policymakers and consumer advocates that come to use such terms do not necessarily share this vision of restraint. Tracing the use of the terms of *medicalization* and *pharmaceuticalization* in both scholarly and popular literatures, one finds the negative implications of the term far outweigh the small number of studies documenting any "positive medicalization" (Bell and Figert 2012a, 2012b; Williams, Martin and Gabe 2012). Meanwhile, a term like "essential drugs," it would appear, has moved in the opposite direction – a term initially intended as a political critique of existing structures of marketing, pricing, and private property in public health has instead become apolitical, as useful to the production of new marketing tactics as it is to their critique.

Attending to the contested history of essential drugs, then, serves to remind us that the problems pharmaceuticals pose at the conjunction of the biological and social cannot fully be captured in abstract, timeless, placeless terms. They need to be located in time, and in place, and in the complexity of new positions for agency that new forms of biomedical technology bring into being. As with so many other fields of inquiry at the intersection of social science and biomedical technology, the emerging field of pharmaceutical studies requires attention to this context as well as structure, the old as well as the new.

Notes

1 Some of the material in this chapter is based on an article I published in *BioSocieties* in 2010 and re-presented at a conference at Bowdoin College in September of 2013 on "Big Pharma, Big Medicine and Technoscience"; the material has been reworked to address the themes of pharmaceuticalization in light of old critiques and new engagements. On the emerging ethnography of antiretroviral rollout, see Fassin (2007), Biehl (2009), Gould (2009), Nguyen (2010) and Crane (2013); on neglected diseases see Webel (2013). On pharmaceuticals for chronic disease see Yach et al. (2004).

2 On the Cold War politics of international health agencies, see Douglas (1987), Mingst (1990), Siddiqi (1995), Amrith (2006) and Chorev (2012).

3 On the postwar "drug explosion" in the global North and the ensuing difficulties of distinguishing therapeutic innovation from innovative repackaging, see Bud (2007), Greene and Podolsky (2009) and Greene (2014).

4 For broader contemporary critiques of medicine and capitalism, see Navarro (1976) and Waitzkin and Sharratt (1977).

5 Omran (1983) later recognized the role of Sri Lanka's form transformation (driven by mortality decline rather than fertility decline) in an update to his theory of epidemiological transition.

6 By the early 1970s, Pakistan, Mozambique and Sri Lanka had each attempted to establish restricted formularies of generic drugs with tight controls on pharmaceutical imports. Each nation was subsequently subjected to highly unfavorable positions within international trade and either swiftly abandoned these efforts (as in Pakistan), or gave up such strategies after the outbreak of war (as in Mozambique) or a series of government collapses and, ultimately, civil war (as in Sri Lanka). See Muller (1982), Medawar (1984) and Kanji et al. (1992).

7 The IFPMA also protested the anti-commercial tone of the essential drugs concept, and suggested that the existence of any essential drugs list would "ultimately restrict all access to medicines, depriving those dependent on public sector health care of the drugs which they might individually need and lending impetus to similar measures affecting the private sector" (Egli 1978:3). "The pharmaceutical industry is not aware of any *developed* nation where regulatory authorities can provide assurance of the bioequivalence or interchangeability of the drug supply within their jurisdiction; and the state of regulatory effectiveness in most developing countries is substantially less advanced. Because of this reality, governments, the medical profession, and the patient must rely upon the reputations of companies with consistent histories of producing high quality products as the best assurance of safety and therapeutic effectiveness

... To discourage [the use of brand names] as the WHO Report does would have grave repercussions for the quality of pharmaceutical supplies and health care, whether in developed or developing nations" (Egli 1978:3).

8 The foundational International NGO Seminar on Pharmaceuticals in Geneva took place immediately following the 1981 World Health Assembly in Geneva, and included over fifty organizations from twenty-six countries. See Fazal (2006).

9 For example, Brooks (1985) and Mingst (1990).

10 See, for example, Kaler's (2003) history of colonial and postcolonial critiques of contraceptive deployment in Zimbabwe, which built on earlier critical accounts of reproductive technologies in global North and South, including Mamdani (1972), Mass (1976), McDonald (1986), among others.

11 TRIPS, or the Agreement on Trade-Related Aspects of Intellectual Property Rights, is an international treaty first negotiated at the Uruguay Rounds of the World Trade Organization in 1994. In 2001, the Doha Rounds clarified the scope of the TRIPS agreement to set out pathways for access to essential medicines through parallel importation and compulsory licensing, particularly in situations of national health emergencies.

12 Noting the diversity of offerings in pharmacophilanthropic programs, Sturchio (2006) describes that Abbott had launched "Abbott Access" in 2001, and offered Kaletra and Norvir as well as a rapid HIV test branded "Determine® HIV"; Boehringer Ingelheim had made the Virammune® Donation Programme available free of charge for the prevention of mother to child transmission of HIV, though much of the other programs were dependent on "sustainable preferential pricing," and Bristol-Myers Squibb, GlaxoSmithKline and Boehringer Ingelheim have granted licenses to generic manufacturers in South Africa. Merck's own contribution, titled the "African Comprehensive HIV/AIDS Partnership," established in partnership with the Bill & Melinda Gates Foundation, involved a direct donation program to the Botswana national antiretroviral therapy program. Hoffmann-La Roche, moreover, had shifted its patent policy to (a) not file any patents for any Roche medicines in low-income nations and sub-Saharan Africa, and (b) promise not to take action in these countries against the sale or manufacture of generic HIV medicines.

13 Even in 1978, as the IFPMA was actively denying the possibility of a list of essential drugs, a few pharmaceutical firms had approached the WHO unilaterally to lobby for admission to the essential drugs list, leading the WHO to censure companies on more than one occasion for the use of the essential drugs logo for promotional purposes. Eaton Laboratories lobbied the WHO for "inclusion of nitrofurantoin macrocrystals as a primary drug in the management of urinary tract infections in the WHO Essential Drug List." American Cyanamid sent a similar list of four of their own products (leucovorin, minocycline, chlortetracycline and traimcinolone) that they suggested to be added to the list. Each of the companies met with some success – both nitrofurantoin and chlortetracycline were included in the 1979 revision of the essential drugs list. See Keenan (1978), Affleck (1978) and WHO (1979b).

14 Pfizer responded to their low ranking on the 2008 Access to Medicines Index, "We recognize that we have yet to meet our full potential, as reflected in pharmaceutical company rankings such as the Access to Medicines Index ranking, and value the feedback and insights provided by the many stakeholders we engage and partner with on access to medicine issues." www.pfizer.com/responsibility/cr_report/access.jsp (accessed April 10, 2010); Merck has posted a similar report: http://www.merck.com/corporate-responsibility/summary-data-resources/kpis-gri-atmi-mdgs/atmi-2008-index.html (accessed April 10, 2010).

15 As cited on the ATMF website: www.atmindex.org/index/what_leaders_are_saying (accessed April 10, 2010).

References

Access to Medicines Foundation (ATMF). 2008. *Access to Medicines Index 2008*. Haarlem: Access to Medicines Foundation.

Adams, V. 2010. "Against Global Health." Pp. 40–60 in *Against Health: How Health Became the New Morality*, edited by Jonathan Metzl and Rebecca Herzig. New York: New York University Press.

Affleck, J. to H. Mahler. 1978. Letter, June 8. E 19 81 1, folder 1, WHO Archives, Geneva.

Amrith, S. S. 2006. *Decolonizing International Health: India and Southeast Asia, 1930–1965*. Cambridge: Cambridge University Press.

Anderson, W. 2014. "Making Global Health History: The Postcolonial Worldliness of Biomedicine." *Social History of Medicine* 27(2):372–84.

Associated Newspapers of Ceylon. 1978. *Pharmaceutical Reform in Pharmaceuticals: A Third World Experience*. Lake House: Associated Newspapers of Ceylon.

Avorn, J. L. 2004. *Powerful Medicines: The Costs, Benefits, and Risks of Prescription Drugs*. New York: Knopf.

Barnet, R. J. and R. Muller. 1976. *Global Reach: The Power of Multinational Corporations*. New York: Simon & Schuster.

Bell, S. E. and A. E. Figert. 2012a. "Medicalization and Pharmaceuticalization at the Intersections: Looking Backward, Sideways, and Forward." *Social Science & Medicine* 75:775–83.

Bell, S. E. and A. E. Figert. 2012b. "Starting to Turn Sideways to Move Forward in Medicalization and Pharmaceuticalization Studies: A Response to Williams et al. (2012)." *Social Science & Medicine* 75:2131–3.

Biehl, J. 2007. "Pharmaceuticalization: AIDS Treatment and Global Health Politics." *Anthropological Quarterly*, 80(4):1083–126.

Biehl, J. 2009. *The Will to Live: AIDS Therapies and the Politics of Survival*. Princeton, NJ: Princeton University Press.

Birn, A. B. 2005. "Gates's Grandest Challenge: Transcending Technology as Public Health Ideology." *The Lancet* 366:514–19.

Breckenridge, A. 2003. Royal Society of Tropical Medicine and Hygiene meeting at the University of Liverpool, Liverpool, March 16, 2001: Debate that "This house believes the essential drug concept hinders the effective deployment of drugs in developing countries." *Transactions of the Royal Society of Tropical Medicine and Hygiene* 97:1.

Brooks, R. 1985. Saving the World Health Organization from a poison pill. November 19. Washington, DC: The Heritage Foundation.

Brown, T., M. Cueto and E. Fee. 2006. "The World Health Organization and the Transition from 'International' to 'Global' Health." *America Journal of Public Health* 96(1):62–72.

Bud, R. 2007. *Penicillin: Triumph and Tragedy*. New York: Oxford University Press.

Chirac, P. 2003. "Translating the Essential Drugs Concept into the Context of the Year 2000." *Transactions of the Royal Society of Tropical Medicine and Hygiene* 97:11–12.

Chirac, P. and R. O. Laing. 2001. "Updating the WHO Essential Drugs List." *The Lancet* 357(9262): 1134.

Chorev, N. 2012. *The World Health Organization between North and South*. Ithaca, NY: Cornell University Press.

Cochrane, A. L. 1979. "Medicine's Contribution from the 1930s to the 1970s: A Critical Review." Pp. 1–11 in *Medicines for the Year 2000*, edited by G. Telling-Smith and N. Wells. London: Office of Health Economics.

Collins, K. L. 2004. "Profitable Gifts: A History of the Merck Mectizan Donation Program and Its Implications for International Health." *Perspectives in Biology and Medicine* 47(1):100–9.

Crane, J. T. 2013. *Scrambling for Africa: AIDS, Expertise, and the Rise of American Global Health Science*. Ithaca, NY: Cornell University Press.

Cruickshank, P. 2011. "The Teleology of Care: Reinventing International Health, 1968–1989." Unpublished PhD dissertation, Harvard University, Cambridge, MA.

Daemmrich, A. A. 2003. *Pharmacopolitics: Drug Regulation in the United States and Germany*. Chapel Hill, NC: University of North Carolina Press.

Douglas, W. 1987. *The Specialized Agencies and the United Nations: The System in Crisis*. New York: St Martin's Press.

Egli, J. to V. Fatturoso. 1977. Untitled letter, December 2. E 19 81 1, folder 1, WHO Archives, Geneva.

Egli, J. to H. Mahler. 1978. Statement as adopted by the IFPMA Council, April 13. E 19 8 81, folder 1, WHO Archives, Geneva.

Evatt, G. J. H. 1881. "The Portability of Drugs in Field Service." *The Lancet* 118(3031): 608.

Farmer, P. 2001. *Infection and Inequalities: The Modern Plagues*. Berkeley, CA: University of California Press.

Farmer P., F. Leandre, J. S. Mukherjee, M. Claude, P. Nevil, M. C. Smith-Fawzi, S. P. Koenig, A. Castro, M.C. Becerra, J. Sachs, A. Attaran and J. Y. Kim. 2001. "Community-based Approaches to HIV Treatment in Resource-poor Settings." *The Lancet* 358(9279):404–9.

Fassin, D. 2007. *When Bodies Remember: Experiences and the Politics of AIDS in South Africa*. Berkeley, CA: University of California Press.

Fazal, A. 1983. "The Right Pharmaceuticals at the Right Price." *World Development* 11(3): 265–69.

Fazal, A. 2006. "Global Action on Health: The Story of the Birth of Health Action International." Pp. 1–7 in *Fast, Flexible, and Furious: The Story of Health Action International (HAI) 1981– 2006.* Amsterdam: HAI.

Fox, R. C. 2014. *Doctors without Borders: Humanitarian Quests, Impossible Dreams of Médecins Sans Frontières.* Baltimore, MD: Johns Hopkins University Press.

Garrett, L. 2007. "The Challenge of Global Health." *Foreign Affairs* 86(1):14.

Gould, D. B. 2009. *Moving Politics: Emotion and ACT UP's Fight against AIDS.* Chicago, IL: University of Chicago Press.

Greene, J. A. 2010. "Making Medicines Essential: The Emergent Centrality of Pharmaceuticals in Global Health." *BioSocieties* 6(1):10–33.

Greene, J. A. 2014. *Generic: The Unbranding of Modern Medicine.* Baltimore, MD: Johns Hopkins University Press.

Greene, J. A. and S. H. Podolsky. 2009. "Keeping Modern in Medicine: Pharmaceutical Promotion and Physician Education in Postwar America." *Bulletin of the History of Medicine* 83(2): 331–77.

HAI. 1981. Press statement, May 29, 1981.

Hardon, A. 1992. "Consumers versus Producers: Power Play behind the Scenes." Pp. 48–64 in *Drugs Policy in Developing Countries,* edited by N. Kanji, A. Hardon, J. W. Harnmeijer, M. Mamdani and G. Walt. London: Zed Books.

Hey, N. to H. Mahler. 1978. IMSWORLD manuscript, September 20. P 5 348 1, WHO Archives, Geneva.

Hilton, M. 2009. *Prosperity for All: Consumer Activism in an Era of Globalization.* Ithaca, NY: Cornell University Press.

Horton, J. 2003. "Proposing the Motion." *Transactions of the Royal Society of Tropical Medicine and Hygiene* 97:12–13.

Howard, N. J. and R. O. Laing. 1991. "Changes in the World Health Organization Essential Drug List." *The Lancet* 338:743–45.

IFPMA. 1978. IFPMA Annual Report 1978. P 5 348 4 f3, WHO Archives, Geneva.

Illich, I. 1975. *Medical Nemesis: The Expropriation of Health.* New York: Pantheon.

Kaler, A. 2003. *Running After Pills: Politics, Gender, and Contraception in Colonial Zimbabwe.* Minneapolis, MN: University of Minnesota Press.

Kanji N., A. Hardon, J. W. Harnmeijer, M. Mamdani and G. Walt. 1992. *Drugs Policy in Developing Countries.* London: Zed Books.

Keenan, R.E. to H. Mahler. 1978. Letter, January 23. E 19 81 1, folder 1, WHO Archives, Geneva.

Koch, Erin. 2013. *Free Market Tuberculosis: Managing Epidemics in Post-Soviet Georgia.* Nashville, TN: University of Nashville Press.

Lasagna, L. 1980. "The World Health Organization List of 'Essential Drugs.'" *Annals of Internal Medicine* 93(2):368–9.

Ledogar, R. 1975. *Hungry for Profits.* New York: IDOC.

McDonald, K., ed. 1986. *Adverse Effects: Women and the Pharmaceutical Industry.* Toronto: Canadian Scholars Press.

McNeil, D. J. 2010. "Ally for the Poor in an Unlikely Corner." *The New York Times,* February 8.

Mahajan, M. 2010. "Governing through the Non-governmental." Manuscript in possession of author.

Mahler, H. 1975. "Address to the 28th World Health Assembly." Geneva: World Health Organization, A28/11.

Mamdani, M. 1972. *The Myth of Population Control: Family, Caste, and Class in and Indian Village.* New York: Monthly Review Press

Mass, B. 1976. *Population Target: The Political Economy of Population Control in Latin America.* Toronto: Latin American Working Group.

Medawar, C. 1979. *Insult or Injury: Enquiry into the Advertising and Marketing of British Food and Drugs in the Third World.* London: Greener Books.

Medawar, C. 1984. *Drugs and World Health.* The Hague: IOCU.

Melrose, D. 1982. *Bitter Pills: Medicines and the Third World Poor.* Oxford: OXFAM.

Mingst, K. A. 1990. "The United States and the WHO." Pp. 205–30 in *The United States and Multilateral Institutions: Patterns of Changing Instrumentality and Influence,* edited by M. P. Karns and K. A. Mingst. Boston, MA: Unwin Hyman.

Mintz, M. 1965. *The Therapeutic Nightmare.* Boston, MA: Houghton-Mifflin.

Muller, M. 1982. *The Health of Nations: A North-South Investigation.* London: Faber & Faber.

Myrdal, G. 1967. *The Asian Drama: An Inquiry into the Poverty of Nations*. New York: Pantheon Press.

Navarro, V. 1976. *Medicine under Capitalism*. New York: Prodist Press.

Nguyen, V.-K. 2010. *The Republic of Therapy: Triage and Sovereignty in West Africa's Time of Crisis*. Durham, NC: Duke University Press.

Omran, A. R. 1971. "The Epidemiologic Transition: A Theory of the Epidemiology of Population Change." *Milbank Memorial Fund Quarterly* 49(4):510–22.

Omran, A.R. 1983. "The Epidemiologic Transition Theory: A Preliminary Update." *Journal of Tropical Pediatrics* 29(6):305–16.

Packard, R. M. 1997. "Visions of Postwar Health and Development and Their Impact on Public Health Interventions in the Developing World." Pp. 93–115 in *International Development and the Social Sciences: Essays on the History and Politics of Knowledge*, edited by F. Cooper and R. M. Packard. Berkeley, CA: University of California Press.

Peretz, S. M. 1983. "An Industry View of Restricted Drug Formularies." *Journal of Social and Administrative Pharmacy* 1(3):130–3.

Quick, J. D. 2003. "Essential Medicines Twenty-Five Years on: Closing the Access Gap." *Health Policy and Planning* 18(1):1–3.

Quick, J. D., H. V. Hogerzeil, G. Velásquz and L. Rägo. 2002. "Twenty-Five Years of Essential Medicines." *Bulletin of the World Health Organization* 80(11):913–14.

Redfield, P. 2008. "Vital Mobility and the Humanitarian Kit." Pp. 147–72 in *Biosecurity Interventions*, edited by A. Lakoff and D. J. Collier. New York: Columbia University.

Redfield, P. 2013. *Life in Crisis: The Ethical Journey of Doctors without Borders*. Berkeley, CA: University of California Press.

Reich, M. R. 1987. "Essential Drugs: Economics and Politics in International Health." *Health Policy* 8:39–57.

Reidenberg, M. M. 2006. "Are Drugs for Rare Diseases 'Essential'?" *Bulletin of the World Health Organization* 84:686.

Robertson, J. and S. R. Hill. 2007. "The Essential Medicines List for a Global Patient Population." *Clinical Pharmacology & Therapeutics* 82(5):498–500.

Ross, W. 2007. "Arming Advocates." *Medical Marketing and Media* 42(9):11–12. Accessed April 10, 2010 (www.mmm-online.com/arming-advocates/article/35537).

Samsky, Ari. 2015. "The Drug Swallowers: Scientific Sovereignty and Pharmaceuticalization in Two International Drug Donation Programs." Pp. 112–36 in *Reimagining (Bio)Medicalization, Pharmaceuticals and Genetics: Old Critiques and New Engagements*, edited by Susan E. Bell and Anne E. Figert. New York: Routledge.

SCRIP. 1977. *SCRIP World Pharmaceutical News* 259:23.

SCRIP. 1986. *SCRIP World Pharmaceutical News* N. 1152:18.

Seers, Dudley. 1969. "What Are We Trying to Measure?" *Journal of Development Studies* 8(3): 21–36.

Siddiqi, J. 1995. *World Health and World Politics: The World Health Organization and the UN System*. Columbus, SC: University of South Carolina Press.

Silverman, M. and P. Lee. 1976. *The Drugging of the Americas: How Multinational Drug Companies Say One Thing about Their Products to Physicians in the United States and Another Thing to Physicians in Latin America*. Berkeley, CA: University of California Press.

Steiger, W. to H. Hogerzeil, August 13 2001. Accessed April 10, 2010 (http://dcc2.bumc.bu.edu/ richardl/WHO_Select_docs/backgrnd_docs.htm).

Stolk, P., M. J. C. Willemen and H. G. M. Leufkens. 2006. "'Rare Essentials': Drugs for Rare Diseases as Essential Medicines." *Bulletin of the World Health Organization* 84:745–51.

Sturchio, L. 2006. "Partnership for Action: The Experience of the Accelerating Access Initiative, 2000–04, and Lessons Learned." Pp. 178–97 in *The Economics of Essential Medicines*, edited by B. Granville. London: Royal Institute of International Affairs.

t'Hoen, E. 2002. "TRIPS, Patents, and Essential Medicines: A Long Way from Seattle to Doha." *Chicago Journal of International Law* 32:27.

Teitelbaum, M. S. 1975. "Relevance of Demographic Transition Theory for Developing Countries." *Science* 188:420–5.

The Lancet [editorial]. 2006. "Abortion Drugs Must Become WHO Essential Medicines." *The Lancet* 365:1826.

Tiefembacher, M. 1979. "Problems of Distribution, Availability, and Utilization of Agents in Developing Countries: Industry Perspectives." Pp. 211–27 in *Pharmaceuticals for Developing Countries*. Washington, DC: IOM.

United Nations Conference on Trade and Development (UNCTAD). 1982. *Guidelines on Technology Issues in the Pharmaceutical Sector in the Developing Countries*. UNCTAD TT 49. New York: United Nations.

Varmus, H., R. Klausner, E. Zerhouni, T. Acharya, A. D. Daar and P. A. Singer. 2003. "Grand Challenges in Global Health." *Science* 302:5644.

Vatican. 1986. Drugs for Human Life. Conference Proceedings to the *First International Conference on the Ethical and Moral Problems of Pharmacotherapy*, Vatican City. Found in the Louis Lasagna Papers, box 10, folder 4, University of Rochester, Rochester, NY.

Waitzkin, H. and J. Sharratt. 1977. "Controlling Medical Expansion." *Society* 14:30–5.

Webel, M. 2013. "From Colonial Disease to NTD: Sleeping Sickness and Global Health in Historical Perspective." Paper presented at the Annual Meetings of the American Association for the History of Medicine, Atlanta, GA.

Weisz, G. and J. Olshenko-Gryn. 2010. "The Theory of Epidemiologic Transition: The Origins of a Citation Classic." *Journal of the History of Medicine and Allied Sciences* 65:287–326.

WHO. 1976. "Consultation on the Selection of Essential Drugs." Geneva, October 11–13. SPM 76.1, Geneva: WHO Archives.

WHO. 1977. "The Selection of Essential Drugs." WHO Technical Report Series no. 615. Geneva: World Health Organization.

WHO. 1978. EB 63 18.

WHO. 1979a. "The Selection of Essential Drugs." WHO Technical Report Series no. 641. Geneva: World Health Organization,.

WHO. 1979b. *A Summary of Proposed Changes to the Model List of Essential Drugs* WHO DPM/WP/79.1, March 26, 1979. Geneva: WHO Archives.

Wickremansinghe, S. A. and S. Bibile. 1971a. *The Management of Pharmaceuticals in Ceylon*. Colombo: Ceylon Industrial Development Board.

Wickremansinghe, S. A. and S. Bibile. 1971b. "The Management of Pharmaceuticals in Ceylon." *British Medical Journal* 3:757–9.

Williams, J., P. A. Martin and J. Gabe. 2011. "The Pharmaceuticalization of Society? A Framework for Analysis." *Sociology of Health and Illness* 33:710–23.

Williams, J., P. A. Martin and J. Gabe. 2012. "Medicalization and Pharmaceuticalization at the Intersections: A Commentary on Bell and Figert." *Social Science & Medicine* 75:2129–30.

Yach, D., C. Hawkes, C. L. Gould and K. J. Hofman. 2004. "The Global Burden of Chronic Diseases: Overcoming Impediments to Prevention and Control." *Journal of the America Medical Association* 291(21):2616–22.

6

The Drug Swallowers
Scientific Sovereignty and Pharmaceuticalization in Two International Drug Donation Programs

ARI SAMSKY

Political Narratives

Drought and the memory of water mark the hills near Gairo, in the Morogoro region of Tanzania. I am sitting with my friend Donatus, a bilingual Tanzanian nongovernmental organization (NGO) consultant, and a village health officer named Penford.[1] We are discussing the spectral, puzzling presence of two huge international drug donation programs, the Mectizan donation to treat river blindness and the Zithromax donation to treat trachoma. The programs have reached from high-tech labs in New York and New Jersey all the way here to East Africa, and they have marked and changed local people, local systems of knowledge and local power structures. They have done this by providing free drugs. Our conversation went like this:

> Penford: We should have services in the community – it shouldn't matter how many of us there are. We should have things like schools, and health facilities, and they should be nearby. And as citizens, it is important that we have a dispensary here. We shouldn't have to go all the way to Gairo. And when you get to Gairo, the clinic is crowded and you have to wait for hours before you see a doctor.

> Donatus: Well, there's a program starting, you heard what President Kikwete said right?

> Penford: What did he say?

> Donatus: That every village should have its own dispensary.

> Penford: I have heard that.

Penford and Donatus continued, back and forth, joined by a woman who also served as a village health worker and a man who is a member of the village council. I sat silently, listening, taking notes, watching each speaker in turn.

Penford: It is true that this program [the drug donation] has come to help us. We agreed, and we still agree, to serve our community [by volunteering for the donation]. But at least they should look at our case. We have agreed to serve the community, but there should be at least something small for us, for all the work that we are doing.

Donatus: For what you are doing for the community?

Penford: Yes. The drugs come once a year, and they gather us together in a seminar and that is the only time that they give us something. Twenty-five hundred shillings [about US$1.50]. They should give us something better.

Council member: Before he answers our visitor: this is a community project, OK? It is a project that has been brought to the community, and the community members must realize that it is their responsibility to look after the people who are helping them, the drug distributors. The government, together with the donors, has brought this service to the people, just like a school. They knew that you could not afford the drugs, so they have brought you the drugs, just like they give you teachers and other things for development. So that's why they are saying that the village [instead of the international drug donation program] should find a way to remunerate the drug distributors. The government supports you in giving you drugs, transporting the drugs and educating you all so you know about the drugs, how they work and how to take care of them. And the importance of the drugs. That's what I understand, and that's the reality.

Penford: That's just politics.

Council member: No, it's not politics.

This conversation and the story told in it can shed light on cracks and fissures of unjust political and social structures located in a complex web of global health inequality.[2] It echoes a story recounted by Didier Fassin in *When Bodies Remember*. Fassin relays the words of a woman named Puleng, a South African who later died of complication from AIDS, alone in a subterranean apartment in a township (Fassin 2007). Without much prompting Puleng told Fassin her life story, a narrative filled with pain, with missed chances and cruelty; she told Fassin this story not to elicit his pity, but to illuminate the injustice of what happened to her, and what was happening to so many others around her. I recount the previous conversation, and some of the following narratives, in a similar interpretative spirit. Like Fassin, I am interested in how these stories, told spontaneously and with a certain degree of frank self-interest, can trouble and add to technical narratives of the life of these two international drug donation programs. I follow Fassin here, among many other ethnographers and anthropologists, in trying to make many parts of a complex story speak to and with one another, and specifically in trying to put together a hybrid political narrative, a bricolage of voices from many actors (organizers, recipients and scholars of these international humanitarian interventions) that attempts, in a spirit of respectful criticism, to chart and examine the "unspoken orthodoxies" (Stirrat and Henkel 1997) that drive the donation programs.

These stories take place in a complex international web of humanitarian agreements, scientific knowledge, political and economic power, and puzzling, fraught corporate generosity. The two donation programs in question provide drugs, free of charge, to populations suffering from two tropical diseases: onchocerciasis (a blinding parasitic disease transmitted by black flies) and trachoma (a blinding eye infection spread through infected ocular discharge). I provide more detail on the history and structure of the donation programs below; but I would like to begin with another political narrative, this one from an executive of Williams Pharmaceuticals, the corporation that manufactures and donates Zithromax for the control of trachoma.

In 2006, I spoke over lunch with a research scientist on the Zithromax team in New London, Connecticut. We sat in an alcove drinking coffee; he had walked me there from his office, led me there in fact, because the interior of the building lacked signs or other points of reference. Its architects had designed it with curved walls and disorienting starts and stops, none of the usual furniture of a working office; this was supposed to provide a physical impediment to espionage.

The Zithromax Donation Program is massive – 225 million doses have been distributed to date (International Trachoma Initiative 2014). The researcher was excited about his corporation's charitable work; he was excited that a product with which he strongly identified himself was being given away, and was being absorbed so usefully into so many bodies. He asked me why I hadn't asked why his company didn't donate more drugs or other drugs, then provided an explanation as if I had. He argued that if the corporation began donating all its drugs it would "shut its doors" within a year or two, and would be unable to pay its researchers, or to continue manufacturing its existing products. Total donation, in the researcher's view, would remove the corporation from the sustaining cycle of for-profit research. Of the recipients of this hypothetical largesse the researcher said, "They will live – and their children will have no chance at a better life." In the researcher's conception the continual innovation of the pharmaceutical industry promised to provide this "better life," and it could not do so without commercial structures of profit.

This statement among many other similar ones led me to ask two questions that I hope will help connect drug donation programs to ideas of property and ownership. We know that the donation programs are organized around giving, but one of my questions follows Mauss, Godelier and Weiner in asking, "what do the donations keep?" (Weiner 1992; Godelier 1999; Mauss and Halls 2000). The other asks, "what do the donation programs say about public and private property in humanitarian interventions?" The answers to both questions reveal the paradoxically conservative nature of the donation programs. Although they are novel and create new relationships (not exactly partnerships, as in the Harvard public health scholar Michael Reich's work on public-private partnerships, 2002), they do so in tune with the well-worn values of neoliberal capital. They appear to be yoking private industry and public service, but they do not, or they do so in a way that reaffirms public and private identities, rather than bringing them into question.

I found in my fieldwork that the employees of Big Pharma, and their colleagues in the NGOs that operated the donation programs day to day, thought deeply and spoke volubly about injustice; they, too, were interested in telling their stories in a way that emphasized issues of justice and morality, even though they often refused to engage directly with these themes. As I recount the many perspectives that came together across stark power differentials to create and administer the donation programs, I keep this angle of analysis at the forefront; critically, I interpret and collect these narratives following an emerging body of scholarship on pharmaceuticalization, which we might think of most simply as the reduction of healthcare to the provision of drugs (Biehl 2006, 2007, 2013; Bell and Figert 2012). It is fruitless to think about the drug donation programs without accounting for the incredible power and importance of the drugs as central actors in the programs.

In the many narratives of the history of the drug donation programs I collected in my fieldwork, the same few themes emerged from the multiply-positioned speakers: the surprising power of the drug, the complex process of marrying a donated pharmaceutical product with a disease and a treatment or control technique (on the scale of public or global health) and finally the construction of new organizations or partnerships to administer the donation. I sketch these processes here for the two drug donation programs in this study.

Ivermectin and River Blindness

In 1988 Daniel Bishop, then the CEO of Kurtis Pharmaceuticals, inaugurated an international donation of the drug Ivermectin, or Mectizan, for the control of river blindness, also called onchocerciasis. Ivermectin is a deworming drug that Kurtis initially developed for veterinary use, then later adapted to control human parasites. Ivermectin controls and cures river blindness with one yearly dose. The drug reaches its recipients through a complex network of organizations involving client governments, international blindness NGOs, a purpose-built foundation/NGO called the Mectizan Donation Program and of course the drug company itself. Since the 1980s the model of drug donations disbursed through mass drug administration has become increasingly important in global health.

Zithromax and Trachoma

Ten years later, in 1998, Williams Pharmaceuticals began its own drug donation program. Williams gives away the antibiotic Azithromycin (Zithromax) to control trachoma, a blinding bacterial eye infection endemic to Africa and parts of Asia. Williams' donation relies on a public health technique called the SAFE strategy (Emerson et al. 2006). SAFE combines medication with corrective surgery and a few simple hygiene techniques (face washing and "environmental" cleanliness, usually referring to digging and using communal latrines and tidying households) to cure and control trachoma. Williams partnered with the Edna McConnel Clark Foundation to create the International Trachoma Initiative, an NGO tasked with disbursing the donated drug.

In order to chart and understand both of these programs I spoke with retired and current pharmaceutical, foundation and NGO executives, attended seven international meetings of disease-control experts, and visited Tanzania, where I met with regulatory, NGO and Ministry of Health officials, and interviewed Tanzanian citizens in the Morogoro region. Some of these local people volunteered for the donation efforts, and some simply received the drugs as part of the yearly distributions. I did this research between 2006 and 2009; I was in Tanzania in September and October of 2007.

One of my enduring interests in this research was charting what the provision of donated pharmaceutical products did to personhood, citizenship and the human body, on a literal and also on an epistemological scale; that is, I wanted to understand what impact the donation programs had on the imagination of what is possible in global health. It was very clear from the beginning that the drug donation programs, which made extreme claims on the stage of global health and development (see Amazigo 2008; International Trachoma Initiative n.d.), were part of an emerging global trend of pharmaceuticalization. The programs struggled constantly, on the level of operations and also on the level of self-presentation and PR rhetoric, with the extent of their mission and whether what they were doing was "merely" drugging, or whether they could claim a more comprehensive humanitarian effect. What's more, on a political and global level, they were treating a highly multifactorial problem (the ill health of the world's poorest) as essentially a technical challenge. This technical challenge was even more narrowly framed as a specifically medical challenge, and more specifically still as pharmaceutical one.

Actors situated at different parts of the donation projects expressed different opinions on the issue of what exactly the drugs were doing and who they benefited (the drug companies, international NGOs, the recipients, client ministries of health). The same actors told the story from multiple points of view. Others, like Nathan Rangan and Mohammed Bahraini of the International Trachoma Initiative, emphasized broad development benefits when they told me proudly that their donation programs benefited young women and girls particularly, since they prevented blindness and thus freed socially subordinated family members to go to school. This allowed some rhetorical room to maneuver within the narrow field of responsibility of the programs; program officers could speak about development without taking responsibility for it.

Today the International Trachoma Initiative website features a page detailing comprehensively how the trachoma intervention engages with the much-debated Millennium Development Goals, making claims that the intervention integrates tightly with and substantially benefits all eight goals: embracing poverty eradication, primary education, gender equality, improvement of child mortality rates, promotion of maternal health, combat against disease (HIV, malaria and others), environmental sustainability and global development partnerships. Again, this is striking coming from a humanitarian intervention that focuses solely on a single disease and that does not claim any direct expertise in or authority on development per se and, again, it contributes to a discourse that medicalizes and pharmaceuticalizes a social phenomenon that we might term inequality or poverty (International Trachoma Initiative n.d.).

In the rest of this chapter, I chart some of the ways in which human bodies and the drugs that affected them took center stage in the rhetoric of the donation programs. I explore what is at stake when a large corps of developed world health professionals harnesses the economic, biomedical and political power of pharmaceuticals to elaborate and export a notion of the body that does not necessarily match local ideas in the developing world.

What Is at Stake in the Donation Programs?

The key to understanding how the donation programs engage with publics and imagine their own work is analyzing their technical practices and rhetoric. The Mectizan Donation Program uses a technique called CDTI (community-directed treatment with Ivermectin); the Zithromax donation relies on a similar technique called SAFE (standing for surgery, antibiotics, face washing and environmental cleanliness). Both drugs cure other diseases, especially Zithromax, which is a broadly useful antibiotic (interlocutors in Tanzania reported grinding the pills up and rubbing the powder into cuts, for instance; they also told me that they knew they were not supposed to do it). But in these drug donation programs, the drugs are not for patients; they are for regions made up of bodies marked by a particular global public health logic (see also Frost 2002 for a discussion of conflict between patient and population in the early days of the Mectizan donation).

The central approach for both donation programs is usually called a "mass drug administration." Mass drug administration's basic requirement is that the drug must be consumed by the entire eligible population. In these two donation programs, the drugs are administered only once a year. Populations become eligible based on geographical surveys of disease endemicity – for example, in the case of onchocerciasis, practitioners measure this endemicity through a technique called REMO, rapid epidemiological mapping of onchocerciasis (Noma et al. 2002). In both donation programs, the geographic areas must demonstrate an endemicity higher than a certain arbitrary threshold (20 percent in the case of onchocerciasis); once this threshold is reached, all members of the community receive the drug, whether or not they actually have the disease.

In mass drug administration, human bodies become adjuncts to more or less artificial geographic imaginings of disease, and they lose their individual embodiedness to a startling extent. They become spaces into which "the donation" moves, a geographic area accessed by mouths rather than by roads. Although the donations are ostensibly concerned with health, they rarely focus on the body as meaningful except as a pathway to access disease. The tool that works upon the diseases found in these multiple bodies is the drug.

As we drove from Dar es Salaam to the Morogoro region to conduct interviews I asked Donatus, who had worked closely with onchocerciasis and trachoma control programs in Tanzania for years, what the Kiswahili word for participants in the donation programs was: "wamezadawa," he told me, meaning "drug swallowers." The word recurred in the rest of my fieldwork in Tanzania – in the offices of the Tanzania Food and Drug Administration, the Ministry of Health, at clinics and dispensaries at which we paid courtesy calls on the way to the five villages in Morogoro and in conversation with village health workers and ordinary people who received the donated drugs. The technical and popular discourse of the drug donation programs did not meaningfully characterize the targets of international health aid as patients or citizens, people with rights or desires or thinking, acting subjects. The name for donation recipients in Tanzania, "wamezadawa," "drug swallowers," derived from the powerful goods that they received, and from a narrow understanding of what they ought to do with the drugs.

The Mectizan Donation Program for river blindness approaches the individual body as a site of area-based, highly pharmaceuticalized public health. My interlocutors at Kurtis and at various NGOs explained to me that adult *Onchocerca volvulus* worms encyst themselves in their victim's skin, creating the nodes measured by palpation. These cysts cause little harm or discomfort by themselves, but the adult worms also produce multitudes of microfilaria or juvenile worms, which chew their way through the skin and the tissues of the eye, causing horrific itching and, eventually, blindness. The drug Ivermectin paralyzes the microfilaria but does not necessarily kill the adult worm. Since Ivermectin does not kill the adult, a single mass drug administration will not eliminate the disease from a community or from an individual – the adults will, theoretically, survive and give birth to new microfilaria. The encysted adult worms die of old age after about fifteen years. Program administrators and researchers have therefore concluded that fifteen years of yearly treatment with Ivermectin will ensure that the adult worms leave this earth without reproducing, and therefore the disease will be eradicated from an area (biomedical evidence supports this idea; see Diawara et al. 2009).

By dosing individual bodies with drugs the organizers of the donation hope to "cleanse" an area; human bodies become a feature of the natural landscape, an expedient way to come to grips with a foe that lives in a specific region. Previous scholars have noted a reductive impact on healthcare, in which provision of drugs becomes the main mode through which patients experience medical care and, in many cases, the state (Biehl 2004, 2013). In the drug-based environmental hygiene project of the Mectizan donation, we see a pharmaceuticalization of the environment, a way of acting upon natural features of an area, a population of harmful parasites, and the massed bodies of a population all at once, ostensibly for a period of at least fifteen years.[3]

"As if We Were Developing Any Profitable Drug . . ."

As I began to learn about the drug donation programs, I wondered how these tropical or global health efforts fit into the corporate structures of the drug companies. It was clear that Big Pharma was willing to spend enormous amounts of money and effort on these health interventions which, unlike other drug company projects, never promised to yield any profit. How could the authors of the donation reconcile this with their responsibility to manage a for-profit corporation? I saw this question, which my interlocutors never fully or clearly answered, as another way of looking at how the donation programs operated on the imagination of what is possible in global health – and what is possible for corporate charity.

I began research into the world of pharmaceutical donations by talking with policy researcher Laura Frost, who was then a visiting scholar at Princeton's Woodrow Wilson School. Frost had an extensive background in drug donations, having worked closely with leading public-private partnership scholar Michael Reich at Harvard. She told me succinctly and powerfully that mass drug administrations have more going on beneath the surface than one might think – "donations aren't free." Frost's work focuses on the donation of Mectizan, explores early conversations between Kurtis Pharmaceuticals and the World Health Organization (WHO), and charts how the two organizations strove to reconcile corporate cultures and to iron out the difference between treating individual patients (that is, patients with many rights, in a clinical setting) versus conducting a mass drug administration (Frost 2002). The ex-CEO of Kurtis Pharmaceuticals told me a strikingly different story of Mectizan. His account of the early days of the drug donation program reveals the roots of the orthodoxy that places drugs at the center of a massive, continually growing global health intervention that still operates today. I met with Dr Daniel Bishop, who was CEO of Kurtis when the donation began, in his suite in an unassuming corporate park in suburban New Jersey, not too far from Princeton and New York City.

Although Bishop is retired, he maintains this one-man office suite, marked only by his initials on a brass plaque, complete with a receptionist and a tiny waiting room. His actual office is spacious and beautiful, decorated with a career's worth of awards – I was relieved when we sat around a small coffee table instead of on opposite sides of his imposing desk. Bishop had responded eagerly to my email inquiries about the Mectizan donation. I was to learn that this was one of his proudest accomplishments.

When research on Ivermectin began, Bishop was head of Kurtis' labs; he became CEO later, after distinguishing himself as a superb research director, a man who bridged corporate and scientific interests and attracted and fostered incredibly talented pharmaceutical researchers.[4] Bishop began the story of the Mectizan Donation Program with the origin of the drug itself, as a veterinary dewormer, an antiparasitic for livestock and pets. He repeatedly called it "an amazing drug" – "the most important animal health drug in history." Bishop told the story of the drug's movement into the world of global health avidly and passionately. He spoke rapidly, with emphasis, clearly, fluently, as if he had told this account before many times but still became bound up in the telling:

> Initially we had high hopes that this drug would be important for humans. Because it was an exciting antiparasitic, which had unusual potency. It was probably 100 times more potent than the latest, most exciting drug for killing parasites. So we quickly looked at, investigated all the parasites that might be sensitive to it. All roundworms essentially were sensitive to it, so it was clear that it could be an important drug for all kinds of mammals that have roundworm parasites. We also looked at hookworms and tapeworms in humans, that were important parasites in humans, and they were not very sensitive, so it early became apparent that it was not going to be, it might not be important for humans, so it was essentially put on the shelf.

The story continues with Dr Mohammed Aziz, a researcher on the Ivermectin team, who had spent some time doing tropical health work with the WHO. Aziz wondered if Ivermectin would be useful to control a different class of tropical parasites (see Newland et al. 1988) and Dr Bishop supported him:

> ... he asked to take a small sample of the drug in the form of a tablet (we didn't have any tablets at the time, we made some tablets for him), he went to Dakar in Senegal, which is the Western tip of Africa ... And there he did an experiment with a small number of patients, I forget how many, he took skin snips over the hip and counted the number of microfilaria per snip, and then he came back in a month [after treatment with Ivermectin] and he did a skin snip on the other side and found that the microfilaria were all gone. It was very exciting. We called in the WHO folks and told

them about our exciting results. And they pooh-poohed the results. They did not think that this was an important observation for several reasons.

Bishop went on to sketch the details of early corporate conversations around Mectizan. He told me that he had approached the Kurtis Pharmaceuticals marketing team with the information that Mectizan could be useful for tropical disease among the world's poorest people; he told me that the marketers reported, with great excitement, that it would be indeed be possible to market the drug, at a very low price: "They said of course they could [sell the drug] and of course they could not, they were completely wrong, they could not, we didn't at the end think we could get the drug to the people at ten cents a year!"

Already, in this narrative, it appears that Bishop thought of the drug donation as inevitable; with this in mind he had decided that Ivermectin was going to become an important, perhaps historically important, public health drug no matter what the WHO thought of it (for early WHO opposition see Rougemont 1982).

The conflict between Kurtis Pharmaceuticals and the WHO took shape in the early 1980s, when the WHO was transitioning away from primary healthcare and into "selective primary" care, moving towards the "global health" paradigm of the 1990s (Brown, Cueto and Fee 2006). Dr Bishop described a long process of wrangling and arguing with the WHO, which was already running a pesticide-based intervention, the Onchocerciasis Control Program (OCP). An experienced fieldwork interlocutor from Christian Blind Mission told me that the WHO's OCP had been quite effective – the program had hired pilots, in some cases veterans of the Vietnam war, to drop pesticides in black-fly infested rivers, thus eliminating the "vector" of onchocerciasis without directly intervening on individuals (that is, treating an infestation of an area rather than patients). The OCP had its problems and critics – it was expensive, the pesticides were toxic and it seemed possible that either the parasites or the black flies would develop resistance to the poisons. But the program did work, measurably eliminating the parasites and flies without using potentially expensive drugs. This was recognized and confirmed by participants at an expert committee meeting (an independent group of tropical health experts who met yearly to assess the Mectizan Donation's progress and practices) that I attended in Atlanta in 2007. Dr Bishop and his team from Kurtis Pharmaceuticals wanted to change all that – they envisioned a cheaper, dramatically more effective intervention relying on donated Ivermectin, thus effectively pharmaceuticalizing what had formerly looked like a regional hygiene problem. In the end they got what they wanted.

In my interview with him, Dr Bishop spoke with some bitterness of what he saw as attempts by the WHO to seize credit for the creation of the new, drug-based intervention – they had tried to "steal" the program, in his words. He would "not allow it"; he recalled particularly a conflict over an early publication about the donation program: "So I saw a draft of this letter, and I called them up and told them that if that paper were published, I would publish a rebuttal and I would take them out of the program. So they revised the manuscript and put in the correct data, and we continued working in a friendly fashion." He described working with the WHO as a necessary, but unpleasant alliance – "they had access to all the clinics in the thickets of Africa," he explained, but other than that he had little positive to say about the WHO. The essential conflict was between a traditional view of tropical hygiene (espoused by the WHO) and an ostensibly new idea of treating tropical disease with huge amounts of drugs. For example, Rougemont, writing for the WHO in 1982, clearly stated that Ivermectin would never be useful as a treatment for river blindness. As it turned out, he was quite wrong (Rougemont 1982).

What are we to make of the ambitious, talented CEO of an international drug firm and his fraught alliance with a global health organization experiencing a crisis of leadership and value (see Brown et al. 2006, for the WHO's troubles at this time)? One interpretation is a kind of foreshadowing of pharmaceuticalization of public health. Dr Bishop wanted to get his drug out to as many people as possible, ideally to everyone suffering from the parasitic infection that it treated. The WHO, with its waning but still salient emphasis on primary care and the development of health infrastructure was an impediment, a slow, outmoded, fractious organization that stood in the way of a sweeping new arrangement of medicine, economics and politics. It was a hurdle to be leapt as quickly and cleanly as possible, in Bishop's version (which is, perhaps, an extreme retelling of this story), not a partner in Reich's sense (Reich 2000) but a means to reach the "thickets of Africa" with their bodiless mouths ready to swallow pills.

The internal history of the Ivermectin, that is its history as a commodity researched and marketed by a for-profit firm, reveals another dimension of pharmaceutical power. When I spoke with my colleagues about my research on drug donations they almost always asked me why the drug companies had decided to give away drugs in the first place – why manufacture a product only to give it away? Many of my pharmaceutical company interlocutors anticipated this question. They gave me various answers ranging from "corporate social responsibility" as an implicitly valuable project to the advantage that the programs conferred on recruitment and employee morale; but no one response was definitive. The decision to turn a for-profit veterinary drug into a costly humanitarian mass drug administration meant many different things to different actors within Kurtis Pharmaceuticals (the same goes for the later, parallel process with Azithromycin). Dr Bishop's version of the Mectizan program origin myth continually emphasized the power of the drug Ivermectin itself, as something that challenged and escaped conventional corporate understanding but that might, ultimately, have been converted into a tame, conservative corporate commodity despite itself. "We developed it as if we were developing any profitable drug," he told me, though his remarks on the impossibility of selling the drug seemed to contradict this.

Many scholars have remarked on the paradox of developing drugs to treat the diseases of the very poor – even if the will, science and funding is there, the market is not, and the inventor firm stands to lose its investment, or to recoup it unacceptably slowly (Light and Lexchin 2004; Petryna 2009; Pogge 2008; for a historical look at drug access see Greene 2015, Chapter 5, this volume). In the Mectizan case the donation plan benefited indirectly from a market: Ivermectin was a blockbuster veterinary drug, so sales from the veterinary market could support the donation for humans. Various NGO interlocutors speculated that the enormous rewards for Ivermectin on the veterinary market must have more than compensated for any costs involved in manufacturing and donating Mectizan for human beings. No one at Kurtis Pharmaceuticals would comment directly on the finances involved here.

Dr Bishop continued his narrative, explaining that he had pushed the donation through using his own power and charisma despite the market failure of human Mectizan; a point of crisis came when he learned that the drug was about to receive regulatory approval for use in humans for treatment of river blindness from the French Food and Drugs Administration (at this time the US Food and Drugs Administration had not yet approved the drug for this use). Bishop explained that he had to get Kurtis Pharmaceuticals to make a lasting decision on whether to sell the drug or to give it away:

> So we had essentially no time to prepare for anything other than that we had to make a decision. Our decision was that if we put a price on it it wasn't going to be used, no government was going to get behind it, and therefore this *drug had the potential not to be adequately and appropriately distributed throughout the people who needed it*, and so [Kurtis] could only make one decision and that was that they'd give it away free, contribute it to anybody who needed it for as long as it was required, anywhere in the world. (Emphasis mine)

I understood this to mean that market logics compelled a fast decision – for drug companies, the time that a drug is under patent and on the market is supremely valuable, since the price drops so quickly after the patent expires. So if Kurtis Pharmaceuticals were to *sell* Ivermectin they would need to be ready to make use of the markets opened by regulatory approval from day one. Things turned out very differently.

Months earlier, at Williams Pharmaceuticals' high-rise Manhattan headquarters, I had asked the Williams point person for the Zithromax donation for trachoma what she thought of the ethics of giving away drugs. She thought for a moment and then told me, "I don't think corporations can have ethics." Ethics, she explained, applied only to persons, and corporations were made up of so many people working in such complex ways that she didn't think it was even possible to think in terms of ethics.

In the drug donation programs we see new and old concepts being questioned, reframed, elaborated and reconfigured. Specifically in the story of the Ivermectin donation we see traditional notions in tropical medicine being challenged at the planning and political level and altered in practice – care of patients gets remade as mass drug administration, medical intervention becomes a partnership between state and corporate actors, hygiene as a health practice tied to specific areas becomes part of a global or regional package of drugs and behavior change, and disease endemicity becomes a pharmaceutical, rather than environmental or epidemiological, issue. Similarly, in the political economy of Big Pharma we see ubiquitous ideas like commercial manufacture of drugs and medicine as part of a liberal market being interrogated and deconstructed. The changes, both practical and ideological, happen sometimes in a sidelong or indirect way, sometimes more directly, as in Nicholson's contemptuous description of the WHO. Moreover, the Ivermectin donation reconfigured the bodies of patients – where the WHO's pesticide program treated human beings as inhabitants of an area afflicted with dangerous, disordered biological forms, the Ivermectin donation proposed an idea of suffering African people as a kind of hygiene patient, as bodies in need of drugs, but also closely linked to the sanitation of a landscape. I will describe more of what happens to bodies in the donation programs below. The trachoma donation program is even more striking in its handling of bodies than the river blindness program.

Trachoma Treatment: Biopolitics and Citizenship

I turn now to the trachoma control efforts that I studied both internationally and in Tanzania. In the Morogoro region, trachoma control and river blindness control operated in close coordination, most obviously because the Ministry and community health workers who carried out one donation program usually worked on the other as well (this was true in every one of the five villages where I conducted interviews). On the ground, both programs operated mainly as mass drug administrations; in fact, many interlocutors referred to them interchangeably, and others who understood that they focused on different diseases still classed them as the same kind of activity. The crucial difference between the two programs, which was expressed much more clearly in technical literature and PR pamphlets than it was in practice, was the comprehensive hygiene strategy associated with trachoma control. The river blindness program lacked this component (though my contacts at Kurtis Pharmaceuticals and the Mectizan Donation Program spoke hopefully, if somewhat vaguely, of the value of "behavior change" in efforts to control river blindness).

In my fieldwork, I spoke extensively with the officers of the International Trachoma Initiative, visiting their midtown Manhattan office many times over the course of my fieldwork (they have since relocated to Atlanta, to the same building as the Mectizan Donation Program). A pair of conversations with Joseph Mensah, a Ghanaian epidemiologist and logistics expert, stuck in my mind as I thought over this material years later. Mensah was friendly, expansive, entertaining – he spoke energetically whether he just gotten off a transatlantic flight or had simply come into the office from his family home. He told me, early in my inquiry, that he came from a "dextral people" in Ghana, a group that privileged the right hand over the left. Antibiotics, the donated drugs, he told me, were the weak, sinister hand of trachoma control. The strong right hand, surgery, face washing and environmental cleanliness had to "support" the rest of the program – the part involving drugs.

Mensah told me an anecdote about the history of trachoma control in Africa. Previous regimes of trachoma control, again associated with the WHO, had used antibiotic ophthalmic ointment to treat the disease. This technique was effective, but required people to apply medicated ointment to their eyes, often several times a day. Trachoma disproportionately afflicts geographically dry areas, Mensah explained to me, so the prospect of putting ointment into your eyes in a region of blowing sand and grit was not appealing. He described to me desolate, disused granaries filled with useless antibiotic ointment, now long expired, being kept in the Kenyan bush because no one knew what to do with them, or no one could afford to dispose of them.

The International Trachoma Initiative's treatment strategy, SAFE, involves four components: Surgery (a simple procedure to reverse the inversion of eyelids caused by advanced trachoma, usually not necessary for most people living in trachomatous regions), Antibiotics (the donated drug), Face washing (a traditional public health "behavior change" encouraging frequent face washing with clean water and separate washcloths for all household members) and Environmental cleanliness (use of latrines and general cleaning to keep flies down) (Emerson et al. 2006). Clearly SAFE focuses quite strongly on the body, first and foremost as a generator of unclean or polluting matter. In fact, SAFE fragments and analyzes the body on a surprisingly minute level, calling to mind Latour's celebrated remarks on scientific scale (see Latour 1999); SAFE calls upon its participants to think of their own bodies in new ways, both as a site of public health intervention and as a source of polluting matter (Samsky 2011). In this program, SAFE is seen as safer and more effective than mass drug administration alone. The Mectizan donation is a mass drug administration that promises to treat environmental ills through careful attention to the inside of the human body, or to human bodies as representatives of a population. The Azithromycin donation makes the body itself an important site of pollution (following a distressingly long tradition in tropical health – see Anderson 1992, 1995). With trachoma control, ocular discharge and feces become medicalized as they are absorbed under the gaze of public health. Here we can see an emerging negotiation between "traditional" modes of public health, as exemplified by the hygiene of imperial and tropical medicine and the self-consciously new forms of mass drug administration (Farley 2003).

From the perspective of institutional history, the trachoma control program was a treatment strategy looking for a better drug (SAFE predated the Zithromax donation) where the Mectizan donation was a drug looking for a disease. But in both cases it appears that the drug ultimately drove the explosive success of the programs. The International Trachoma Initiative, backed by the power of the donated drug and its parent company, recently celebrated fifteen years of trachoma control, and "the distribution of 340 million doses of Zithromax® to 28 countries in Africa and Asia" (International Trachoma Initiative 2014). I understood Mensah when he said that the drugs were the weak left arm of the donation, and that the behavior change and environmental portions of SAFE were more important. Likewise, I understood Bjorn Thylefors (head of the Mectizan Donation Program) and Jeffrey Hald (Kurtis Pharmaceuticals' director of Mectizan donation), when they emphasized that behavior change and a strong public health message were vital parts of the Mectizan donation. But the facts on the ground seemed to belie this hopeful and more expansive message of public health and development.

Donated drugs brought these diseases to international attention, but they also caused a curiously flattening effect on bodies and health in the areas and national health systems where they operated. There is nothing false about their achievements – both programs really have dramatically reduced incidence of their target diseases. In fact, the International Trachoma Initiative has boldly promised to end trachoma by 2020 (International Trachoma Initiative 2014). Chad McArthur, an officer of Helen Keller international with extensive experience in tropical medicine in Africa, clearly and powerfully acknowledges the primary importance of the drugs in both interventions. McArthur entirely dismisses behavior change and public hygiene in the Mectizan donation, and explained to me that the trachoma control program relies quite heavily on donated drugs, and that it probably could work without the S (surgery), F (face washing) and the E (environmental cleanliness) components.

Instead of using SAFE techniques to change the behaviors and environment of people affected by the disease, the Zithromax Donation Program effectively medicalizes certain familiar bodily processes. It invites its constituents to consider everyday functions of the body as part of a public health or sanitation action. It transforms basic yet nonetheless intimate practices – such as washing one's face and using the toilet – into participation in state rituals of health, a difficult to interpret set of practices related to what Vinh-Kim Nguyen calls "resource-seeking behavior," itself part of his concept of therapeutic citizenship (Nguyen 2007). In Nguyen's examples, local people from Burkina Faso and Côte D'Ivoire take up the orthodox procedures and practices of international humanitarian movements in order to qualify for resources (money, expert advice, educational materials). These processes of international mimesis become locally useful after a while, but ultimately relate to structures of obligation, clientship and control coming from abroad (see also Whyte et al. 2013); I saw a similar process happening in Tanzania, though it was distressingly less like the cosmopolitan, conversational phenomena that Nguyen described. Tanzanian drug recipients with whom I spoke explained to me that their adherence to international disease control strictures (defecating in latrines, washing their faces, consenting to swallow pills once a year) was an action that took place in a reciprocal gift economy – that is, they expected to get something in return from the architects of the donations. One recipient stated: "We have agreed to serve the community, but there should be at least something small for us, for all the work that we are doing." The difference between what Nguyen found in Burkina Faso and Côte D'Ivoire and what I found in Tanzania is striking. Unlike Nguyen's informants, the Tanzanians did not know who had given them the drugs, who had invented the disease control techniques or how to communicate their desires to the center of the donation program (see Samsky 2011). Therefore, it was hard to know to whom they were obligated – and from whom they might be able to demand reciprocation.

With Mectizan and the fight against river blindness, the pill and the disease become part of a new epistemology and relationship to the state, understood and experienced as a reaction between pills and bodies. In trachoma control and Zithromax, the relationship of mass drug administration to the state becomes even clearer – the body itself becomes a site of the juridical presence of political authority. The SAFE strategy mandates clean faces, clean houses and latrine use; in the five villages that I visited the local governments had enacted bylaws that assessed a fine or jail time to citizens who refused to comply with the programs:

> Jacob (village health worker, drug distribution volunteer): Here, first of all we give the person the drugs if they are there. If he isn't there then he is pursued and he is also fined.
>
> Donatus: About how much?
>
> Jacob: Mostly, according to the bylaw, it's five thousand shillings [about US$3.00]. It also depends on your financial status, how well off the person is.
>
> Ari: Five thousand Tanzanian shillings?
>
> Donatus: Yeah. You get the drugs, and then you pay the fine.

My interlocutors told me that the authorities rarely actually went through with these punishments, and they seemed mostly focused on ensuring that residents swallowed the donated drugs. Yet people with whom I spoke told me that at least in theory, they could be fined for having a dirty face, or for relieving themselves in the bushes. The same type of penalty for failure to take the medication went for the Ivermectin mass drug administration – but in that case the fine was more narrowly applied only to people who refused to swallow the drugs.

These local bylaws were not part of the international donations' plan – no part of the official international structure of either program mandated or encouraged legal enforcement of its strictures. Yet nonetheless all five of the Tanzanian villages where I conducted interviews had the same set of bylaws, laws that compelled bodies into certain theoretically pleasing configurations, and compelled drugs into human bodies in both programs.

Bodies and Populations

At Kurtis Pharmaceuticals' headquarters in New Jersey, at the WHO in Geneva and at the Carter Center in Atlanta stand the same bronze statues representing an aged African man following a young boy, each holding the end of a long stick. Jeffrey Hald, my first contact at Kurtis Pharmaceuticals explained the symbolism behind the statue to me during one of our early conversations. We had encountered the statue on the ground floor of Kurtis Pharmaceuticals' enormous lobby, a glass box towering several stories at the center of a carefully maintained, lush corporate campus large enough to be called a park. Flowering trees and dense greenery lined the singularly beautiful drive to the security checkpoint and the small cluster of office buildings where I met with my Kurtis company interlocutors. The statue occupied a prominent place in the lobby; beside it stood a few informational placards explaining the corporation's role in the fight on river blindness. Hald told me that the statue represented the sad past of onchocerciasis. In the conventional public health imagination the disease river blindness causes primary morbidity (itching skin and blindness) and also a second order of morbidity, conceived as the burden of blind relatives on families already near the edge of poverty. He explained that the statue represented the wasted life of a little boy who would spend years leading around a blind elder instead of attending school. The Mectizan donation was intended to erase this misfortune; memorializing it in bronze was a clear comment on the political and moral power of the donation program; it was also a way of linking single-disease intervention to broad ideas of development.

Although it is not memorialized in bronze, I saw the same narrative operate in the Azithromycin donation, which in fact made identical claims about the family and economic impact of blindness. Trachoma Initiative rhetoric took a particularly gendered stance on the link between development and mass drug administration – Nathan Rangan emphasized the gendered nature of trachoma suffering (the disease disproportionately affects women and small children, probably through transmission via ocular discharge). As mentioned earlier in the chapter, one of the major benefits of trachoma control was freeing young women and girls from the responsibility of caring for older, blind family members, much as in the situation ambiguously memorialized by the Mectizan statue.

The evidence for a link between mass drug administration and broad economic development is not robust. Two sets of implicit claims operate in the world of the drug donations: one, that they are improving health where they operate; and two, that they are motivators or proxies for "development," conceived in very broad terms as neoliberal economic growth and an approach to an economy and standard of living that more closely corresponds with broadly understood "standards" of life in the global North. In an address in 2008 Margaret Chan, director general of the WHO, articulated this relationship with crystal clarity:

> Safe and powerful drugs are being donated through public-private partnerships or made available at very low cost. Integrated approaches have been devised for tackling several diseases at once, with limited demands of health systems and staff. Delivery mechanisms piggyback on existing systems.
>
> A strategy of mass preventive chemotherapy, aimed at reaching all at risk, rivals the protective power of immunization. Research continues to document the gains in poverty reduction and economic productivity achieved when these diseases are controlled. A perfect rainbow really can end in a pot of gold. (Chan 2008)

Bjorn Thylefors, an experienced tropical disease ophthalmologist and, at the time, the head of the Mectizan donation, wrote in a special issue of *Tropical Medicine and International Health* that "the link to primary healthcare is still needed" (Thylefors 2008:43). Other actors in the donation world expressed more pointed concerns. Chad McArthur explained to me that one of the ways in which mass drug administration based international health donations are attempting to fulfill ideas of development and access to primary care is through "horizontal" program structures, which during my intensive fieldwork were beginning to link to emerging ideas of "sustainability." Horizontal programs contrast with "vertical" programs. In a vertical program, an outside entity targets one particular disease or issue and builds a management apparatus and infrastructure to address it. In the case of the drug donation programs this might involve building refrigerated warehouses, commissioning trucks to ship pills around the country and training local people in the distribution of pills during the once-yearly treatment season. Horizontal collaboration emphasizes sharing of resources and intelligent collaboration – for instance, with the two programs in question in this chapter it would be an expedient horizontal collaboration to ask the same village volunteer health worker to handle the disbursement of both Ivermectin and Azithromycin. Horizontal collaboration exerts a powerful attraction for NGO executives and, according to these executives, to international grant-making foundations. Fieldworkers and executives discussed it at every steering meeting I attended from 2006 through 2009. But experienced field workers like McArthur had their doubts about it – he confessed to me that he thought that on the ground "horizontal" programs, or "sustainable" programs or other gestures towards efficiency and synergy might end up simply overburdening village health volunteers, who were in almost all cases true volunteers, in the sense that they didn't get paid.

Elsewhere I have documented the resentment and anger that volunteers and drug recipients experience as a result of this strategy in mass drug administration (Samsky 2011). Tanzanians with whom I spoke envisioned a donation program in which their health work would be rewarded – in the local conception distributing or swallowing the drugs was a kind of labor done to repay the donor corporations, but also to invite further reciprocal gifts, very much as found in work by Mauss, and later Godelier and Weiner. For the local people, more than drugs circulated – ideas, values and labor also moved around within the donation, though often in ways that local people found puzzling or incomplete (Samsky 2011).

But the drugs, and ideas of ownership and generosity attached to the drugs, are really at the center of the programs. Each pharmaceutical company very carefully defines its role in the donations – they agree to donate drugs only in endemic areas, and only for two particular diseases, river blindness and trachoma. The donated drug for trachoma is Azithromycin, a powerful and broadly useful antibiotic, but its parent corporation provides it only for the treatment of trachoma. Executives at the International Trachoma Initiative, the NGO that disburses the drugs, praised Azithromycin's ability to cure lung infections, skin infections and genital chlamydia, but they identified this ability only as an added bonus for drug recipients who live in trachomatous areas. Dr Bishop similarly praised the power of Ivermectin over skin infections and intestinal parasites, yet the donation focused solely on areas afflicted with the particular parasite that causes river blindness.

Godelier and Weiner ask anthropologists to attend to what is kept in gift exchange; in the pseudo-exchange of the drug donation programs, the donor corporations give the drug but they keep the authority to determine how it is used, and they certainly keep its patent rights. My fieldwork convinced me that this is part of a strategy to preserve, elaborate and reaffirm the market structures of Big Pharma, and especially the articulation of patent ownership, social responsibility and the market. The donation programs give the drug companies a way to bring up and then immediately dismiss the complex relationship between their products and people who need them but cannot afford them. The programs provide a pantomime of humanitarian morality while refusing to engage with issues of human rights, the right to health or the essential cruelty of a market commodity system for life-saving technologies.

Donated drugs, which are given with "strings attached" fit into the regimes of ownership and property that the fact of donation appears to question but ultimately reinforces. The drugs enter bodies and create value: publicity value, life value in Fassin's biolegitimacy sense, public/global health value in the form of statistics, the spectral and difficult to trace state value that articulates citizenships in ill-understood systems of clientship and so on. The articulation between drugs, disease and bodies generates new forms of biopower, a new arrangement of state and private power mediated through broad ideas of humanitarianism and more focused work that redefines the role of the state as an executor and junior partner to corporate interests acting in the name of life itself (see Biehl's "intermediary power formations" for a similar arrangement in the treatment of HIV in Brazil; see also Fassin's remarks on biolegitimacy: Biehl 2007; Fassin 2009).

Conclusion

Official and technical discourse in the donations works to reinforce particular conceptions of health and, perhaps as a byproduct, to suppress the body. In the rhetorical world of the donation programs disease, health and treatment become confused. The simple fact that the donations of these two drugs target only populations in areas suffering from particular endemic diseases confirms Canguilhem's (2008) ideas on public disease as a more recognizable and internationally interesting phenomenon than public "health." It also starkly illuminates the particular politics that inform this branch of international humanitarianism: "healthy" people, that is people living in areas free from trachoma and onchocerciasis, do not merit free drugs, even if they suffer terribly from other disease, violence, economic privation and other structural ills. "Sick" people living in areas with endemic trachoma or onchocerciasis are conceived as bodily reservoirs of the bacteria or parasite and receive the drugs whether they want them or not, and whether or not they individually, personally have the disease.

A very distinctive symbolic order is established here, one that maintains traditional neoliberal economic, political and social claims. First, drug companies own the drugs and may do with them anything that they wish. Second, individuals have a significant responsibility to society to manage their own health in harmony with approved scientific ideas. Finally, perhaps paradoxically members of communities ought to give of themselves in order to help their neighbors (the health workers who distribute the drugs in both programs are all volunteers). I often wondered during fieldwork why the drug companies both worked so closely with client country ministries of health and placed such tight constraints on what recipient health systems could do with the drugs. Jane Ewing at the Mectizan Donation Program explained to me in great detail the application process for states that wanted to receive free Mectizan to treat their citizens; they had to prove, exhaustively, that they could distribute the drugs appropriately, that they would not let them spoil and that they knew where the disease could be found. Why not, I wondered, just give the drugs to ministries of health and trust them to use them appropriately?

The answer given by developers of the donation program is that the donated drugs, as valuable and complex goods tied to the reputation of their Big Pharma owners, required intensely responsible management; managers of both donations told me that if the drugs were to be "diverted" (stolen) or squandered it would be a disaster for the programs. On an ideological level I understood that this tight control was authorized by what donation architects saw as the implicit good of the programs; provision of health pharmaceuticalized as access to pills. The Tanzanians with whom I spoke did not wholly agree that they were getting access to "health" through the donations – they asked strongly for clinics, wells and, tellingly, for drugs to treat other diseases. Similarly, in the international discourse of the donation programs bodies exist as populations, as cases, as a source of danger and as battlegrounds, but not as subjective or important ways of experiencing the world. This rhetorical position has not displaced local and personal understandings of the body. The Tanzanians with whom I spoke still understand their own bodies as locations of individual suffering, gauges of treatment efficacy, and sites of more or less effective palliation of pain and disability. It is nonsensical to "disagree" with either side; yet I think it is important to ask what is lost and what comes into being when a scientific, earnest conception of bodiless disease control goes abroad, taking with it the power and influence of pharmaceuticals.

This negotiation between bodies, populations, drugs and the state seems to me to represent the movement between disciplinary societies, biopower and whatever comes next that Deleuze described so passionately in his "Postscript on Control Societies," and that Foucault also began to address with his concept of security (Deleuze 1995; Foucault 2007). The basic fact is that the donation programs demonstrate a contemporary way in which governments operate on the biology of populations. Moreover, they show us how people transform into populations, how health and biology make that possible and how that process takes place in a new terrain of negotiations between the market, medicine and the state.

That said, in a way the hygiene of the mass drug administration seems less postmodern than either Deleuze's concept of control or Foucault's of security. The discipline that the donations exert over Tanzanians living in populations marked by disease is, in a way, modern. It is very much of a piece with the nineteenth- and twentieth-century concentrative disciplines that Foucault described – hygiene strictures, the control of the bowels and the cleanliness of the face seem utterly disciplinary and, in a way, old fashioned. Scholars like Anderson, Cueto and Greene can help us think through the intellectual and practical continuities that tie these ostensibly new and innovative health interventions to a world history of tropical health and hygiene – tellingly, a history marked by domination and colonization (Anderson 1992, 1995; Cueto 2014; Greene 2015). Yet this minute state modulation of behavior takes place not in sites of coercion, not in factories or hospitals, but in the home, in the village, in daily life, and in fact in the body itself. Exactly as Foucault wrote, the state has taken an interest in human biology – but in the example of the donations, the state's interest is interpenetrated with international humanitarianism, which is itself motivated by and reliant on seemingly inexplicable generosity coming from pharmaceutical companies.

In "Postscript on Control Societies," Deleuze predicts a high-tech future in which governments will track individuals through passwords rather than through hard checkpoints. In the world of the donations this has not exactly come to pass, yet in the improvisational messiness of these programs' engagement with bodies there is more of the routinized disorder of Deleuze's control or Foucault's security than the tidiness of classical discipline. Foucault argues that mechanisms of security (arising as early as the eighteenth century with the French state's initial attention to tracking smallpox), allow for a certain play and modulation in the populations that they address – security, unlike discipline, does not expect perfection. It allows for death and disorder. I remember vividly Jeff Hald telling me, in his office in New Jersey, that "you can't sacrifice the good for the perfect" in disease control – meaning, broadly, that one must not waste time searching for a fully equitable, scientifically acute and sustainable solution for chronic global health problems; one must act now, with the tools at hand. These tools, implicitly, are drugs such as Zithromax and Ivermectin.

The drug donation programs described in this chapter root themselves firmly in this disease-based, immediately active concept of public health or global health. Both drug donation programs act on disease more than they do on health, and perhaps this is why in the donations the body becomes a battlefield rather than a site of meaning production, or of joy, or of negotiation. Most of all it becomes a site of pharmaceutical consumption. The tools at hand, the drugs, constrain the mission; drug donation programs link themselves to ideas of health and development while disavowing any direct responsibility for these goals writ large, and while limiting the use of their products to specific diseases. Ownership of drugs, treatment strategies and programs is extrinsic to the local situation. It provides in and of itself a powerful moral and political justification for action. The value of the drug, its marvelous biological power, its equally marvelous financial or economic power, drives this arrangement, which I argue contributes to a changing political sovereignty of health, and to a conservative, neoliberal idea of the role of drug companies in the world. This reinforces rapidly globalizing regimes of intellectual property (Sell 2003) and the more philosophical relations that obtain in the commodity market of pharmaceuticals. Ultimately, only the person who owns the drugs can decide who swallows them and conditions under which they are swallowed.

Acknowledgments

I would like to express my deep gratitude to Princeton University's Center for Health and Wellbeing, the Princeton Institute for International and Regional

Studies, the Princeton Center for Migration and Development and the Office of the Dean of the Graduate School of Princeton University for their support of this research. I also thank the Tanzania National Institute for Medical Research. I thank the Global Health Studies Program at the University of Iowa and the Department of Anthropology at Washington University in St Louis for supporting me during writing. My thanks especially to João Biehl and Erica Prussing for their invaluable aid in thinking through this project.

Notes

1 I have changed the names of people and corporations in this chapter to obscure the identities of my informants.
2 For more on the specific economy of healthcare, humanitarian aid and communitarian action in Tanzania see Sanders (2003). The World Bank classes Tanzania as a low-income country – 28 percent of the population lives in poverty, only 44 percent have access to an improved water source, and the gross per capita income is US$570 as of 2012. Life expectancy is sixty-one years (World Bank 2014; see also Fassin 2009, for a discussion of how life expectancy expresses life value).
3 Things, of course, could be otherwise – a previous onchocerciasis control program administered by the World Health Organization (called the Onchocerciasis Control Program or OCP) relied on aerial spraying of pesticides into rivers to accomplish the same goal; the Ivermectin-based mass drug administration carefully discredited and replaced these prior efforts, but the goal remained the same: to destroy a population of worms. After pesticides left the scene human bodies became the vehicle for environmental improvement. Dr Frank Richards of the Carter Center, an onchocerciasis expert, remarked to me at a lunch at the WHO in Geneva that the cessation of pesticide application may not have been wholly positive from the perspective of the local people – they would have been very pleased to bid farewell to the black flies, whose bites were painful even if they didn't happen to be infectious.
4 Theodore Nicholson and Dieter Meyer, the lead biologist and molecular chemist on the Ivermectin development team, praised Bishop's leadership extensively in my interviews with them.

References

Amazigo, U. 2008. "The African Programme for Onchocerciasis Control (APOC)." *Annals of Tropical Medicine & Parasitology* 102(Suppl. no. 1):S19–22.
Anderson, Warwick. 1992. "Where Every Prospect Pleases and Only Man Is Vile: Laboratory Medicine as Colonial Discourse." *Critical Inquiry* 18(3):506.
Anderson, Warwick. 1995. "Excremental Colonialism: Public Health and the Poetics of Pollution." *Critical Inquiry* 21(3):640.
Bell, Susan E. and Anne E. Figert. 2012. "Medicalization and Pharmaceuticalization at the Intersections: Looking Backward, Sideways and Forward." *Social Science & Medicine* 75(5):775–83.
Biehl, João. 2004. "The Activist State: Global Pharmaceuticals, AIDS, and Citizenship in Brazil." *Social Text* 22(3):105–32.
Biehl, João. 2006. "Pharmaceutical Governance." Pp. 206–39 in *Global Pharmaceuticals: Ethics, Markets, Practices*, edited by A. Petryna, A. Lakoff and A. Kleinman. Durham, NC: Duke University Press.
Biehl, João. 2007. "Pharmaceuticalization: AIDS Treatment and Global Health Politics." *Anthropological Quarterly* 80(4):1083–126.
Biehl, João. 2013. "The Judicialization of Biopolitics: Claiming the Right to Pharmaceuticals in Brazilian Courts." *American Ethnologist* 40(3):419–36.
Brown, Theodore M., Marcos Cueto and Elizabeth Fee. 2006. "The World Health Organization and the Transition from 'International' to 'Global' Public Health." *American Journal of Public Health* 96(1):62–72.

Canguilhem, Georges. 2008. "Health: Crude Concept and Philosophical Question." *Public Culture* 20(3):467–77.

Chan, Margaret. 2008. Statement from the Director General. USAID Stakeholder's Meeting on Neglected Tropical Disease. Washington, DC.

Cueto, Marcos. 2014. *Cold War, Deadly Fevers: Malaria Eradication in Mexico, 1955–1975.* Washington, DC: Woodrow Wilson Center Press.

Deleuze, Gilles. 1995. "Postscript on Control Societies." Pp. 177–82 in *Negotiations, 1972–1990.* New York: Columbia University Press.

Diawara, Lamine, Mamadou O. Traoré, Alioune Badji, Yiriba Bissan, Konimba Doumbia, Soula F. Goita, Lassana Konaté, Kalifa Mounkoro, Moussa D. Sarr, Amadou F. Seck, Laurent Toé, Seyni Tourée and Jan H. F. Remme. 2009. "Feasibility of Onchocerciasis Elimination with Ivermectin Treatment in Endemic Foci in Africa: First Evidence from Studies in Mali and Senegal." *PLoS Neglected Tropical Diseases* 3(7):E497.

Emerson, Paul and Laura Frost, with Robin Bailey and David Mabey. 2006. *Implementing the SAFE Strategy for Trachoma Control.* Atlanta, GA: The Carter Center.

Farley, John. 2003. *Bilharzia: A History of Imperial Tropical Medicine.* Cambridge: Cambridge University Press.

Fassin, Didier. 2007. *When Bodies Remember: Experiences and Politics of AIDS in South Africa.* Berkeley, CA: University of California Press.

Fassin, Didier. 2009. "Another Politics of Life Is Possible." *Theory, Culture & Society* 26(5):44–60.

Foucault, Michel. 2007. *Security, Territory, Population: Lectures at the Collège de France, 1977–78.* Basingstoke: Palgrave Macmillan.

Frost, Laura. 2002. "A Partnership for Ivermectin." Pp. 87–112 in *Public-Private Partnerships for Public Health,* edited by M. Reich. Cambridge, MA: Harvard Center for Population and Development Studies.

Godelier, Maurice. 1999. *The Enigma of the Gift.* Cambridge: Polity Press.

Greene, Jeremy A. 2015. "Vital Objects: Essential Drugs and Their Critical Legacies." Pp. 89–111 in *Reimagining (Bio)Medicalization, Pharmaceuticals and Genetics: Old Critiques and New Engagements,* edited by Susan E. Bell and Anne E. Figert. New York: Routledge.

International Trachoma Initiative. 2014. "ITI 2013 Year in Review." Accessed May 2, 2014 (http://archive.constantcontact.com/fs170/1101417198815/archive/1116320748296.html).

International Trachoma Initiative. n.d. "Trachoma and the MDGs." Accessed May 2, 2014 (http://trachoma.org/trachoma-and-mdgs).

Latour, Bruno. 1999. "Give Me a Laboratory and I Will Raise the World." Pp. 258–75 in *The Science Studies Reader,* edited by M. Biagioli. New York: Routledge.

Light, Donald and Joel Lexchin. 2004. "The International War on Cheap Drugs." *New Doctor* 81:1.

Mauss, Marcel and W. D. Halls. 2000. *The Gift: The Form and Reason for Exchange in Archaic Societies.* New York: W. W. Norton.

Newland, H. S., A. T. White, B. M. Greene, S. A. D'Anna, E. Keyvan-Larijani, M. A. Aziz, P. N. Williams and H. R. Taylor. 1988. "Effect of Single-dose Ivermectin Therapy on Human Onchocerca Volvulus Infection with Onchocercal Ocular Involvement." *British Journal of Ophthalmology* 72(8):561–9.

Nguyen, V.-K. 2007. "Antiretroviral Globalism, Biopolitics, and Therapeutic Citizenship." Pp. 124–44 in *Global Assemblages,* edited by A. Ong and S. J. Collier. Oxford: Blackwell Publishing.

Noma, M., B. E. Nwoke, I. Nutall, P. A. Tambala, P. Enyong, A. Namsenmo, J. Remme, U. V. Amazigo, O. O. Kale and A. Sékétéli. 2002. "Rapid Epidemiological Mapping of Onchocerciasis (REMO): Its Application to the African Programme for Onchocerciasis Control (APOC)." *Annals of Tropical Medicine and Parasitology* 96(1):29–39.

Petryna, Adriana. 2009. *When Experiments Travel: Clinical Trials and the Global Search for Human Subjects.* Princeton, NJ: Princeton University Press.

Pogge, Thomas Winfried Menko. 2008. "Could Globalisation Be Good for World Health?" *Global Justice: Theory Practice Rhetoric* 1(1):1–10.

Reich, Michael. 2000. "Public-Private Partnerships for Public Health." *Nature Medicine* 6(6):617–20.

Reich, Michael, ed. 2002. *Public-Private Partnerships for Public Health.* Cambridge, MA: Harvard Center for Population and Development Studies.

Rougemont, A. 1982. "Ivermectin for Onchocerciasis." *The Lancet* 320(8308):1158.

Samsky, Ari. 2011. "'Since We Are Taking the Drugs': Labor and Value in Two International Drug Donation Programs." *Journal of Cultural Economy* 4(1):27–43.

Sanders, Todd. 2003. "Invisible Hands and Visible Goods: Revealed and Concealed Economies in Millennial Tanzania." Pp. 148–74 in *Transparency and Conspiracy: Ethnographies of Suspicion in the New World Order*, edited by H. G. West and T. Sanders. Durham, NC, and London: Duke University Press.

Sell, Susan K. 2003. *Private Power, Public Law: The Globalization of Intellectual Property Rights*. Cambridge: Cambridge University Press.

Stirrat, R. L. and Heiko Henkel. 1997. "The Development Gift: the Problem of Reciprocity in the NGO World." *The Annals of the American Academy of Political and Social Science* 554: 66–80.

Thylefors, B. 2008. "The Mectizan Donation Program (MDP)." *Annals of Tropical Medicine & Parasitology* 102(Suppl. no. 1):S39–44.

Weiner, Annette B. 1992. *Inalienable Possessions: The Paradox of Keeping-While-Giving*. Berkeley, CA: University of California Press.

Whyte, Susan Reynolds, Michael A. Whyte, Lotte Meinert and Jenipher Twebaze. 2013. "Therapeutic Clientship: Belonging in Uganda's Projectified Landscape of AIDS Care." Pp. 140–65 in *When People Come First: Critical Studies in Global Health*, edited by João Guilherme Biehl and Adriana Petryna. Princeton, NJ: Princeton University Press.

World Bank. 2014. "Tanzania Data." Accessed June 15, 2014 (http://data.worldbank.org/country/tanzania).

7

Pharmaceutical Technologies and the Management of Biological Citizens in Chile

COURTNEY A. CUTHBERTSON

The hospital's head psychiatrist, Dr Muñoz,[1] held appointments with patients in his office, a small, ten-foot by twelve-foot rectangular space, crowded with furniture.[2] The psychiatrist's desk had two chairs on either side. The cabinets mounted on the wall at eye level behind the psychiatrist's desk housed multiple books about psychiatry and mental health, including a copy of the Diagnostic and Statistical Manual, 3rd edition.[3] *An entire cabinet space was heaping full with muestras, boxes of free samples of various drugs from pharmaceutical companies which had been haphazardly tossed in upon receipt – Sertac (sertraline), Arilex FT (aripiprazole), Traviata XR (paroxetine), Noptic (eszopiclone) and Aceptran (clonazepam) were the most recent arrivals. A calendar on the bookshelf advertised Cymbalta (duloxetine manufactured by Eli Lilly) and on the psychiatrist's desk was a calendar for Aroxat (paroxetine produced by GlaxoSmithKline). The desk featured a laptop computer set up next to a box of tissues advertising for Wellbutrin (bupropion manufactured by GlaxoSmithKline) and coasters displaying Pfizer's logo. Among the seemingly disorganized piles of paper on the right side of the desk were a paper brochure from Janssen-Cilag about Attention Deficit/ Hyperactivity Disorder and another brochure underneath from Laboratorios Andrómaco. A year-at-a-glance calendar on the back of the door came from Globe Chemicals Company in Germany. Each of these items had been gifted to the psychiatrist during regular visits from representatives of pharmaceutical companies. It was within these walls that patients would come, sit down and consult with Dr Muñoz, often revealing significant or traumatic life experiences, in hopes of finding some resolution to their suffering within their fifteen- to thirty-minute appointment.*

Pharmaceutical intervention for illness, disease and disorder is not a new phenomenon, although its increasing presence in healthcare represents part of the changes in health, illness and medicine related to biomedicalization

(Clarke et al. 2010). Biomedicalization is a series of processes leading to an intensification of health-oriented discourses, sciences and technologies, where new technologies are enabled to compartmentalize pieces of the body on smaller and smaller scales to pinpoint the place of and intervene against illness. Additionally, biomedicalization is attentive to how more human conditions are coming under the medical gaze, managed through advances in technoscience such as pharmaceutical interventions that act upon chemical compounds within a person's body. Pharmaceuticalization is a more recently explored trend within medicalization more broadly, wherein drug treatments are deemed necessary or considered as best practices in the management and resolution of illness, disease and disorder (Bell and Figert 2012a).

The expanding biomedicalization literature has largely examined the shape of technoscientific advances in health within the US context. More recently scholars have called for increased attention to health, medicine and technoscience around the world, in non-Western settings as well as to the study of how technoscience and biomedicine operate through public health (Clarke et al. 2010; Bell and Figert 2012a). Drawing from six months of fieldwork in the psychiatry departments of two public hospitals in Santiago, this chapter contributes to the biomedicalization literature by addressing recent calls for transnational, public health-oriented studies through an examination of the role of biomedical technologies in the treatment of mental illness, and depression specifically, in Chile.

Scholars have argued that societies structured around responsible management of population health through the use of medical treatments will lead individual people to interpret their problems through the lens of biological ailments and to demand care for their ailments from the government, a concept called biological citizenship (Petryna 2002, 2004; Rose and Novas 2005; Rose 2007). This chapter evaluates the shape of biological citizenship within a specific Chilean context; drawing from empirical examples, I propose a modified, more dynamic vision of biological citizenship.

Mental Illness and the Pharmaceutical Market in Chile

Narratives of global mental health have touted Chile as a success story. Part of the cited success of Chile is the increase in the number of people treated for depression over time, from around 29,000 in 2001 to over 275,000 in 2009 (Minoletti, Rojas and Sepúlveda 2011). From 2004 to 2007 the number of new patients seeking treatment each year for mental illnesses went up almost 350 percent, primarily because of depression (Minoletti, Sepúlveda and Horvitz-Lennon 2012). Global mental health researchers and the World Health Organization (WHO) anticipate that through the nation's involvement in various mental health initiatives, including expanding access to psychiatric services and treatment within primary care, psychiatric knowledge would "trickle down" to the level of the general population.

Several studies have documented the rise of depression in Chile, making use of different metrics. The prevalence of depression disorders went from 4.6 percent in 1992 (Florenzano Urzua et al. 1995) to over 9 percent in 2002 (Vicente et al. 2002). In 2006, the lifetime prevalence of psychiatric disorders in Chile was 31.5 percent; almost a third of these cases were depression (Vicente et al. 2006). By 2009, 17.2 percent of Chileans had experienced some symptoms of depression in the past year; at that time, depressive symptoms were found among 8.5 percent of men and 25.7 percent of women (MdS 2010). In 2010, Chile had one of the highest rates of Years of Life Lived with Disability (YLD) in the Americas due to dysthymia (chronic mild depression) and major depressive disorder (Ferrari et al. 2013).

Explanations for this seeming explosion of depression diagnoses and prevalence in Chile are located within recent developments in healthcare in the country, which is the other component considered successful in narratives of global mental health. In 2001, the national program for depression was unveiled, and in 2005 the new national healthcare program (AUGE/GES, Regime of Explicit Health Guarantees) included a pilot program for depression that was officially incorporated in 2006. AUGE originally provided free or low-cost treatment for four of the most common mental illnesses: depression, schizophrenia, alcohol and drug abuse.[4] Antidepressants are offered by the public health system as part of AUGE, most of which are given a grade of "A" by the Ministry of Health's Clinical Guide for the Treatment of Depression.[5] In light of these recent developments in healthcare coverage, it may not be that the number of people with depression increased so suddenly, but that the provision of mental healthcare services for low or no cost has made treatments more accessible, especially among the poor. In the context of a population with an average expendable income of just over US$11,000 per year (OECD 2014), for poorer families the US$75 sometimes required for hospitalization would still be quite expensive.[6]

Even before AUGE was in place, the use of antidepressant medications in Chile had skyrocketed over 470 percent from 1992 to 2004 (Jirón, Machado and Ruiz 2008). In 2009, the private sector had pharmaceutical sales over US$1 billion while the public or institutional market reached US$400 million (Hartwig, Quirland and Dickens 2009). By 2012, the retail pharmaceutical market in Chile reached approximately US$1.5 billion (CENAFAR 2013). The pharmaceutical industry is competitive in Chile, with local laboratories such as Bagó and Royal Pharma accounting for 58 percent of private sector sales (Hartwig et al. 2009).

On average, 55 percent of Chileans' healthcare costs for any diagnosis are for pharmaceutical treatments (CENAFAR 2013). Recent political developments are shaping the current pharmaceutical context in Chile, as there are commitments to enable lower prices of drug treatments (CENAFAR 2013) and a bioequivalents (generics) campaign to spread the word about cheaper and equally effective, chemically identical drugs (www.bioequivalentes.cl/home.

html, accessed May 5, 2014). The Ministry of Health is working on a Pharmaceuticals Law to guarantee the availability of generic pharmaceuticals, which has been estimated to potentially save Chilean families over US$3,000 per year and over US$300 per year on antidepressants specifically (Rojas 2013).

During my six months of fieldwork in the clinics, I observed that representatives from various pharmaceutical companies would come to speak with the doctors nearly once a week. The company representatives would come in between outpatient consultations for a brief visit of no more than five minutes, sharing a pamphlet about a new drug, giving Dr Muñoz (the hospital's head psychiatrist) promotional merchandise such as highlighters or chocolates and inevitably ending in leaving some samples at the office. The pharmaceutical samples left at the hospitals made it possible for mental health professionals to provide free treatments to a financially strapped patient base, especially for cases where the AUGE program did not provide coverage. The heavy presence of pharmaceuticals within the space represents a new form of pharmaceutical governance enabled by neoliberalism (Biehl 2006); the state program governing wellness through the provision of mental healthcare involving low-cost or free access to antidepressants is accompanied by the promotion of self-reliance and responsibility in using them to achieve wellness.[7] This could be considered pharmaceuticalization of psychiatric care. That is, antidepressant medications were strongly promoted in the space and were relied upon as the primary means of care for depression; all other treatments, such as psychotherapy, supplemented pharmaceutical therapies. A turn towards pharmaceutical solutions for illness, the marketing and promotion of such solutions, along with physician and government support of pharmaceuticals have all been documented as processes of pharmaceuticalization (Abraham 2010; Busfield 2010).

Studies in biomedicalization posit that as a result of society's intensifying focus on health through technoscience both knowledge and identities are transformed (Clarke et al. 2003, 2010). A key concept for understanding this transformation is biological citizenship, originally theorized by Adriana Petryna (2002, 2004). Biological citizenship represents an identity produced when individuals come to understand their problems in terms of health and illness and to urge the national government to provide care for these problems. Rose and Novas (2005) and Rose (2007) further theorized biological citizenship as an extension of biopolitical governance. That is, within a biopolitical system, society is managed with an emphasis on maintaining the health and well-being of the population, with health defined simultaneously in economic, political and scientific ways. Biopolitical systems and biomedicalization encourage individuals to seek the care of trained professional healthcare providers as experts who have been empowered as knowledgeable about health (Foucault 1990, 2003; Rabinow and Rose 2006).

Biopolitics goes beyond management of society and into a way of socializing individuals how to think of themselves. In biopolitical societies, individuals are encouraged to regulate themselves in accordance with the good of the whole. It is through being socialized in this system, Rose (2007) theorizes, that biological citizenship takes shape. Rose's (2007) conception of biological citizenship as the outcome of socialization within a power structure utilizing biopolitics means that individuals within such a context will express their concerns in terms of problems in biological processes that are interpreted as illnesses. As citizens, people would also make demands upon the state as the primary agent of governance to intervene on behalf of the population's health. The experiences of two patients, Gloria and Pamela, as presented in the next section, demonstrate how reliance upon pharmaceutical interventions in the AUGE program helped to shape biological citizenship in the Chilean context. One effect of the state's policies for coverage of psychiatric care is the creation of a unique biological citizenship.

Diagnostics and the Dispensation of Medications

Gloria was referred to the inpatient clinic directly from an appointment at her neighborhood's consultorio in Las Condes. She stood approximately five feet, ten inches tall in knee-high black boots with black tights, and a purple and blue slinky dress that stopped short of her knees. Her wavy, black hair was cut short with wisps falling down the back of her neck. Although Gloria had accomplished a postsecondary technical degree, she was not working at the time she entered the inpatient facility. That day, she spoke openly and almost conversationally about the recent events in her life. Her father had been very sick, and died in her arms only five months before. She had been wanting to commit suicide, with a plan to throw herself in front of a subway train while holding her son in her arms. She explained to the head nurse and occupational therapist that she had previously been diagnosed and hospitalized, and pharmaceutical interventions did not work for her. "Drugs are almost useless," she said, before saying that she wanted electroshock therapy. The intake interview then ended abruptly, and after the occupational therapist escorted Gloria out of the room, the head nurse asked me what I thought about the new arrival. "It is interesting that she wants TEC [terapia electroconvulsiva, electroconvulsive therapy]," I said. The head nurse responded that it was common that patients ask for electroconvulsive therapy because of the "show" of it, going to a different area of the hospital for the sessions, having to sign forms and being informed about a unique, exotic treatment. For some patients, she said, the spectacle alone worked great. "So it's more a placebo effect?" I asked. "Yes, the placebo effect works wonders," she responded.[8]

Gloria's connection between negative emotional states and desire for suicide with a globally recognized, official psychiatric diagnostic label and her knowledge of acceptable treatment options within psychiatric standards and healthcare service capabilities demonstrates the co-constitution of new forms of knowledge, technoscientific interventions and services characteristic of biomedicalization (Clarke et al. 2010). Notably, her strategies exemplify a key component of biomedicalization, to optimize her performance.

Gloria's insistence on the necessity of biomedical intervention for her survival along with her knowledge of particular kinds of interventions as ineffective for her represents a level of transformation of her own identity and subjectivity as part of the processes of biomedicalization of depression in the context (Clarke et al. 2010). Gloria had familiarized herself, perhaps through previous experiences in mental health treatment, with the languages of biomedicine as the socially and medically acceptable mechanisms for recovery. Her knowledge of possible biomedical treatments works simultaneously to produce personal empowerment as her own expert, to become fluent in speaking the same languages as care providers and to demonstrate that she is a proper biological citizen who speaks the dominant language of health and personal responsibility for her own health. Gloria could potentially find validation by aligning her view of possibilities with medical professionals', although as this example shows Gloria was discredited due to her uncredentialed, patient status. The head nurse's seeming dismissal of Gloria's request for electroconvulsive treatment asserted a classic power differential between patient and provider. In biopolitical terms, this interaction indicates that from the expert perspective it was really the provider, rather than the patient, who knew best which intervention to utilize, and that the best intervention would include pharmaceuticals.

In the following Monday's rounds of interviews the entire staff arranged to speak with Gloria. After the weekend in the hospital, she looked tired as she shuffled slowly into the staff room with her eyes slightly closed. Gloria sat down and the interview commenced, with four medical students and the head psychiatrist listening attentively. Gloria described herself as overly demanding and perfectionistic. While she was employed, she would often work from 8:00 am to 11:00 pm instead of 6:00 pm out of sheer desire for her work. Gloria first experienced depression six years earlier, at age thirty, when her brother had an accident and was in a coma for twenty days. The same year she gave birth to her son. During her pregnancy, she had problems with her partner and although she broke up with him, he continued to bother her. Gloria's father, she said, died recently of a lung infection and had advanced Parkinson's disease. His passing greatly affected Gloria, even though during her childhood he drank alcohol often, causing her to lose trust in him as a provider, meaning she had to mature early. She came to the hospital the past Friday because she found herself unable to cry and felt she had a depression she could not get rid of. Gloria had tried twice previously to kill herself by taking seventy pills and cutting her arms. This time, she wanted to throw herself in front of the subway train with her son, because she could not bear the thought of her son being on his own after her suicide. It would be better, she reasoned, if he died then too. Killing herself, she told the doctors, would solve her problems without bothering anyone. Gloria said she didn't want to be hospitalized a long time; she just wanted electroconvulsive therapy and to go home to her son, whom she missed terribly. "I want to stabilize myself quickly, to be with him." Over the course of the weekend she was prescribed and began taking five pharmaceuticals, including risperidone, clonazepam and paroxetine. She reported that her body was shaking a lot, and she was not sure why. "I needed to hospitalize myself but I didn't want to just take pills," Gloria said. "I want to put my emotions in order and I want to be able to withstand more."

For Gloria, engaging in biomedical, technoscientific interventions such as pharmaceuticals or electroconvulsive therapy was not about changing the conditions of her life that led her to feel depressed, but for her to be able to continue in her life without such conditions having the same effect on her. In other words, Gloria was seeking to optimize or enhance her ability to tolerate undesirable circumstances, for her to be made to "live better" through technoscience (Clarke et al. 2010). Often pharmaceutical interventions are utilized in maintaining rather than changing a lifestyle (Dumit 2012), but in Gloria's case it was more about desensitizing herself to the unchanging or unchangeable conditions around her than it was about keeping her physical body functioning in a socially desirable way. This is similar to the case of male sexual performance and other drugs that work to keep male bodies functioning as if in perpetual youth (Conrad 2007; Clarke et al. 2010). Gloria's desire to be able to withstand more through biomedical interventions to desensitize herself is noteworthy because such desire indicates how powerless Gloria felt to change the environment around her. Rather, she was claiming power over the situation by seeking biomedical modifications to her body that would have an effect on her psychological coping. Optimization in this instance means the ability to be productive, to work and to go through normal routines. Events weighing on Gloria reduced her productive capacities so desensitizing herself to her surrounding circumstances in this case was to optimize her productive potential.

When I was able to interview Gloria about her diagnosis she stated:

Depression is a, for me, is a state in which one enters, in which one needs tranquility, needs therapy, needs value, a lot of value as a person, because that causes anxiety and much shame. That is super important. It's when one reaches the bottom, when one reaches the bottom, and has, have a very large anxiety in the soul [from which] one cannot move forward alone. You have to do it with someone else. To help yourself . . . They say the causes are genetic.

What would you tell someone who has depression?

That it's an illness, so negative, so negative, but that you have to ask for help. Ask for help. Ask for help because many people who develop depression don't ask for help. That they see to solving their problems because that will happen with time. Get treatment whether in short or long term but so they can get a solution to their problems. [Help means] with doctors, or psychiatrist, or psychologist, that are really important, like psychotherapy, and that you take *fármacos* [medication/drugs].

Gloria's account points to several thematic elements that swept across other patients' descriptions of their experience as well as their explanations for depression, including reliance upon medical doctors, psychiatrists and psychologists as mental health experts and the seeming contradiction between perceived causes and suggested interventions for depression.

Outpatient appointments and inpatient interviews with mental health providers were similar to Gloria's experience: patients would come in to discuss what had been bothering them, describing symptoms and the environmental or social circumstances around them. Care providers in both settings swiftly made diagnostic decisions based on the patients' symptom complaints, the severity of those symptoms (how much the symptoms impact people around the individual, or the individual's social interactions), and any response to previous drug treatments as indicated by whether the original symptoms and severity persisted or worsened. In outpatient appointments, new patients would get detailed instructions on how much and how often to take the drug they were prescribed – take one in the morning, one in the afternoon, and one at night, for example – and returning patients would discuss how well their current medication seemed to be working for them, often to have their dosages or schedules changed.

The combination of symptoms, severity and response to any previous medication were not considered in isolation. Often, psychiatrists would consider the patient's ability to pay for medication, as few specific drugs were covered by the government program for depression. One patient from a lower socioeconomic class could not afford Wellbutrin medication. "It will work best for him [of options available], but it is expensive," Dr Muñoz explained. Whereas most samples are meant to last perhaps a few days, the psychiatrist gave all four boxes of Wellbutrin he had to the patient, to last for the month. Pharmaceutical decisions were made by considering symptoms, their severity and the individual's response to previous medication, all in combination with the economic constraints of the individual as demonstrated through this next example.

Pamela came to the hospital after having been referred to Dr Muñoz through her comuna's mental health center. At thirty-seven, she was separated from her husband and had two children aged ten and fifteen. Pamela did not like that her daughter had gone to live with her father, and Pamela reported that she often felt anxiety about her situation in life and specifically about her children. The head psychiatrist stopped the interview with Pamela and turned to face me. "You see," he said, "She does not have depression. But I am diagnosing her with depression for administrative reasons so she can get the drugs for free, because otherwise they are not available to her." Pamela nodded along as the psychiatrist spoke. He explained that the same drugs to treat depression that were available through AUGE would help Pamela, although they were not as beneficial as some pharmaceuticals manufactured explicitly for anxiety. The psychiatrist turned back to Pamela and to his desk, and began filling out a diagnostic processing form for depression, to allow Pamela to leave momentarily with a prescription to fill for free at the hospital's pharmacy.

As mentioned earlier, the AUGE program originally included treatment for depression, schizophrenia, alcohol and drug abuse, and was later expanded to include bipolar disorder. As developed in the next section, the program's provision of medical consultation and treatment, although limited, effectively preempts claims-making by Chilean citizens that the government is obligated to provide healthcare. When asked about the AUGE program, patients at times did not know what it was, much less argue it was the responsibility of the state to provide the mental health coverage to them. However, citizens did engage in an implicit form of staking claims by utilizing the system, because it creates economic costs the government must pay. Dr Muñoz intentionally misdiagnosed Pamela so she too would have low-cost access to some treatment, thus eliminating the need for Pamela to lay claims with the state for the coverage of psychiatric care for her anxiety as a biological problem in order to receive pharmaceutical interventions. While such explicitly stated intentional misdiagnoses were not common in observations, they were perceived as common by many of the mental healthcare providers because of AUGE's coverage for only a few mental illnesses, in combination with poor economic backgrounds of many patients and the desire of practitioners to provide what help they could.

Biological citizenship has been constructed within academic literature as a formulation of self where the individual person is responsible for making biologically oriented claims to the state for healthcare. In Pamela's case, the demand on the state or assertion the state should be responsible for her care is being made implicitly by the psychiatrist who has access to diagnostic and prescription documents, while Pamela's role as patient, as recipient of services, continues, seemingly without change. Pamela made no statements to the doctor that she should have, or that the government program was obligated to provide mental healthcare, but she readily accepted the doctor's arrangement for her to receive free psychiatric medications through diagnostic alteration.

Daniel, a social worker at one of the hospitals, explained that he would rather work with someone diagnosed with psychosis, because it is more difficult to work with patients needing more than pharmaceutical treatments – such as those with depression. He stated: "It's easier to work with a person with psychosis than a depressed person … they [those experiencing depression] always have a need for psychotherapy, they don't take the drugs, it's much more complicated than you'd think." He explained that it was challenging to work with patients who have depression because of the interference in biomedical treatments. At times, Daniel said, patients with depression did not understand why they would take or did not want to take antidepressants, and the symptomatic negative outlook would hinder the treatment process. Abandonment of pharmaceutical use was common among Daniel's patients with depression, and this would cause the recovery period to lengthen substantially.

In many outpatient interviews, patients told Dr Muñoz that they had stopped taking medications because they began to feel better. The standard response Dr Muñoz gave was to point out the corrective lenses he wore. He would tell his patients that he could not see properly, so he got prescription eyeglasses. Quickly abandoning pharmaceutical treatment for depression would be like removing his eyeglasses because with them suddenly he could see again. The effect, the psychiatrist explained, is that because he was no longer using the glasses, he was unable to see. Wearing the glasses was required for him to see, just as using antidepressants was necessary for patients to feel well.

In summary, a key component of biomedicalization is transforming the meaning and use of pharmaceutical drugs and treatment strategies, from having been used to *subdue or eliminate* symptoms for the restoration of health to the use of such interventions for *optimization, enhancement and preservation* of health (Fosket 2010). Dr Muñoz implored his patients to use the antidepressants beyond the time of experiencing symptoms; even when symptoms had subsided, the patient would continue to take the antidepressants for a period of time as part of his or her management of wellness. Although the doctor would eventually lower dosages, this was not immediately presented to patients when they arrived and received their prescriptions. Once the psychiatrist considered a patient stabilized, which was often several weeks or months beyond the report of no experienced symptoms of depression, dosage levels would slowly be lowered until the patient was instructed to no longer take the drug(s). Pharmaceutical interventions were primary components of treatment, requiring a patient's commitment and self-regulation to the doctors' expert recommendation and authority as a professional in mental health.

Constructing Depression

Teresa was a newcomer to the inpatient facility, having been admitted through the emergency room the night before for being wildly out of control, fighting with her husband and throwing things. Teresa looked younger than her forty-seven years, with dirty blonde hair that curled as it reached past her shoulders. It was a cold day, so she sat wearing both a brown mock neck sweater and a coat. She sat in a chair against the wall while the psychiatrist interviewed her. "I feel useless. It pains me, it makes me mad," she said. "I feel very guilty, very useless. I'm good for nothing." Teresa had her hands in her coat pockets as she spoke, making eye contact with the doctor. "I'm scared to go back home," she said, as she explained that she was worried that she would be abused by her spouse, who uses a handful of illegal drugs and alcohol. He's been fairly controlling of her, obsessing over her schedule and calculating where she should be. "He tells me I'm unfit, I'm not able to work," Teresa said, describing him as a chauvinist. Sharing background about her life, Teresa mentioned that she first experienced depression around the age of fourteen or fifteen. "All of my life, I've had a very big sorrow," she sighed. "What do you hope for with this hospitalization?" the psychiatrist asked her. "To settle myself," Teresa said. With her right index finger she pointed to her temple, saying, "There's something here that doesn't work well. What is it I have? Why do I think what I think? Why am I not like other people I see who smile, but have some problems and don't want to kill themselves, but have hope? . . . As I am, I don't have a life. It's horrible not to feel that one wakes up [from this]. It's not that it's another day, it's torture."

Teresa described her life and her experiences of depression as intertwined, although she did not point to the social conditions of her life as the cause of her sorrows. In spite of the social conditions of her life that may have contributed to her feeling hopeless and sad, such as her abusive and controlling partner, Teresa pinpointed depression as originating somewhere in her head. She reported that she experienced depression for decades, interpreting those feelings as the result of something malfunctioning inside her head, something which she could not understand and could not control. Within a society focusing on one's responsibility for the management of health problems as biologically based, Teresa had appropriately expressed her problems by pointing to biological mechanisms and bodily organs. Although Teresa's formulation of the problems was somewhat unusual in the observations, her explanation for her distress as rooted in something not working properly inside her head falls more closely in line with what would be expected in a biopolitical society.

Patients often described issues in their lives causing them distress – a boss who was abusive or insulting, domestic violence, interpersonal communication problems. "[Depression] could be [caused by] a need, of an absent parent . . . problems of class can also produce depression. Abuse too, sexual abuse," said María, who was in treatment for depression.[9] Patients most often understood their depression as being caused by social issues. In that regard, going to the psychiatrist or other mental health professional can be seen as resolving those social issues that then were reinterpreted as personal, medical problems. Some went to psychotherapy with psychologists but not all, because as a "talking cure," psychiatrists in the project understood it to take more time and resources from the hospital. Sometimes patients were unable or unwilling to return for subsequent sessions. Pills were seen as an integral component of recovery by both patients and professionals.

Biologically oriented, technoscientific interventions such as pharmaceuticals target specific components of individual bodies for treatment, such that the effect will lead to an individual's wellness, or at least lessening of symptoms. Pharmaceutical treatments in the context of depression work to change an individual's emotional and sometimes physical responses to their environments, and thus can be seen as desensitizing patients to often unfortunate social circumstances, such as in Gloria's case (discussed earlier).

Participants who had been diagnosed with depression felt that depression was being seen more and more like an illness, comparable to any other physical illness, such as diabetes. As Claudia explained, "for all of us it's an illness, and just a bad illness." Estefania expressed gratitude that this perception was widely shared in society: "It's understood that depression is a state of illness." Estefania continued:

> I think that it's a big help, that depression would be like an illness, that it's not a state of madness or schizophrenia for people … That they see it as a normal illness, but rather as if they saw it as a freak, it would be, I think, much more that people would fall into depressions from which they would not be able to recover … In the current time, thanks to God, it's seen as an illness and not as madness.

Interestingly, the terms Estefania used connoted a distancing of general society from people with depression, along with a lack of understanding, and a lack of willingness to help those suffering. Estefania felt that the more heavily stigmatized depression was, the more difficult it would be for people to return to their previous well-being. In her view the medicalization of depression worked to reduce stigma.

A student, Cristina, who had not experienced depression, similarly felt society saw depression as an illness:

> I think that now it's seen more as an illness than before. I mean, I think that before they didn't realize, because no, no, no, I don't know, for example now the psychiatrists say depression and the people are like "ahh, that person has depression," but before it was like due to laziness that they don't go to work, or something, because of laziness they don't do this. That's how I would say for now it's taken more, more as an illness, and it's taken as prisoner by doctors.

Historically, depression would have been interpreted as an unwillingness to work or handle one's responsibilities, but taken as an illness, the inability to manage one's duties is interpreted to mean the individual is no longer in control of his or her life because of a physical, internal, biological problem. Cristina felt that the term "depression" was understood by the population without the necessity of explanation. The statement that Cristina makes about depression being a "prisoner" to doctors indicates that the medical model may now be the only acceptable manner for handling depression, and that doctors have staked claims over expertise on depression; she implies that this may not be an entirely positive phenomenon.

The idea that depression was an illness meant that it was seen socially through more of a medical model than many mental illnesses had been historically; that depression was interpreted through a medical model rather than mere deviance demonstrates depression had been medicalized (Conrad and Schneider 1992; Conrad 2007) in the popular imaginary. Viewing depression as an illness meant seeing something was wrong with the body which required one to seek attention from a licensed care provider or doctor, along with the notion that people with mental illnesses are patients who should follow the orders of their doctors and through those treatments, people would recover. In other words, patients and people outside the medical settings alike saw those with depression as being obligated to take on the sick role (Parsons 1951).

If depression is an illness one needs to see an expert, explain their symptoms and have those symptoms identified as a disease process in the body to be treated with medical interventions such as antidepressant medications. To be an illness also implies that the experience is beyond the control of the individual, as something that must work its course through the body to be relieved. Depression being viewed as an illness indicates that there is an acceptable, accessible and respectable method of treatment. Whereas historically depression was seen as insanity, being a freak or laziness, and thus something from which most would distance themselves, depression as an illness makes the experience more understandable to those who do not have it, with the population having the impression that depression was caused by a biological problem in the body, not a moral failing of the individual. In this case, biomedicalization moves the issue from deviance to a physical, bodily dysfunction, with the effect of absolving one's "poor character" or morality of fault unlike many other health conditions (Metzl 2010).

Advice for Others

Although the people interviewed for this project largely understood depression as an illness related to social problems, their advice for someone who may be facing depression was often entirely given in terms of "look for professional help" or "get treated." When asked about what advice they would give to someone who has depression, overwhelmingly they responded that one should look for help, and most often, help from a medical professional. "That they look for help … Each person knows how they can help themselves" (Estefania, patient). Carmen (patient) explained "[w]ell, that they have to get treated … with the general physician." Carmen would advise someone to advance through the different levels of healthcare by beginning first in primary care.

One patient elaborated by saying that the healthcare services are useful and that it has become so easy to receive the services that accessibility should not be an issue. "What I would say first, that they get treated ... That the hospital's *policlínico* is really good ... It's not difficult to enroll. You have to do it" (María, patient). There was no question to María that medical interventions at the hospital were necessary to overcome depression. Although this contradicts how most of the patients interpreted the causes of their own depression as social, it is not entirely surprising as pharmaceutical interventions have become normalized not only within psychiatric practice but also in everyday life (Orr 2010).

Estefania felt that she was often told she could overcome depression on her own, to be healthy and continue in life, but that others would explain that she should get professional help. "Many people tell you, eh, 'you can leave, you are capable of leaving,' but there are other people who say help. Look for help, look for professional help, or something, someone who understands you." In this case, professional help means that one finds assistance from another individual who is trained and licensed to comprehend and deal with the problems at hand. At the same time, this statement may still express a sense of being stigmatized for experiencing depression as one could infer that *only* a mental health professional was able to understanding depression, and others were not.

Even while patients would recommend to others that they seek psychiatric help and utilize pharmaceutical remedies, they had mixed feelings about the pharmaceutical interventions with which they were faced. One patient, Carlos, believed the drugs helped him to feel better, but those drugs created an unwanted feeling of requiring the drugs to feel good or normal. "With the drugs that they gave me I feel really good, but the problem is that I quit taking them, and I returned, like, I went backwards. Like I depend on the drugs." Carla, another patient, felt that pills worked well for a while, but she also disliked having to take them. "For two or three years the pills worked really well for me. Trying out different drugs and quantities never did good for anyone. I prefer not to take so many ... It's bad for the spirit." Pharmaceuticals are appreciated for their ability to lessen the symptoms of depression, but produced feelings of guilt and a sense that the patient, as an individual human being, is harmed by taking them.

Those participants who had not been diagnosed with a mental illness expressed similar faith in medical professionals, although divergent in their more detailed justifications drawing from biomedical and "atomized" (Clarke et al. 2010) reasoning, explaining their stances through references to internal processes and neurochemicals only mental health professionals were capable of properly understanding. Juliana, who had not been diagnosed with depression, felt that professional healthcare providers had a unique ability to assist individuals in removing the depression inside of them: "What would I say.

Hmm. I don't know, go to get treated, go to some doctor, a psychologist, reach down and try to take out what you have inside, try to get better … Get a professional who can help you not to continue in that same state. To overcome it." To Juliana, experts would be able to help individuals to rid their bodies of depression so those individuals could continue in their lives, as healthy people.

Drawing from biological notions that depression may be about lacking a vitamin in the brain, Veronica believed it might be important to understand what was causing a severe depression. "For a severe depression maybe go to the psychiatrist, and there are studies to see really if your brain is lacking some type of vitamin … see a psychiatrist and a psychologist to combine a, some type of therapy." Veronica saw therapies from psychiatrists and psychologists as the best solution.

Vicente had a more urgent feel to his sentiment that people with depression should see health professionals who use science to facilitate the healing process. "Well, I would tell them first that, that turn off the car, stop the car, right? And that, and that they put their problems in the hands of science, in the hands of people who effectively can support them and help without shame … The professionals are there so they can help leave more quickly, leave better, and leave without wounds." To Vicente, people with depression needed to suspend their lives temporarily to ask for help from experts. Vicente's statement implies that mental health professionals, by relying on science to support the care they provide, avoid placing stigma and blame on patients. People will be able to be healthier and be less harmed by relying on mental health experts than attempting recovery by other means.

Reimagining Biological Citizenship

Constructing depression through the language of illness shows an interpretation of depression as caused by biological dysfunction, although patients do not rely on descriptions of neurotransmitters or neurochemicals. Rather than using atomizing language (Clarke et al. 2010) which locates depression within neurochemical functions of the brain, Teresa's explanation of something not working correctly inside her brain came the closest to the languages of biomedicalization by focusing on the functioning of biological processes outside of the control of individual will as a problem in need of professional medical assistance. As an illness, the diagnosis of depression obligates patients to use pharmaceutical treatments for recovery although they many times felt drug therapies were harmful to their personhood. Explicit statements that the government is responsible for providing healthcare for its citizens were absent in these accounts. Only non-patient Vicente expressed something close in his statement that if he were to become depressed, he could do so "calmly … because the illness is financed." The reality is that patients did, however, create financial demands on the state through utilizing the AUGE program.

First, those suffering from depression did not elaborate depression as solely biological, or in specific terms relating to biological processes within the body. By not fully explaining depression in a biological way, in a context where it has been stigmatized, depression is still shrouded in mystery; it requires relying on experts to aid in its interpretation, management and resolution. Second, those suffering from depression were not actively asserting that the state should be held responsible for their healthcare. In Petryna's original articulation of biological citizenship (2002, 2004), victims from the Chernobyl explosion were arguing for medical coverage they believed the government should have provided, because it did not already exist. The patients in my study were recipients of the relatively recent, although preexisting, AUGE program to help in the treatment of depression.

Theories of biological citizenship explain the concept as an active, ongoing process created from the bottom up by individuals who are reframing their problems in terms of health and consciously petitioning the state to care for those needs. The creation of communities or social groups around health statuses as elaborated through the concept biosociality (Rabinow 1996) is similarly an active process. In the current study, individuals understood depression as an illness and utilized the national healthcare program to receive free services for depression; however, depression was not a galvanizing force for people in the ways that conditions such as breast cancer have been (Klawiter 2000, 2008). The dispensation of and beliefs around pharmaceuticals helped to construct biological citizenship in this context.

Biological citizenship in this context has not taken shape as would be predicted by social theorists (Clarke et al. 2003, 2010; Rose and Novas 2005; Rose 2007). Rather, the specific local sociopolitical historical context has overridden any "trickle down" of knowledge or sense of who is responsible for the health and well-being of citizens. The history of social medicine in Chile may help to explain why biological citizenship is different in this case. As early as Salvador Allende's 1939 publication *The Chilean Medico-Social Reality*, health issues were examined through their connections with larger social problems such as poverty and unemployment. This perspective held popularity in the public eye until the dictatorship period, when political violence and repression squashed portions of the social medicine movement as leaders lost their jobs, were forced into exile, or were tortured (Waitzkin et al. 2001). Due to the violence of the dictatorship, people may have been unwilling to make demands upon the state as this could be seen as making a potentially costly – or fatal – political statement.

Chile's recovery from the totalitarian, repressive governmental regime could be playing a large role in the shape of biological citizenship. The dictatorship represented a time when the general population experienced a "cultural blackout" (Timerman 1987) and large-scale fear of the government and its agents. Additionally, Pinochet's "Chicago Boys"[10] helped to enable neoliberal capitalism through economic "shock treatments" (Klein 2007). While this traumatic national history does not preclude the development of biological citizenship, the types of neoliberal programs and policies enacted during Pinochet's time may be playing a larger role in how people conceptualize themselves, their health and their needs today. Similarly, the social structural changes in China during the Cultural Revolution led people to feel distrustful, and neurasthenia as an illness became an acceptable expression of complaint (Lee 2011). That the logic of self-regulation has moved from economic or political realms into healthcare, inspired by the use of various therapies including pharmaceutical ones, demonstrates a sort of medical neoliberalism (Fisher 2007) congruent with biopolitical goals.

Biological citizenship described by Petryna (2002, 2004) as co-constituted through active processes among people affected by Chernobyl who explicitly stated their problems in biological terms and made clear demands on the state for healthcare, does not entirely fit with the findings of this study. Rather, this empirical case showed mixed reliance on biological languages, and demands on the state which, instead of being stated outright, were implicit through the use of and benefits from the provision of care through the AUGE program. With a health program in place to help people resolve their illnesses, disorders and diseases, the participants in this study may have felt that the government was already fulfilling an obligation for care, and did not pursue options to engage in activism against the state on this matter. However, as is well documented, more and more people have been receiving treatments for depression through the AUGE program. Because of the financial cost associated with paying for antidepressant pharmaceuticals and reimbursements to hospitals, this too is a demand on the state, although it is quite different from the demands made by those affected by Chernobyl (Petryna 2002, 2004). The original theory of biological citizenship is elaborated as an active process where individuals are cognizant of the biological ways they describe their problems and demands on the state. However, in this study, most patients indirectly described depression as biological through the language of illness, still looking to state supported pharmaceutical solution for treatment and as an obligation for care. Thus, the findings of this research point to the need for modifications to biological citizenship as a theoretical concept. As such, I suggest a new *gradational biological citizenship* to capture a wider range of experiences within biopolitical societies where people both express their health using biological language and make demands upon the state for care, although in new or different ways than originally theorized. This gradational biological citizenship takes into consideration how active or explicit such claims and claims-making are by those experiencing a particular problem, and as such exists along a spectrum from active to passive. A number of factors may influence how active and explicit or passive and implicit the processes of biological citizenship may be, including:

1 The types of languages used by those affected by a health condition, including whether such languages are overt and explicit or implied and assumptive regarding both biological definitions of health and claims-making for formal, state-provided care.

2 The level of involvement or activism of those considered to have the health condition, disease or disorder, in making healthcare an obligation of the state.

3 The degree to which access to healthcare services is already granted by the state.

4 The interaction of the experienced symptoms with one's involvement in the social world. For example, withdrawal from activities, people and social engagements are characteristic of depression, which may have the effect of lessening one's likelihood of making demands for care.

Gradational biological citizenship also enables the consideration of multiple levels and types of power from the bottom up, as well as the notion of power working discreetly, in line with Foucault's argument that power is diffuse and dispersed, not held by solely one entity but used across a field of social relations by many different actors (Foucault 2004).

Where biological citizenship is a concept that captures the processes of producing a successful biopolitical society through the construction of health issues as biological in origin and the demand for formalized state care, *gradational biological citizenship* adds dimensionality through the evaluation of the processes as active or passive in considering how explicitly people acknowledge and express their concerns using biological languages as well as their demands on the state for care. Further research may demonstrate that gradational biological citizenship captures a wide spectrum of biological citizenship. This modification to the original theory allows for the presence of biological citizenship in situations where the state has already adopted responsibility for the well-being of citizens through the provision of healthcare.

Conclusion

Pharmaceutical management orients the gaze inward to biological mechanisms as the targets of intervention. The use of such interventions assumes that they should work and if they have not, doctors have targeted the wrong biological mechanism, so long as the lack of responsiveness is not due to user error. The assumption that another drug treatment will surely be the answer reinforces the notion of depression as a biological entity. Within these treatment logics, patients expect and are expected to relinquish their decision-making and ownership of experience to the mental health professionals as experts of the brain, who simultaneously rely on patients to regulate themselves in accordance with the outline set by the expert. Pharmaceutical management redefines needs in terms of what the patient should require to experience a lessening of mental illness symptoms, and determining pharmacological need through self-reports of social engagement and interactions in combination with a patient's economic circumstances. Finally, by focusing on biological mechanisms, pharmaceutical treatment of depression works to obscure any social conditions/causations by internalizing mental illness as individual pathology.

At the same time that patients largely perceive problems in their lives to have caused the depression they experience, they construct their depression as an illness within a system of care that reduces any recommendations for what a person with depression should do to seeking medical care and using pharmaceutical interventions. When patients used biologically colored languages to talk about depression, it is through tropes of illness. As part of being an illness, depression means inexplicably being out of control of emotions and thoughts. Technoscientific interventions such as antidepressant drugs are expected as part of treatment and have become ubiquitous. The reliance primarily on intervention strategies targeted at the level of individual physical bodies and processes through the use of scientific, technological tools and the inclusion of those tools in the AUGE program demonstrates a biomedicalization of public health for mental illness and not just physical diseases or disorders.

The pharmaceuticalization of depression through the national healthcare program both encourages the biological construction of the illness and preempts political and social claims-making that is part of active biological citizenship found in other settings. Participants implicitly make demands on the state when they utilize the public healthcare program that provides them with free or low-cost treatments. The findings from this project suggest the need for a gradational model of biological citizenship, wherein the self-descriptive languages and demands on the state are implicit, covert or passive. Biopolitical societies problematize populations through health, encouraging the use of "biologically-colored languages" (Rose 2007:140) and requiring individuals to regulate themselves for the public good. Within such a system, where health problems are widespread enough as to be seen as normal, passive biological citizenship may be the sign of effective biomedicalization and pharmaceuticalization.

Notes

1 All names in this chapter are pseudonyms, to protect the confidentiality of participants.
2 This chapter comes from part of a larger ethnographic study examining global mental health, biopolitics and depression in Chile, which included eighty interviews with people diagnosed with depression, mental healthcare providers and people outside of the medical settings who did not have depression. People who were outside of medical settings were interviewed to capture the extent of a biopolitical frame towards depression within the local context. Fieldwork locations inside the hospitals included inpatient and outpatient services, the psychiatric

emergency room and the psychiatric day hospital. Passages are truncated, edited compilations of field notes and quotes from project interviews.

3 The *Diagnostic and Statistical Manual* (*DSM*), 3rd edition, published in 1980, represented a paradigm shift in psychiatry as it adopted a new system of diagnosis and classification of mental illnesses, drawing from a medical model with categories of symptoms as indicators of discrete, pathological mental disorders (Mayes and Horwitz 2005). The fifth edition of the *DSM* was released in 2014.

4 The AUGE program has been updated and now includes coverage for bipolar disorder.

5 Electroconvulsive therapy and half of the psychosocial interventions in the Clinical Treatment Guide are also given the grade of "A."

6 Antidepressant medications have taken on additional social meaning for those in poor communities. For some poor families in Santiago, the sharing of such pharmaceuticals is a demonstration of care for other people when general resources are scant (Han 2013).

7 This is not to say that pharmaceuticals are ineffective. Pharmaceuticals can be critical to the management of illness, disease and disorder (Williams, Gabe and Martin 2012; Bell and Figert 2012b). The points of interest here are the complex social relationships between actors involved with pharmaceuticals, and how the increasing focus on and promotion of pharmaceuticals as management tools shape interactions and ways of living.

8 Electroconvulsive therapy is generally accepted in psychiatry as an effective treatment for severe depression, with some studies showing it is effective in the short term (UK ECT Review Group 2003; Weiner and Falcone 2011). Other evidence regarding the effectiveness of electroconvulsive therapy is mixed; changing parameters of electroconvulsive therapy (bilateral or unilateral, level of stimulus intensity) produce varying results, where some have found benefits in symptom reduction and to rates of relapse, while others have found few or no benefits (Sackeim et al. 1993, 2001; UK ECT Review Group 2003; Greenhalgh et al. 2005; Ross 2006; McCormick et al. 2009). One comparison study between electroconvulsive therapy and pharmacotherapy found the two equally effective, and both more effective than placebos (Kellner et al. 2006). Read and Bentall (2010) argued that due to the combination of inconsistent results and the potential for persistent, permanent brain damage that electroconvulsive therapy should not be used. What is important in the context of Gloria's treatment is her insistence that electroconvulsive therapy would more effectively intervene in her biology to reduce or eliminate her depression, in contrast with the nurse's belief that the effectiveness of electroconvulsive therapy was more psychological than biological, perhaps as a self-fulfilling prophecy.

9 Some also expressed that through changes associated with economic development, society inspired people to become more competitive, individualistic and superficial (which has been described by Lakoff (2006) as neoliberal subjectivity), leading to increased levels of depression, which Han (2011) calls neoliberal depression.

10 The "Chicago Boys" were a group of Chilean economists, trained at the University of Chicago, who were expected to help Pinochet develop social reforms to advance neoliberalism throughout Chilean society after the 1973 coup (Valdés 1995; Taylor 2006).

References

Abraham, John. 2010. "Pharmaceuticalization of Society in Context: Theoretical, Empirical, and Health Dimensions." *Sociology* 44(4):603–22.

Bell, Susan E. and Anne E. Figert. 2012a. "Medicalization and Pharmaceuticalization at the Intersections: Looking Backward, Sideways, and Forward." *Social Science & Medicine* 75(5):775–83.

Bell, Susan E. and Anne E. Figert. 2012b. "Starting to Turn Sideways to Move Forward in Medicalization and Pharmaceuticalization Studies: A Response to Williams et al. (2012)." *Social Science & Medicine* 75:2131–3.

Biehl, João. 2006. "Pharmaceutical Governance." Pp. 206–39 in *Global Pharmaceuticals: Ethics, Markets, Practices*, edited by Adriana Petryna, Andrew Lakoff and Arthur Kleinman. Durham, NC: Duke University Press.

Busfield, Joan. 2010. "'A Pill for Every Ill': Explaining the Expansion in Medicine Use." *Social Science & Medicine* 70(6):934–41.

CENAFAR, Centro Nacional de Farmacoeconomía. 2013. *Medicamentos en Chile: Revisión de la Evidencia del Mercado Nacional de Fármacos* (*Medications in Chile: Review of the Evidence of the National Drug Market*); CENAFAR Report, Institute of Public Health, December. Santiago, Chile: Ministry of Health.

Clarke, Adele E., Janet K. Shim, Laura Mamo, Jennifer Ruth Fosket and Jennifer R. Fishman, eds. 2003. "Biomedicalization: Technoscientific Transformations of Health, Illness, and U.S. Biomedicine." *American Sociological Review* 68(2):161–94.

Clarke, Adele E., Laura Mamo, Jennifer Ruth Fosket, Jennifer R. Fishman and Janet K. Shim, eds. 2010. *Biomedicalization: Technoscience, Health, and Illness in the U.S.* Durham, NC: Duke University Press.

Conrad, Peter. 2007. *The Medicalization of Society.* Baltimore, MD: Johns Hopkins University Press.

Conrad, Peter and Joseph W. Schneider. 1992. *Deviance and Medicalization: From Badness to Sickness.* Philadelphia, PA: Temple University Press.

Dumit, Joseph. 2012. *Drugs for Life: How Pharmaceutical Companies Define Our Health.* Durham, NC: Duke University Press.

Ferrari, Alize J., Fiona J. Charlson, Rosana E. Norman, Scott B. Patten, Greg Freedman, Christopher J. L. Murray, Theo Vos and Harvey A. Whiteford. 2013. "Burden of Depressive Disorders by Country, Sex, Age, and Year: Findings from the Global Burden of Disease Study 2010." *PLOS Medicine* 10(11):1–12.

Fisher, Jill A. 2007. "Coming Soon to a Physician near You: Medical Neoliberalism and Pharmaceutical Clinical Trials." *Harvard Health Policy Review* 8(1):61–70.

Florenzano Urzua, R., J. Acuña Rojas, C. Fullerton Ugalde and C. Castro Muñoz. 1995. "Results from the Santiago de Chile Centre." Pp. 247–63 in *Mental Illness in General Health Care: An International Study*, edited by T. B. Üstün and Norman Sartorius. New York: Wiley & Sons.

Fosket, Jennifer Ruth. 2010. "Breast Cancer Risk as Disease: Biomedicalizing Risk." Pp. 331–52 in *Biomedicalization: Technoscience, Health, and Illness in the U.S.*, edited by Adele E. Clarke, Laura Mamo, Jennifer Ruth Fosket, Jennifer R. Fishman and Janet K. Shim. Durham, NC: Duke University Press.

Foucault, Michel. 1990. "Right of Death and Power over Life." Pp. 133–60 in *The History of Sexuality, Volume 1: An Introduction.* Trans. Robert Hurley. New York: Random House.

Foucault, Michel. 2003. "17 March 1976." Pp. 239–64 in *Society Must Be Defended: Lectures at the Collège de France, 1975–1976*, edited by Mauro Bertani and Alessandro Fontana. English series editor: Arnold I. Davidson. Trans. David Macey. New York: Picador.

Foucault, Michel. 2004. "The Subject and Power." Pp. 126–44 in *The Essential Foucault: Selections from Essential Works of Foucault, 1954–1984*, edited by Paul Rabinow and Nikolas Rose. New York: The New Press.

Greenhalgh, J., C. Knight, D. Hind, C. Beverley and S. Walters. 2005. "Clinical and Cost-effectiveness of Electroconvulsive Therapy for Depressive Illness, Schizophrenia, Catatonia and Mania: Systematic Reviews and Economic Modelling Studies." *Health Technology Assessment* 9(9): 1–156, iii–iv.

Han, Clara. 2011. *Life in Debt: Times of Care and Violence in Neoliberal Chile.* Berkeley, CA: University of California Press.

Han, Clara. 2013. "Labor Instability and Community Mental Health: The Work of Pharmaceuticals in Santiago, Chile." Pp. 276–301 in *When People Come First: Critical Studies in Global Health*, edited by João Biehl and Adriana Petryna. Princeton, NJ: Princeton University Press.

Hartwig, Guillermo, Andrés Quirland and Carlos Dickens. 2009. *Chilean Pharmaceutical & Medical Devices Market Overview 2009.* OSEC Business Network Switzerland, October.

Jirón, Marcela, Márcio Machado and Inés Ruiz. 2008. "Consumo de antidepresivos en Chile entre 1992 y 2004" (Consumption of Antidepressants in Chile between 1992 and 2004). *Revista médica de Chile* 136:1147–54.

Kellner, Charles H., Rebecca G. Knapp, Georgios Petrides, Teresa A. Rummans, Mustafa M. Husain, Keith Rasmussen, Martina Mueller, Hilary J. Bernstein, Kevin O'Connor, Glenn Smith, Melanie Biggs, Samuel H. Bailine, Chitra Malur, Eunsil Yim, Shawn McClintock, Shirlene Sampson and Max Fink. 2006. "Continuation Electroconvulsive Therapy vs Pharmacotherapy for Relapse Prevention in Major Depression: A Multisite Study from the Consortium for Research in Electroconvulsive Therapy (CORE)." *Archives of General Psychiatry* 63(12): 1337–44.

Klawiter, Maren. 2000. "From Private Stigma to Global Assembly: Transforming the Terrain of Breast Cancer." Pp. 299–334 in *Global Ethnography: Forces, Connections, and Imaginations in a Postmodern World*, edited by Michael Burawoy. Berkeley, CA: University of California Press.

Klawiter, Maren. 2008. *The Biopolitics of Breast Cancer: Changing Cultures of Disease and Activism.* Minneapolis, MN: University of Minnesota Press.

Klein, Naomi. 2007. *The Shock Doctrine: The Rise of Disaster Capitalism.* New York: Picador.

Lakoff, Andrew. 2006. *Pharmaceutical Reason: Knowledge and Value in Global Psychiatry.* New York: Cambridge University Press.

Lee, Sing. 2011. "Depression: Coming of Age in China." Pp. 177–212 in *Deep China: The Moral Life of the Person: What Anthropology and Psychiatry Tell Us About China Today*, edited by Arthur Kleinman, Yunxiang Yan, Jing Jun, Sing Lee, Everett Zhang, Pan Tianshu, Wu Fei and Guo Jinhua. Berkeley, CA: University of California Press.

Mayes, Rick and Allan V. Horwitz. 2005. "DSM-III and the Revolution in the Classification of Mental Illness." *Journal of the History of the Behavioral Sciences* 41(3):249–67.

McCormick, Laurie M., Michael C. Brumm, Ajith K. Benede and Jerry L. Lewis. 2009. "Relative Ineffectiveness of Ultrabrief Right Unilateral Versus Bilateral Electroconvulsive Therapy in Depression." *Journal of ECT* 25:238–42.

MdS, Ministerio de Salud. 2010. "Encuesta Nacional de Salud" (National Health Survey). Report. Santiago, Chile: MINSAL.

Metzl, Jonathan M. 2010. "Introduction: Why 'Against Health'?" Pp. 1–14 in *Against Health: How Health Became the New Morality*, edited by Jonathan Metzl and Anna Kirkland. New York: New York University Press.

Minoletti, Alberto, Graciela Rojas and Rafael Sepúlveda. 2011. "Notas sobre la Historia de las Políticas y Reformas de Salud Mental en Chile" (Notes on the History of Mental Health Policies and Reforms in Chile). Pp. 132–55 in *Apuntes de la Historia de la Psiquiatría en Chile*, edited by María Alejandra Armijo Brescia. Santiago, Chile: Royal Pharma.

Minoletti, Alberto, Rafael Sepúlveda and Marcela Horvitz-Lennon. 2012. "Twenty Years of Mental Health Policies in Chile: Lessons and Challenges." *International Journal of Mental Health* 41(1):21–37.

OECD. 2014. "Better Life Index: Chile." Accessed January 9, 2014 (www.oecdbetterlifeindex.org/countries/chile/).

Orr, Jackie. 2010. "Biopsychiatry and the Informatics of Diagnosis: Governing Mentalities." Pp. 353–79 in *Biomedicalization: Technoscience, Health, and Illness in the U.S.*, edited by Adele E. Clarke, Laura Mamo, Jennifer Ruth Fosket, Jennifer R. Fishman and Janet K. Shim. Durham, NC: Duke University Press.

Parsons, Talcott. 1951. "Illness and the Role of the Physician: A Sociological Perspective." *American Journal of Orthopsychiatry* 21(3):452–60.

Petryna, Adriana. 2002. *Life Exposed: Biological Citizens after Chernobyl.* Princeton, NJ: Princeton University Press.

Petryna, Adriana. 2004. "Biological Citizenship: The Science and Politics of Chernobyl-Exposed Populations." *Osiris* 19:250–65.

Rabinow, Paul. 1996. "Artificiality and Enlightenment: From Sociobiology to Biosociality," Pp. 234–52 in *Essays on the Anthropology of Reason*. Princeton, NJ: Princeton University Press.

Rabinow, Paul and Nikolas Rose. 2006. "Biopower Today." *BioSocieties* 1:195–217.

Read, John and Richard Bentall. 2010. "The Effectiveness of Electroconvulsive Therapy: A Literature Review." *Epidemiologia e Psichiatria Sociale* 19(4):333–47.

Rojas, O. Catalina. 2013. "Según estudio del Minsal una familia puede ahorrar más de 2 millones anuales gracias a bioequivalentes" (According to a MINSAL study, a family could save over 2 million [pesos] annually thanks to bioequivalents). *La Tercera* November 14. Accessed August 5, 2014 (www.latercera.com/noticia/nacional/2013/11/680-551703-9-segun-estudio-del-minsal-una-familia-puede-ahorrar-mas-de-2-millones-anuales.shtml).

Rose, Nikolas. 2007. *The Politics of Life Itself.* Princeton, NJ: Princeton University Press.

Rose, Nikolas and Carlos Novas. 2005. "Biological Citizenship." Pp. 439–63 in *Global Assemblages: Technology, Politics, and Ethics as Anthropological Problems*, edited by Aihwa Ong and Stephen J. Collier. Malden, MA: Blackwell Publishing.

Ross, C.A. 2006. "The Sham ECT Literature: Implications for Consent to ECT." *Ethical Human Psychology and Psychiatry* 8(1):17–28.

Sackeim, Harold A., Roger F. Haskett, Benoit H. Mulsant, Michael E. Thase, John Mann, Helen M. Pettinati, Robert M. Greenberg, Raymond R. Crowe, Thomas B. Cooper and Joan Prudic. 2001. "Continuation Pharmacotherapy in the Prevention of Relapse Following

Electroconvulsive Therapy: A Randomized Controlled Trial." *Journal of the American Medical Association* 285(10):1299–307.

Sackeim, Harold A., Joan Prudic, D. P. Devanand, Judith E. Kiersky, Linda Fitzsimmons, Bobba J. Moody, Martin C. McElhiney, Eliza A. Coleman and Joy M. Settembrino. 1993. "Effects of Stimulus Intensity and Electrode Placement on the Efficacy and Cognitive Effects of Electroconvulsive Therapy." *New England Journal of Medicine* 328:839–46.

Taylor, Marcus. 2006. *From Pinochet to the "Third Way": Neoliberalism and Social Transformation in Chile*. Ann Arbor, MI: Pluto Press.

Timerman, Jacobo. 1987. *Chile: Death in the South*. New York: Vintage Press.

UK ECT Review Group. 2003. "Efficacy and Safety of Electroconvulsive Therapy in Depressive Disorders: A Systematic Review and Meta-analysis." *The Lancet* 361:799–808.

Valdés, Juan Gabriel. 1995. *Pinochet's Economics: The Chicago School in Chile*. New York: Cambridge University Press.

Vicente, Benjamin, Pedro Rioseco, Sandra Saldivia, Robert Kohn and Silverio Torres. 2002. "Estudio chileno de prevalencia de patología psiquiátrica (DSM-III-R/CIDI) (ECPP)." *Revista médica de Chile* 130(5):527–36.

Vicente, Benjamin, Robert Kohn, Pedro Rioseco, Sandra Saldivia, Itzhak Levav and Silverio Torres. 2006. "Lifetime and 12-Month Prevalence of DSM-III-R Disorders in the Chile Psychiatric Prevalence Study." *American Journal of Psychiatry* 163:1362–70.

Waitzkin, Howard, Celia Iriart, Alfredo Estrada and Silvia Lamadrid. 2001. "Social Medicine Then and Now: Lessons from Latin America." *American Journal of Public Health* 91(10): 1592–601.

Weiner, Richard D. and Grace Falcone. 2011. "Electroconvulsive Therapy: How Effective Is It?" *Journal of the American Psychiatric Nurses Association* 17(3):217–18.

Williams, Simon, Jonathan Gabe and Paul Martin. 2012. "Medicalization and Pharmaceuticalization at the Intersections: A Commentary on Bell and Figert (2012)." *Social Science & Medicine* 75:2129–30.

8
Commentary and Reflections: The Ongoing Construction of Pharmaceutical Regimes

MATTHEW E. ARCHIBALD

Introduction

Institutional change in biomedicine has a specific historical character that hinges on the socioeconomic and political reconstitution of the field. This field has witnessed, among other dramatic transformations, jurisdictional expansion and technological rationalization, the rise of new sources of biomedical knowledge and the production of new identities based on health (Clarke et al. 2010; Bell and Figert 2012). I draw on these transformations to call attention to the contingent processes of institutional change as described in the chapters by Greene (2015, Chapter 5, this volume), Samsky (2015, Chapter 6, this volume) and Cuthbertson (2015, Chapter 7, this volume). More narrowly, the focus of this discussion will be the recent emergence of pharmaceutical medicine as a form of health governance. The basic premise is that new forms of socioeconomic and political relations emerge at the juncture of pharmaceutical medicine and health which produce a realignment of power relations in the field of biomedicine under the burgeoning pharmaceuticalization of health (Biehl and Eskerod 2007).

Two central processes underlie the dynamics of this realignment in the field of biomedicine. The first describes the struggle between socioeconomic and political organizational actors to structure the field of biomedicine after their own interests. In this framework, transformation in the field occurs following shifts in the relative costs of exchange that lead actors to alter the rules of the game through which exchange takes place (North 1990). These institutional rules are rights and prohibitions, rewards and sanctions, norms and conventions and other social structures that shape human interaction in socioeconomic and political exchanges. They reduce uncertainty because they constrain certain kinds of behavior such as free riding (Phelps 1985). They also constitute the very components of the field of action (Scott and Davis 2010). Strategically, change occurs as a result of marginal adjustments to rules, norms and sanctions that comprise institutional life. This interest-driven perspective involves actors and organizations that develop sufficient bargaining strength to use the polity to maximize their objectives. Naturally, the rules of the game, including formal and informal constraints, tend to be highly stable in many areas of modern life and are therefore resistant to marginal adjustments. For example, the corporate founders of the Mectizan Donation Program Samsky (2015) interviewed inveighed against the World Health Organization (WHO) over its perceived encroachment on their program and chaffed at their dependence on it. This dependence was unavoidable since the WHO "had access to all the clinics in the thickets of Africa" (Samsky 2015:122). Similarly, resistance to marginal adjustments occurred when the WHO was pressured by the International Federation of Pharmaceutical Manufacturers Association (IFPMA), among others, to reduce its "activist" stance vis-à-vis the use of off-patent medicines as essential medicines because of its waning authority to direct global health (Greene 2015).

The second process by which institutional change occurs is at the level of ideologies and ideas. Like price changes, ideational transformation serves to restructure both the formal rules of socioeconomic and political interaction as well as norms of behavior, customs and traditions. Pharmaceutical philanthropy is a good example of one such normative transformation in the field. Pharmaceutical companies such as Merck and Hoffman-La Roche are in the business of manufacturing, marketing and selling pharmaceuticals, not giving them away. Yet, by the early 2000s, these companies had become enthusiastic proponents of pharmaceutical donation programs, (seemingly) contrary to their own business interests. Moreover, some of them began to call themselves global health companies (Greene 2011). This kind of pharmaceutical philanthropy signifies the extent to which ideological shifts can transform the rules of the game in an institutional sector.

One method for understanding these transformations in the biomedical sphere is to highlight historical trends. Greene focuses on the program of essential medicines to show how various processes, such as sociopolitical transformation, jurisdictional expansion and technological rationalization have been wrought by the intersection of interests around this program (see Greene 2011, 2015). Samsky and Cuthbertson use another approach to investigate institutional change in biomedicine. They employ a case-study strategy and examine particular programs such as donated medicine or particular practices such as depression diagnostics to locate the overarching structure of institutional change in those programs and practices (see Samsky 2015; Cuthbertson 2015).

Both methodological perspectives articulate nicely with the conceptual dimensions of Clarke et al.'s (2003) schema of biomedicalization. The central idea, for example, that institutional change in biomedicine entails transformation in knowledge and practices, signaling resistance to monopolistic control of medicines can be located in Greene, Samsky and Cuthbertson's different approaches to addressing pharmaceutical inequities. Information about pharmaceuticals proliferates through every kind of available media. This expansion produces an increasingly heterogeneous body of knowledge and practices. In turn diversification of knowledge and practices mobilizes health social movements including patient rights' groups, self-help and contested illness movements to wrest control of healthcare from traditional providers (see Brown et al. 2004; Banaszak-Holl, Levitsky and Zald 2010).

This is not to suggest that corporate hegemony disappears following the widespread diffusion of medical knowledge by popular healthcare initiatives. Although Greene shows that the essential drug concept revealed global North-South inequities in healthcare and that this served to rally non-aligned nations in the 1970s, corporate interests were persistent in their attempts to control knowledge and practices, if not the market itself. The Accelerating Access Initiative, a donation program led by Abbott Laboratories, Bristol-Meyers Squibb, Merck and other companies, illustrates one among many strategies for gaining the upper hand in struggles over control of the distribution of pharmaceutical medicine.

Furthermore, since the 1970s, new standards for drug approval and new linkages between public and private agencies have transformed knowledge and practices in biomedicine. Today corporate revanchism takes place through the practice of co-opting public entities as Samsky's discussion of "Dr Bishop's" clash with the WHO over the Ivermectin Donation Program demonstrates. Because knowledge and practices have changed so dramatically, regulation is uneven and market share can still determine who creates the terms under which the sector operates even when the state intervenes. Cuthbertson's discussion of the AUGE/GES programs in Chile shows that although the Chilean government authorized the widespread provision of depression medication, its implementation was thoroughly dependent on pharmaceutical companies, such as GlaxoSmithKline, Pfizer and Laboratorios Andrómaco.

In the remaining sections of this commentary, I address the emergence of pharmaceutical health governance by delineating some important conceptual issues related to institutional change in biomedicine and then link them to Greene's analysis of essential medicines and access, Samsky's investigation of the Mectizan and Zithromax Donation Programs and Cuthbertson's study of depression in Chile.

Institutions and Institutional Change

The institutions of biomedicine consist of cognitive, normative and regulative structures and activities that provide stability and meaning to social behavior (Scott and Davis 2010). These repeatable, stable patterns of behavior are based on rules, norms, values and shared understandings or shared knowledge about common practices in the field. In its earliest formulation, medicalization described a process of structural formation whereby the medical profession was able to establish hegemonic practices largely aimed at expansion of jurisdictional authority (Conrad 2005). The expansion of medical judgment, observation and control into nearly all life processes in modern societies results from the combined success of science and technology, the decline of traditional moral paradigms, the rise of higher education and the burgeoning of the profession and related fields. Science, as the dominant account of the ordering of the natural world, provides medicalizing processes with a powerful cognitive anchor. It is probably not too much of an exaggeration to claim that, despite residual spiritual beliefs, people in Western societies tend to take a scientific-secular paradigm for granted. This paradigm hinges on the incompatibility of scientific rationality with irrational (i.e., traditional) beliefs. Moreover, the social power of the paradigm is based on the efficaciousness of its technologies. Any incompatibility that is too great will lead to the erosion of support for traditional moral reasoning in the face of technical-scientific rationality. Since biomedicine presents itself as nothing if not rational, the expansion of medical authority in formerly protected institutional spheres seems inevitable.

By the late 1980s medicine had paradoxically become more institutionalized yet more prone to de-institutionalization or institutional change (Clarke et al. 2003, 2010). Many of the medical innovations that ushered in biomedicalization were created by organizational actors whose interests now differed markedly from those of the profession of physicians and other medical professionals. For example, health social movements and advocacy groups, corporations and the state have all worked to erode the hegemony of medical professionals in one way or another. Consequently, much recent institutional change in the health field has been driven by a variety of organizational actors with crosscutting purposes. It is not just the engines of medicalization that have shifted but the project of transforming medicine itself has changed (Clarke et al. 2010). In Greene's chapter, social movement actors appropriated the controversial essential medicines concept and used it to legitimate distributing antiretroviral drugs to fight HIV/AIDS in Africa, while in Samsky's chapter pharmaceutical philanthropists had to surmount public programs already in place which defined the parameters of healthcare provision for onchocerciasis and trachoma. In Cuthbertson's chapter, the state provided free or low-cost treatment for mental health through neoliberal programs that gave pharmaceutical companies unrestricted access to new markets.

In all these cases, the transformation of the medical field has been so thorough that it has taken on a heterogeneous character marked by decentered institutional and organizational governance regimes, greater commodification, new social forms of practice and new forms of subjectivity, among other aspects (Clarke et al. 2003). Importantly, it involves the transformation of the social, political, economic and cultural organization of not only medicine but adjacent societal sectors that provide its resources.

Pharmaceuticalization

This transformation is particularly apparent with respect to the burgeoning power and authority of pharmaceutical medicine. Pharmaceuticalization is a process that emerges from a pharmaceutically informed definition of health and illness. Over the past thirty years pharmaceutical companies and their agents have acquired considerable political, economic and biomedical authority as a result of both increasing market power, and a cultural narrative that promotes pharmaceuticals as central to treatment of health disorders. Pharmaceuticalization is often depicted as a reduction of healthcare to the treatment of disease solely with medicines. Yet, other dimensions of pharmaceuticalization include questions about what constitutes treatment access, what its socioeconomic and political prerequisites are and what its implications are for definitions of health and disease. Samsky describes how mass drug administration in Tanzania is aimed at a community such that the environment becomes pharmaceuticalized in much the same way that earlier sanitation, pesticide and clean water campaigns sought to purge unhealthy areas of disease. Cuthbertson describes another aspect of pharmaceuticalization in which the biomedicalization of public health (depression in this case) is shaped by the alignment and misalignment of the corporate interests of pharmaceutical companies alongside those of the Chilean state.

One question that arises from these chapters is whether pharmaceuticalization is a rationalizing myth that serves to garner society-wide legitimacy for an array of actors with vested interests in this particular form of healthcare delivery (Meyer and Rowan 1991[1977]). The purpose of a rationalizing myth is to explain why efficiency concerns are abandoned in favor of social rules that structure coordination and control activities. Programs, professions and technologies are dependent on socioeconomic and political support such that any set of relevant actors seeking legitimacy will have to show how their enterprise meets societal expectations in these domains. Many of the policies, programs and technologies of biomedicine are enforced by public opinion, depend on constituent support, and are legitimated by the educational system, social prestige and law. For example, in Cuthbertson's research, the Chilean depression patients' experiences of a change in their social status, their biological citizenship, is instructive. This change is based on a burgeoning global taken-for-grantedness of depression as a physiological dysfunction that needs a pharmaceutical corrective, rather than a psychotherapeutic or social one.

Pharmaceuticalization and Access to Medicine

Pharmaceutical treatment has also become institutionalized as a preeminent and often preferred form of healthcare. In these chapters, access is an opening into the impact of pharmaceuticalization processes on changes in the institutional character of healthcare. Healthcare access entails the systemic availability or provision of health-related services as well as an individual's right or opportunity to utilize those services. In addition to an adequate supply of services, economic, organizational, social and cultural factors promote or hinder individuals' capacity to acquire services (Gulliford et al. 2002).

At the heart of contemporary pharmaceutical governance issues is the concept that everyone has a right to medicine. To deny people that right is to deny them not only health but the right to biosocial citizenship. Health is a commodity and an individual goal with attendant social and moral responsibilities. For the psychiatric patients in Cuthbertson's research, receipt of antidepressant medication legitimates their inclusion in the biopolity and secures resources to which they would otherwise not be entitled. Gloria's demand for ECT rather than routine antidepressant medication and Pamela's receipt of a depression diagnosis for an anxiety disorder simply to provide her with free care, however misaligned with her symptoms, are indicators of the taken-for-granted quality of pharmaceutical treatment. Treatment with pharmaceuticals is expected as a matter of course, even when it is resisted, in Gloria's case, or ineffectual, in Pamela's case. For the informants in Samsky's research, health is defined as pharmaceutical access to pills which has an unlikely geographical component – only individuals living in an area targeted for drug control might legitimately assert their right to healthcare treatment, at least for the two illnesses of trachoma and onchocerciasis, even if paradoxically individual diagnosis showed no presence of a disease. In this context, simply being at risk was enough to guarantee membership in that micro biopolity of Morogoro.

Socioeconomic and Political Transformation of the Sector

Pharmaceutical provision is as much a consequence of socioeconomic and political policy serving organizational interests as it is intricately linked with the publics' right to pharmaceuticals. Organizational actors' interests and their ability to make those interests the preeminent concern of the field entails investigation of the struggle between them along the dimensions specified by Clarke et al. (2003).[1]

Rationalization processes also result in fragmented health services because some types of care are less profitable than others (e.g., outpatient care, home health, nursing homes). This results in further stratification of an already hierarchical system of healthcare access and provision. For example, Greene investigates the question of essential medicines (what should be included in the list) to reveal the more divisive questions of access (who should get them) and provision (how should they be allocated). Compounding the questions of who should get essential medicines worldwide and what rules should be put in place to guide production and allocation is the difficulty of identifying which entities should legitimately lay claim to serving global public health. Do the familiar actors of previous epochs, e.g., the WHO, UNRAA and UNICEF best represent the interests of today's global public health sector? What about Health Action International (HAI), Partners in Health and Médecins Sans Frontières (MSF)? More provocatively, should the IFPMA, Pfizer and similar corporate interests be permitted to call themselves global health companies? Which entities would have authority to grant or withhold permission?

The core concept of pharmaceutical therapeutics as essential medicines and the questions it raises in Greene's chapter serves to illuminate how biomedical technologies in the form of drug delivery have become hegemonic processes. The prominence of essential drugs/medicines as a "boundary object" (Star and Griesemer 1989) around which issues of global access and governance unfold, has a history rooted in the very idea of medical supplies, colonialism and the interests of both public and private sector actors in pharmaceutical intervention. The concept of essential medicines emerged as a form of critical discourse. It functioned as a site of contestation initially within Cold War politics of international health and then among actors in the burgeoning global health sector (Greene 2011). No central agent like the WHO consolidated enough power to regulate and control pharmaceuticals. This may be a function of the shifting goals of the WHO as well as the ability of more flexible less bureaucratic organizations to take advantage of the WHO. Instead an array of actor interests growing out of multiple overlapping private, public, public-private institutions, struggle to create and control global access to essential medicines.

Samsky's discussion of drug donation programs reveals the tension between these private and public worlds. Samsky argues that corporate sponsored drug donation programs reformulate the implicitly moral questions of human rights and inequality in light of the more benign but obfuscating technical question of accessibility. Drug donation programs serve as a key emerging technology in global health governance and pharmaceuticalization largely because they maintain the values of neoliberal capitalism in keeping with their for-profit organizational goals. Exploring why they donate medicines at all is a strategic way of understanding why some but not all medicines are donated. Samsky uses two international donation programs, the Mectizan and Zithromax programs, to illustrate these contradictions in corporate sponsored mass drug administration programs. Mectizan is an antiparasitic for livestock and pets that turned out to be an effective treatment for humans with onchocerciasis, a blinding parasitic disease. Zithromax is an effective treatment for trachoma, a blinding eye infection. Both proved to be highly effective when aimed at targeted populations. Samsky's interlocutors give him a range of unclear and somewhat self-serving answers that usually end with a statement about it being the right thing to do. Ironically, they proceed to disparage any discussion with him about ethics when it comes to corporate donation programs. Samsky argues that despite the appearance of providing the longed-for link between the private sector and public health services, these programs simply reaffirm the private-public divide. They do so largely because the issue of pharmaceutical philanthropy is one of property rights that, however efficacious a particular treatment, results in monopolistic practices. As Samsky notes, "the donor corporations give the drug but they keep the authority to determine how it is used, and they certainly keep its patent rights" (2015:130). In his field study of the distribution of these two drugs in the Morogoro region of Tanzania, Samsky discovers that disease, health and treatment tend to become conflated. The very notion of health becomes invisible in the face of intensified surveillance of populations with marked disease prevalence or at risk. Borrowing from Canguilhem (2008), the issue is that:

> "healthy" people, that is people living in areas free from trachoma and onchocerciasis, do not merit free drugs, even if they suffer terribly from other disease, violence, economic privation and other structural ills. "Sick" people living in areas with endemic trachoma or onchocerciasis . . . receive drugs whether they want them or not, and whether or not they individually, personally have the disease. (Samsky 2015:131)

Here is a good example of how pharmaceutical governance operates. It takes the social phenomenon of place of residence, problematizes it with respect to socioeconomic inequities and then organizes its solution to those problems in the form of Ivermectin and Azithromycin regimes.

As the political economy and social structure of biomedicine is transformed by increasing corporatization and commodification, the processes of stratified biomedicalization generate new modes by which medical markets, and therefore social life, are structured, based on any number of individual and group characteristics (Clarke et al. 2003). In these cases explored by Samsky, the relevant characteristic is whether one is an inhabitant of a particular region with a clear community health problem that can be resolved through pharmaceutical intervention. Paradoxically, this translates into one group's greater access to particular medicines through the donation programs' targeting of epidemiological catchment areas, even for those who do not need treatment, while excluding other groups residing beyond those areas that may have significant healthcare needs as well.

Pharmaceutical Governance

One way of understanding the details of how these contests for market advantage, political benefit and popular goodwill emerge is through the kind of fine-grained ethnographic research that Cuthbertson undertakes in her research of Chilean hospitals (2015). Cuthbertson's research explores the micro-level ramifications of the macro- and meso-level processes depicted in Greene's and Samsky's research. As a result of the corporatization of medicine under the flourishing of managed care and the pharmaceutical industry, when patients became patient-consumers, the question of whether pharmaceuticals or some other regimen provides the best treatment is quickly superseded by market concerns.

Cuthbertson's research illustrates the globalization of biomedical mental health models through the explosive growth of antidepressant use in Chile. A key theme here, as in the chapters by Greene and Samsky, is pharmaceutical governance. The idea of pharmaceutical governance is that health problems, diseases, epidemics and the like produce local markets for medical treatments and these local markets are linked to global ones through the medical technologies that are presumed to address the problem (in this case antidepressants). Organizations that mediate between local and global markets are international public organizations such as the WHO, the World Bank, the International Monetary Fund and the United Nations Programme on HIV/AIDS (UNAIDS). Local agencies serve as mediators as well, and their own private-public partnerships have led to greater organizational reach at the meso-level (Clarke et al. 2003). As the state, in the form of its public health agencies, health departments and ministries, seeks to provide healthcare to the populace, novel forms of private-public partnerships emerge. These partnerships are capable of providing better access to pharmaceuticals, which are being demanded by an increasingly knowledgeable and mobilized set of patients, their advocates and other stakeholders. In the case of treatments for depression in Chile, state policy is shaped by expectations attached to the biosocial rights to unrestrained access to antidepressant medication.

The role of corporate interests in pharmaceuticalizing depression provides a fitting example of medico-technological intervention as medical neoliberalism. Antidepressants are the primary form of treatment in this context and Lilly and GlaxoSmithKline representatives serve as beneficent providers offering free doctor's office samples (to stimulate demand), which doctors dispense to indigent patients who by then have come to expect pharmaceutical treatment. The use of free samples (which show up in Cuthbertson's study) to enhance pharmaceutical access is also supplemented by a state-run program (AUGE) that provides free or low-cost treatment for depression (as well as schizophrenia and substance abuse).[2]

One of the key observations in Cuthbertson's work on Chilean psychiatric practices is that the disjuncture between psychiatric symptomatology of the patient and the economic constraints on patient care result in organizational workarounds in which diagnostic practices are undermined because of access problems. For example, the patient Pamela visits Dr Muñoz with symptoms consistent with a diagnosis of an anxiety disorder. The doctor turns to Cuthbertson and remarks that the patient presents with anxiety, she does not have depression and yet "I am diagnosing her with depression for administrative reasons so she can get the drugs for free, because they are otherwise not available to her" (Cuthbertson 2015:145). By expanding markets for antidepressants companies have fostered patient expectations for their products and shaped patient knowledge and identities. This in turn reverts to organizations that realign their policies and infrastructures to meet demand.

Pharmaceutical Philanthropy

Pharmaceutical philanthropy can be understood as an instance in which the ideals of humanism inherent in charity and good works meet those of the commodities market to create new forms and practices. For example, in 2004 Wal-Mart began to provide 300 "basic" prescription drugs for US$4 each (Greene 2011). These included medications for gastrointestinal and heart problems, diabetes, asthma, mental health and thyroid conditions. What is problematic about pharmaceutical philanthropy, according to Greene (2015) and Samsky (2015) is that the question of access to health technologies gets mired in a discussion of what would make for a more efficient pipeline for drug delivery. The real issue is that a host of social structural inequalities that shape health and healthcare access circumscribe that pipeline. These inequalities are intractable because of the extent to which they are embedded in multiple overlapping fields of vested interests which privilege a certain (technical) solution to healthcare provision over others. Thus, donation is problematic in that "to truly engage the social factors that determine the development, production, regulation, distribution, utilization and consumption of essential medicines is to engage with a project of understanding health disparities and the challenges of strengthening complex health systems at the most detailed level" (Greene 2011:29). This is reminiscent of the condemnation of the relatively benevolent public health technocracy that fails to solve world health problems because of its focus on technical solutions and its failure to address infrastructural ones (Farmer 2003).

Conclusion

As these three chapters by Greene, Samsky and Cuthbertson show, the process of institutional change in biomedicine concerning pharmaceutical technologies is discontinuous and uneven. The global political economy and culture both fosters and resists the institutionalization of pharmaceutical technologies. On the one hand are powerful corporate and national economic interests. On the other hand are social movement actors poised to challenge those interests. The burgeoning global society in which corporations like Pfizer and Novartis are hegemonic is challenged by movements like Partners in Health and MSF that have been successful in their resistance to global corporatization.

Greene, Samsky and Cuthbertson show that institutional change in biomedicine, in part, follows from the struggle of actors in the pharmaceutical industry to shape its sociopolitical, jurisdictional, technological, informational and interpersonal dimensions. Organizations such as the WHO, MSF and the IFPMA struggle to determine access and control over field resources. These struggles shape the behaviors of, and socioeconomic, political and health outcomes for, individual, corporate and bureaucratic actors. For these actors, the social and economic logics of their relationships may be crosscutting and surprisingly counterintuitive, especially when we take into account the social context in which seemingly utilitarian maximizing exchanges take place. Pharmaceuticalizing processes and hence governance regimes are thus neither monolithic nor unidirectional. They are even sometimes built on contradictory logics.

Over time pharmaceutical companies and their agents have acquired considerable political economic and biomedical authority as a result of both increasing market power and a cultural narrative that promotes pharmaceuticals as central to treatment of health problems. Since pharmaceuticals are usually manufactured by private for-profit firms they depend on markets that are created by professionals and cater to individuals, vis-à-vis humanitarian rather than monetary concerns. Institutions like medicine, philanthropy and commodities markets have contradictory narratives that govern the actors that create and are subject to them. Greene finds the WHO and its affiliated nongovernmental organizations in the odd position of being compelled to compete with a number of individual and corporate actors, such as the IFPMA, the American Enterprise Institute and the Heritage Foundation, to justify its authority over essential medicines. Individuals and organizations can exploit these tensions to alter the institutional relations of biomedicine. The evolution of essential medicines, the Mectizan and Zithromax Donation Programs, and AUGE in Chile, all demonstrate the extent to which crosscutting alliances and their underlying narratives create, reinforce and sometimes relieve the tension between various institutional actors.

Another way of thinking about the dynamics of pharmaceuticalization is to note that in these three studies, questions about the socioeconomic and political implications of the morality of pharmaceutical access are apparent as they play out at the levels of distribution and consumption. The morality of medicine raised in Greene's chapter concerning essential medicines is about how structural constraints may limit individuals' and groups' access while in Samsky's and Cuthbertson's studies it is about how groups and individuals (respectively) view their own medicine-taking on a moral continuum. With regard to pharmaceutical authority, moral considerations entail that corporations meet societal expectations vis-à-vis the right of access to healthcare in the form of medicines.

As mentioned earlier, policies, programs and technologies of biomedicine are enforced by public opinion and depend on constituent support. Since pharmaceuticals are manufactured by private for-profit firms they depend on markets. However, since they concern public goods, their manufacture is hedged in with putative humanitarian concerns, or at least an accompanying rhetoric that points to the importance of noting those purposes. The requisite of joining a pharmaceutical commodity with a disease and its treatment and inserting that product into the public sphere creates a particular tension that Greene, Samsky and Cuthbertson are well-suited to explicate at various levels of analysis. Greene provides us with the core concept of pharmaceutical therapeutics as essential medicines and the questions it raises serve to illuminate how biomedical technologies in the form of drug delivery have become heterogeneous processes. Samsky's discussion reveals that drug donation programs are implicitly moral questions of human rights and inequality, while Cuthbertson's chapter neatly illustrates how health problems, diseases, epidemics and the like produce local markets for medical treatments that are linked to global ones precisely through the insertion of pharmaceuticals into the public sphere. These studies in sum provide clear evidence for understanding how pharmaceuticals and their agents have acquired their enviable socioeconomic, political and cultural authority. And yet, importantly, they also show how the field of biomedicalization is still in the process of being made and unmade as a host of new forms of socioeconomic and political relations produce a realignment of power relations in the field under the emerging pharmaceuticalization of health.

Notes

1 The first element concerns changes in the political economy of biomedicine. Its research, products and services are becoming increasingly corporatized and privatized, as opposed to state-funded. These products and services themselves are created by technoscientific innovation, which itself is increasingly corporatized and privatized. Health subsequently becomes more commodified and access to healthcare (including pharmaceuticals) is stratified along a number of socioeconomic, political, racial, geographic and gender dimensions. The nature of commodification depends on multinational corporate entities. Globalization of the biomedical model and biomedical processes are core objectives of sector corporations such as those opening markets in pharmaceuticals. Private corporate entities appropriate more areas of the health sector that used to be state-funded, shifting the center of sector governance, management and control away from the public. Ironically, the costs of corporate hegemony are borne by the public as the state underwrites corporate expenditures. In addition, centralization and rationalization of healthcare services through mergers and acquisitions leads to the demise of community, public and not-for-profit agencies.

2 Pharmaceutical and biotechnology firms have always been involved in promoting their products, but this was previously done at the behest of physicians who ultimately prescribed their medicines and technologies. With relaxation of regulations in many countries, pharmaceutical companies have more latitude to market products for off-label uses as well as to market products directly to consumers. Consequently, pharmaceutical companies can create markets for their products without the gatekeeper function of physicians.

References

Banaszak-Holl, Jane, Sandra Levitsky and Mayer Zald, eds. 2010. *Social Movements and the Transformation of American Health Care.* Oxford: Oxford University Press.

Bell, Susan E. and Anne E. Figert. 2012. "Medicalization and Pharmaceuticalization at the Intersections: Looking Backward, Sideways and Forward." *Social Science & Medicine* 75(5):775–83.

Biehl, João G. and Torben Eskerod. 2007. *Will to Live: AIDS Therapies and the Politics of Survival.* Princeton, NJ: Princeton University Press.

Brown, Phil, Stephen Zavestoski, Sabrina McCormick, Brian Mayer, Rachel Morello-Frosch and Rebecca Gasior Altman. 2004. "Embodied Health Movements: New Approaches to Social Movements in Health." *Sociology of Health and Illness* 26:1–31.

Canguilhem, Georges. 2008. "Health: Crude Concept and Philosophical Question." *Public Culture* 20(3):467–77.

Clarke, Adele E., Janet K. Shim, Laura Mamo, Jennifer Ruth Fosket and Jennifer R. Fishman. 2003. "Biomedicalization: Technoscientific Transformations of Health, Illness, and U.S. Biomedicine." *American Sociological Review* 68:161–94.

Clarke, Adele, Laura Mamo, Jennifer Ruth Fosket, Jennifer R. Fishman and Janet K. Shim, eds. 2010. *Biomedicalization: Technoscience, Health, and Illness in the U.S.* Durham, NC: Duke University Press.

Conrad, Peter. 2005. "The Shifting Engines of Medicalization." *Journal of Health and Social Behavior* 46(1):3–14.

Cuthbertson, Courtney A. 2015. "Pharmaceutical Technologies and the Management of Biological Citizens in Chile." Pp. 137–59 in *Reimagining (Bio)Medicalization, Pharmaceuticals and Genetics: Old Critiques and New Engagements*, edited by Susan E. Bell and Anne E. Figert. New York: Routledge.

Farmer, Paul. 2003. *Pathologies of Power: Health, Human Rights, and the New War on the Poor.* Berkeley, CA: University of California Press.

Greene, Jeremy A. 2011. "Making Medicines Essential: the Emergent Centrality of Pharmaceuticals in Global Health." *BioSocieties* 6(1):10–33.

Greene, Jeremy A. 2015. "Vital Objects: Essential Drugs and Their Critical Legacies." Pp. 89–111 in *Reimagining (Bio)Medicalization, Pharmaceuticals and Genetics: Old Critiques and New Engagements*, edited by Susan E. Bell and Anne E. Figert. New York: Routledge.

Gulliford, M., J. Figueroa-Munoz, M. Morgan, D. Hughes, B. Gibson, R. Beech and M. Hudson. 2002. "What Does 'Access to Health Care' Mean?" *Journal of Health Services Research and Policy* 7(3):186–8.

Meyer, John W. and Brian Rowan. 1991[1977]. "Institutionalized Organizations: Formal Structure as Myth and Ceremony." *American Journal of Sociology* 83(2):340–363. (Reprinted in *The New Institutionalism in Organizational Analysis*, edited by Walter W. Powell and Paul J. DiMaggio.)

North, Douglass. 1990. *Institutions, Institutional Change and Economic Performance.* Cambridge: Cambridge University Press.

Phelps, Edmund S. 1985. *Political Economy.* New York: W. W. Norton & Co.

Samsky, Ari. 2015. "The Drug Swallowers: Scientific Sovereignty and Pharmaceuticalization in Two International Drug Donation Programs." Pp. 112–36 in *Reimagining (Bio)Medicalization, Pharmaceuticals and Genetics: Old Critiques and New Engagements*, edited by Susan E. Bell and Anne E. Figert. New York: Routledge.

Scott, W. R. and G. F. Davis. 2010. *Organizations and Organizing: Rational, Natural, and Open System Perspectives.* Upper Saddle River, NJ: Pearson Prentice Hall.

Star, Susan Leigh and James R. Griesemer. 1989. "Institutional Ecology, 'Translations' and Boundary Objects: Amateurs and Professionals in Berkeley's Museum of Vertebrate Zoology, 1907–1939." *Social Studies of Science* 19:387–420.

III
Genetics/Genomics

9
Biomedicalization and the New Science of Race

CATHERINE BLISS

In the 1990s–2000s, developments in genetic science and technology ushered in a new era of DNA research focused on "genomics" – the science of DNA sequences – and a massive drive to create technoscientific medicine for the world. Throughout these developments, debates about race dominated the large-scale sequencing efforts that underpinned research and development in the USA. In particular, the US National Institutes of Health (NIH) led the broadest international efforts to simultaneously characterize human biodiversity with genomics and redefine biomedical understandings of race. In this chapter, I explore how a new medical science conducted under the auspices of Western preoccupations about human difference led to critical developments in biomedicalization, namely new forms of what Rose (2007) calls "technologization" and "responsibilization" – the growth and expansion of technological and moral imperatives in science and society – that have placed the definition and management of an increasing number of social processes in the hands of a narrow corridor of DNA science.

I begin the chapter by discussing the theoretical implications of a race-based and genetics-based biomedicalization associated with classification and identification processes of genetics and race. I then investigate biomedicalization in four domains – racial genome projects, health disparities research, gene–environment research and personal genomics. These four areas cement the appropriation of essentialist notions of life in medical science and their legitimization in public health governance. They also obfuscate the social factors contributing to social processes of race such as institutionalized racism and racial inequality and suggest the dominance of a sociologically inadequate framework for assessing and managing the relationship between health and the environment. Finally, I demonstrate that groups, as much as individuals, are politically disadvantaged by these present developments in biomedicalization, especially around issues of group formation and political advocacy.

Medicalization Meets Racialization

A vast sociological literature has emerged to track the ways medicine has expanded its authority to define and govern social processes (cf. Conrad 1992, 2000; Lock 2004). Studies of medicalization, or "the processes through which aspects of life previously outside the jurisdiction of medicine come to be construed as medical problems," show that these processes are intensifying and being transformed "from the inside out" by new technosciences (Clarke et al. 2003:162). In the present genomic era, medicine is increasingly aimed at personal biology and health, sold to the individual based on privately profiled information and distributed through informatic networks connected to intricate research and health databases (Atkinson, Glasner and Lock 2009; Schnittker 2009; Conrad and Stults 2010; Clarke et al. 2010). Internet-based genetic health communities have sprung up as test-buyers struggle to interpret their personal risk profiles and plan their biological futures (Miah and Rich 2008; Reardon 2009; Rabinow and Rose 2006). Thus, scholars who previously illuminated the rapid expansion of the role of medicine in everyday life via physicians' professional expansion, the rise of health social movements and physicians' organizational claims-making have now shifted to studying the way emerging technosciences are changing the nature of that expansion (Clarke et al. 2003; Conrad 2005). New institutions like the pharmaceutical industry, biotechnology and managed care have become major players in the distribution of medical resources and health policy (Moynihan and Henry 2006; Williams, Gabe and Davis 2008; Pollock 2011). Medicalization is now so technologized that it may be better viewed in some instances as "biomedicalization" (Clarke et al. 2003; also see Bell and Figert 2015, Chapter 1, this volume).

The postwar growth of a molecularized "Biomedical TechnoService Complex" has brought a distinctly genetic form of medicalization (Clarke et al. 2003) – a "geneticization" of social processes in which genetics has become a central lens in interpreting their meaning (Lippman 1991, 1992) and in which genetic findings have displaced prior sociological explanations for those processes (Duster 2006; Goodman 2007). The idea that genetics are responsible for processes like homosexuality or learning disabilities (Hedgecoe 2000; Rapp 2011) has created essentialist notions in the broader society that human traits and behaviors are innate and immutable (Hubbard and Wald 1999; Kay 2000). The development of genetic tests for common traits and behaviors has furthered the belief that individuals must move beyond acknowledgment of their biological destiny and take responsibility for it (Rose 2007). In this environment, the individual management of people's own health through consumptive practices has thus not only ensured but also comes with a moral imperative (Clarke et al. 2003). As Rose argues, the rise of the new genetic sciences ushers in a technologization and responsibilization unlike any seen before:

> For even if no revolutionary advances in treatment are produced, once diagnosed with susceptibilities the asymptomatic individual is enrolled

for a life sentence in the world of medicine – of tests, of drugs, of self-examination and self-definition as a prepatient suffering from a proto-sickness. (Rose 2007:94)

Those that identify as "at-risk" for a specific disease or share a similar chromosomal code are compelled to interact with each other based on their genetic profiles. As they co-manage their somatic selves, new "biosocial" identities arise that are formulated around genetic practices (Rabinow 1996). Such combinations of technologization and responsibilization make for a tenacious form of biomedicalization especially when connected with race.

Racialization is another process that becomes an important aspect to understand in relationship to biomedicalization. Racialization, the process by which social processes are assigned racial meaning, is not new (Omi and Winant 1994). But in the contemporary moment racialization intersects with geneticization and thereby expands biomedicalization's imperative to interpret life as genetically determined and thus in dire need of biomedical expertise. The simultaneous racialization of genetics and the geneticization of race encourages even stronger essentialist forms of categorization – the process by which people are grouped according to perceived similarities in traits and behaviors – and identification – the process by which individuals identify with social categories (Daynes and Lee 2008). In today's world, categories that are ascribed to individuals and groups are reconstituted in stark DNA terms (Bliss 2011; Roberts 2011). Individuals and groups internalize these categories and interact based upon a biologically essentialist notion of what a human is and what their own selves are all about.

In this chapter, I examine the ways classification in public health, government-sponsored industry and the public creates a system in which people are recognized by and recognize themselves in terms of new biomedical technologies of the gene. This analysis reveals an even more autonomized and marketized imperative at play than that witnessed before the genomic turn in which a highly rarified technoscientized corner of the medical profession drives the medicalization of social processes, and individuals and groups are prevented from seeing the social and political conditions affecting their lives (Bliss 2013).

Biomedicalizing Race

In the latter half of the twentieth century, as genetic technologies proliferated and new genetic sciences assumed responsibility for defining race, meanings of race rapidly changed in science and society. Starting in the postwar period, the notion that race was a social and political construction took hold within the sciences, displacing earlier definitions that race was biologically determined (Morning 2011). The policies of Affirmative Action in public institutions and legal protections, and campaigns for inclusion of minorities in public health, created an environment in which race began to be viewed not as a biological difference but in terms of institutionalized discrimination, socioeconomic status and neighborhood effects (Krieger 2011). Yet with the advent of recombinant DNA science in the 1990s, the question of race's biological foundation reemerged (El-Haj 2007). Conceptual debates between evolutionary scientists about the biological foundations of race that had continued to unfold below the radar of major government institutions and the public were once again more publicly debated. Placed within this context, they arose to become public health priorities and policies (Reardon 2005).

The first decade of the twenty-first century witnessed a proliferation of scientific discourse on the biological definition, validity and utility of race (Braun 2002; Hunt and Megyesi 2008; Williams 2011). From the frontiers of genetic science, scientists began exploring how new technologies would affect prior notions of ancestry and evolution (Bliss 2012; Fujimura and Rajagopalan 2011). In addition, public health departments across the world partnered with pharmaceutical and biotech companies in search of new biological models for understanding racial health disparities (Fullwiley 2007a, 2007b; Lee 2007; Whitmarsh 2008). Federal agencies like the NIH and the Food and Drug Administration (FDA) spurred scientific innovation by funding lines for research into racial drug dosage disparities and biomarkers (Bliss 2009), while health organizations co-sponsored race-based clinical trials (Kahn 2012). The consequence of all of these discussions and partnerships was that the social object of race was drawn into the realm of technoscience and medicine, becoming property of the genetic domain and not of social analysis or policymaking.

Nowhere was this shift more apparent than in the burgeoning genetic subfield of genomics. Genomics launched in the late 1980s with a project to map the human genome. At the start of the project, the field did not examine or even debate race (Jackson 2000). Rather, it treated all human DNA as "equal." The Human Genome Project's reference genome was comprised of DNA samples of convenience solicited from various regions of the world (Bliss 2012). In the opening years of the project, its leaders did not participate in public health debates over whether to use federal race standards in research and the clinic (Bliss 2012).

Yet, in the early 1990s, the leading agencies of the US Public Health Department, such as the Department of Health and Human Services (HHS), the NIH and Centers for Disease Control and Prevention (CDC), began to make the implementation of federal race classifications a public health priority. These agencies created policies requiring researchers to use federal race categories in all publicly funded research (NIH 1993; also see CDC 1993; Shim et al. 2015, Chapter 3, this volume). In response, genomic researchers began to reflect on the relevance of race to their science and their science to race. The Human Genome Diversity Project, originally conceived as a diversity-focused complement to the Human Genome Project, criticized genomics for proliferating a dangerous biomedical form of Eurocentrism (Roberts 1992; UNESCO 1994).

The Polymorphism Discovery Resource, formed in 1997 by a cadre of Human Genome Project chief scientists, assumed the federal mandate to create racially apportioned sample sets based on the federal race classifications (Collins, Brooks and Chakravarti 1998). When the leaders of the Human Genome Project began to bring the project to a close in 2000, they started planning the next major global project with project directors from around the world. They decided to base their project for the new millennium, the International HapMap Project, on the same US federal race standards about which genomic science formerly had nothing to say (Bliss 2012). The result was that they established and became the voices of a new science of race.

An important result of the biomedicalization of race was that as scientific projects became racialized and race became geneticized, the moral imperative to biomedicalize race amplified among the elite community of scientists responsible for its biomedicalization. As Eric Lander, leader of the Human Genome and HapMap projects, and founding director of the Broad Institute, Millennium Pharmaceuticals, maintained, "If we shy away and don't record the data for certain populations, we can't be sure to serve those populations medically" (Wade 2001). Lander directed the field into the territory covered by projects like the NIH's US$33 million heart disease study and US$22 million cancer study focused on African Americans, where the imperative to use race in biological terms was not only assumed, but equated with and couched within a language of social justice. Genomic leaders promised to create racial health equity, and thus social equality, through research inclusion. They spoke of inclusion in genome projects as a kind of health-focused Affirmative Action wherein groups would be targeted as racial groups until more personalized medical technologies were available.

The moral imperative rhetoric of the scientists is also apparent in comments made by collaborators in the NIH Pharmacogenomics Research Network. In a series of policy pieces published in the field's flagship journal *Genome Biology* and the *New England Journal of Medicine*, Pharmacogenomics Research Network scientists argued, "A 'race-neutral' or 'colorblind' approach to biomedical research is neither equitable nor advantageous, and would not lead to a reduction in disparities in disease risk or treatment efficacy between groups" (Risch et al. 2002:A17). Like Lander, these pharmaceutically focused project directors popularized the belief "that ignoring race and ethnic background would be detrimental to the very populations and persons that this approach allegedly seeks to protect" (Burchard et al. 2003:1174).

As the field turned its sights toward gene–environment interactions and whole-genome sequencing, more leading scientists echoed the sentiment that biomedicine needed to use race "as a starting point" (Burchard et al. 2003:1174). Amid the launch of two major international sequencing projects, the 1000 Genomes whole-genome sequencing project and the function-mapping ENCODE Project, then-Director of the NIH National Human Genome Research

Institute (NHGRI), Francis Collins, argued that scientists had to take subjects' race into account in order to characterize health and illness:

> We need to try to understand what there is about genetic variation that is associated with disease risk, and how that correlates, in some very imperfect way, with self-identified race, and how we can use that correlation to reduce the risk of people getting sick. (Quoted in Henig 2004)

Collins also claimed that genomics was the field best positioned to study race in an ethical manner:

> I think our best protection against [racist science] – because this work is going to be done by somebody – is to have it done by the best and brightest and hopefully most well attuned to the risk of abuse. That's why I think this has to be a mainstream activity of genomics, and not something we avoid and then watch burst out somewhere from some sort of goofy fringe. (Quoted in Henig 2004)

In launching new projects to the public and arguing for the field's responsibility as a leading science of biomedicine and public health, genome scientists coined a new kind of responsibilization more stringent and essentialist than ever before. From here on, doing something about race would mean not only understanding it from a biomedical perspective, but specifically studying it with DNA science. Genomic leaders posited themselves both as ethical stewards for the public in matters having to do with race and as models for the use of new biomedical knowledge about race in the construction of biomedical apparatuses with public health ramifications (Bliss 2011). They simultaneously created the content of that knowledge and the moral framework for using the knowledge and subsequently publicized it to the world.

Biomedicalizing Disparity

Health disparities research is a related biomedical domain that has experienced racialization matched with a rapid and stark geneticization. When the field of health disparities science arose in the late 1980s and early 1990s (Carter-Pokras and Baquet 2002; Braveman 2006), genomics was busy with its own launch of the Human Genome Project. Just as they initially ignored the institutionalized of federal race categories across US public health in the form of minority inclusion policies in all publicly funded research, the new genetic sciences took no notice of the growing efforts to implement a health disparities framework in biomedical research. Thus disparities research developed with a focus on social epidemiological methodologies and environmental factors, including the critical interrogation of what was then defined as social categories like race (Krieger 2005; James 2009).

Yet, at the close of the Human Genome Project in 2000, the NIH began to reexamine health disparities from a more resolutely biological standpoint by bringing genomic science to bear. The NIH began by mandating minority community consultation in all new genetic studies (NIH 2000) and instituting trans-institute and institute-specific Strategic Research Plans to Reduce and Ultimately Eliminate Health Disparities from a genomic angle (see, for example, NHGRI 2004). These strategic plans effectively geneticized all of the major research funding agencies by stating that the new priority issue of health disparities research would involve the release of funds for genomic research. A total of US$1.3 billion was issued to federal institutes that would dually use a genomics and racial health disparities approach. The HHS and Institute of Medicine (IOM) also put their stamps of approval on the newly minted "health disparities genomics" approach by circulating their own initiatives to eliminate racial and ethnic disparities (HHS 1998; IOM 2002). By 2003, genetics and health disparities were tightly coupled across America's mainstay biomedical institutions.

The characterization and study of health disparities became so ensconced "in the trenches" of emerging genomic science that the HHS turned to the production of race-based medicine as a salve for health inequities. Genome scientists lauded the inclusionary aspects of race-based drug development at the same time as they sung its praises for its potential to save drug makers billions of dollars in clinical trials expenses (Stolberg 2001). As Genaissance Pharmaceuticals' Gualberto Ruaño argued, in a genetically and racially retrofitted biomedicine "efficacy could be proven in small cohorts instead of populations in the thousands" (Weiss 2000:A1). Ruaño and other leading drug makers equated race-based medicine with access to life-saving therapies that racial minorities would otherwise not obtain (also see Goldstein and Weiss 2003).

The FDA has required drug makers to use federal race categories in clinical trials of new drugs since 1998 (see FDA 1998). Yet, its 2005 approval of the race-based medicine BiDil signaled the crystallization of the US government's moral imperative to use technoscience as the ultimate resource for social processes associated with race and inequality even, as I show, at the expense of careful science (Bliss 2013). BiDil is a fixed-dose combination of a generic antihypertensive and a generic vasodilator that was developed solely for use in people of African descent. The ethics of this more expensive combination of two safe and efficacious generics was debated immediately (Kahn 2012). However, after a blacks-only randomized clinical trial demonstrated a 43 percent relative one-year mortality decrease in research subjects, the drug was slated for approval without further debate or research (Temple and Stockbridge 2007).

BiDil's "success" cannot be attributed to a successful race-based clinical trial, because drug makers had already proved that its components worked in all populations. BiDil was successful for the same reasons of responsibilization witnessed in the case of racial genome projects, where scientists appropriated social justice language and targeted racial advocacy groups to popularize their products. BiDil's makers were able to recruit the most powerful race-based advocacy organizations to support their cause, thereby sedimenting the moral imperative to biomedicalize health disparities and race across governance and within the public (Rusert and Royal 2011).

Throughout its clinical trials, representatives of the National Association for the Advancement of Colored People (NAACP), the Association of Black Cardiologists and the premiere African American health advocacy organization, the National Medical Association, publicized the benefits BiDil would have for rectifying racial health disparities. The NAACP went so far as to donate US$1.5 million to BiDil's maker, NitroMed, for three years of exploratory health disparities research (Rusert and Royal 2011). As BiDil's principal scientist and patent-holder, Jay Cohn, remarked, revealing the prevailing sentiment in science, public health and the extant advocacy leadership:

> Here we have the black community accepting the concept that African Americans need to be studied as a group, and then we have the science community claiming that race is dead ... It seems to me absolutely ludicrous to suggest that this prominent characteristic that we all recognize when we look at people should not be looked at. (Quoted in Stolberg 2001)

Cohn's statement exposed the extent to which scientists, policymakers and the public supported the biomedicalization of health disparities. To them, race-based pharmacogenomics was the most race-aware weapon against health disparities, and thus the only truly socially responsible choice in addressing social processes of inequality.

In the wake of BiDil's 2005 approval, the FDA and the American College of Medical Genetics have petitioned drug makers to reanalyze their blockbuster drugs – drugs that make over US$1 billion in revenue per year – using federal race categories. The HHS has also partnered with a range of regulatory agencies, health justice groups and community-based organizations in support of race-based medicine (Kahn 2013). Statements from a representative of the National Minority Health Month Foundation further express the moral tone of this position:

> Underrepresentation of African Americans in clinical studies might partially explain the development of a standard treatment for heart failure that has proved to be less effective for them ... Race may be the coarsest of discriminators, but it now has proven life saving potential for heart-failure patients. The evidence that convinced the FDA predicts a dramatic increase in black patients' survival rate. (Puckrein 2006:371–2)

Racial advocacy organizations have since further coalesced in support of accepted biomedical definitions of race and set their political sights on fighting disparities from a biomedical angle. Exclusion from genomics research has become the new target of minority justice campaigns.

Even racial advocates most known for their work on the sociological factors that contribute to inequality have come on board the genomics bandwagon. In a spate of mini-series and television shows, famed African American Studies scholar Henry Louis Gates, Jr has featured race-based genomics in his recent efforts to draw critical attention to racial inequality in the USA. Gates first loaned his intellectual and political celebrity to a two-part mini-series that mapped the genealogies of famous African Americans, called "African American Lives."[1] This series popularized genetic ancestry tests that assign continental origins to personal DNA, thereby creating a racial DNA profile with which to redefine a person's racial ancestry in genetic terms. Gates has since launched his own line of genetic ancestry tests that he has used for his prime-time television series "Faces of America."[2] Gates is also a board member of a pharmacogenomics company that targets diseases in people of African descent. Gates has not only put his money where his mouth is, but also put his body into his message, becoming the first African American to have his whole genome sequenced. Gates' efforts illuminate how the moral imperative associated with contemporary constructions of race and disparity reconfigures biomedicalization in deeply essential ways that draw on a personal and individual sense of responsibility (Bliss 2013).

Commodification has also proven fundamental to the new biomedicalization, as scientists whose research or products are simultaneously academic, industry and government sponsored have created therapies and technologies that they characterize as social justice weapons and use across these domains in the service of profit to biomedical and pharmaceutical companies. Successful political framing of therapies and technologies like BiDil generates chains of legitimacy, authority and monetary gain (Bliss 2013). For example, when another "blacks only" clinical trial of the race-based pharmacogenomic beta-blocker Bystolic showed efficacy in a study population of self-identified blacks, the FDA approved its maker, Forest Pharmaceuticals, for further race-specific trials of Mexican Americans. Forest Pharmaceuticals then went on to file a number of race-specific patents for new drug applications (Kahn 2009). The president of the Association of Black Cardiologists, Paul Underwood, would later herald the Association's support for Bystolic, stating: "We're excited to add another therapeutic tool to the armamentarium in the treatment of high blood pressure in African-Americans" (British Cardiovascular Society 2012). The Association of Black Cardiologists and other minority advocacy groups have continued to petition insurance companies to place race-based medicine on their formularies, and target minority physicians to prescribe them.

The result of all of this is that a number of international bioethics advocates have now asked pharmaceutical companies to create race-based medicine for the developing world as a stopgap solution to what they refer to as the growing "genomic divide" between regimes in the global North and South. Some have even voiced support for drug makers to investigate "whether their unsuccessful chemical combinations [can be] resuscitated" and repackaged for distribution in markets of the global South (Daar and Singer 2006). These ethicists recommend racial analysis "to perform a sort of economic triage to focus on those for whom the test is most likely to produce a useful result" (Kahn 2009:82). Framing race-based drugs as a necessary shortcut to leveling the playing field, they encourage the fight for rights and resources through the further production and consumption of pharmacogenomics. Such neoliberal strategies plug racialization and geneticization into uneven market dynamics, effectively allowing market forces to determine how health disparities will be handled and how race will be defined.

All these changes create a highly racialized transnational biomedical system, replete with racialized databases, protocols and standards in the service of biomedicalization – a system in which the questions asked and answers sought are entirely focused on the body. The sociological concerns with transgenerational health effects, institutionalized forms of discrimination and social environments disappear from the research and debate. The quality of food supplies in various neighborhoods, discrimination-related stress, access to jobs with clean and safe working environments and items that cannot fit on a genomic "microarray" assay are but some of the issues that are pushed out from under the scientific gaze of biogenetics.

This new form of biomedicalization also means that systemic racialization and geneticization are more than the scientific sum of their parts. Social processes associated with health disparities and racial inequality are not only cast as race-related or genetic, they are imbued with a technologization and responsibilization that only allow for genomic biomedical solutions, such as pills and genetic tests. Neither the state nor the public holds any responsibility for health disparities in this moral framework beyond facilitating the work of genomic science. Government agencies fund it, while the public consumes it. Genomics is the great fixer.

Biomedicalizing the Environment

The combined racialization and geneticization of race, and conceptions and approaches to health disparities research, have implicated another object of biomedicalization: that of the environment. The past decade witnessed a turn in genomic science toward study of gene–environment interactions, epigenetics and translational medicine (see Richardson and Stevens 2014). Just as public health agencies increasingly prioritized the study of race and health disparities from a genetic perspective, federal mandates came to highlight the need to fund research that examines genes in context (HHS 2011, 2012). Yet, with the continuing emphasis on funding health disparities genomics approaches, gene–environment research has only served to divest in studying the environment, in ways that further the authority of the genomic profession and detract from social and political forms of knowledge, actions and policies.

The major large-scale sequencing gene–environment projects and funding mechanisms of the US public health establishment's leading health disparities genomics initiatives are cases in point. The Gene–Environment Initiative, initiated by the HHS in 2006 (NIH 2007), and its National Human Genome Research Institute branch, GENEVA, touts "pathways to disparities in health outcomes" as one of its three foundational aims (GENEVA 2012; HHS 2012). However, its objects of analysis are genetic variants and epigenetic pathways, garnered from genome-wide association and whole-genome sequencing technology. Nowhere do these projects examine social hierarchies, the politics of race or institutionalized discrimination.

Similarly, The NIH Common Fund, the central trans-institute administration that was initially launched to bring genomic funding to all federal health institutes, has also issued funding strategies that prioritize projects that take a genomic tack in studying noncommunicable chronic diseases that exhibit a disparity between whites and blacks. For example, its cornerstone project, the Synthetic Cohort for the Analysis of Longitudinal Effects of Gene–Environment Interactions, targets three diseases for health disparities gene–environment research – diabetes, hypertension and prostate cancer – and supports a range of projects that include what genomicists refer to as "next generation sequencing" (see FUSION, FBPP and C-GEMS partnerships in NIH 2012). Again, these studies all seek to apply novel sequencing technologies to the question of genetic determinants of health in ways that stay intricately tied to the body.

Even the most systems-biological and developmental approaches with which the NIH rationalizes its gene–environment approach to health disparities genomics allude to the environment, but do not provide guidance for its analysis. The NIH states:

> [E]nvironmental exposures are varied … Disadvantaged populations may experience greater exposure to these hazards and exhibit higher rates of disease incidence, morbidity and mortality. Understanding and modulating this risk in humans during critical windows of development offers the promise of primary prevention for many of these [noncommunicable chronic diseases] and may result in reducing health disparities. (NIH 2012)

While this statement makes clear that trans-institute projects must include a biomedical health disparities component to their gene–environment and epigenetic programs, it does not require measures for exposure that go beyond analysis of biomarkers (see Shostak and Moinester 2015, Chapter 11, this volume). The NIH instead argues that epigenetics and intrauterine interactions communicate the necessary information about the environment in the context of developmental or systems biology approaches (also see HHS 2012).

In 2010, the NIH hosted a Global Health Research Meeting wherein gene–environment research was lauded as the basis of a new global health science that would eradicate the polarization between the global North and South. The meeting's participants, a veritable Who's Who of biomedicine, listed "RNAi, small molecule screening, genomics of pathogens, and vaccine development" as the world's biggest hopes for global health equity (NIH 2010). Microbiomics, epigenetics and genomic health disparities research were their newly minted "Priority Areas." DNA technologies of the gene were the only strategies discussed for understanding the environment–gene interaction.

The HHS has since backed up its aims with the launch of the first gene–environment international sequencing project, the Human Health and Heredity in Africa Project, or "H³Africa." Launched in 2010 by the NIH and UK Wellcome Trust, H³Africa sponsors research into functional genomics in order to reduce the communicable and noncommunicable disease burden in populations of African descent. A recent 2013 examination of the research that it has thus far funded shows that only one study has measured an environmental variable that is not associated with genetic markers (Bliss 2014).

The biomedicalization of the environment is inextricably linked to the institutionalization of the biomedicalization of race and health disparities. Since 2003, the NIH has funded Centers for Population Health and Health Disparities programs across the USA. By 2008, five centers had been funded and ten more were scheduled (HHS 2007). In the award's funding opportunity announcement reissue we see the slippage from environment to biological metrics:

> The first funding period of the [Centers for Population Health and Health Disparities] Program has enabled us to understand the persistence of health disparities and to begin to identify approaches to address these inequities . . . Some of these studies have begun to explain how the social and built environments impact biological processes, such as epigenetic modifications, gene expression, endocrine function, inflammation, tumor growth, and cancer-related health outcomes. These types of information are crucial in developing appropriate prevention, early detection, and treatment intervention programs to mitigate cancer disparities. (NIH 2009)

These multimillion dollar institutional awards only fund studies that utilize the latest DNA sequencing technologies to characterize health disparities in terms of biological functions.

Also since 2003, the NHGRI, Department of Energy and National Institute for Child Health and Human Development have funded Centers of Excellence in Ethical, Social and Legal Issues Research. This institutional funding program initially provided over US\$20 million in grants to study issues such as breast cancer and asthma in people of African descent, and has since funded a number of research centers focused on gene–environment research into diabetes, prostate cancer and sickle cell anemia in minority communities. From the outset, Centers of Excellence in Ethical, Social and Legal Issues research sites were envisioned to be hubs of gene–environment health disparities genomics research. Yet, the award has focused on facilitating the spread of the new genetic sciences to new populations by way of increasing access to genomic information, increasing minority community support for genomics and exploring informed consent and decision-making in the absence of a broader understanding of the relationship between environmental contexts and health. Provisions have not been made for sociological research of the built environment in these awards.

Finally, the HHS has established two intramural federal research centers entirely focused on health disparities gene–environment research. In 2007, the NIH inaugurated the Intramural Center for Health Disparities Genomics, now renamed as the Center for Research on Genomics and Global Health. The center began by focusing its gene–environment studies on people of African descent. Today it focuses its efforts more broadly on epigenomics in minority populations. The CDC also established the Office of Public Health Genomics "to convey the importance of engaging communities, investing in [community-based public research] and ensuring that social justice be central to public health genomics" (CDC 2011). In 2011, the office stated racial stratification as one of its foci of gene–environment inquiry.

Taken together, these institutions have steered and ensured the biomedicalization of the environment and moved away from the study of sociological factors. They also standardized racialization and geneticization across American public health. Finally, the sheer amount of funding available for analysis of environments (far outranking other funding mechanisms such as social and behavioral funding offered by the National Science Foundation and other public agencies), has produced a world in which social epidemiologists and other biomedical and nonmedical experts of the built environment must align with genomic science or trade in their nongenomic approaches for genomic expertise.

Biomedicalizing Ancestry

These three instances of biomedicalization dovetail with the burgeoning consumer market of ancestry, or the recreational pursuit of personal genealogy. Through a series of academic-industry partnerships and enterprises, genome scientists have sold racialized and geneticized interpretations of select sequences of consumer DNA, making ancestry and any politicization around it a matter of personal DNA and genomic expertise. Since the turn of the millennium, leading genomic scientists have worked to transfer foundational population-defining technologies such as mitochondrial DNA and Y-chromosome technologies, which assess the non-recombinant portions of the genome, to the private sector in the form of ancestry tests. One type of test that has dominated the market is the *haplogroup test*. Since haplogroup tests are only able to report on the consumer's maternal or paternal lineage – a mere 2 percent of an individual's ancestry – companies have specifically capitalized off of a client base of African Americans and others who have limited records of their more distant family history. Another popular ancestry test relies on a technology called *admixture mapping*. In admixture mapping, companies select a set of ancestry informative markers, or "AIMs" – gene variants that present approximately 30 percent more frequently in one continental population – and create panels with which to assign admixture profiles. Admixture mapping can also be conducted on groups of samples using principle-components software.

The first genetic genealogy companies on the market positioned themselves as biomedical experts who had the key to knowledge about ancestry that traditional historical genealogy did not have. Companies established a pattern of promising to unlock customers' questions about their biological core, while providing the tools to recreate the public personae, social ties and political narratives about which identity-based groups have raised consciousness (Bolnick et al. 2008; Nelson 2008a, 2008b). Oxford Ancestors, an early company on the scene, characterized itself as the only expert team in the world that could explain ancestral lineages of the British Isles (Sykes 2002). Its founder, Oxford University geneticist Bryan Sykes, released tests alongside a series of bestselling books designed to aid consumers in reading the "truth" of their DNA (Sykes 2002, 2007a, 2007b). Other companies, such as the American firm, African Ancestry, Inc., offered "Certificates of Ancestry," and developed online social networking Web forums to legitimize consumer belief in the meaning and significance of their tests.

The routinization of the genomic technologies used in scientific labs across the world opened the possibility of decoupling the racialization and geneticization associated with modern genomics by generating populations based on statistical clustering instead of using lay or even governmental racial categories. Yet, although companies marketed their ancestry tests as keys to a person's true self, they built business models that used emerging technologies to recode consumer data in racial terms. Companies with names like "African DNA" and "DNA Tribes" not only used mitochondrial DNA and Y-chromosome tests to determine haplogroup membership, but they imparted a racial connotation by interpreting haplogroup affiliation in terms of continental race (e.g., "African" and "tribal") (Bliss 2013). Other companies like Roots for Real, a European company that targets African American root seekers, and DNAPrint Genomics, an American company known for its forensic technologies that have been used by police agencies around the world, marketed their admixture tests as indicative of unknown racial ancestry (Roberts 2011; Bliss 2012). Companies were thus not only positing tests as better than historical or genealogical knowledge, but they were also positing them as better than social knowledge.

In fact, from the outset, companies portrayed their tests as tools useful for consumers who would like to change or confirm their racial identity. For example, DNAPrint Genomics acquired the indigenous American forensics company Trace Genetics, Inc., so that it could be the leading firm to test for Native American tribal membership. Many companies advertised to people who suspected they had indigenous American origins in order to sell them proof of this "biological citizenship." For example, DNAPrint claimed its tests could produce credentials with which to register for tribal membership so that nonmembers could petition for resources from tribal councils or the US government (TallBear and Bolnick 2004). DNAPrint Genomics also encouraged clients to use their personal ancestry reports to petition for Affirmative Action consideration and to inform medical decision-making (TallBear and Bolnick 2004). By 2006, Oxford Ancestors and African Ancestry followed suit (Harmon 2006). In encouraging consumers to take advantage of an affirmative action policy or a legacy clause, or to use their newfound ancestral profiles to support their college admissions, these companies more tightly coupled the ensuing racialization and geneticization in biomedicine's new realms, pushing yet another brick into the wall of a social justice ethics based on DNA code. To date there have been no published statistics on how many genetic genealogy consumers use tests to this end, but in 2006 *The New York Times* ran an article exposing the practice (Harmon 2006). The article demonstrated that companies were encouraging customers to associate their reported ancestry with governmental classifications by using federal classifications to represent their test findings.

In their marketing of ancestry tests, companies have also more systematically relied on racial models that embed the foundations of genomic technology. While companies have purported to target the individual by tailoring genomic knowledge to the individual consumer's personal DNA, all have offered medical readings of consumer DNA. They have also made probabilistic claims about the individual's genome based on the body of genome-wide association literature that uses the racial terms of the global genome projects. Many companies have even required consumers to affiliate themselves with a preestablished racial group before running the tests in order to triage their analyses. In all cases, consumers have either had their results read or have had to actively read their results through a racial rubric.

Still, the clearest way that ancestry has been biomedicalized is in the move from traditional genealogy practices to the creation of online DNA racial "families." As companies have opened up databases and social networking platforms to encourage socializing and launched products that match "genetic cousins" in their databases, consumers have moved racial organizing, socializing and health advocacy online. In 2011, the Google-backed personal genomics company 23andMe – a firm that also reports personal genetic susceptibilities data by race – launched a race-specific research campaign "Roots into the Future." Roots into the Future challenged African Americans to "Be part of a 10,000 person movement to power genetic research for African Americans" (23andMe 2013). The project promised to create a black database within its research branch, 23andWe, to spur race-focused medicine and technologies. 23andMe partnered with the founders of AfricanDNA and African Ancestry, Inc., to foster a new era of bioinformatic social organizing. "Roots into the Future" set a precedent for linking direct-to-consumer marketing, a commodified version of personal genomics, with calls for the altruistic lending of one's personal DNA for a racial cause.

The availability of these new personal genealogy tools and racial political forums has not displaced prior forms of root-seeking (Nelson 2014). However, it has succeeded in infiltrating the domains where historical genealogy is used, serving as a supplement to historical claims. It has also succeeded in gaining entrance into minority community centers, where academic-industry partners and science "reps" and advisors have garnered new markets for their research and community support for their biomedical enterprises (Bliss 2012).

Biomedicalization thus has serious consequences for racial and personal identity processes. Sociological research on race has established that identity is made and remade through a dialectic of classification and identification (Omi and Winant 1994; Brubaker 2009; Daynes and Lee 2008). Individuals see themselves in terms of the social categories ascribed to them. Groups form around shared conceptions, practices, treatment and experiences. Against this knowledge, in the current climate, racial classifications are conceived as entirely inherent in the unchanging DNA code with which a person is born. Their ideas, experiences and action are to be interpreted in terms of the genetic ancestral cluster a particular technology assigns them. Their sense of belonging to a group thus forms around an idea of innate biology. With genetic race as the official classification frame, and the guiding framework for biomedicine, the most authoritative notions of identity become synonymous with innate biology.

As seen in the discussion above, individuals are affected, but so are groups. New racialized groups are formed through virtual participation and membership instead of social action, activism and collective experience. Groups align with and through genomic science. Thus, the responsibility for group formation is relinquished to genomic scientists, or the uppermost elite experts of DNA science. People in racial groups will know no more about the basis of their groupness than the aggregate designations of membership that genomic scientists have provided them.

This model of genetic "groupness" biomedicalizes former conceptions of relatedness, such as familial and communal notions of connectedness, on a political level as well (cf. TallBear and Bolnick 2004; TallBear 2008). Even racial groups that have traditionally put a high value on cultural and familial kinship are turning to DNA and replacing former notions of social connectedness. In the case of Native American polities, which typically require proof of familial descent from one or more registered grandparents, or some proportion of maternal or paternal lineage, genomic ancestry tests have become a new way of evaluating kinship (TallBear 2013). Some of these polities have publicly encouraged individuals to use tests as proof of membership in order to amplify numbers and gain US Bureau of Indian Affairs recognition, or to limit the circulation of tribal resources to genetic nonmembers (TallBear and Bolnick 2004). Genetic proof and biological citizenship are fully equated and encouraged or required.

Conclusion

In this chapter, I have shown that new intersections between geneticization and racialization are creating new domains of biomedicalization – the biomedicalization of race, disparity, environment and ancestry – but also a new *form* of biomedicalization itself. Because today's biomedicalization is based on DNA technoscience, it creates more fixed and essentialized notions of racial identity and difference. Further, it puts the onus of responsibility on genomic scientists to interpret inequality and the social environment in DNA terms, and on individuals to manage their biological predestination with DNA solutions. It also shifts debates about societal impacts on healthcare disparities to the province of science and scientists.

The result of the four strands of biomedicalization discussed in this chapter is that basic politics, such as articulating and petitioning for equal rights, increasingly filter through genomics. The field is continually providing new biomedical angles for social justice, which governments are adopting as frontline weapons against inequality. Leading advocates are accepting pharmaceuticals and biotechnologies as solutions to the social ills that their constituents face. They are replacing talk of broader environmental and social factors of racial inequality with drug-seeking advocacy for individual constituents potentially affected by diseases characterized as racial. Genetic claims about race increasingly serve as the dominant language and the dominant framework for understanding and managing inequality in biomedicine, public health and the wider public sphere.

The new biomedicalization results in an individualization of identity and groupness and a depoliticization of advocacy. Accessing rights shifts from being a matter of political participation to scientific participation, specifically DNA science participation. That these changes in politics are attached to the construction of racial meaning only serves to reify essentialist notions that DNA is the key to understanding individuals, groups and disparities between them, and the social and built environment. Genetics is the arbiter of a person's race and a person's environmental experience.

These developments have important consequences for how individuals conceptualize race, and thereby interact based on race, but also for groups' formation and deliberation. For individuals, political action around race is geneticized and individualized at the level of demands pertaining to personal DNA. Taking genetic tests and buying pharmacogenomics become personal priorities. For some groups, making tests and drugs readily available to their constituents become political priorities. Furthermore, group affiliation via DNA identification comes to serve as the indication of legitimate membership. For both groups and individuals personal experience and political organizing around shared social experiences recede. Thus even collective disputation is individualized and made real in terms of DNA. In sum, changing forms of technologization and responsibilization make for a powerful biomedicalization in which alternative social relations and conceptualizations are pushed out in favor of a highly specialized framework of expertise.

Acknowledgments

My deepest gratitude goes to Troy Duster and Phil Brown for careful mentorship of the research and writing process. Thanks are also due to Anne Figert and Susan Bell for their astute stewardship of this volume. This research was supported by the National Science Foundation, Andrew Mellon Foundation and Howard Hughes Medical Foundation.

Notes

1   www.pbs.org/wnet/aalives/ (accessed March 31, 2012).
2   www.pbs.org/wnet/facesofamerica/ (accessed March 31, 2012).

References

23andMe. 2013. "Roots into the Future." Accessed April 12, 2013 (www.23andme.com/roots/).
Atkinson, P., P. E. Glasner and M. M. Lock. 2009. *Handbook of Genetics and Society: Mapping the New Genomic Era*. New York: Routledge.
Bell, Susan E. and Anne E. Figert. 2015. "Moving Sideways and Forging Ahead: Reimagining '-Izations' in the Twenty-First Century." Pp. 19–40 in *Reimagining (Bio)Medicalization, Pharmaceuticals and Genetics: Old Critiques and New Engagements*, edited by Susan E. Bell and Anne E. Figert. New York: Routledge.
Bliss, C. 2009. "Genome Sampling and the Biopolitics of Race." Pp. 322–9 in *A Foucault for the 21st Century: Governmentality, Biopolitics and Discipline in the New Millennium*, edited by S. Binkley and J. Capetillo. Cambridge, MA: Cambridge Scholars Publishing.
Bliss, C. 2011. "Racial Taxonomy in Genomics." *Social Science & Medicine* 73(7):1019–27.
Bliss, C. 2012. *Race Decoded: The Genomic Fight for Social Justice*. Stanford, CA: Stanford University Press.
Bliss, C. 2013. "The Marketization of Identity Politics." *Sociology* 47(5):1011–25.
Bliss, C. 2014. "Defining Health Justice in the Postgenomic Era." Pp. 271–96 in *Postgenomics*, edited by S. S. Richardson and H. Stevens. Durham, NC: Duke University Press.
Bolnick, D. A., D. Fullwiley, J. Marks, S. M. Reverby, J. Kahn, K. TallBear . . . and P. Ossorio. 2008. "The Legitimacy of Genetic Ancestry Tests – Response." *Science* 319(5866):1039–40.

Braun, L. 2002. "Race, Ethnicity, and Health: Can Genetics Explain Disparities?" *Perspectives in Biology and Medicine* 45(2):159–74.

Braveman, P. 2006. "Health Disparities and Health Equity: Concepts and Measurement." *Annual Review of Public Health* 27(1):167–94.

British Cardiovascular Society. 2012. "Beta-blocker for Blacks Is Effective." *British Cardiovascular Society.* Accessed July 16, 2012 (www.bcs.com/pages/news_full.asp?NewsID=2228).

Brubaker, R. 2009. "Ethnicity, Race, and Nationalism." *Annual Review of Sociology* 35:21–42.

Burchard, E. G., E. Ziv, N. Coyle, S. L. Gomez, H. Tang, A. J. Karter, J. L. Mountain, E. J. Pérez-Stable, D. Sheppard and N. Risch. 2003. "The Importance of Race and Ethnic Background in Biomedical Research and Clinical Practice." *New England Journal of Medicine* 348(12): 1170–5.

Carter-Pokras, O. and C. Baquet. 2002. "What Is a 'Health Disparity'?" *Public Health Reports* 117(5):426–34.

CDC. 1993. *Use of Race and Ethnicity in Public Health Surveillance Summary of the CDC/ATSDR Workshop.* Accessed October 7, 2014 (www.cdc.gov/mmwr/preview/mmwrhtml/00021729. htm).

CDC. 2011. "Public Health Genomics." Accessed November 1, 2013 (www.cdc.gov/genomics/).

Clarke, A. E., J. K. Shim, L. Mamo, J. R. Fosket and J. R Fishman. 2003. "Biomedicalization: Technoscientific Transformations of Health, Illness, and US Biomedicine." *American Sociological Review* 68:161–94.

Clarke, Adele, Laura Mamo, Jennifer Ruth Fosket, Jennifer R. Fishman and Janet K. Shim, eds. 2010. *Biomedicalization: Technoscience, Health, and Illness in the U.S.* Durham, NC: Duke University Press.

Collins, F. S., L. D. Brooks and A. Chakravarti. 1998. "A DNA Polymorphism Discovery Resource for Research on Human Genetic Variation." *Genome Research* 8(12):1229–31.

Conrad, P. 1992. "Medicalization and Social Control." *Annual Review of Sociology* 18(1):209–32.

Conrad, P. 2000. "Medicalization, Genetics, and Human Problems." Pp. 322–33 in *Handbook of Medical Sociology*, edited by C. E. Bird, P. Conrad and A. M. Fremont. Upper Saddle River, NJ: Prentice Hall.

Conrad, P. 2005. "The Shifting Engines of Medicalization." *Journal of Health and Social Behavior* 46(1):3–14.

Conrad, P. and C. Stults, 2010. "The Internet and the Experience of Illness." Pp. 179–91 in *Handbook of Medical Sociology,* edited by C. E. Bird, P. Conrad, A. M. Fremont and S. Timmermans. Vanderbilt, TN: Vanderbilt University Press.

Daar, A. S. and P. A. Singer. 2006. "Ethics and Geographical Ancestry: Implications for Drug Development and Global Health." *UNESCO* 6(3):77.

Daynes, S. and O. Lee. 2008. *Desire for Race.* Cambridge and New York: Cambridge University Press.

Duster, T. 2006. "Comparative Perspectives and Competing Explanations: Taking on the Newly Configured Reductionist Challenge to Sociology." *American Sociological Review* 71(1):1–15.

El-Haj, N. A. 2007. "The Genetic Reinscription of Race." *Annual Review of Anthropology* 36(1): 283–300.

FDA. 1998. *Investigational New Drug Applications and New Drug Applications.*

Fujimura, J. H. and R. Rajagopalan. 2011. "Different Differences: The Use of 'Genetic Ancestry' versus Race in Biomedical Human Genetic Research." *Social Studies of Science* 41(1):5–30.

Fullwiley, D. 2007a. "Race and Genetics: Attempts to Define the Relationship." *BioSocieties* 2:221–37.

Fullwiley, D. 2007b. "The Molecularization of Race: Institutionalizing Human Difference in Pharmacogenetics Practice." *Science as Culture* 16(1):1–30.

GENEVA. 2012. "GENEVA Study Overview." Accessed September 30, 2012 (www.genevastudy.org/ StudyOverview).

Goldstein, A. and R. Weiss. 2003. "Howard U. Plans Genetics Database." washingtonpost.com. Accessed September 30, 2012 (www.washingtonpost.com/ac2/wp-dyn/A46122-2003 May27?language=printer).

Goodman, A. 2007. *Presidential Address.* Accessed March 31, 2012 (www.aaanet.org/president. htm).

Harmon, A. 2006. "Seeking Ancestry in DNA Ties Uncovered by Tests." *The New York Times* April 12. Accessed September 30, 2012 (www.nytimes.com/2006/04/12/us/12genes.html).

Hedgecoe, A. M. 2000. "The Popularization of Genetics as Geneticization." *Public Understanding of Science* 9(2):183–9.

Henig, R. M. 2004. "The Genome in Black and White (and Gray)." *The New York Times* October 10. Accessed September 30, 2012 (www.nytimes.com/2004/10/10/magazine/10GENETIC.html).

HHS. 1998. *Healthy People 2010 Objectives: Draft for Public Comment.* HHS, Office of Public Health and Science.

HHS. 2007. HHS Strategic Plan, 2007–2012. Accessed September 30, 2012 (http://aspe.hhs.gov/hhsplan/2007/).

HHS. 2011. "FY 2012 President's Budget for HHS." Accessed September 30, 2012 (www.hhs.gov/about/hhsbudget.html).

HHS. 2012. "FY 2013 President's Budget for HHS." Accessed September 30, 2012 (www.hhs.gov/budget/).

Hubbard, R. and E. Wald. 1999. *Exploding the Gene Myth: How Genetic Information is Produced and Manipulated by Scientists, Physicians, Employers, Insurance Companies, Educators, and Law Enforcers.* Boston, MA: Beacon Press.

Hunt, L. M. and M. S. Megyesi. 2008. "The Ambiguous Meanings of the Racial/Ethnic Categories Routinely Used in Human Genetics Research." *Social Science & Medicine* 66(2):349–61.

IOM. 2002. "Unequal Treatment: Confronting Racial and Ethnic Disparities in Health Care." *Institute of Medicine.* Accessed April 24, 2014 (www.iom.edu/Reports/2002/Unequal-Treatment-Confronting-Racial-and-Ethnic-Disparities-in-Health-Care.aspx).

Jackson, F. L. C. 2000. "Anthropological Measurement: The Mismeasure of African Americans." *The ANNALS of the American Academy of Political and Social Science* 568(1):154–71.

James, S. A. 2009. "Epidemiologic Research on Health Disparities: Some Thoughts on History and Current Developments." *Epidemiologic Reviews* 31(1):1–6.

Kahn, J. 2009. "Beyond BiDil: The Expanding Embrace of Race in Biomedical Research and Product Development." *Saint Louis University Journal of Health, Law, and Public Policy* 3:61–92.

Kahn, J. 2012. *Race in a Bottle: The Story of BiDil and Racialized Medicine in a Post-genomic Age.* New York: Columbia University Press.

Kahn, J. 2013. "The Politics of Framing Health Disparities: Markets and Justice." Pp. 25–38 in *Mapping "Race": Critical Approaches to Health Disparities Research,* edited by L. E. Gómez and N. López. Piscataway, NJ: Rutgers University Press.

Kay, L. E. 2000. *Who Wrote the Book of Life?: A History of the Genetic Code.* Stanford, CA: Stanford University Press.

Krieger, N. 2005. "Stormy Weather: Race, Gene Expression, and the Science of Health Disparities." *American Journal of Public Health* 95(12):2155–60.

Krieger, N. 2011. *Epidemiology and the People's Health: Theory and Context.* Oxford: Oxford University Press.

Lee, S. S. 2007. "The Ethical Implications of Stratifying by Race in Pharmacogenomics." *Clinical Pharmacological Therapeutics* 81(1):122–5.

Lippman, A. 1991. "Prenatal Genetic Testing and Screening: Constructing Needs and Reinforcing Inequities." *American Journal of Law and Medicine* 17:15–50.

Lippman, A. 1992. "Led (Astray) by Genetic Maps: The Cartography of the Human Genome and Health Care." *Social Science & Medicine* 35(12):1469–76.

Lock, M. 2004. "Medicalization and the Naturalization of Social Control." Pp. 116–25 in *The Encyclopedia of Medical Anthropology,* Vol. 2, edited by C. R. Ember and M. Ember. New York: Kluwer Academic.

Miah, A. and E. Rich. 2008. *The Medicalization of Cyberspace.* New York: Routledge.

Morning, A. J. 2011. *The Nature of Race: How Scientists Think and Teach about Human Difference.* Berkeley, CA: University of California Press.

Moynihan, R. and D. Henry. 2006. "The Fight against Disease Mongering: Generating Knowledge for Action." *PLoS Medicine* 3(4):e191.

Nelson, A. 2008a. "Bio Science: Genetic Genealogy Testing and the Pursuit of African Ancestry." *Social Studies of Science (Sage)* 38(5):759–83.

Nelson, A. 2008b. "The Factness of Diaspora." Pp. 253–269 in *Revisiting Race in a Genomic Age,* edited by B. Koenig, S. S.-J. Lee and S. S. Richardson. Piscataway, NJ: Rutgers University Press.

Nelson, A. 2014. *The Social Life of DNA.* Boston, MA: Beacon Press.

NHGRI. 2004. *NHGRI/NIH Health Disparities Strategic Plan (2004–2008).* Washington, DC: NHGRI.

NIH. 1993. *The NIH Revitalization Act of 1993* (Vol. PL 103–43). Washington, DC: NIH.

NIH. 2000. "Report of the First Community Consultation on the Responsible Collection and Use of Samples for Genetic Research." Accessed March 28, 2012 (www.nigms.nih.gov/News/Reports/community_consultation.htm).

NIH. 2007. "Genes, Environment and Health Initiative Invests In Genetic Studies, Environmental Monitoring Technologies." *NIH News*. Accessed September 30, 2012 (www.nih.gov/news/pr/sep2007/nhgri-04.htm).

NIH. 2009. "RFA-CA-09-001: NIH-Supported Centers for Population Health and Health Disparities (CPHHD) (P50)." Accessed September 30, 2012 (http://grants.nih.gov/grants/guide/rfa-files/RFA-CA-09-001.html).

NIH. 2010. "Global Health Meetings." Accessed September 30, 2012 (http://commonfund.nih.gov/globalhealth/researchmeeting.aspx).

NIH. 2012. "NIH Common Fund." Accessed September 30, 2012 (http://commonfund.nih.gov/proteomics/author/Admin.aspx).

Omi, M. and H. Winant. 1994. *Racial Formation in the United States: From the 1960s to the 1990s.* New York: Routledge.

Pollock, A. 2011. "Transforming the Critique of Big Pharma." *BioSocieties* 6(1):106–18.

Puckrein, G. 2006. "BiDil: From Another Vantage Point." *Health Affairs* 25(5):w368–w374.

Rabinow, Paul. 1996. *Essays on the Anthropology of Reason.* Princeton Studies in Culture/Power/History. Princeton, NJ: Princeton University Press.

Rabinow, P. and N. Rose. 2006. "Biopower Today." *BioSocieties* 1(2):195–217.

Rapp, R. 2011. "Chasing Science: Children's Brains, Scientific Inquiries, and Family Labors." *Science, Technology & Human Values* 36(5):662–84.

Reardon, J. 2005. *Race to the Finish: Identity and Governance in an Age of Genomics.* Princeton, NJ: Princeton University Press.

Reardon, J. 2009. "Finding Oprah's Roots, Losing the World: Beyond the Liberal Anti-Racist Genome." Accessed September 30, 2012 (http://globetrotter.berkeley.edu/bwep/colloquium/papers/FindingOprahLosingWorld%20Oct%203%202009%20PDF.pdf).

Richardson, S. and H. Stevens. 2014. *Postgenomics: Biology after the Genome.* Durham, NC: Duke University Press.

Risch, N., E. Burchard, E. Ziv and H. Tang. 2002. "Categorization of Humans in Biomedical Research: Genes, Race and Disease." *Genome Biology* 3(7):comment2007.1–12.

Roberts, L. 1992. "How to Sample the World's Genetic Diversity." *Science (New York, N.Y.)* 257(5074):1204–5.

Roberts, D. 2011. *Fatal Invention: How Science, Politics, and Big Business Re-create Race in the Twenty-First Century.* New York: New Press.

Rose, N. S. 2007. *The Politics of Life Itself: Biomedicine, Power, and Subjectivity in the Twenty-First Century.* Princeton, NJ: Princeton University Press.

Rusert, B. M. and C. D. M. Royal. 2011. "Grassroots Marketing in a Global Era: More Lessons from BiDil." *The Journal of Law, Medicine & Ethics: A Journal of the American Society of Law, Medicine & Ethics* 39(1):79–90.

Schnittker, J. 2009. "Mirage of Health in the Era of Biomedicalization: Evaluating Change in the Threshold of Illness, 1972–1996." *Social Forces* 87(4):2155–82.

Shim, J. K., K. Weatherford Darling, S. L. Ackerman, S. Soo-Jin Lee and R. A. Hiatt. 2015. "Reimagining Race and Ancestry: Biomedicalizing Difference in Post-Genomic Subjects." Pp. 56–78 in *Reimagining (Bio)Medicalization, Pharmaceuticals and Genetics: Old Critiques and New Engagements,* edited by Susan E. Bell and Anne E. Figert. New York: Routledge.

Shostak, S. and M. Moinester. 2015. "Beyond Geneticization: Regimes of Perceptibility and the Social Determinants of Health." Pp. 216–38 in *Reimagining (Bio)Medicalization, Pharmaceuticals and Genetics: Old Critiques and New Engagements,* edited by Susan E. Bell and Anne E. Figert. New York: Routledge.

Stolberg, S. G. 2001. "The World: Skin Deep: Shouldn't a Pill Be Colorblind?" *The New York Times* May 13. Accessed September 30, 2012 (www.nytimes.com/2001/05/13/weekinreview/the-world-skin-deep-shouldn-t-a-pill-be-colorblind.html).

Sykes, B. 2002. *The Seven Daughters of Eve: The Science That Reveals Our Genetic Ancestry.* London: W. W. Norton & Co.

Sykes, B. 2007a. *Blood of the Isles.* London: Corgi Books.

Sykes, B. 2007b. *Saxons, Vikings, and Celts: The Genetic Roots of Britain and Ireland.* London: W. W. Norton & Co.

TallBear, K. 2008. "Native-American-DNA: In Search of Native American Race and Tribe." Pp. 235–52 in *Revisiting Race in a Genomic Age,* edited by B. A. Koenig and S. S. Richardson. Piscataway, NJ: Rutgers University Press.

TallBear, K. 2013. "Genomic Articulations of Indigeneity." *Social Studies of Science* 43(4):509–33.

TallBear, K. and D. A. Bolnick. 2004. "'Native American DNA' Tests: What Are the Risks to Tribes?" *The Native Voice* D2:3–17.

Temple, R. and N. L. Stockbridge. 2007. "BiDil for Heart Failure in Black Patients: The U.S. Food and Drug Administration Perspective." *Annals of Internal Medicine* 146(1):57–62.

UNESCO. 1994. Human Genome Diversity Project, address delivered by Luca Cavalli-Sforza, Stanford University, to a special meeting of UNESCO, September 21. Accessed September 30, 2012 (www.osti.gov/bridge/servlets/purl/505327-ILeo4n/.../505327.pdf).

Wade, N. 2001. "Genome Mappers Navigate the Tricky Terrain of Race." *The New York Times* July 20. Accessed September 30, 2012 (www.nytimes.com/2001/07/20/science/20GENO.html).

Weiss, R. 2000. "The Promise of Precision Prescriptions; 'Pharmacogenomics' Also Raises Issues of Race, Privacy Series: The Human Blueprint; Matching Drugs to Genes." *Washington Post*, June 24:A1.

Whitmarsh, I. 2008. *Biomedical Ambiguity: Race, Asthma, and the Contested Meaning of Genetic Research in the Caribbean*. Ithaca, NY: Cornell University Press.

Williams, J. E. 2011. "They Say It's in the Genes: Decoding Racial Ideology in Genomics." *Journal of Contemporary Ethnography* 40(5):550–81.

Williams, S. J., J. Gabe and P. Davis. 2008. "The Sociology of Pharmaceuticals: Progress and Prospects." *Sociology of Health & Illness* 30(6):813–24.

10
Racial Destiny or Dexterity?
The Global Circulation of Genomics as an Empowerment Idiom

RUHA BENJAMIN

In 2001 at the World Conference on Racism in Durban, South Africa, a heated dispute ensued between representatives of the Indian government and the Dalit movement (formerly "untouchables") over whether caste discrimination should be included on the international agenda as a form of oppression akin to racism. This was the latest iteration of a longstanding debate that pits the view that caste is an ancient, naturalized hierarchy against the idea that it is a colonial fabrication built upon existing social fault lines. Some Dalit activists have made appeals to ancient genetic divisions, emphasizing the outsiderness of the upper caste, in order to legitimize their grievances, undermine the authority of powerful actors and build solidarity with other racialized groups. Representatives of the Indian government, in turn, have resisted the latter appeals and were largely successful in eliminating any mention of caste discrimination in the World Conference against Racism, Racial Discrimination, Xenophobia and Related Intolerance proceedings and outcomes document (Egorova 2009). Although the inherited position of caste is tied to one's work, it is also an embodied status such that lower castes are often considered "impure" and "untouchable" with numerous implications for social life. But until very recently there was little scientific evidence to support the notion that caste groupings were biologically distinct in the way that US racial groupings have historically been construed. In 2009, when the Durban Review Committee convened in Geneva to evaluate progress towards the conference goals, a sizable delegation of Dalit representatives traveled to Geneva to "raise their voices against the wall of silence they [were] met with at the Durban Review Conference" (Human Rights Watch 2009). In this case, advancing the idea that group differences are biologically real is a way to assert social divisions as consequential, and therefore requiring redress. To the extent that socially subordinate groups find it necessary to claim recognition and assert rights in genomic terms, it is both a form of co-optation *of* and capitulation *to* science as the authority on group boundaries.

In this chapter, I explore how genomics is both powerful and problematic due to its epistemic agility (making competing knowledge claims) and normative dexterity (asserting conflicting political claims), rather than due to the field's strict enforcement of hierarchically stable categories. While those at the bottom of the Indian social hierarchy have seized upon genomic findings to bolster their oppressed group identity (Egorova 2009), those who monopolize power and status in India have also used population genomics to support their claims to indigeneity when that was called in to question. Genomic claims are used at both ends of the lines of power, where the meaning of biological difference and the rights sought by different groups are negotiated and contested. But despite the seeming short-term empowerment that genomics claims seem to hold for marginalized social groups, the long-term political implications of describing centuries-old social divisions as "genetic diversity" are unclear. In what follows I discuss national genomic initiatives in Mexico and India, which marshal already existing national discourses about biological and cultural affinity in their quest to genetically map variation in the population. I compare their different conceptions of heterogeneity, one focusing on diversity and the other on mixture, to show how political and scientific actors in both contexts must contend with the ways in which linking genetic and social groupings become politically controversial.

Since the World Conference on Racism, some in the Dalit movement have welcomed genomics research that supports the theory of Aryan migration, seeing in it:

> proof of the idea that "upper castes" were alien to the subcontinent. At the same time, the Hindu right favoured the studies which suggest that the "European" contribution to the South Asian gene pool was minimal, and hence could be construed as supporting the Aryan indigenousness hypothesis. (Egorova 2010:34)

Population genomics in this context has become an unlikely ally on both sides of a very heated and at times deadly struggle over the legitimate parameters of citizenship. On the one side, there are Hindu nationalists of purportedly Aryan ancestry, and on the other, Dalit activists of purportedly Dravidian ancestry. The dexterity of genomics, supporting as it does two competing accounts of Indian peoplehood, suggests it is important to examine the wider context in which population genomics is taking shape.

Whereas many social scientists and racial justice advocates have spent decades working to denaturalize race and highlight its social construction, the new biopolitics of race are "new" in part because the relationship between biological knowledge and political power is decoupled. That is, the logic of biological difference and social subordination are not so tightly knit as they were in previous eras characterized by explicit forms of eugenic ideology (Hammonds and Herzig 2008). As Rose cautions, it is important to avoid painting contemporary developments in the life sciences as a new genetic determinism; instead, current debates over race and genomics should be located within the biopolitics of the twenty-first century that "does not seek to legitimate inequality but to intervene upon its consequences" (Rose 2007:167). This is what Bliss (2012:15) aptly calls an "antiracist racialism, or the idea that there is no rank to races but there are nevertheless discrete populations worth studying" as a prevailing ethos among both genomicists and other social justice activists. Focusing upon just such interventions, the following discussion examines the "new-fangled" relations between race and genomics with a sober eye towards the way such attempts to intervene in the name of the dispossessed may sediment longstanding inequalities in unexpected ways. It builds upon work by Roberts and others cautioning that our newfound ability to intervene upon life in unprecedented ways is not necessarily cause for celebration, because this new form of biocitizenship "threatens to replace active, collective engagement to create a better society with providing information to the biotech industry and consuming its goods and services" (Roberts 2011:225). The biopolitics of race are one set of developments within the broader context of "racial neoliberalism" (Goldberg 2009) that marks a shift away from state-sanctioned medical experimentation, towards the privatization of health research in which the onus is on individual biocitizens to opt in or out. But the seeming empowerment of individuals can serve as a ruse, drawing our attention away from the inequitable social contexts in which individuals exercise circumscribed agency. For example, the US pharmaceutical industry outsources clinical trials to places that have "pharmaceutically naïve" populations to test drug efficacy because Americans already consume too many drugs to make them useful test subjects (Petryna 2005). Another countervailing process is pharmaceutical development situated *in* postcolonial contexts, where the location of drug discovery comes to matter for the researchers and the knowledge produced (Pollock 2014). But, due to persistent global inequalities, the actual fruits of such research are out of reach for many of those whose bodies are the experimental substrate of science. Such disparities – between those who bear the risks and those who reap the benefits of experimental life sciences – will likely persist in the context of genomic medicine.

Making the Biopolity

It is tempting to embark upon an investigation of the biopolitics of race in the post-genomics era as if the "polity" at the heart of biopolitics were self-evident and stable. But one of the features that sets it apart from other political fields is that it involves a simultaneous struggle over the parameters of both rights and bodies (Benjamin 2013). So that claims about what governments, for example, owe particular groups or conversely what citizens are responsible for as members of a society are intimately connected to the question of *what constitute groups* in the first place. Whether on the basis of genes, geographical proximity or census results – to name but a few – how groups are imagined and produced is at the heart of biopolitical struggles. The possible forms of group-making, in turn, are negotiated and contested by a host of social agents – scientists, activists and politicians among them – who vie for legitimacy and authority with and against one another. While advocates of population genomics in postcolonial settings typically appeal to progress, profit and public health as the desired aims of the field, there are unintended social and political consequences that do not fit neatly in to a development narrative of science.

Strictly speaking, population genomicists seek to understand how "evolutionary processes . . . influence variation across genomes and populations" (Kumar 2012) by sampling and genotyping individuals in the hope of finding patterns that may eventually relate to disease susceptibility and drug response. As a first step in understanding population genomics, it is important to recognize that it is not simply a new discipline, but part of a broader social field with political implications that exceed the intentions of researchers. The growth of the field is tied to the crises faced by the global pharmaceutical industry, wherein an estimated US$140 billion worth of drugs will lose their patents between 2012 and 2017 (Kulkarni 2012). Companies are under pressure to reconfigure their business models and find new markets as blockbuster drugs fall over the "patent cliff."[1] The one-size-fits-all model of drug development is giving way to a niche marketing strategy in which companies are turning to "growth potential in specialty markets and in emerging nations" (Wilson 2011). This approach is often undertaken in the name of helping "the underserved," as exemplified by prominent Canadian health policy officials Daar and Singer:

> Developing countries are not only potentially huge markets for drug therapeutics but are also depositories of important human genetic diversity. Understanding this diversity is valuable because it better defines those population subgroups that will benefit more from a particular drug than others, and allows the detection of side-effects that might not be seen in populations that are mainly Caucasian. (2005:245)

Such appeals to marginalized racial groups as the purported beneficiaries of genomic medicine avert critical attention from the broader political economy of pharmaceuticals in which "the public health paradigm shifted from prevention to treatment access, [and] political rights have moved towards biologically-based rights" (Biehl and Eskerod 2009:10).

A focus on the political economy of drug development reveals that, in resuscitating intellectual property and establishing niche markets, racialized understandings of biological difference become the value added, as a justification for extending patent life. In "How a Drug Becomes 'Ethnic'" (2004), Kahn describes how the role of law and commerce in creating race-based medicine becomes "masked both by well-meaning concerns about perceived health disparities and by an imprudent reliance on erroneous or incomplete statistical data" (2004:3). His in-depth case study of the first race-based prescription in the

USA, BiDil, illuminates how legal and marketing imperatives incentivize racial packaging even, or especially, when the scientific grounds for doing so are shaky. As Rajan explains, "the more things get reduced to their molecular components ... the more one needs to reply on statistical, population-based data to 'individualize' therapy. This means that one can individualize therapy *only* on the basis of population classifications" (2006:163). So although "personalized medicine" is the umbrella under which many of these practices fall, many analysts caution that race serves as a permanent "detour" to individualized treatments (Collier 2012). Kahn points out that as companies attempt to "tailor therapies ever more closely to the genetic profile of individuals or groups of consumers, identifying racial or ethnic correlations with disease are becoming big business" (2006:118). In terms of "tailoring" drugs to consumers, *groups* not individuals comprise the necessary markets.

In response, a number of postcolonial nations seek to control the terms in which researchers and pharmaceutical companies approach their populations as resources for genetic samples and as markets for new drugs by asserting "genomic sovereignty" over their population's genome. In addition to the economic implications, proponents of genomic sovereignty in India and Mexico expressed a sense of exclusion from the US-based International Haplotype Mapping project, "a partnership of scientists and funding agencies from Canada, China, Japan, Nigeria, the United Kingdom and the United States to develop a public resource that w[ould] help researchers find genes associated with human disease and response to pharmaceuticals."[2] As I have described elsewhere, scientists from a number of countries, including Mexico and India, questioned the generalizability of this initiative because it did not include samples from their populations (Benjamin 2009). In Mexico, where a Genomic Sovereignty amendment to the national constitution was passed, foreign researchers are subject to fines and prison time for collecting genetic samples without the necessary permission. Spokesmen for the new policy have made claims about the uniqueness of the "Mexican Genome" as a justification for protecting Mexican genetic samples (Schwartz-Marin and Restrepo 2013). Governments are approaching the genomic data produced from their citizens' bodies as a national resource vulnerable to capitalist piracy, in the same way that plants and minerals have been regarded for some time (Hayden 2003; Foster 2014). In response, one US-based investor lamented that the expansion of Big Pharma in to foreign markets has "hit a roadblock: Nationalism" (D'Altorio 2011).

Some of the countries with genomic sovereignty policies are part of the "emerging seven" – China, Indonesia, Brazil, Turkey, Russia, India and Mexico – that global capital regards as its new "Promised Land" (Pharmaceutical Technology 2009). US business journals discuss this in terms of companies needing to develop strategies to capitalize on the "new" illnesses resulting from the higher standards of living in these societies. The financial consulting firm PricewaterhouseCoopers (PwC) estimates that by 2020 the "emerging seven" may account for as much as one-fifth of global sales. PwC says "the number of diabetes suffers in India is projected to reach 73.5 million people by 2025, with the direct cost of treating each individual at about $420 per person per year, and that if these costs remain the same, India's total bill for diabetes alone would be about $30 billion by 2025" (Pharmaceutical Technology 2009).

Montoya (2007) cautions that the "emerging market" trope is a "commonly accepted demographic truism," and that to succeed, businesses must now appeal to the ethnic market. So instead of a standard regime of HIV treatment, for example, genomicists investigate how vaccines may differ among population subgroups because of genetic differences (Gonzalez et al. 2001). These genetic differences, in turn, are routinely mapped on to ethno-racial differences – a "strategic calibration" that is not simply careless reification of race but part of the long-term strategy of creating markets for drugs (Benjamin 2009). That is, part of what makes a product "novel, useful, non-obvious, and specific" (in the language of patent development) is the introduction of race as a genetic category. Precisely because social scientists have so thoroughly established the notion that race is socially constructed, intellectual property claims can rest on the logic of race-as-genetic because the latter appears to offer something new and valuable (Kahn 2013).

The need to protect intellectual property by regulating the flow of genomic data is also motivated by the promise of health interventions that may save countries' healthcare expenditures and generate profits from "tailored" drug development in the long term. Genomic sovereignty policies, in turn, implicitly brand nations as biologically distinct from other nations, even as the science itself seeks to discern clinically meaningful subgroup differences within each country. In these "bioethnic" markets (Montoya 2007) human bodies are classified as neither part of a universal nor as individuals, but as biologically meaningful social groups (Epstein 2007). In the process, new biopolitical entities are being imagined. "Mexican DNA" and "Indian DNA," among others, are part of a biopolitical imaginary that is strategically calibrating existing social differences such as race-ethnicity with genetic groupings. On the surface, genomic sovereignty asserts a deeply nationalist sentiment of self-determination in a time of increasing globalization. It implicitly "brands" national populations as biologically distinct from other populations, naturalizing nation-state boundaries to ensure that countries receive the economic and medical benefits that may result from this new science. But as Aoki urges, "invocations of nations' sovereignty vis-à-vis an international order are always, foundationally, wrapped up in the question of nations' sovereignty over the subjects contained within their jurisdiction" (Aoki 1996; cf. Ghosh 2005:15). So instead of celebrating genomic sovereignty as postcolonial empowerment, such claims are better examined for the kinds of power relations that they at once hide, rather than combat.

Whether it relates to Amerindians in Mexico or Dalits in India, political assertions about indigeneity and sovereignty are embedded in genomic claims about patrimony. But *whose* claims will gain traction as authoritative knowledge – those who exercise state power or those seeking to contest it – is directly tied to preexisting social hierarchies. Although this discussion highlights the role of epistemic dexterity as a feature of biopolitics, it is important to emphasize that not all assertions that draw upon genomics carry equal weight. As TallBear explains, "in the 'real world' of power and resource imbalances, in which some peoples' ideas and knowledge are made to matter more than others, genetic markers and populations named and ordered by scientists play key roles in the history that has come to matter for the nation and increasingly the world" (2013:7). So while genomic findings are available to members of different social groups to make competing claims about belonging and personhood, and may on the surface appear empowering to disenfranchised groups, the extent to which those claims become authoritative depends, in part, on who directs the flow of political and economic resources in the first place.

Bioconstitutional Moments

By examining the emergence of genomic sovereignty claims as a form of what Jasanoff and colleagues term *bioconstitutionalism,* novel life sciences and new rights claims that are "redefining the obligations of the state in relation to lives in its care" are drawn into the same analytic frame (2011:3). In doing so, it is important to extend beyond the realm of official policy and legislative enactment, to include bioconstitutional *moments* in scholarly analysis, where struggles over who "we" are, what we are owed and what we are responsible for, as both objects and subjects of scientific initiatives, take place all around us. In the more mundane work of developing sampling protocols, reporting scientific findings in the mass media or lobbying the state for social and political redress as the Dalit movement in India has attempted to do, the meaning of life and the entitlements owed to the living are negotiated and contested.

Expanding the biopolitical terrain beyond the bounds of official genomic sovereignty policy, old forms of social domination are reproduced and, at times, resisted. In postcolonial contexts, claims about the relative proportion of indigenous or European genes in a population continue alongside efforts to map and celebrate nations' ethno-racial mixture. The persistence of biological claims about racial-ethnicity, not as a Western imposition but as an empowerment idiom, should alert us to the political dexterity of racial idioms at the heart of biopolitics. Genomic sovereignty claims are used to exercise some measure of control over the rapacious appetite of Big Pharma and Global Science – a means by which non-Western groups "can be at the table, not simply on the table" of novel life sciences (Benjamin 2013:10). Even so, when marginalized groups adopt the logic of racial difference, intra-national hierarchies based on caste or race are granted the "seductive imprimatur of molecular genetic precision" (Duster 2003:153). Patterns of social domination in education, housing and healthcare, for example, are overshadowed by a narrative of biological difference and kinship; rather than address how disparities in illness and death arise out of the "fatal couplings of power and difference" (Gilmore 2002:18), such inequities are approached in terms of genetic predisposition towards disease. Histories of social domination, in this way, are increasingly euphemized as biological diversity; for example, Erasmus critiques a South African documentary on ancestry testing saying, that "despite its reference to the racial violence of apartheid, the documentary declares 'you might even say that differences between races are all merely cosmetic', implying such differences have no real historical, political and material effects on people's lives" (2013:45). It is necessary, then, to look beyond the empowering rhetoric that often surrounds genomics, at the way genetic histories serve as a *moral prophylactic* – protecting the state and dominant social groups against charges of domination and displacement by focusing on seemingly benign patterns of migration and kinship.

In the most prominent assertion of genomic sovereignty to date, the Mexican Senate established the National Institute of Genomic Medicine and unanimously approved reforms to the General Health Law in 2008, which makes "the sampling of genetic material and its transport outside of Mexico without prior approval . . . illegal" (Seguin et al. 2008:6). The Genomic Sovereignty amendment states that Mexican-derived human genome data are the property of Mexico's government, and prohibits and penalizes its collection and utilization in research without prior government approval. It seeks to prevent other nations from analyzing Mexican genetic material, especially when results can be patented. The law's enforcement comes with a formidable bite in the form of prison time and lost wages. In addition to Mexico, countries such as India, Thailand, South Africa, China and others have also issued policy statements or passed legislation that seek to develop genomic infrastructure explicitly to benefit their national populations (Seguin et al. 2008). So while the term "genomic sovereignty" is used primarily in Mexico at this time, its conceptual underpinnings are emerging in other nations (Slabbert and Pepper 2010; de Vries and Pepper 2012).

Unlike pan-indigenous advocacy groups that have asserted group sovereignty claims to opt out of genomics research, government genomic sovereignty policies set out proactive research agendas to stimulate health and economic gains, thereby opting to participate but only under their own terms. In this way, the biology of the population becomes a "natural resource" and genomics serves as a nation-building project maximizing the potential of this resource. Unlike other nationalisms, the point of postcolonial genomics is not to posit the nation as "pure" (as in the Iceland case, cf. Fortun 2008), but as a unique genetic mixture (i.e., "admixed") when compared to other nations (Wade et al. 2014). But in addition to their stated aims, genomic initiatives have the potential to naturalize social hierarchies and disparities within the respective countries. Debates surrounding genomics in Euro-American contexts – whether or not it legitimates social inequalities – still remain relevant to the arena of postcolonial genomics (Soo-Jin Lee, Mountain and Koenig 2001; Foster and Sharpe 2002; Reardon 2004; Duster 2005; Kahn 2006, 2013; El-Haj 2007; Montoya 2007; Fujimura, Duster and Rajagopalan 2008; Fullwiley 2008; Hamilton 2008; Harding 2013; TallBear 2013; Wade et al. 2014). As a science policy born of existing global power inequality, postcolonial genomics can also be understood as having a mixed genealogy and trajectory that is at once innovative and retrograde in its assertions. Diversity maps serve as a "naturalizing" cartography of the nation that aims to account for the accumulated genetic inheritance of a people; they also act as social maps for contemporary anxieties about social fragmentation and future cohesion.

For example, the first major task of the Mexican HapMap Project was to investigate the common haplotypes distributed across six states. Mexican newspaper reports drew upon the Mexican Institute for Genomic Medicine's public communications and stated that "due to the race, there is a pronounced difference between the populations of various states within the country. In Sonora they have the highest prevalence of European genes, 58%, while in Guerrero, their population presents a major index of African genes, 22%" (Fupen 2007). Some scientists at the Mexican Institute criticize the newspaper's use of "race," preferring "population" as a more scientifically valid substitute. Yet the Institute's public statements and academic publications continue to describe Mexico as a predominantly "mestizo" nation. Wade and colleagues explain that:

> [D]espite the fact that most geneticists in Latin America actively deny the
> validity of race as a biological category, genetic science might produce
> knowledge and interpretations that, while they appear nonracial to
> genetic experts, might look a lot like race to the nonexpert in genetics . . .
> Even when scientists explicitly deny the association between ancestry and
> race, the way genetic knowledge reaches society at large can give
> unintended but public salience to a notion of race based on ancestry.
> (2014:2)

As in much of Latin America, population genomics in Mexico rests upon the scaffold of *mestizaje*; so that the Mexican Genome is said to "admixed" – more indigenous in the South, more African on the coast and more European in the northern regions. Not simply "north" as in geographically higher, but also in the way that whiteness confers a higher position in the social order, and lighter members of the mestizo body politic monopolize political and economic power. As Figueroa explains, "Mestizaje enables whiteness to be experienced as both normalized and ambiguous, not consistently attached to the (potentially) whiter body, but as a site of legitimacy and privilege" (2010:387).

Soon after the founding of Mexico's National Institute for Genomic Medicine in 2004, researchers initiated an ambitious program to collect DNA samples from more than 2,000 individuals, an initiative dubbed the National Crusade Genomic Map of Mexico. Representatives of the agency and a battalion of health workers visited states in which governors and local leaders had agreed, through prior consultation and negotiation, to allow the agency to recruit blood donors. As an official Institute document reports, the Crusades were "intended primarily to collect blood samples of 100 men and 100 women originally from each of the participating states ... They turned into academic events of three days during which were given public presentations and discussion tables in universities, high schools and public forums, both for the student community, as for the general public" (Benjamin 2009:350). During the sampling process, some agency officials and observers expressed heightened anxieties about human subjects' protection for indigenous communities, such that local elders and community representatives (often anthropologists with connections to the group) were recruited as intermediaries and consent documents were translated from Spanish into the local languages. In addition, the informed consent process placed emphasis on explaining to the communities that their donations would be used to map the genetic diversity of the country and for research as yet unknown, but that they should expect no direct medical benefit from their participation (Schwartz-Marin 2011).

In earlier stages of Mexican nation-building, *mestizaje* was utilized by the national intelligentsia as "a potential route to national consolidation and as a positive mark of national identity" contra notions of "hybridity as degenerate" (Lund 2006:86). The recent popularity of calculating levels of ethno-racial mixture in genomics (rather than determining pure types), gives added value to the Mexican genome brand within the global scientific community. But as in previous nation-building projects, genomic mapping both includes and excludes racialized others. Lund describes the salience of the "indigenous question" for Mexico's national identity and collective biology, as "an included exclusion that forms the very logic of mestizaje ... The Indian participates in the building of a new race and a new spirit, yet is excluded from the modern" (2006:83). In a similar vein, Erasmus (2013) critiques researchers who attempt to tell a prehistory of South African populations that reinforces contemporary power dynamics. She refers specifically to a rural nomadic group, Karretjiemense (translated as the Cart People), who due to a number of socioeconomic factors are among the poorest in the country:

> They position Karretjiemense at a point in linear time when they could be considered not-yet-historical. From this place, "these people," "these Others" are – before the beginning of History – "expelled as prehuman ... without meaning or time ... This anti-political and anti-historical conceptual frame underlies most studies that attempt to link 'identity' primarily to genetics." (2013:45)

Implicit in the framework of genomic mapping exercises, "first people" are spoken *of* in the past tense but not spoken *to* as citizens of the modern body politic. An evolutionary narrative positions them both *before* and *below*, so that their subordinate social position appears to be a function of their primitiveness, rather than state policies that relegate them as second class. The "indigenous question," in short, complicates genomic nation-building as an empowering exercise, revealing the intra-national hierarchies that are reinscribed through biological race-making.

Related to issues of informed consent and future access to therapies, an even more fundamental set of bioconstitutional issues arise, over what donors think their DNA represents versus what their tissue is *made* to represent in the framework of national genomics. During the Mexican Institute's outreach and sampling, anthropologist Ernesto Schwartz-Marin reports a situation in which a Tepehuanes (indigenous) elder who was serving as community spokesman at one of the blood sampling sites in the state of Durango asserted, "We are not Mexicans. We are Tepehuanes, and you are looking for the genome of the Tepehuanes!" The elder's statement contrasts that of the project director who, when asked whether indigenous research subjects require special defense against harm or discrimination, replied "the protection is the same, finally they are Mexicans, the same as us" (Schwartz-Marin 2011). There is a tension between the ethos of nationalist unity and hybridized homogeneity expressed by the government representative versus the genomic self-determination of an indigenous gatekeeper attempting to appropriate the scientific gaze to assert a more "local" biopolitical identity. As Schwartz-Marin and Restrepo deftly illustrate, the Mexican genome initiative's "nationalistic and sovereign discourse made it possible to make an extensive sampling of Mexico's indigenous communities without any major setback, despite open opposition from indigenous activists" (2013:11). As in other cases around the world, tissue from indigenous populations, what Erasmus incisively refers to as "designer descendants" (2013:50), are often considered valuable as repositories of genetic information about the larger "admixed" population. But, in most contexts, it remains extremely difficult for indigenous representatives to substantively shape the classificatory schemas and governance structures that oversee such projects. In the example above, the elder's and the director's statements floated past one another, with only one of their claims mapping on to the official record – a bioconstitutional moment in which the *power to define* life and the *power to assert* political rights based on that definition are co-constituted (Reardon 2004).

To the extent that genomics is the lingua franca of the life sciences, and national elites have the political power to enact silences on socially subordinate groups in the governing process, it is possible to amend the classic postcolonial query, and ask *whether the subaltern's genome can code*. In the Mexican case, the different points of view between researchers and Tepehuanes participants over the relationship of an indigenous group to the national body politic did not thwart collection of indigenous blood samples. This reveals how the very elaborate community engagement and informed consent protocol that characterize such initiatives are not designed to address fundamental classificatory conflicts that call in to question who "we" are that is being mapped. Such bio-constitutional moments reveal how interventions meant to empower the national body politic vis-à-vis an international order can, at once, further dispossess already marginal social groups.

Recasting the Biopolity

Whereas the indigenous-mestizo divide frames population genomics in Mexico, each national or regional initiative is constructed around social divisions that are salient in that context. In this next section, I return to the case of India where the Indian Genome Variation Project seeks to map a notoriously heterogeneous, and highly stratified, population. Project director Samir Brahmachari commented that, "In fact the term 'Indian' is a misnomer in population genetic studies, as it indicates the population to be homogenous. This is evidently now untrue" (Koshy 2008). Dubbed the largest, most comprehensive genome initiative in the world to date, Indian researchers collected blood samples from 15,000 unrelated individuals drawn from what it calls "well-defined ethnic groups that were chosen to represent the entire spectrum of diversity within the Indian population" (Indian Genome Variation Consortium n.d.). And, although India is comprised of nearly 28,000 endogamous populations, scientists say that the choice of fifty-five subpopulations, defined through a mix of caste, tribe and religious affiliation, has been done in a way to represent only a quarter of India's genetic diversity.

Unlike the insistence by the head of Mexico's Institute that the country's indigenous populations are "Mexican," in India project director Brahmachari was eager to denaturalize the nation-state and admit the ways in which social groupings do not calibrate with scientifically produced groupings. Even so, the Indian director's rhetoric should not be viewed as a straightforward exercise in questioning the "logic of difference" that animates much of genomics. Rather, it draws upon and strategically deploys historical tensions implicit to Indian nationalism. Indian nationalism is such that one prominent commentator refers to as a "rare animal … the nationalism of an idea – rooted in the spirit of diversity" (Tharoor 2007). This contrasts with the history of Mexican nationalism, which is rooted in hybridity, that is, the merging of differences. The latter celebrates the absorption of European, Amerindian and African lineages in to a single "mestizo" population. But as Mexican scholars and activists critical of the genome project assert, "A project attempting to prove that there is a 'mestizo genome' will fail if it pretends to correlate race and disease. Mestizo is a label, not a race."[3]

Like Mexico's Genomic Sovereignty legislation, India's Human Genome Regulatory Bill was developed in the wake of concerns over biopiracy – "where genetic resources have been taken without the knowledge and consent of the resource owners" (Indigenous People's Council on Biocolonialism n.d.). The Indian consortium was also motivated by concerns that the US-led International HapMap project lacked adequate South Asian genetic samples in its database, thereby limiting the accessibility of genomically tailored medicine to South Asian populations. The director of the Indian Genomic Variation Consortium notes that, "We've shown that [International] HapMap studies cannot always be applied to the Indian context" (Koshy 2008). Like genomic sovereignty proponents elsewhere, the implication is that India's exclusion from the International HapMap is a precursor to what Ecks (2005:241) has called "pharmaceutical marginalization," caused by a lack of access to, in this case, future drug therapies and as a site for potential drug testing.

While the Indian Genomic Variation Consortium is one hub of research that combines evolutionary and biomedical foci similar to Mexico's National Institute of Genomic Medicine, the logic of genomic sovereignty extends beyond this set of institutional actors. There are also partnerships between Indian and non-Indian scientists which are not necessarily affiliated with the Consortium, who collaborate through other public and private institutions on an intermittent basis. The controversial findings of a number of these studies have been enrolled in political battles such as the one between Hindu nationalists and the Dalit movement described above. In one of the first genomic studies to attract widespread attention in the mass media, Bamshad et al. concluded that the datasets they analyzed "show a trend toward upper castes being more similar to Europeans, whereas lower castes are more similar to Asians" (2001:994) based upon samples taken from a relatively limited number of groups from one particular region. In a *Times of India* newspaper article reporting on the Bamshad et al. study, the headline exclaimed, "Upper caste Indian male more European, says study" (Rajghatta 2001), in which the findings were interpreted as relevant to the entire caste system, despite their limited scope.

Subsequent genomic studies have been used by activists on both sides of the political spectrum to intervene in this debate. The Hindu right has used particular findings to build up a case for shared ancestry and the "indigenousness" of the Hindu tradition, pointing to evidence that suggests:

> the recent external contribution to Dravidian- and Hindi-speaking caste groups has been low. The sharing of some Y-chromosomal haplogroups between Indian and Central Asian populations is most parsimoniously explained by a *deep, common ancestry between the two regions*, with diffusion of some Indian-specific lineages northward. The Y-chromosomal data consistently suggest a *largely South Asian origin for Indian caste communities and therefore argue against any major influx*, from regions north and west of India, of people associated either with the development of agriculture or the spread of the Indo-Aryan language family. (Sahoo et al. 2005:843; my emphasis)

Leaders of the Dalit movement have referenced Bamshad's study as scientific proof that upper-caste Hindus are "'foreigners' and 'new-comers' on the subcontinent," which has a long history in Dalit activism (Egorova 2009:427). By appealing to genetically determined group identity, Dalit representatives also attempt to link caste subordination to racism in order to "attract the attention of the international community" (Egorova 2010:426). But, as Erasmus warns, "[t]his amounts to doing history and politics through genetics" (2013:40). Efforts to appropriate genomic knowledge fail to question the underlying assumption that legitimate forms of group identity, history and solidarity must necessarily be sought in the genome.

In a high-profile article in *Nature*, a team of researchers from Harvard University and the Centre for Cellular and Molecular Biology in Hyderabad, India, provided "strong evidence for two ancient populations, genetically divergent, that are ancestral to most Indians today. One population, the 'Ancestral North Indians' (ANI), is genetically close to Middle Easterners, Central Asians, and Europeans, whereas the other population, the 'Ancestral South Indians' (ASI), is as distinct from ANI and East Asians as they are from each other" (Reich et al. 2009:489) The social and political implications of this seemingly straightforward finding cannot be apprehended without first understanding how "in popular discourse and in political debates, the populations of the North and of the South of India are perceived as both culturally and 'biologically' different, with 'northerners' (and upper castes in the South) being allegedly descended from Eurasians and having fairer skin, and southerners being the dark-skinned descendants of ancient Dravidians" (Egorova 2010:38). Despite the seeming confirmation of these associations by Reich et al.'s findings, they have been interpreted to support two opposing claims: a convergent claim that all Indians shared these two ancestral lines has been used to make unifying claims such that "there was no need to speak separately about Aryans and Dravidians" (Egorova 2010:40). At the same time, proponents of a divergent claim assert that the *proportion* of these ancestral contributions distinguishes Indian subgroups in meaningful ways. Crucially, the latter emphasize "the proportion of [Ancestral North Indian] of the tested groups correlates with their position in the caste system" (Egorova 2010:41). The idea that the more Aryan one is, the higher one's caste appears, on first glance, to revive eugenic ideas about racial fitness. But the divergent hypothesis that those with greater Ancestral North Indian lineage are not indigenous to the subcontinent has been used by some in the Dalit movement to call in to question the political legitimacy of Hindu nationalists. For example, an article in *Dalit Voice* referred to studies which suggested "Brahmins were not of Indian origin and hence 'should not be allowed to occupy any constitutional position in India'" (Egorova 2009:417). In the same way that the "indigenous question" in Mexico positions subordinate groups as *before* and *below* the modern mestizo, the "caste question" in India positions dominant social groups as *above* and *apart* from the body politic through an unexpected cooptation of genomics by Dalit activists.

As I have shown using the cases of India and Mexico, biological definitions of group belonging are marshaled in bioconstitutional struggles, but not in any deterministic way that would allow us to predict how scientific findings are going to be interpreted and used. Lack of scientific consensus, in fact, means that the field has more, not less, influence as it becomes enrolled on competing sides of political struggle. Likewise, "objective science" cannot tell us how society should be organized and resources distributed. This is the case even when researchers themselves seem to be explicitly supporting one historical narrative over another. For example, Reich et al. claim that, "Some historians have argued that 'caste' in modern India is an invention of colonialism ... However, our results indicate that many current distinctions among groups are ancient and that strong endogamy must have shaped marriage patterns in India for thousands of years" (2009:490). In so doing, they unintentionally provide "ammunition to those who support 'racialist' explanations for the existence of the caste system" (Egorova 2010:39). Its social and political underpinnings are said to draw on older, biologically inscribed distinctions that can be identified in the genome. But socially subordinate groups such as the Dalits may draw upon such findings in unexpected ways, forging political alliances with other racialized subgroups to call for an end to systemic discrimination and seek restorative justice (Prashad 2000; Reddy 2005).

Conclusion

In the context of new biopolitical regimes, biological race is not so much destiny, as it is dexterous. The field of population genomics serves as a political lightening rod for growing anxieties over economic development, health crises and citizenship more broadly and it is used in bioconstitutional struggles over who "we" are, what we are owed and what we are responsible for as objects and subjects of science. As with the Mexican genome initiative, Indian population genomics is justified in terms of its future medical benefits. In stressing the importance of analyzing homegrown data sets rather than those produced by US-led consortia, namely the International HapMap Project, many researchers implicitly draw upon the idiom of genomic sovereignty as a basis for intellectual property claims.[4] In this process, biological notions of race are resuscitated in service to new kinds of biopolitical regimes that have received little critical attention partly because of the emancipatory rhetoric in which they come packaged. The investment here is not in hierarchy and exclusion but commodification and inclusion, with the explicit goal of producing tailored medicine for niche markets. Despite the seeming empowerment of genomic sovereignty claims, we must nevertheless contend with the way that the parameters of this social field, its rules and doxa, are being constituted around a narrow definition and commodification of patentable life in to which longstanding social divisions are euphemized as "genetic diversity."

The cases of India and Mexico discussed in this chapter illustrate how genomics serves as an empowerment idiom for nations and subordinate groups to assert authoritative claims around sovereignty, indigeneity and uniqueness as well as make demands for medical attention and resources. For social scientists wary about the resurgence of biological determinism in the wake of genomics, this discussion directs attention to the wider biopolitical arena, focusing on the inter- and intra-national power dynamics that give rise to claims around genomic group identity. It has argued that the conventional sociological concern with determinism overlooks the dexterity of genomics – the way that study findings can be mobilized by competing political actors. The agility, not the fixity of genomic claims, underpins their authority and power and should therefore be the focus of ongoing critical engagement.

Notes

1   A "patent cliff" refers to the potential for a firm's revenue to plummet when one of their products goes off-patent. The latter can result in the product being replicated and sold cheaply by other firms.
2   International HapMap Project, http://hapmap.ncbi.nlm.nih.gov/ (accessed July 31, 2014).
3   Interview with Leon Olive, bioethicist at Mexico's National Autonomous University, cited from Mothelet and Herrera (2005:1030).
4   Reich et al. "give an example of a genetic marker which increases heart-failure risk by about sevenfold and which occurs at 4 per cent in India and is practically absent elsewhere. It is concluded that it is therefore imperative to conduct a full gene-mapping in India to identify 'clinically significant' alleles that cannot be discovered by studying genetic variation outside of India. Thus, the paper constructs Indian populations as genetically different from the rest of humanity and explicitly advocates the importance of conducting genetic population surveys in India, rather than relying on DNA data from other countries" (Egorova 2010:39).

References

Aoki, Keith. 1996. "Notes toward a Cultural Geography of Authorship." *Stanford Law Review* 48(5):1293–355.

Bamshad, Michael, Toomas Kivisild, W. Scott Watkins, Mary E. Dixon, Chris E. Ricker, Baskara B. Rao, J. Mastan Naidu, B. V. Ravi Prasad, P. Govinda Reddy, Arani Rasanayagam, Surinder S. Papiha, Richard Villems, Alan J. Redd, Michael F. Hammer, Son V. Nguyen, Marion L. Carroll, Mark A. Batzer and Lynn B. Jorde. 2001. "Genetic Evidence on the Origins of Indian Caste Populations." *Genome Research* 11(6):994–1004.

Benjamin, Ruha. 2009. "A Lab of Their Own: Genomic Sovereignty as Postcolonial Science Policy." *Policy & Society* 28(4):341–55.

Benjamin, Ruha. 2013. *People's Science: Bodies and Rights on the Stem Cell Frontier.* Palo Alto, CA: Stanford University Press.

Biehl, João and Torben Eskerod. 2009. *Will to Live: AIDS Therapies and the Politics of Survival.* Princeton, NJ: Princeton University Press.

Bliss, Catherine. 2012. *Race Decoded: The Genomic Fight for Social Justice.* Palo Alto, CA: Stanford University Press.

Collier, Roger. 2012. "A Race-based Detour to Personalized Medicine." *Canadian Medical Association Journal* 184(7):E351–3.

Daar, Abdallah S. and Peter A. Singer. 2005. "Pharmacogenetics and Geographical Ancestry: Implications for Drug Development and Global Health." *Nature Reviews Genetics* 6:241–6.

D'Altorio, Tony. 2011. "Big Pharma Faces Major Roadblock in India." Accessed September 19, 2011 (www.investmentu.com/2011/April/indias-pharmerging-market.html).

de Vries, Jantina and Michael Pepper. 2012. "Genomic Sovereignty and the African Promise: Mining the African Genome for the Benefit of Africa." *Journal of Medical Ethics* 38(8):474–8.

Duster, Troy. 2003. *Backdoor to Eugenics.* New York: Routledge.

Duster, Troy. 2005. "Race and Reification in Science." *Science* 307(5712):1050–1.

Ecks, Stefan. 2005. "Pharmaceutical Citizenship: Antidepressant Marketing and the Promise of Demarginalization in India." *Anthropology & Medicine* 12(3):239–54.

Egorova, Yulia. 2009. "De/geneticizing Caste: Population Genetic Research in South Asia." *Science as Culture* 18(4):417–34.

Egorova, Yulia. 2010. "Castes of Genes? Representing Human Genetic Diversity in India." *Genomics, Society and Policy* 6(3):32–49.

El-Haj, Nadia A. 2007. "The Genetic Reinscription of Race." *Annual Review of Anthropology* 36: 283–300.

Epstein, Steven. 2007. *Inclusion: The Politics of Difference in Medical Research.* Chicago, IL: University of Chicago Press.

Erasmus, Zimitri. 2013. "Throwing the Genes: A Renewed Biological Imaginary of 'Race', Place, and Identification." *Theoria* 60(3):38–53.

Figueroa, Monica M. 2010. "Distributed Intensities: Whiteness, Mestizaje and the Logics of Mexican Racism." *Ethnicities* 10(3):387–401.

Fortun, Michael. 2008. *Promising Genomics: Iceland and deCODE Genetics in a World of Speculation.* Berkeley, CA: University of California Press.

Foster, Laura. 2014. "Critical Cultural Translation: A Socio-Legal Framework for Regulatory Orders." *Indiana Journal of Global Legal Studies* 21(1):79–105.

Foster, Morris W. and Richard R. Sharpe. 2002. "Race Ethnicity, and Genomics: Social Classifications as Proxies of Biological Heterogeneity." *Genome Research* 12:844–50.

Fujimura, Joan. H., Troy Duster and R. Rajagopalan. 2008. "Race, Genetics, and Disease: Questions of Evidence, Matters of Consequence." *Social Studies of Science* 38:643–56.

Fullwiley, Duana. 2008. "The Biologistical Construction of Race: 'Admixture' Technology and the New Genetic Medicine." *Social Studies of Science* 38(5):695–735.

Fupen, Orietta. 2007. "Los más europeos." Accessed June 17, 2014 (http://yoexpreso.com/ediciondigital/index2.php?cual=5&sdia=10&smes=03&sanio=2007&seccion=1).

Ghosh, Rishab, ed. 2005. *CODE: Collaborative Ownership and the Digital Economy.* Cambridge, MA: MIT Press.

Gilmore, Ruth W. 2002. "Fatal Couplings of Power and Difference: Notes on Racism and Geography." *The Professional Geographer* 54(1):15–24.

Goldberg, David T. 2009. *The Threat of Race: Reflections on Racial Neoliberalism.* Malden, MA: Wiley-Blackwell.

Gonzalez, Enrique, Rahul Dhanda, Mike Bamshad, Srinivas Mummidi, Reni Geevarghese, Gabriel Catano, Stephanie A. Anderson, Elizabeth A. Walter, Michael F. Hammer, Andrea Mangano, Luisa Sen, Robert A. Clarke, Seema S. Ahuja, Matthew J. Dolan and Sunil K. Ahuja. 2001. "Global Survey of Genetic Variation in *CCR5, RANTES,* and *MIP-1a*: Impact on the Epidemiology of the HIV-1 Pandemic." *Proceedings of the National Academy of Sciences* 98(9):5199–204.

Hamilton, Jennifer. 2008. "Revitalizing Difference in the HapMap: Race and Contemporary Human Genetic Variation Research." *The Journal of Law, Medicine & Ethics* 36(3):471–7.

Hammonds, Evelynn M. and Rebecca M. Herzig. 2008. *The Nature of Difference Sciences of Race in the United States from Jefferson to Genomics.* Cambridge, MA: MIT Press.

Harding, Sandra. 2013. "Beyond Postcolonial Theory: Two Undertheorized Perspectives in Perspectives in Science and Technology Studies." Pp. 431–54 in *Women, Science, and Technology: A Reader in Feminist Science Studies,* edited by Mary Wyer, Donna Giesman, Mary Barbercheck, Hatice Ozturk and Marta Wayne. New York: Routledge.

Hayden, Cori. 2003. *When Nature Goes Public: The Making and Unmaking of Bioprospecting in Mexico.* Princeton, NJ: Princeton University Press.

Human Rights Watch. 2009. "United Nations Racism Conference Fails on Caste-based Discrimination." Accessed October 13, 2012 (www.hrw.org/news/2009/04/22/un-racism-conference-fails-caste-based-discrimination).

Indian Genome Variation Consortium. n.d. Accessed October 13, 2012 (www.igvdb.res.in/phase1details.php).

Indigenous People's Council on Biocolonialism. n.d. Accessed June 17, 2014 (www.ipcb.org/issues/intellect_prop/files/igc10_gr.html).

Jasanoff, Sheila, ed. 2011. *Reframing Rights: Bioconstitutionalism in the Genetic Age*. Cambridge, MA: MIT Press.

Kahn, Jonathan. 2004. "How a Drug Becomes 'Ethnic': Law, Commerce, and the Production of Racial Categories in Medicine." *Yale Journal of Health Policy, Law, and Ethics* 4(1):1–46.

Kahn, Jonathan. 2006. "Genes, Race, and Population: Avoiding a Collision of Categories." *American Journal of Public Health* 96(11):1965–70.

Kahn, Jonathan. 2013. *Race in a Bottle: The Story of BiDil and Racialized Medicine in a Post-Genomic Age*. New York: Columbia University Press.

Koshy, Jacob P. 2008. "Indian Gene Map Links Ethnic Groups, Diseases." Accessed June 17, 2014 (www.livemint.com/Home-Page/LebTt30evw3j9jmaGDRWbJ/Indian-gene-map-links-ethnic-groups-diseases.html).

Kulkarni, Kaustubh. 2012. "India's Dr Reddy's Lab Q3 Net Beats Forecasts on US Sales." *Reuters*. Accessed June 17, 2014 (www.reuters.com/article/2012/02/03/dr-reddys-labs-results-idUSL4E8D323320120203).

Kumar, Dhavendra. 2012. *Genomics and Health in the Developing World*. Oxford: Oxford University Press.

Lund, Joshua. 2006. *The Impure Imagination: Toward a Critical Hybridity in Latin American Writing*. St Paul, MN: University of Minnesota Press.

Montoya, Michael J. 2007. "Bioethnic Conscription: Genes, Race, and Mexicana/o Ethnicity in Diabetes Research." *Cultural Anthropology* 22(1):94–128.

Mothelet, Veronica G. and Stephan Herrera. 2005. "Mexico Launches Bold Genome Project." *Nature Biotechnology* 23(9):1030.

Petryna, Adriana. 2005. "Ethical Variability: Drug Development and Globalizing Clinical Trials." *American Ethnologist* 32(2):183–97.

Pharmaceutical Technology. 2009. "The Emerging Seven: Pharma's Promised Land." Accessed June 17, 2014 (www.pharmaceutical-technology.com/features/feature48666).

Pollock, Anne. 2014. "Places of Pharmaceutical Knowledge-making: Global Health, Postcolonial Science, and Hope in South Africa Drug Discovery." *Social Studies of Science*. Published online before print; doi: 10.1177/0306312714543285. Accessed November 9, 2014.

Prashad, Vijay. 2000. "Afro-Dalits of the Earth, Unite!" *African Studies Review* 43:189–201.

Rajan, Kaushik S. 2006. *Biocapital: The Constitution of Postgenomic Life*. Durham, NC: Duke University Press.

Rajghatta, Chidanand. 2001. "Upper Caste Indian Male More European, Says Study." *The Times of India* May 21:4.

Reardon, Jennifer. 2004. "Decoding Race and Human Difference in a Genomic Age." *Differences* 15(3):38–65.

Reddy, Deepa S. 2005. "The Ethnicity of Caste." *Anthropological Quarterly* 78:543–84.

Reich, David, Khumarasamy Thangaraj, Nick Patterson, Alkes L. Price and Lalji Singh. 2009. "Reconstructing Indian Population History." *Nature* 461(24):489–95.

Roberts, Dorothy. 2011. *Fatal Invention: How Science, Politics, and Big Business Re-Create Race in the Twenty-First Century*. New York: The New Press.

Rose, Nikolas. 2007. *The Politics of Life Itself: Biomedicine, Power and Subjectivity in the Twenty-First Century*. Princeton, NJ: Princeton University Press.

Sahoo, Sanghamitra, Anamika Singh, G. Himabindu, Jheelam Banerjee, T. Sitalaximi, Sonali Gaikwad, R. Trivedi, Phillip Endicott, Toomas Kivisild, Mait Metspalu, Richard Villems and V. K. Kashyap. 2005. "A Prehistory of Indian Y Chromosomes: Evaluating Demic Diffusion Scenarios." *Proceedings of the National Academy of Sciences* 103:843–8.

Schwartz-Marin, Ernesto. 2011. "Genomic Sovereignty and the 'Mexican Genome': An Ethnography of Postcolonial Biopolitics." Dissertation, University of Exeter.

Schwartz-Marin, Ernesto and Eduardo Restrepo. 2013. "Biocoloniality, Governance, and the Protection of 'Genetic Identities' in Mexico and Colombia." *Sociology* 47(5):925–42.

Seguin, Beatrice, Billie-Jo Hardy, Peter A. Singer and Abdallah S. Daar. 2008. "Genomic Medicine and Developing Countries: Creating a Room of their Own." *Nature Reviews Genetics* 9: 487–93.

Slabbert, Melodie and Michael Pepper. 2010. "'A Room of Our Own?' Legal Lacunae Regarding Genomic Sovereignty in South Africa." *Journal of Contemporary Roman-Dutch Law* 73: 432–50.

Soo-Jin Lee, Sandra, Joanna Mountain and Barbara A. Koenig. 2001. "The Meanings of 'Race' in the New Genomics: Implications for Health Disparities Research." *Yale Journal of Health Policy, Law, and Ethics* 1:33–75.

TallBear, Kim. 2013. *Native American DNA: Tribal Belonging and the False Promise of Genetic Science.* Minneapolis, MN: University of Minnesota Press.

Tharoor, Shashi. 2007. "Mapping a Nation: Pluralism at 60." *Outlook India.* Accessed June 17, 2014 (http://business.outlookindia.com/article.aspx?99848).

Wade, Peter, Carlos López Beltrán, Eduardo Restrepo and Ricardo Ventura Santos. 2014. *Mestizo Genomics: Race Mixture, Nature, and Science in Latin America.* Durham, NC: Duke University Press.

Wilson, Duff. 2011. "Drug Firms Face Billions in Losses in '11 as Patents End." *The New York Times.* Accessed June 17, 2014 (www.nytimes.com/2011/03/07/business/07drug.html).

11

Beyond Geneticization

Regimes of Perceptibility and the
Social Determinants of Health

SARA SHOSTAK AND MARGOT MOINESTER

Introduction

Many early social scientific critiques of the Human Genome Project (HGP) used the concept of geneticization as their point of departure. Indexing myriad potential negative social consequences – including genetic reductionism, determinism, essentialism and fatalism – the concept of geneticization made strong claims about the potential power of genetic information. Social scientists were especially concerned with the power of genetics to shift scientific research, public understanding and scarce resources away from the social and environmental determinants of health. Two decades after the first writings on geneticization and more than a decade into the post-genomic era, the social and environmental determinants of health remain prominent concerns in both scientific and public arenas. For a wide array of scientists, "the environment" – varyingly defined – and its effects on health are primary research foci. We do not see this as a simple repudiation of the geneticization thesis. Rather, we contend that in the current moment, addressing the critical concerns at the heart of the concept of "geneticization" demands new conceptual frameworks.

Simply put, the assumption of the geneticization critique that genes and environments are mutually exclusive explanatory frameworks for human health and illness is an insufficient conceptual basis for contemporary analyses of biomedical research and practice. For while "the environment" is a focal concern across disciplines in the life sciences and social sciences, there is no consensus within or across disciplines as to how it should be conceptualized or operationalized. Indeed, some operationalizations of the environment render it an internal, individual attribute that conveys health risks at the molecular level – very much like a gene. As such, it is now clear that merely focusing research on environmental or social determinants of health does not necessarily lead to social structural understandings of health and illness as implied by the concept of geneticization. Rather, much depends on how genes, environments and their interactions are conceptualized and operationalized in biomedical research.

Consequently, in order to understand contemporary practices in biomedical science, we need analytic frameworks that support inquiry into "historical ontology," that is, an examination of the history of things – such as "genes," "the environment" and "the social determinants of health" – as they are formed in relationship to specific epistemological traditions and practices (Mitman, Murphy and Sellers 2004). Drawing on work in the history of science, we deploy the concept of "regimes of perceptibility," which directs analytic attention to questions about what factors, or levels of analysis, are made visible or obscured by specific scientific techniques and technologies. We make our case for this approach by applying it to three determinants of health – diet, toxic chemicals and stress – that scientists from different disciplines have investigated at varying levels of analysis. Further, we argue that this framework can be extended to ask questions about how a *political economy of perception* may favor particular conceptualizations and operationalizations of the environment.[1] Thus, while moving on from now outdated assumptions embedded in the concept of geneticization, we envision new scholarly engagements that maintain fidelity to some of its central social justice concerns. We begin with a review of the concept of geneticization and the wealth of empirical studies it has generated.

The Geneticization Critique

The concept of geneticization entered social scientific research through the work of Abby Lippman, a professor of epidemiology at McGill University and a dedicated women's health activist. As introduced by Lippman, geneticization refers to "an ongoing process by which differences between individuals are reduced to their DNA codes, with most disorders, behaviours, and physio-logical variations defined, at least in part, as genetic in origin" (1991:19). Lippman understood the concept of geneticization as a jumping off point for a broad "social justice critique" of the new genetics. In an interview with the Canadian Women's Health Network in 1999, she defined geneticization as "the tremendous extent to which 'genetics' is taking precedence over how we see health and social problems."[2] Similarly, prominent social scientists and human-ists highlighted the potential of genetics to supplant public health approaches to complex diseases and to undermine efforts to identify the social and environ-mental determinants of health (Conrad 1999; Sherwin and Simpson 1999). In an oft-cited work, Duster (2003) argued that extensive public sector investment in genetic research would disproportionately and negatively impact Blacks by diverting attention and resources away from social and environmental factors that contribute to increasing rates of lung cancer and cardiovascular disease in the African American population (see also Conrad 1999; Duster 2006).[3]

In these early writings, geneticization further served as connotative short-hand for various related concerns about how new genetic findings might be understood and used, including:

1 *genetic reductionism*, in which a complex and ecumenical under-standing of the causes of human development is supplanted by one in which genes are perceived as the "true cause" of difference[4] (Sloan 2000:17),

2 *genetic determinism*, in which genes are taken as inevitably implying traits and behaviors (Lippman 1992; Alper and Beckwith 1993; Rothman 2001; Nelkin and Lindee 2004),

3 *genetic essentialism*, in which genetics becomes a dominant way "to explore fundamental questions about human life" and "to talk about guilt and responsibility, power and privilege, intellectual or emotional status" (Nelkin and Lindee 2004:16).

Lippman believed that much of the new genetics was motivated by "two E's … economics and eugenics." As a women's health advocate, she hoped that "there's enough strength in the women's community, and enough belief that this is not the way to go, so that we can mobilize and put brakes on geneticization."[5]

Unsurprisingly, given the critical stance built into the original formulation of the concept, there has been debate about whether the term "geneticization" can be used to neutrally characterize social phenomena (Freese and Shostak 2009).[6] At issue is whether "geneticization" is too "ethically loaded" or "morally circular" to serve as a framework for empirical research (Hedgecoe 1998). Some writers have suggested that it should be understood as "a heuristic tool" in a moral debate (Ten Have 2001). Others have countered that conceptual writings about geneticization are replete with claims that can be evaluated with the tools of empirical research (Hedgecoe 2001) and social scientists have generated a substantial literature towards that end.

This empirically oriented literature reveals that genetic concepts, technologies and practices have multiple and contradictory effects (Freese and Shostak 2009). Analyses of biomedical research articles have found that genetic information can reshape disease categories (Hedgecoe 2002) and that scientists privilege genetic explanations over non-genetic explanations, at least in part because genetic causes are seen as more easily specified and researched (Hedgecoe 2001; see also Shim 2005). Content analyses of newspaper articles find that media coverage of research on gene–environment interaction selectively emphasizes the gene "half" of the interaction and largely ignores environmental causes of disease (Horwitz 2005). There are discrepancies among studies that seek to assess whether geneticization in the print media is increasing. For example, Duster (2003) found an increase in articles invoking a genetic explanation of crime in the late 1970s and early 1980s. Condit, Ofulue and Sheedy (1998) found, over a longer timespan, that, if anything, discourse about heredity may be becoming less deterministic. Research by Phelan and colleagues (2013) demonstrates that news articles discussing racial differences in genetic bases of disease increased significantly between 1985 and 2008 and were significantly less likely than non-health-related articles about race and genetics to discuss social implications. However, Condit (1999) has warned against any presumption that the use of supposedly geneticized metaphors in the media (e.g., "genetic blueprint") implies that public conceptions of genetic causation are correspondingly deterministic or reductionistic.

There is clear evidence that people attribute individual health and social outcomes to genetics (Shostak et al. 2009). However, research that moves from the relative simplicity of the printed word to the messy realities of clinics, patient advocacy groups and the daily experiences of those living with illness – or the risk of illness – has suggested that neither the lived realities nor the broad implications of genetics are as simple as early writings suggested. Against the notion that geneticization is an inevitable consequence of genetic research, empirical analyses have highlighted the power of daily practices of diagnosis and treatment of disease to enable or impede geneticization, even for conditions with simple (i.e., autosomal dominant) genetic etiologies (Cox and Starzomski 2004; Kerr 2005).[7] In contrast to prior conceptualizations of genetics as a deterministic discourse, this research points to the enduring power of local knowledge (Rapp 2000), national health policy regimes (Parthasarathy 2007) and the institutional embeddedness (Shostak, Conrad and Horwitz 2008) and social meanings (Sankar et al. 2004) of medical conditions in shaping lay understandings of and responses to genetic information. In an explicit challenge to the assumption that genetic information will lead to fatalism, a growing cadre of researchers contend that genetic information creates new obligations to act on knowledge to protect health and to maximize quality of life (Novas and Rose 2000; Frosch, Mello and Lerman 2005; Rose 2006; Gibbon 2007).

Moreover, many users of genetic testing appreciate the nuances of probabilistic risk and predictive uncertainty, and are correspondingly circumspect in their interpretations of genetic information. This appears to be the case even in regard to prenatal genetic testing, arguably the clinical setting wherein genetic testing is the most routinized (Markens, Browner and Press 1999; Rapp 2000; Franklin and Roberts 2006; Thompson 2007). Parents of children with genetic conditions (e.g., Klinefelter, Turner and fragile X syndromes) may simultaneously accept the authority of molecular genetic test results and create a space for uncertainty about the condition by emphasizing variation between diagnosed children, the individuality of their diagnosed child and his or her accomplishments, and other ambiguities in prognosis that complicate the significance of genetic information (Whitmarsh et al. 2007; see also Timmermans and Buchbinder 2013). Even when individuals embrace the idea that a disease "runs in the family," they interpret information about genetic susceptibility in the context of their own beliefs about the multiple causes of illness, patterns of inheritance and observable risk factors in their families (Meiser et al. 2005; Lock et al. 2006; Shostak, Zarhin and Ottman 2011).

While two decades worth of empirical research point to the need to revisit and revise the concept of geneticization, transformations in the life sciences also highlight the need for new conceptual frameworks. As we detail below, the assumption that "genetic" and "environmental" explanations of human health and illness are mutually exclusive – existing in a zero-sum relationship – is an insufficient analytic lens for contemporary scientific research on the processes and consequences of gene–environment interaction. Additionally, the environment is often molecularized in research on gene–environment interaction, becoming a trait of the individual that, like a gene, is measured inside the human body and at the molecular level (Shostak 2013). This underscores the importance of questions about how the environment is conceptualized, operationalized and made knowable and actionable in contemporary biomedical research.

A Place for the Environment

In contrast to the early predictions of the geneticization thesis, the genomic revolution has not resulted in a complete erasure or "undoing" (Frickel et al. 2010) of the environment in research on human health and illness. In fact, as noted by researchers across the life sciences and social sciences, genomics has had the paradoxical effect of calling attention to the importance of social and environmental factors vis-à-vis health (Olden and White 2005; Pescosolido 2006; Schwartz and Collins 2007; Bearman 2013). As scholarly observers of the contemporary life sciences have noted, "It is almost ironic that the deeper biologists delve into the human body and the more fine-grained and molecularised their analyses of the body become, the less they are able to ignore the many ties that link the individual body and its molecules to the spatio-temporal contexts within which it dwells" (Niewöhner 2011:290). Within the life sciences, researchers assert that current research makes it absolutely clear that "the genome cannot operate independently of its environmental contexts – both external and internal to the body" (Meaney 2010, in Lock 2013). Indeed, a hallmark of the post-genomic era is the imperative that scientists elucidate the role of the environment in shaping the processes and outcomes of gene action (Shostak and Moinester 2015).

In fact, soon after the completion of the Human Genome Project (HGP) in 2003, the leadership of the National Human Genome Research Institute (NHGRI) began making statements about the importance of understanding gene–environment interactions. In a paper entitled "Welcome to the Genomics Era," Guttmacher and Collins noted that it "bears repeating" that "even in the genomic era, it is not genes alone but *the interplay of genetic and environmental factors* that determines phenotype (i.e., health or disease)" (2003:997; emphasis added). In pursuit of better understanding this "interplay," the NHGRI convened a "Gene Environment Interplay Workshop" in 2010. This meeting brought together 150 scientists, representing a wide array of fields, to evaluate the state-of-the-science in the study of gene–environment interactions in complex diseases, and make recommendations regarding research priorities, challenges and next steps (Bookman et al. 2011). The participants at the workshop called for an "integrative" model of complex diseases, emphasizing particularly the need to bring measures of environmental exposures into biomedical research. Today, the leadership of the NHGRI also advocates for the "integration" of genomic information" with "environmental exposure" in order to generate "a much fuller understanding of disease aetiology" (Green, Guyer and National Human Genome Research Institute 2011:208).

This may be especially true for research which seeks to understand the persistent challenge of health disparities in the USA, many of which are associated with inequities in social and environmental conditions (Williams 2005; Brulle and Pellow 2006). Leading public health scientists have noted that integrating environmental measures and interventions into biomedical research will be critical to efforts to remediate health disparities: "a more nuanced understanding of how genes interact with each other and with environments is necessary to fully understand if and how genetic variation contributed to health disparities" (Diez Roux 2011:1628). Writing in *Nature*, the director of the NHGRI observes that "Most documented causes of health disparities are not genetic . . ."; consequently, "as genomics continues to be applied in global healthcare settings, it must not be mistakenly used to divert attention and resources from the many non-genetic factors that contribute to health disparities, which would paradoxically exacerbate the problem" (Green et al. 2011:210).

It has not escaped the notice of researchers that this emergent intellectual agenda will require new and perhaps novel conceptualizations – and measurements of – the environment in gene–environment interaction (Boardman, Daw and Freese 2013; Fletcher and Conley 2013). This has led to calls for better measurements of environmental exposures and for the inclusion of exposure data in large databases, including, but not limited to, those being used in genomics research (Wild 2005; Schwartz and Collins 2007; Rappaport and Smith 2010). These calls often emphasize that understanding common, complex diseases requires "that both environmental exposures and genetic variation be reliably measured" (Wild 2005:1847). At the same time, scientists note that the disproportionate investment, to date, in genetics research, means that they often use "cutting edge" genomics technologies to assess genetic variation and gene expression, while using self-report questionnaires to characterize environmental exposures (Rappaport and Smith 2010:460).

However, cross-disciplinary scientific consensus about the importance of understanding "the environment" in gene–environment interaction is not the same as a cross-disciplinary scientific consensus about how the environment should be conceptualized or measured. For example, within the life sciences, the environment may refer to the cell (the environment of the gene), endogenous hormonal profiles (the environment of the cells), indoor or outdoor physical environments (the environment of the human body) or stressful life situations (the social environment).

Additionally, social scientists argue that "actually thinking about the environment" (Bearman 2013:S12) requires consideration of how environments change over the life course and how individuals are embedded in multiple social networks. Put differently, social scientists assert that actual lived environments are more than "little Petri dishes" but rather include dynamic processes unfolding across time and place (Bearman 2013:S12). From this perspective, understanding the environment in gene–environment interaction requires "a multilevel, multidomain, longitudinal framework that accounts for upstream processes influencing health outcomes" (Boardman et al. 2013:S1). Further, social scientists emphasize "the potentially important role that characteristics of intermediate levels of social organization, such as neighborhoods, schools, and the workplace, have to play" (Boardman et al. 2013:S1).

Simply put, there is a remarkable degree of heterogeneity in the levels of analysis at which a single concept – "the environment" – can be operationalized. Insofar as the geneticization framework implies a mutually exclusive relationship between genes and environments in explanations of human health and illness, this heterogeneity, along with the increasing focus across disciplines on the interplay of genetic and environmental factors, is potentially obscured. By directing analytic attention instead to questions regarding the factors and levels of analysis made more or less visible by specific scientific techniques and technologies, the concept of "regimes of perceptibility" (Murphy 2006) provides greater analytical leverage for investigating the diverse processes and outcomes of contemporary biomedical research about genes, environments and human health and illness.

Regimes of Perceptibility

The concept of "regimes of perceptibility" comes from historian Michelle Murphy's research on the emergence of Sick Building Syndrome in the 1980s (2006). Murphy's analysis contrasts scientific, corporate and laypersons' approaches to apprehending the presence and effects of chemical exposures inside the office buildings where (mostly female) workers reported a constellation of health problems, such as headache, rashes and immune system disorders. She demonstrates how specific techniques of measurement make particular aspects of the environment more and less visible, with consequences for what dimensions of the environment are perceived as more or less real and actionable. As she notes, domains of imperceptibility are the "inevitable result" of the tangible ways that domains of perceptibility are established: "the history of how things come to exist is intrinsically linked to the history of how things come not to exist, or come to exist with only uncertainty or partiality"

(Murphy 2006:9). By regularizing, standardizing and sedimenting the contours of perception and imperception within academic disciplines, regimes of perceptibility determine which objects have the opportunity to populate the worlds of the lab, the clinic and the community – and which do not (Murphy 2006).

The concept of "regimes of perceptibility" points to a new set of questions about how genes and environments are studied in research on human health and illness. It suggests that we must ask not only "is it genes or the environment?" but also consider how the environment is conceptualized, how it is operationalized and, consequently, which dimensions of the environment can be seen and which become invisible. Likewise, we may ask questions about how regimes of perceptibility make some actors – whether individual or institutional – more or less credible witnesses and with what consequences for different kinds of action. As such, the concept of regimes of perceptibility also offers analytic leverage on how some objects or situations, such as the environment, become imbued with "complexity" or "uncertainty," while others, such as genes, are perceived to be more easily ascertained and actionable.[8]

Perceiving Exposures

We deploy the concept of "regimes of perceptibility" to examine three kinds of environmental exposure – diet, toxics and stress – relevant to health disparities. In each case, we describe different materializations of the environment in contemporary research on human health and illness. We find that some materializations of these environmental exposures include social institutions, contexts and processes, while others render "the environment" an internal, individual attribute. Taken together, these brief case studies demonstrate how environmental exposures may be made more or less social in nature, depending on the techniques and technologies that scientists use to study them. These renderings, in turn, have consequences for how scientists, policymakers and the public may understand human health and seek to ameliorate health disparities. Therefore, we contend that the underlying social justice concerns of the geneticization critique now demand a different kind of inquiry, one focused on regimes of perceptibility and how they shape knowledge production and policymaking regarding the social and environmental determinants of health.

Diet

Nutrition was among the earliest foci of public health efforts in the USA (Rosen 1993). More recently, concern about the rising incidence of obesity has highlighted the role of diet in a wide variety of diseases, including diabetes, cardiovascular disease and certain types of cancer. There are marked health disparities for these diseases, which often include earlier onset of illness and more severe disease among minorities compared to Whites (Williams et al. 2010).

A robust literature on the neighborhood food environment in social epidemiology and the social sciences examines the social institutions and processes that structure opportunities for access to different types of diets. Specifically, these lines of research investigate "how the structure and organization of the neighborhood food environment ... might influence food purchasing patterns and hence diet and diet-related chronic diseases" (Thompson et al. 2013:116). Drawing on a variety of methods, this research calls attention to the accessibility, availability, affordability and quality of food in local environments (McKinnon et al. 2009). It also highlights social processes and symbolic relations between individuals and food environments in order to examine the "dynamic relationships between meaning and action" regarding food purchasing behavior (Thompson et al. 2013:117). Collectively, this line of research conceptualizes "spatial variations in exposure to aspects of the local food environment as an underlying explanatory factor for social and spatial inequalities in diet and related health outcomes" (Cummins 2007:196).

At the same time, a very different line of research – the emergent field of nutritional epigenetics – has rendered diet an "environmental exposure" that is assessed at the molecular level (Landecker 2011:167). Indeed, in nutritional epigenetics, "food stands in for the environment in the dyad of 'gene–environment interactions'" (Landecker 2011:168). It is against this background that we can make sense of a recent paper in the *Annual Review of Nutrition* that calls diet "*the greatest single source of chemical exposures*, including nutrients, nonnutritive chemicals, pesticides, and others" (Jones, Park and Ziegler 2012:186; emphasis added).

As highlighted by Landecker, nutritional epigenetics "proposes a specific molecular route from outside to inside, and suggests a mechanism by which the wars and famines and abundant harvests of one generation can affect the metabolic systems of another" (2011:178). Such models have clear implications for theorizing how dimensions of social organization, such as race, class and gender, become biologically embedded and heritable. Research cited by health disparities scholars as an exemplar of the integration of levels of analysis (Williams et al. 2010), proposes that epigenetic mechanisms can account for specific racial disparities in health, as well as their intergenerational transmission (Kuzawa and Sweet 2009). In Landecker's evocative phrasing, the models recast "social suffering" as "molecularly heritable" (2011:179). The proposition here is that complex social institutions and processes become biologically embedded, not only in those who experience them, but in their offspring. Further, maternal experiences – often recast in this research as "environmental exposures" – may have long-term consequences for their children, such as increased risk for adult onset diseases.

Epigenetics thus directs scientific analysis to "biography and milieu" as the conditioning contexts of gene expression and action (Niewöhner 2011). However, while it calls attention to the role of "the outside world" – including the social environment – in shaping human health and illness, the experimental formalization of nutritional epigenetics requires that the world be measured at the molecular level (Landecker 2011). Thus, even as it offers a means of conceptualizing how socioeconomic differences – as manifest in differences in sociomaterial environments – become embodied, in practice it simultaneously renders those very socioeconomic differences as a "fuzzy background" for bioactive molecules. In these accounts, purportedly focused on the social environment, methyl groups, histones, etc. nonetheless emerge as the "real" actors shaping human bodies, and their vulnerabilities (Landecker 2011:184).

In this case, the concept of regimes of perceptibility directs analytic attention to disciplinary differences in how "diet" is rendered as an environmental exposure with consequences for human health. It highlights how certain aspects of diet – such as neighborhood food environments or methyl groups – become researchable objects that populate the worlds of the lab, the clinic and the community, while others do not. Additionally, in this case, the concept of regimes of perceptibility also allows us to ask questions about the molecularization of the social and environmental determinants of health in contemporary biomedical research, such as epigenetics. At issue is not whether complex social and environmental phenomena are a focus of epigenetic research; clearly they are. Rather, the issue is how these complex phenomena are made amenable to the demands of contemporary laboratory research, and the consequences of this for science and society (Landecker 2011). If "what we are witnessing here is the attempt to operationalise instances of social change according to criteria taken from the practice of molecular biological research" (Niewöhner 2011:291), then we must engage seriously with the consequences of these operationalizations, both in the laboratory and beyond. Similarly, as we describe next, research that centers on environmental chemicals – and their interactions with human genetic material – tends to molecularize the environment. As such, while environmental exposures and their molecular effects may be more comprehensively documented, the social institutions and processes that make people vulnerable to exposure may begin to fade from view.

Toxic Chemicals

In the USA, both race and socioeconomic status are well-established predictors of exposure to a wide range of suboptimal environmental conditions, including hazardous wastes and other toxins, ambient and indoor air pollutants, water quality, ambient noise, residential crowding, and poor housing quality, educational facilities, work environments and neighborhood conditions (Brulle and Pellow 2006). There has been strong evidence of associations between race, class and proximity to known environmental hazards since the late 1980s. In the social scientific research on "environmental justice," race is particularly identified as a powerful predictor of exposure to environmental chemicals.[9] A meta-analysis of the literature on race, class and environmental exposures found that "whether using a general proximity measure or a precise distance measure, race has an independent effect on the locations of waste sites and proves to be a stronger predictor than income" (Brown 1995:18). A similar pattern is observed for exposure to air pollution: "Blacks face higher exposures at all income levels than Whites" (Brown 1995:20). Research on the regulation, amelioration and cleanup of toxic waste sites also indicates significant inequities associated with race (Lavelle and Coyle 1992). Additionally, research has found that there are race and class differences in siting proposals for new incinerators, hazardous waste sites and nuclear storage sites, with communities facing sitings more likely to be Black, Latino or Native American (Brown 1995).[10] Consequently, researchers have suggested that integrating data on environmental inequality and its health impacts into the existing research on health disparities is critical to efforts to understand the causes of and identify solutions to the ongoing problem of health disparities between demographic groups in the USA (Brulle and Pellow 2006).

Exposomics is an emergent post-genomic field that seeks to assess "the whole environment we have inside our bodies" (Harmon 2010:2). Advocates of exposomics propose a reconceptualization of environmental exposures that encompasses a wide variety of external and internal factors relevant to human biological processes and their health effects. The focal object of exposomics – the exposome – consists of every exposure that an individual experiences, from conception to death (Wild 2012). In contrast to the research undertaken by environmental justice advocates, and their allies in the social sciences, exposomic research is an epistemological intervention. It is designed and intended to improve scientists' ability to measure environmental exposures across the life course and their capacity to speak credibly about the human health effects of environmental exposures (Shostak 2013).

The broadest definition of the exposome includes *internal exposures* (e.g., processes internal to the body such as metabolism, endogenous circulating hormones, body morphology, physical activity, gut microflora, inflammation, lipid peroxidation, oxidative stress and aging), *specific external exposures* (e.g., radiation, infectious agents, chemical contaminants and environmental pollutants, diet, lifestyle factors (e.g., tobacco, alcohol), occupation and medical interventions) and *general external exposures*, defined as wider social, economic and psychological influences on the individual (e.g., social capital, education, financial status, psychological and mental stress, urban–rural environment and climate) (Wild 2012). More narrow definitions of the exposome emphasize the internal consequences of individual behaviors, discounting factors from both the "specific internal" and "general internal" domains described above (Rappaport et al. 2010). However, under both the more expansive and the more narrow definition of "exposures," the environment in exposome research is defined as a characteristic of individuals and measured as a discrete biomarker inside the human body.

Indeed, scientists articulate the exposome as the "complement" to the genome (Wild 2005): "Whereas the genome gives rise to a programmed set of molecules ... in the blood, the exposome is functionally represented by *the complementary set of chemicals derived from sources outside of genetic control*" (Rappaport 2012:2; emphasis added). Advocates of exposomics argue that "We need to be able to analyze 'the environment' in a way analogous to the genetics' community analysis of variation" (Balshaw 2010:8) rather than "relying on questionnaires to characterize 'environmental exposures'" (Rappaport and Smith 2010:460). They call for a "Human Exposome Project," similar in scope to the Human Genome Project, to improve assessment of how the environment affects human health (Arnaud 2010).

As with stress and diet, "in body" measurements of chemical exposures, such as the exposome, raise questions about whether the social processes and institutions that make people vulnerable to exposure to environmental chemicals become imperceptible when scientists take up molecular operationalizations of the environment. In the words of medical anthropologist Margaret Lock, "there is a distinct possibility that it is the apparent molecular endpoints of such variables that will capture most attention, without shedding light on the complex factors implicated in the perturbations of these molecular barometers" (2013:1896–7). Again, in this case, the concept of "regimes of perceptibility" directs analysis towards the consequences of different ways of operationalizing the environment, which may be individualized, and biomedicalized, when it is measured inside the body and at the molecular level.

Stress

Exposure to chronic stress has long been emphasized as an important determinant of disease (Miller, Chen and Zhou 2007) and is a focus of contemporary research on gene–environment interaction and human health. Across disciplines, scientists seek to identify the biological mechanisms by which stress "gets under the skin" (Taylor, Repetti and Seeman 1997), as well as how these stressors are ecologically patterned (Hill, Ross and Angel 2005; Matheson et al. 2006).

Biomedical scientists have primarily focused on the regulation of stress-related biological pathways, such as cortisol, epinephrine and norepinephrine secretion. Within this literature, the release of cortisol through the hypothalamic-pituitary-adrenocortical (HPA) axis has received the most attention, in part because of its widespread regulatory function in the central nervous system, the metabolic system and the immune system (Miller et al. 2007). There is also a quickly growing literature that examines the effects of stress on gene expression, in relation to a wide variety of health and social outcomes (Cole 2010; Hunter 2012).

In contrast, a rich tradition of scholarship in the social sciences focuses on the "ecology of stress." This body of work views stressful circumstances and events as rooted in and arising out of the structural contexts of people's lives (Pearlin 1989). By focusing on features of the contexts, places and locations in which individuals are embedded, these studies make visible geographies of exposure and susceptibility (Jerrett and Finkelstein 2005). Such work holds promise for revealing the social institutions and processes that structure exposure to stress. However, it may ignore the biological mechanisms by which stress gets under the skin to affect gene expression.

Due to technical and methodological developments in the collection of biological samples in community-based settings, scholars are increasingly integrating these two approaches (National Research Council 2001). This line of research seeks to shed light on the reciprocal and potentially reinforcing links between environments and health by uncovering the specific physiological pathways through which social contexts exert their influence on health. Furthermore, advocates of this approach argue that implementing "objective, 'hard science' data" into social science research, "may be particularly effective in mobilizing the attention of policy makers and informing interventions around important social issues" (McDade, Williams and Snodgrass 2007:901).

As social scientists have begun collecting biomarkers of stress, such as cortisol levels, and analyzing it in conjunction with survey data, they have identified new complexities in the relationship between stress and health. In contrast to laboratory-based research, which has consistently found that cortisol increases in response to acute stressors (Dickerson and Kemeny 2004), these studies find that exposure to chronically stressful environments leads to a blunted pattern of cortisol secretion (Ranjit, Young and Kaplan 2005; DeSantis et al. 2007; Karb et al. 2012). Scholars suggest several possible theories to explain the etiology of the blunted cortisol pattern. Some posit that this pattern may be adaptive, helping to protect against the effects of chronic exposure to stressful environments (Karb et al. 2012). Others argue that this pattern could result from stress exposure during early childhood, whereby exposure at a young age may permanently alter one's psychological response to subsequent stressors (DeSantis et al. 2007). Though the specific implications of this pattern for individual health depend on why cortisol levels are low or stress responses blunted, evidence suggests that this pattern may predict increased vulnerability to depression and anxiety and pose a risk to physical and neurological development (Gunnar and Vazquez 2001).

The case of stress thus illustrates how the interplay between social environmental factors and the body's stress response system is significantly more complex than previously thought. Given this complexity, research on gene–environment interaction that focuses wholly on measuring levels of biologically active chemicals in the body's internal environment may be missing a key piece of the puzzle. "In body" analyses make visible the levels of stress hormones present in human subjects, with the aim of identifying the pathways linking stress and health outcomes. However, as suggested by research that moves outside of the laboratory, these levels are difficult to interpret and may obscure the extent and types of exposure to stress that subjects have experienced (Gunnar and Vazquez 2001; Ranjit et al. 2005; DeSantis et al. 2007; Karb et al. 2012).

By employing the concept of regimes of perceptibility, we can see how stress is differentially operationalized in the life sciences and social sciences. Both lines of research focus on an environmental variable – stress – and both are important to understanding the relationships between exposure to stress, gene expression and human health and illness. The challenge of the current moment is to integrate more "distal" social factors and life experiences into research that focuses on the biological mechanisms through which stress comes to matter (Miller, Chen and Cole 2009). Collecting biomarkers in observational studies represents one step towards meeting this challenge. At the same time, as seen through the conceptual lens of "regimes of perceptibility," the integration of biomarker data as a measurable object in social science research raises important questions about how to define and operationalize stressful environments, and their biological consequences. At stake is not only whether, or to what extent, social environments are individualized and biomedicalized in this research. The validity and utility of the science itself may hinge on scientists' ability to work across levels of analysis, in order to account for subjects' life histories of exposure to stressful environments. As we discuss in the conclusion, the case of stress thus also points to the analytic utility of the concept of "regimes of perceptibility" in regard to interdisciplinary research, in which scientists attempt to bring together multiple levels and foci of analysis.

Towards a Political Economy of Perception

One of the primary motivating concerns of the geneticization thesis was the possibility that the social and environmental determinants of health would be obscured by the emergence of genetic research. Two decades after the formulation of the geneticization critique, it is clear that social and environmental determinants are central foci in contemporary research on population health. To be sure, there are genetics research agendas that purport to address health inequalities with little or no attention to the social determinants of health (Sankar et al. 2004). However, in domains as diverse as epigenetics, environmental health science and stress research, the environment is a focal concern of research on health and health disparities. Consequently, we suggest that insofar as geneticization implies a "zero-sum" relationship between genes and environments as determinants of human health and illness, it has the potential to obfuscate important trends in contemporary biomedical research.

To be clear, we do not advocate for a total abandonment of the concept of geneticization. As demonstrated in our review, research that used geneticization as its theoretical jumping off point has made significant contributions to our understanding of the development and implications of genetic science. Further, we acknowledge that there are instances in which it is important to investigate whether genetic research transforms (i.e., via geneticization) individual, familial or popular understandings of a health condition (Meiser et al. 2005; Lock et al. 2006; Shostak et al. 2011); such investigations may be particularly salient in the case of conditions that were stigmatized prior to the identification of genetic causes (Phelan 2005). Likewise, the geneticization of race remains an important concern in contemporary sociological research (Phelan et al. 2013). As such, we suggest that geneticization is the right conceptual tool for analyses that seek to assess the process by which conditions (e.g., mental or physical illness) and social categories (e.g., race) are attributed to genetic causes, as well as the social and political consequences of such attributions (Shostak et al. 2009; Phelan et al. 2013).

More broadly, however, we contend that contemporary scholarship in the sociology of science, technology and medicine must take as its point of departure not the question "is it genes or the environment?" but rather "how are genes and/ or the environment conceptualized and operationalized in this research?" As we have shown, the environment is conceptualized and operationalized in tremendously varied ways across disciplines. To date, there are tensions between molecular and "in body" approaches to measurement, more common in the life sciences, and the meso- and macro-level foci of social epidemiology and the social sciences, with their concern for social institutions, processes and categories of inequality. Such differences reflect the historical division of labor, and traditional regimes of perceptibility, among the disciplines.

Regimes of perceptibility create the conditions of possibility for how social and environmental determinants of health may be understood and can be acted upon – and by whom. As such, they are centrally important to understanding both the daily operations and the social justice implications of biomedical research. In our concluding comments, we point to two ways that the concept of "regimes of perceptibility" might itself be extended, in light of the dynamics we have identified in our case studies of research on diet, toxics and stress, and their consequences for population health.

First, we note that, in each of these cases, there is at least a possibility that molecular measurements – of epigenetic modification, the exposome and stress hormones – could be used to "point outward" to the more distal social, economic and political factors that are the conditioning contexts of the body and its cells. To date, "distal variables have not received the same degree of minute attention as have cellular environments" (Lock 2013:1896). However, as Niewöhner observes, "the emergence of methylation and histone modification as a plausible mode of action and a measurable molecular endpoint" linking social context to human health has meant that some molecular biologists have begun "to extend their gaze from the molecular level and the lab towards suitable objects of study out in the real world" (2011:291). There is a clear conceptual rationale for "bridging" regimes of perceptibility in this way; as social epidemiologist Nancy Krieger notes, "We live embodied: 'genes' do not interact with exogenous (that is, outside of the body) environments – only organisms do, with consequences for gene regulation and expression" (Krieger 2005:351).

Insofar as researchers seek to develop modes of investigation that can more effectively encompass both "distal" and "proximal," "social" and "molecular" factors (Miller et al. 2009), the concept of "regimes of perceptibility," which assumes that perception is anchored in disciplines, will need to be adapted to account for interdisciplinary and transdisciplinary research. In the contemporary moment, there are multiple instances of – and warrants for – research that crosses traditional disciplinary boundaries. These include the advent of social scientists using genetic techniques (see, for example, Kaplan, Spittel and Spotts 2013), the claims of epigenetic researchers to speak to "the entanglement of nature/nurture that exists throughout every human life" (Meaney 2010, in Lock 2013:1896), and emerging research agendas that seek to "methodically piece together both the psychosocial and biological sides in a way that paints a detailed picture of the linear progression from social environment to disease outcome" (Miller et al. 2009:512). Along with this new porousness come opportunities for new engagements for social scientists with the biomedical sciences, and vice versa (European Science Foundation 2012).

Already, there are institutional sites where scholars work across disciplinary boundaries on projects that span regimes of perceptibility; their multilevel scope often is denoted by names such as "neurons to neighborhoods" (Shonkoff and Phillips 2000; Institute of Medicine and National Research Council 2012) and "cells to society."[11] There are some early indications that research that truly spans across disciplines can lead to novel findings in the lab, with important implications for both research and public policy. For example, researchers working together under the auspices of the National Institutes of Health Centers for Population Health and Health Disparities find that "the neighborhood context has a significant effect on individual risk that is independent of individual characteristics" and suggest, therefore, that research on genotypes should include neighborhood contexts (Warnecke et al. 2008:1613). Further, these authors call for the development of "interventions that can address population factors as well as individual behavior and risk" (Warnecke et al. 2008:1614). At the same time, there is concern that biomedical researchers may be "slow to appreciate social scientific approaches, or to engage with them in a meaningful way" (European Science Foundation 2012:3; see also Albert, Laberge and Hodges 2009).

Second, the observation that there are different regimes of perceptibility points to the importance of tracing connections between particular technologies and techniques of measuring the environment and extant social, political and economic concerns and cultural tendencies. Our case studies suggest that there is a *political economy of perception* that favors particular conceptualizations and operationalizations of the environment. Specifically, across the cases examined in this chapter, we observe an individualization of environmental health risks, and their management, which is a hallmark of both contemporary biomedicine (Clarke et al. 2003) and the "dominant epidemiological paradigm" (Brown 2007). With respect to epigenetics, the observation of the intergenerational transmission of health risks via nutrition has already led to calls for the monitoring, modification and potentially the criminalization of the habits and behavior of pregnant women and young mothers (Lock 2013). Thus, even research that points to the ways that history, politics and social environments become biologically embedded (across generations) can be used to hold women individually responsible for the health of their children. Even as it greatly expands the kinds and timing of exposures that genome scientists deem relevant to human health, exposomics simultaneously materializes these exposures as individual attributes that can be assessed and treated by clinicians (Arnaud 2010). While this approach may offer real benefits to people who have been exposed to harmful chemicals, at the same time, it biomedicalizes and individualizes what otherwise might be addressed as important social, political and economic problems. In the case of research on stress, the integration of biomarkers into observational studies represents a significant advancement in social science research. However, measurements of stress hormone levels alone may render less visible the distal social factors and life experiences that shape an individual's stress response system. Thus, by focusing inquiry on whether, or to what extent, the environment is conceptualized and operationalized as an individual attribute, devoid of social structural dimensions (indeed, even in domains of research that seek to understand the social determinants of health), the concept of regimes of perceptibility also leads us to new research questions about the pervasive social, cultural and political dynamics that may contribute to an ongoing individualization and biomedicalization of social determinants of health.

When Lippman formulated the geneticization thesis, it was reasonable to frame analysis in terms of a tension – and perhaps even a zero-sum relationship – between "genes" and "environment" as explanatory frameworks for human health and illness. In the era of gene–environment interaction, such assumptions now seem outdated. New engagements with contemporary biomedical science require analytical frameworks that support inquiry into how genes, environments and other determinants of health are modeled, measured and otherwise made knowable and actionable in different kinds of research, both within and across disciplines. However, we observe also that the same political economy of perception – by which we refer to the social, cultural and economic forces that support individual level rather than social structural understandings of health risks, and clinical rather than population level interventions – that gave genetics its cultural power persists today. As such, fidelity to the social justice concerns that were the bedrock of Lippman's powerful conceptual work now requires the development of new conceptual frameworks that allow us to attend to the perceptibility – and imperceptibility – of specific dimensions of the environment, and other social determinants of health, in biomedical research.

Notes

1 We gratefully acknowledge the insightful comments received on this topic from participants at the workshop "Conceptualizing Environmental Exposure: From Data to Decisions" (Chemical Heritage Foundation, April 2014).
2 At URL: www.cwhn.ca/en/node/39708 (accessed March 4, 2014).
3 A related concern was that information about genetic variation across socially defined racial groups would lead to the geneticization of race (Duster 2003). Phelan et al. (2013) provide an overview of the literature on the geneticization of race and experimental evaluation of this claim.
4 What constitutes a reductive statement is not always clear. The Lippman definition quoted above appears to contend that defining traits as "at least in part" genetically influenced reduces individuals to their DNA.
5 At URL: www.cwhn.ca/en/node/39708 (accessed March 4, 2014).
6 This mirrors the debate on whether "medicalization" implies critique or can be used as a neutral analytic category (Conrad 1992).
7 For example, hereditary polycystic kidney disease (PKD) is a life-threatening, autosomal dominant trait for which genetic testing is available. However, in a case study of the social construction and clinical management of PKD, Cox and Starzomski (2004) noted a striking absence of attention given to the genetic aspects of the disease by healthcare providers, patients and family members. They attribute the mitigation of geneticization to the irrelevance of genetic information to most practical aspects of PKD diagnosis and treatment. The emphasis on disease management may also minimize focus on the hereditary basis of PKD by bringing patients together with others experiencing different types of kidney disease.
8 Our thanks to David Hecht and Rebecca Herzig, for their comments at Bowdoin College in September 2013, which highlighted the importance of making the "complex" or "messy" half of binaries (such as "gene–environment") the focus of analysis.
9 The groundbreaking research in this area was conducted by the Commission on Racial Justice of the United Church of Christ (United Church of Christ Commission for Racial Justice 1987).
10 Recognizing these inequalities, in 1994, President Clinton signed Executive Order 12898, which made environmental justice a part of the mission of the federal agencies. However, in 2004, the Inspector General of the Environmental Protection Agency found that the agency was not doing an effective job of enforcing environmental justice (EJ). Scholars and activists have observed that neither the many local victories of EJ groups nor the establishment of EJ offices at the federal agencies have resulted in significant progress in addressing the broader social processes relevant to ecological protection and social justice (Pellow and Brulle 2005).
11 At URL: www.ipr.northwestern.edu/research-areas/social-disparities-health/ (accessed June 5, 2014).

References

Albert, M., S. Laberge and B. D. Hodges. 2009. "Boundary-work in the Health Research Field: Biomedical and Clinician Scientists' Perceptions of Social Science Research." *Minerva* 47: 171–94.
Alper, J. S. and J. Beckwith. 1993. "Genetic Fatalism and Social Policy: The Implications of Behavior Genetics Research." *The Yale Journal of Biology and Medicine* 66(6):511.
Arnaud, Celia Henry. 2010. "Exposing the Exposome." *Chemical & Engineering News* 88(33):42–4.
Balshaw, David M. 2010. *Making the Case for Advancing the Exposome (or EWAS).* Research Triangle Park, NC: National Institute of Environmental Health Sciences.
Bearman, Peter S. 2013. "Genes Can Point to Environments That Matter to Advance Public Health." *American Journal of Public Health* 103(S1):S11–S13.

Boardman, Jason D., Jonathan Daw and Jeremy Freese. 2013. "Defining the Environment in Gene–Environment Research: Lessons from Social Epidemiology." *American Journal of Public Health* 103(S1):S64–S72.

Bookman, Ebony B., Kimberly McAllister, Elizabeth Gillanders et al. 2011. "Gene–Environment Interplay in Common Complex Diseases: Forging an Integrative Model-Recommendations from an NIH Workshop." *Genetic Epidemiology* 35:217–25.

Brown, P. 1995. "Race, Class, and Environmental Health: A Review and Systematization of the Literature." *Environmental Research* 69(1):15–30.

Brown, Phil. 2007. *Toxic Exposures: Contested Illnesses and the Environmental Health Movement.* New York: Columbia University Press.

Brulle, Robert J. and David N. Pellow. 2006. "Environmental Justice: Human Health and Environmental Inequalities." *Annual Review of Public Health* 27(1):103–24.

Clarke, Adele E., Janet K. Shim, Laura Mamo, Jennifer Ruth Fosket and Jennifer R. Fishman. 2003. "Biomedicalization: Technoscientific Transformations of Health, Illness, and U.S. Biomedicine." *American Sociological Review* 68(2):161–94.

Cole, Steve W. 2010. "Elevating the Perspective on Human Stress Genomics." *Psychoneuroendocrinology* 35(7):955–62.

Condit, Celeste M. 1999. "How the Public Understands Genetics: Non-Deterministic and Non-Discriminatory Interpretations of the 'Blueprint' Metaphor." *Public Understanding of Science* 8(3):169–80.

Condit, Celeste M., Nneka Ofulue and Kristine M. Sheedy. 1998. "Determinism and Mass-Media Portrayals of Genetics." *The American Journal of Human Genetics* 62(4):979–84.

Conrad, Peter. 1992. "Medicalization and Social Control." *Annual Review of Sociology* 18:209–32.

Conrad, Peter. 1999. "A Mirage of Genes." *Sociology of Health & Illness* 21(2):228–41.

Cox, Susan M. and Rosalie C. Starzomski. 2004. "Genes and Geneticization? The Social Construction of Autosomal Dominant Polycystic Kidney Disease." *New Genetics and Society* 23(2):137–66.

Cummins, Steven. 2007. "Neighbourhood Food Environment and Diet – Time for Improved Conceptual Models?" *Preventive Medicine* 44(3):196–7.

DeSantis, Amy S., Emma K. Adam, Leah D. Doane, Susan Mineka, Richard E. Zinbarg and Michelle G. Craske. 2007. "Racial/Ethnic Differences in Cortisol Diurnal Rhythms in a Community Sample of Adolescents." *Journal of Adolescent Health* 41(1):3–13.

Dickerson, Sally S. and Margaret E. Kemeny. 2004. "Acute Stressors and Cortisol Responses: A Theoretical Integration and Synthesis of Laboratory Research." *Psychological Bulletin* 130(3):355–91.

Diez Roux, Ana V. 2011. "Complex Systems Thinking and Current Impasses in Health Disparities Research." *American Journal of Public Health* 101(9):1627–34.

Duster, Troy. 2003. *Backdoor to Eugenics*, 2nd edn. New York: Routledge.

Duster, Troy. 2006. "Comparative Perspectives and Competing Explanations: Taking on the Newly Configured Reductionist Challenge to Sociology." *American Sociological Review* 71(1):1–15.

European Science Foundation. 2012. "'The Good, the Bad and the Ugly': Understanding Collaboration between the Social Sciences and the Life Sciences." Accessed October 8, 2014 (www.esf.org/index.php?id=9388).

Fletcher, Jason M. and Dalton Conley. 2013. "The Challenge of Causal Inference in Gene-Environment Interaction Research: Leveraging Research Designs from the Social Sciences." *American Journal of Public Health* 103(S1):S42–S45.

Franklin, Sarah and Celia Roberts. 2006. *Born and Made: An Ethnography of Preimplantation Genetic Diagnosis.* Princeton, NJ: Princeton University Press.

Freese, J. and S. Shostak. 2009. "Genetics and Social Inquiry." *Annual Review of Sociology* 35: 107–28.

Frickel, Scott, Sahra Gibbon, Jeff Howard, Joanna Kempner, Gwen Ottinger and David Hess. 2010. "Undone Science: Charting Social Movement and Civil Society Challenges to Research Agenda Setting." *Science, Technology & Human Values* 35(4):444–73.

Frosch, Dominick L., Paul Mello and Caryn Lerman. 2005. "Behavioral Consequences of Testing for Obesity Risk." *Cancer Epidemiology Biomarkers & Prevention* 4(6):1485–9.

Gibbon, S. E. 2007. *Breast Cancer Genes and the Gendering of Knowledge. Science and Citizenship in the Cultural Context of the "New" Genetics.* Basingstoke: Palgrave Macmillan. Accessed April 29, 2014 (http://discovery.ucl.ac.uk/12786/).

Green, Eric D., Mark S. Guyer and National Human Genome Research Institute. 2011. "Charting a Course for Genomic Medicine from Base Pairs to Bedside." *Nature* 470(7333):204–13.

Gunnar, Megan R. and Delia M. Vazquez. 2001. "Low Cortisol and a Flattening of Expected Daytime Rhythm: Potential Indices of Risk in Human Development." *Development and Psychopathology* 13(3):515–38.

Guttmacher, Alan E. and Francis S. Collins. 2003. "Welcome to the Genomic Era." *New England Journal of Medicine* 349(10):996–8.

Harmon, Katherine. 2010. "Sequencing the 'Exposome': Researchers Take a Cue from Genomics to Decipher Environmental Exposure's Links to Disease." *Scientific American*. Accessed March 10, 2013 (www.scientificamerican.com/article.cfm?id=environmental-exposure).

Hedgecoe, Adam. 1998. "Geneticization, Medicalisation and Polemics." *Medicine, Health Care and Philosophy* 1(3):235–43.

Hedgecoe, Adam. 2001. "Schizophrenia and the Narrative of Enlightened Geneticization." *Social Studies of Science* 31(6):875–911.

Hedgecoe, Adam. 2002. "Reinventing Diabetes: Classification, Division and the Geneticization of Disease." *New Genetics and Society* 21(1):7–27.

Hill, Terrence D., Catherine E. Ross and Ronald J. Angel. 2005. "Neighborhood Disorder, Psychophysiological Distress, and Health." *Journal of Health and Social Behavior* 46(2): 170–86.

Horwitz, Allan V. 2005. "Media Portrayals and Health Inequalities: A Case Study of Characterizations of Gene X Environment Interactions." *Journals of Gerontology Series B: Psychological Sciences & Social Sciences* 60B:48–52.

Hunter, Richard G. 2012. "Epigenetics Effects of Stress and Corticosteroids in the Brain." *Frontiers in Cellular Neuroscience* 6(8):1–8.

Institute of Medicine and National Research Council. 2012. *From Neurons to Neighborhoods: An Update – Workshop Summary*. Washington, DC: National Academic Press. Accessed June 16, 2014 (http://iom.edu/Reports/2012/From-Neurons-to-Neighborhoods-An-Update.aspx).

Jerrett, Michael and Murray Finkelstein. 2005. "Geographies of Risk in Studies Linking Chronic Air Pollution Exposure to Health Outcomes." *Journal of Toxicology and Environmental Health, Part A* 68(13–14):1207–42.

Jones, Dean P., Youngja Park and Thomas R. Ziegler. 2012. "Nutritional Metabolomics: Progress in Addressing Complexity in Diet and Health." *Annual Review of Nutrition* 32(1):183–202.

Kaplan, Robert M., Michael L. Spittel and Erica L. Spotts. 2013. "Advancing Scientific Inquiry by Blurring Research Boundaries." *American Journal of Public Health* 103(S1):S4.

Karb, Rebecca A., Michael R. Elliott, Jennifer B. Dowd and Jeffrey D. Morenoff. 2012. "Neighborhood-Level Stressors, Social Support, and Diurnal Patterns of Cortisol: The Chicago Community Adult Health Study." *Social Science & Medicine* 75(6):1038–47.

Kerr, Anne. 2005. "Understanding Genetic Disease in a Socio-Historical Context: A Case Study of Cystic Fibrosis." *Sociology of Health & Illness* 27(7):873–96.

Krieger, Nancy. 2005. "Embodiment: A Conceptual Glossary for Epidemiology." *Journal of Epidemiology and Community Health* 59(5):350–5.

Kuzawa, Christopher W. and Elizabeth Sweet. 2009. "Epigenetics and the Embodiment of Race: Developmental Origins of US Racial Disparities in Cardiovascular Health." *American Journal of Human Biology* 21(1):2–15.

Landecker, Hannah. 2011. "Food as Exposure: Nutritional Epigenetics and the New Metabolism." *BioSocieties* 6(2):167–94.

Lavelle, Marianne and Marcia Coyle. 1992. "The Racial Divide in Environmental Law: Unequal Protection." *National Law Journal* 15(September 21):S1–S12.

Lippman, Abby. 1991. "Prenatal Genetic Testing and Screening: Constructing Needs and Reinforcing Inequities." *American Journal of Law & Medicine* 17(1/2):15.

Lippman, Abby. 1992. "Led (Astray) by Genetic Maps: The Cartography of the Human Genome and Health Care." *Social Science & Medicine* 35(12):1469–76.

Lock, Margaret. 2013. "The Lure of the Epigenome." *The Lancet* 381(9881):1896–7.

Lock, Margaret, Julia Freeman, Rosemary Sharples and Stephanie Lloyd. 2006. "When It Runs in the Family: Putting Susceptibility Genes in Perspective." *Public Understanding of Science* 15(3):277–300.

Markens, Susan, Carole H. Browner and Nancy Press. 1999. "'Because of the Risks': How US Pregnant Women Account for Refusing Prenatal Screening." *Social Science & Medicine* 49(3):359–69.

Matheson, Flora I., Rahim Moineddin, James R. Dunna, Maria Isabella Creatorea, Piotr Gozdyraa and Richard H. Glaziera. 2006. "Urban Neighborhoods, Chronic Stress, Gender and Depression." *Social Science & Medicine* 63(10):2604–16.

McDade, Thomas W., Sharon Williams and J. Josh Snodgrass. 2007. "What a Drop Can Do: Dried Blood Spots as a Minimally Invasive Method for Integrating Biomarkers into Population-based Research." *Demography* 44(4):899–925.

McKinnon, Robin A., Jill Reedy, Meredith A. Morrissette, Leslie A. Lytle and Amy L. Yaroch. 2009. "Measures of the Food Environment: A Compilation of the Literature, 1990–2007." *American Journal of Preventive Medicine* 36(4, Suppl.):S124–S133.

Meiser, Bettina, Philip B. Mitchell, H. McGirr, M. Van Herten and Peter R. Schofield. 2005. "Implications of Genetic Risk Information in Families with a High Density of Bipolar Disorder: An Exploratory Study." *Social Science & Medicine* 60(1):109–18.

Miller, Gregory E., Edith Chen and Eric S. Zhou. 2007. "If It Goes Up, Must It Come Down? Chronic Stress and the Hypothalamic-Pituitary-Adrenocortical Axis in Humans." *Psychological Bulletin* 133(1):25–45.

Miller, Gregory E., Edith Chen and Steve W. Cole. 2009. "Health Psychology: Developing Biologically Plausible Models Linking the Social World and Physical Health." *Annual Review of Psychology* 60:502–24.

Mitman, Gregg, Michelle Murphy and Christopher Sellers. 2004. "Introduction: A Cloud over History." *Osiris* 19:1–17.

Murphy, Michelle. 2006. *Sick Building Syndrome and the Problem of Uncertainty: Environmental Politics, Technoscience, and Women Workers*, 1st edn. Durham, NC: Duke University Press.

National Research Council. 2001. *Cells and Surveys: Should Biological Measures Be Included in Social Science Research?* edited by C. E. Finch, J. W. Vaupel and K. Kinsella. Washington, DC: National Academy Press.

Nelkin, Dorothy and M. Susan Lindee. 2004. *The DNA Mystique : The Gene as a Cultural Icon*. New York: W. H. Freeman & Co.

Niewöhner, Jörg. 2011. "Epigenetics: Embedded Bodies and the Molecularisation of Biography and Milieu." *BioSocieties* 6(3):279–98.

Novas, Carlos and Nikolas Rose. 2000. "Genetic Risk and the Birth of the Somatic Individual." *Economy and Society* 29(4):485–513.

Olden, Kenneth and Sandra L. White. 2005. "Health-related Disparities: Influence of Environmental Factors." *The Medical Clinics of North America* 89(4):721–38.

Parthasarathy, Shobita. 2007. *Building Genetic Medicine: Breast Cancer, Technology, and the Comparative Politics of Health Care*, 1st edn. Cambridge, MA: MIT Press.

Pearlin, Leonard I. 1989. "The Sociological Study of Stress." *Journal of Health and Social Behavior* 30(3):241–56.

Pellow, David Naguib and Robert J. Brulle. 2005. "Power, Justice and the Environment: Toward Critical Environmental Justice Studies." Pp. 1–19 in *Power, Justice, and the Environment: A Critical Appraisal of the Environmental Justice Movement*, edited by David N. Pellow and Robert J. Brulle. Cambridge, MA: MIT Press.

Pescosolido, Bernice A. 2006. "Of Pride and Prejudice: The Role of Sociology and Social Networks in Integrating the Health Sciences." *Journal of Health and Social Behavior* 47(3):189–208.

Phelan, Jo C. 2005. "Geneticization of Deviant Behavior and Consequences for Stigma: The Case of Mental Illness." *Journal of Health and Social Behavior* 46:307–22.

Phelan, Jo C., Bruce G. Link and Naumi M. Feldman. 2013. "The Genomic Revolution and Beliefs about Essential Racial Differences: A Backdoor to Eugenics?" *American Sociological Review* 78(2):167–91.

Ranjit, Nalini, Elizabeth A. Young and George A. Kaplan. 2005. "Material Hardship Alters the Diurnal Rhythm of Salivary Cortisol." *International Journal of Epidemiology* 34(5):1138–43.

Rapp, Rayna. 2000. *Testing Women, Testing the Fetus: The Social Impact of Amniocentesis in America*, 1st edn. New York: Routledge.

Rappaport, Stephen M. 2012. "Biomarkers Intersect with the Exposome." *Biomarkers: Biochemical Indicators of Exposure, Response, and Susceptibility to Chemicals* 17(6):483–9.

Rappaport, Stephen M. and Martyn T. Smith. 2010. "Environment and Disease Risks." *Science* 330(6003):460–1.

Rappaport, Stephen M., Sungkyoon Kim, Qing Lan, Guilan Li, Roel Vermeulen, Suramya Waidyanatha, Luoping Zhang, Songnian Yin, Martyn T. Smith and Nathaniel Rothman. 2010. "Human Benzene Metabolism Following Occupational and Environmental Exposures." *Chemico-Biological Interactions* 184(1–2):189–95.

Rose, Nikolas. 2006. *The Politics of Life Itself: Biomedicine, Power, and Subjectivity in the Twenty-First Century*. Princeton, NJ: Princeton University Press.

Rosen, George. 1993. *A History of Public Health*. Baltimore, MD: Johns Hopkins University Press.

Rothman, Barbara Katz. 2001. *The Book of Life: A Personal and Ethical Guide to Race, Normality and the Human Gene Study*. Boston, MA: Beacon Press.

Sankar, Pamela, Mildred K. Cho, Celeste M. Condit, Linda M. Hunt, Barbara Koenig, Patrick Marshall, Sandra Soo-Jin Lee and Paul Spicer. 2004. "Genetic Research and Health Disparities." *Journal of the American Medical Association* 291(24):2985–9.

Schwartz, David A. and Francis S. Collins. 2007. "Medicine: Environmental Biology and Human Disease." *Science* 316(5825):695–6.

Sherwin, Susan and Christy Simpson. 1999. "Ethical Questions in the Pursuit of Genetic Information: Geneticization and BRCA1." Pp. 121–8 in *Genetic Information: Acquisition, Access, and Control*, edited by Alison K. Thompson and Ruth F. Chadwick. New York: Springer.

Shim, Janet K. 2005. "Constructing 'Race' Across the Science-Lay Divide: Racial Formation in the Epidemiology and Experience of Cardiovascular Disease." *Social Studies of Science* 35(3): 405–36.

Shonkoff, Jack P. and Deborah A. Phillips, eds. 2000. *From Neurons to Neighborhoods: The Science of Early Childhood Development*. Washington, DC: National Academies Press. Accessed June 16, 2014 (www.nap.edu/openbook.php?record_id=9824).

Shostak, Sara. 2013. *Exposed Science: Genes, the Environment, and the Politics of Population Health*. Berkeley, CA: University of California Press.

Shostak, Sara and Margot Moinester. 2015. "The Missing Piece of the Puzzle? Measuring the Environment in the Postgenomic Moment." In *Postgenomics*, edited by Sarah Richardson and Hallam Stevens. Durham, NC: Duke University Press (in press).

Shostak, Sara, Peter Conrad and Alan V. Horwitz. 2008. "Sequencing and Its Consequences: Path Dependence and the Relationships between Genetics and Medicalization." *American Journal of Sociology* 114(S1):S287–S316.

Shostak, Sara, Jeremy Freese, Bruce G. Link and Jo C. Phelan. 2009. "The Politics of the Gene: Social Status and Beliefs about Genetics for Individual Outcomes." *Social Psychology Quarterly* 72(1):77–93.

Shostak, Sara, Dana Zarhin and Ruth Ottman. 2011. "What's at Stake? Genetic Information from the Perspective of People with Epilepsy and Their Family Members." *Social Science & Medicine* 73(5):645–54.

Sloan, Phillip R. 2000. "Completing the Tree of Descartes." Pp. 1–25 in *Controlling Our Destinies: Historical, Philosophical, Ethical, and Theological Perspectives on the Human Genome Project*, edited by Phillip R. Sloan. Notre Dame, IN: University of Notre Dame Press.

Taylor, Shelley E., Rena L. Repetti and Teresa Seeman. 1997. "Health Psychology: What Is an Unhealthy Environment and How Does It Get under the Skin?" *Annual Review of Psychology* 48(1):411–47.

Ten Have, Henk A. M. J. 2001. "Genetics and Culture: The Geneticization Thesis." *Medicine, Health Care and Philosophy* 4(3):295–304.

Thompson, Charis. 2007. *Making Parents: The Ontological Choreography of Reproductive Technologies*, 1st edn. Cambridge, MA: MIT Press.

Thompson, Claire, Steven Cummins, Tim Brown and Rosemary Kyle. 2013. "Understanding Interactions with the Food Environment: An Exploration of Supermarket Food Shopping Routines in Deprived Neighbourhoods." *Health & Place* 19:116–23.

Timmermans, Stefan and Mara Buchbinder. 2013. *Saving Babies? The Consequences of Newborn Genetic Screening*. Chicago, IL: Chicago University Press.

United Church of Christ Commission for Racial Justice. 1987. *Toxic Wastes and Race in the United States*. New York: Commission for Racial Justice.

Warnecke, Richard B., April Oh, Nancy Breen, Sarah Gehlert, Electra Paskett, Katherine L. Tucker, Nicole Lurie, Timothy Rebbeck, James Goodwin, John Flack, Shobha Srinivasan, Jon Kerner, Suzanne Heurtin-Roberts, Ronald Abeles, Frederick L. Tyson, Georgeanne Patmios and Robert A. Hiatt. 2008. "Approaching Health Disparities from a Population Perspective: The National Institutes of Health Centers for Population Health and Health Disparities." *American Journal of Public Health* 98(9):1608–15.

Whitmarsh, Ian, Arlene M. Davis, Debra Skinner and Donald B. Bailey, Jr. 2007. "A Place for Genetic Uncertainty: Parents Valuing an Unknown in the Meaning of Disease." *Social Science & Medicine* 65(6):1082–93.

Wild, Christopher Paul. 2005. "Complementing the Genome with an 'Exposome': The Outstanding Challenge of Environmental Exposure Measurement in Molecular Epidemiology." *Cancer Epidemiology Biomarkers & Prevention* 14(8):1847–50.

Wild, Christopher Paul. 2012. "The Exposome: From Concept to Utility." *International Journal of Epidemiology* 41(1):24–32.

Williams, David R. 2005. "The Health of U.S. Racial and Ethnic Populations." *The Journals of Gerontology Series B: Psychological Sciences and Social Sciences* 60(Special Issue 2):S53–S62.

Williams, David R., Selina A. Mohammed, Jacinta Leavell and Chiquita Collins. 2010. "Race, Socioeconomic Status, and Health: Complexities, Ongoing Challenges, and Research Opportunities." *Annals of the New York Academy of Sciences* 1186(1):69–101.

12

Commentary and Reflections: The Lure of the Gene

DAVID K. HECHT

> How can one ... dream of power in any other terms
> than in the symbols of power?
> James Baldwin, *The Fire Next Time* (1963)

Genes are seductive things. They hold the promise of increasing both our understanding of nature and our power to control it. We use genes to explain a dizzying array of personal, medical, social, biological and political phenomena. Sometimes these explanations are quite modest, as in accounts of individual variation in physical traits such as height or eye color. On other occasions, they are much more ambitious, as with complex and politically fraught questions of racial or ethnic identity. And not infrequently, genetic research carries significant, practical consequences. This is perhaps most directly true in the health sector, as genes are important to medical research and patient care. But policy matters often turn on genetic questions as well. The early twenty-first-century successes of gay rights activism in the USA, for example, owe much to an emergent understanding of homosexuality as inborn rather than acquired. Genes are frequently wrapped up in cultural conceptions of what is natural or inevitable (Nelkin and Lindee 2004[1995]). They can be invoked implicitly or explicitly, and as either total or partial explanations. They have become part of our shared cultural heritage: a conceptual apparatus that we can accept, reject or modify – but not ignore.

Accounting for the proliferation of genetic explanations is not a straightforward task. In part, of course, their ubiquity stems from biological reality: they can provide us with accurate and useful information about ourselves. But this is not sufficient explanation for the widespread popularity of genetic stories. Just because something is true does not mean that people will believe it. In fact – as the contemporary politics surrounding climate change and evolution make clear – audiences are quite capable of resisting science that they find uncomfortable or unsettling. The task of understanding the persistent appeal of genes and genetic explanations, therefore, begins but does not end with science. It involves the full range of the humanities and social sciences, because it is ultimately a human story, and a historical one. As explanatory accounts – whether about health, identity or politics – genes proliferate because they conform to audience expectations and desires. Rather than assume inevitability, we might ask about some of the contexts in which genetic explanations have been deemed viable and useful. Who has done so – and why? How have they told their stories, and what have been the consequences of their choices? These are complicated matters, and there is no single answer. But one of the most striking patterns is that genes provide easy basis for reductionist accounts. Genetic stories focus on causal elements that can be reliably isolated, defined and measured. This gives them disproportionate visibility, and tends to obscure other sorts of causal factors. In some cases, this can be politically motivated. But it also stems from the need to provide clear, comprehensible explanations for phenomena whose real origins are too complex to capture fully and easily.

This is not a new phenomenon. Even before the term itself was coined – in 1909, by Wilhelm Johannsen – scientists (and others) had recognized the practical as well as intellectual value of studying genes (Nelkin and Lindee 2004[1995]:3). The eugenicists of the early twentieth century tried to use their limited knowledge of heredity to manage population growth and to cure societal ills (Kevles 1995[1985]; Lombardo 2011). Many of their attempted innovations were discriminatory and elitist, and their most enduring legacy lies in giving this particular brand of social engineering a bad name. And the more extreme policies adopted by the Nazis made the potential dangers of combining biology and ideology clearer still. Every subsequent advocate of genetics' applicability to social policy has had to face this legacy, and they have often been able to move past it. There is much scholarly support for the idea that, as Ruha Benjamin writes, "the relationship between biological knowledge and political power is decoupled" in the modern era (Benjamin 2015:198, Chapter 10, this volume). But the reality here is a complex one, as she also points out the fact that "attempts to 'intervene' in the name of the dispossessed may sediment longstanding inequalities in unexpected ways" (2015:199). Both sorts of interventions are visible in the early twenty-first century, as we find ourselves several decades into a new enthusiasm for genetic explanations that is pervasive if not completely unchallenged. Genes have become social as well as biological reality.

The three chapters in Part III offer an exploration of the social reality of genes. They cover a wide range of topics: race, pharmaceuticals, consumerism, national identity, medical research, expertise, activism. But there is – at least – one common pattern among them. Each chapter focuses on groups of people who seek to challenge the existing politics and practices of genetics, and who ultimately wind up reinforcing many of the things that they hoped to change. Catherine Bliss tells the story of business and government ventures that draw on scientific conceptions of race. Sara Shostak and Margot Moinester detail the efforts of scientists and social scientists to move past a gene–environment binary. Ruha Benjamin writes of national attempts to secure genomic information as country-specific resources. In each instance, the people in question are quite self-conscious about their attempts to redress political inequalities or to increase intellectual and technical sophistication. But the effects of their interventions have been complex, and often surprisingly limited. It has proved rather difficult to dislodge existing conceptualizations of genes. The more they have become our symbols of power, the harder it has become to dream – or to think, talk and conduct research – in any other terms.

Catherine Bliss tells a story in which a diverse range of people – scientists, activists and entrepreneurs – embrace the biomedicalization of race. This embrace is visible in the institutional structures that support genomics research, the development of race-based medicine and the burgeoning field of ancestry searches. Bliss argues that medicalization and racialization have gone hand-in-hand. She cites the words of Human Genome Project veteran Eric Lander: "if we shy away and don't record the data for certain populations, we can't be sure to serve those populations medically" (Bliss 2015:179, Chapter 9, this volume). In this formulation, there is a deep and necessary link between constructing race, doing science and improving health. And this sentiment is not limited to working scientists who may have professional predispositions to believe in the power of genetic explanations. So dominant has the biomedical paradigm become, Bliss writes, that "even racial advocates most known for their work on the sociological factors that contribute to inequality have come on board the genomics band-wagon" (2015:183). Henry Louis Gates, Jr is a prominent example, and Bliss discusses his commitment to mapping genealogies. Consumer interest in ancestry searches is another indication of widespread willingness to accept the authority of genetic information and the racial categories they frequently support. It is critical to understand the extent of the social change that this heralds. Throughout much of the twentieth century, social reformers acted out of a sense that environmental factors rather than genetic ones were the source of many of the inequalities and persistent problems facing modern societies. They thus tended to resist biological explanations for any sort of observed disparity between social groups. This impulse has not disappeared. But much of the present moment is characterized by an attempt to appropriate and modify genetic stories, rather than to reject them. "Exclusion from genomics research," Bliss writes, "has become the new target of minority justice campaigns" (2015:183).

This is not an inevitable state of affairs, but one that has emerged through the science and politics of recent decades. BiDil provides an excellent example of how it works. BiDil is a drug specifically marketed to African Americans for the treatment of heart failure. This is despite the fact that evidence suggests efficacy in all races. Much of the explanation for this limit is commercial, as BiDil promised greater profits as a race-specific drug than as a more general one (Kahn 2007). Many African American advocacy groups – the National Association for the Advancement of Colored People, the Association of Black Cardiologists and the National Medical Association – offered their support (Bliss 2015). In fact, in the view of at least one of the key players involved in the BiDil story, these race-based advocacy groups were more willing than many scientists to support the drug. Bliss quotes Jay Cohn, the chief scientist behind BiDil:

> Here we have the black community accepting the concept that African Americans need to be studied as a group, and then we have the science community claiming that race is dead ... It seems to me absolutely ludicrous to suggest that this prominent characteristic that we all recognize when we look at people should not be looked at. (Bliss 2015:182)

Cohn's words signal his awareness of significant support in the African American community for using race as an analytical category. He invokes the support of the "black community" as a means to recognize the problematic history of race-based medicine and simultaneously assert that past inequities should not preclude contemporary reliance on racial categories should they hold the promise of health benefits. Even more profoundly, however, Cohn's words show his willingness to see the genetic roots of social phenomena. In this formulation, a "prominent characteristic that we all recognize" is thought to have enough biological reality that it can be studied as a separate group. It is the assumption of genetic explanations of human difference that allows the science (and marketing) to proceed. And unlike in eras past, we see members of traditionally disadvantaged groups embracing rather than resisting genetic differentiation.

A similar story emerges in Ruha Benjamin's chapter. She writes of the imagination of "new biopolitical entities" that emerge as countries try to manage the genomic data of their citizens (Benjamin 2015:202). She provides case studies of Mexico and India as examples of a larger trend wherein governments treat this data as a natural (and national) resource. This is meant, in part, to assert national control of the information and "the economic and medical benefits that may result from this new science" (Benjamin 2015:202). Mexico is the most prominent of several examples, having made the export of genetic material illegal (Benjamin 2015). But the notion of local control is a double-edged sword. It asserts national sovereignty in the face of multinational – and often US-led – corporations. But it also has important ramifications, and not always salutary ones, for power relationships among groups within a given country. "In addition to their stated aims," Benjamin writes, "genomic initiatives have the potential to naturalize social hierarchies and disparities" (2015:204–5). But despite this potential, the assertion of genomic rights at the national level seems to be an emergent phenomenon. There is frequently an "emancipatory rhetoric" accompanying the assertion of these rights – and certainly, some political actors gain through controlling access to genomic information at the national level (2015:208). Whatever the dynamics of such national contexts, and Benjamin stresses that they play out differently in different countries, they share at least one important similarity. All recognize the potential power of genes, and accept genetic accounts of group distinctiveness. "Genomic sovereignty," for Benjamin's actors, is quite similar to race-based medicine for Bliss' scientists and advocates (Benjamin 2015). In both cases, assumptions of the validity of genetic stories prompts particular methods of pursuing medical and financial benefits. And the quest itself then further institutionalizes the conceptual frameworks of genetics.

Reliance on established norms is a common tendency in social and political activism. It is also a largely conservative one. Those without power have two routes to achieve it: they can either challenge the terms under which extant power arrangements are constituted, or they can aspire to exploit those terms for their own advantage. The former is more radical, and much more difficult. Hence many groups seek to take the other approach, and appropriate the dominant language and tools for themselves. In the cases of India and Mexico, politicians have acted to capitalize on the science and rhetoric of the genome rather than to challenge it. The specific politics that result from such moves can be quite complex. In the case of India, for example, groups from both ends of the socioeconomic spectrum use population genomics to bolster their arguments. Lower caste Dalits use genomic findings to claim they are indigenous to the Indian subcontinent, thereby casting doubt on the "political legitimacy of Hindu nationalists" whom they depict as newer to the region (2015:209). Those nationalists, generally stemming from upper castes, counter these assertions by pointing to studies which minimize the overall importance of non-South Asian genes in the Indian gene pool. In either case, the importance of genes is assumed – and thus further reinforced. The arguments made by some Dalit activists seem particularly reminiscent of black advocacy for BiDil, in that gene-bolstered racial claims are advanced in the cause of righting historic inequalities. But despite the rhetorical utility of this position for some activists, Benjamin never loses sight of what she aptly calls the "dexterity" of genes (2015). Arguments derived from genomics can frequently be used to support multiple positions, and it is perhaps by reason of this malleability that existing power arrangements tend to be replicated. This is what is happening in the case of Mexico, where elite interest in defining a unitary Mexican population tends to trump the concerns of more local actors who insist on finer distinctions (Benjamin 2015:208). From the vantage point of global politics, the assertion of national genomic independence may well be an emancipatory move – albeit one done in the service of financial as well as medical gain. But when analyzed on a domestic front, the rhetoric and practice of genomics can easily solidify existing hierarchies.

It is important to note that genomic advocacy – whether under national auspices or at the behest of a specific interest group – is often done to secure material benefits for people that may not have them. Thus we need not view the enterprise as a nefarious or ill-intentioned one, even if the results are mixed. In fact, considering the unintended consequences of genomic politics can reveal more than studying overt cases of self-interested maneuvering. Genes also matter in more subtle ways. For example, when multiple sides in caste politics invoke genetics, they may or may not succeed in changing the political culture or their place in it. But they do reify genes as a meaningful category of analysis, and do so in ways that may not be scientifically justified as well as those that are. Similarly, we might sympathize with the desire to improve access to medical treatment at the same time as we grow alert to the fact that commercial concerns often dictate how scientific studies are conducted, packaged and made relevant to the healthcare of individual citizens. At an even deeper level, it may be that genes provide an intellectual framework that influences or even determines how we conceive of reality in the first place. This would be an almost literal instantiation of Baldwin's thought in the epigraph about "symbols of power": that something like a gene has become such a powerful conceptual tool that we cannot abandon the mental pictures and understanding it creates even if we wish to do so. This is one of the important issues raised in Shostak and Moinester's chapter. While the chapters by Bliss and Benjamin highlight the effects of commerce and of politics, Shostak and Moinester consider the attempts by a range of social scientific and scientific researchers to move beyond a gene–environment binary. It should be noted that the authors are ultimately positive about the possibility of replacing this now outmoded conceptualization. But much of their article is given over to the evidence that this has not yet happened. The problem is not that researchers are unaware of the limitations of a gene–environment binary. But understanding the explanatory insufficiency of this framework is not the same thing as designing a new model. In practice, the old ideas continue to assert themselves. "Some operationalizations of the environment," they write, "render it an internal, individual attribute that conveys health risks at the molecular level – very much like a gene" (Shostak and Moinester 2015:216, Chapter 11, this volume). In other words, even when researchers turn their attention to environmental factors, they often look toward elements of the environment that can be conceptualized and measured like genes. In part, this is because techniques for measuring environmental influences tend to be less sophisticated than for genetic ones – a fact that researchers in the field understand (Shostak and Moinester 2015). Furthermore, we do not have "a cross-disciplinary scientific consensus about how the environment should be conceptualized or measured" (2015:221). The environment of the gene is a different thing than the environment of cells, and both are different than the environment of the body or its lived experience (Shostak and Moinester 2015). The recognition of the importance of environmental factors does not always translate to measuring it successfully.

Shostak and Moinester focus on scientific practice, and their analysis runs parallel to the political story that Benjamin tells and the account of institutional inertia and funding patterns in Bliss' article. It is simply difficult to design studies which do justice to the internal world of the body and the external world of the environment without reducing one to the other. Shostak and Moinester discuss the field of exposomics, which "encompasses a wide variety of external and internal factors relevant to human biological processes and their health effects"

(2015:226). These can be narrow, "internal exposures" such as physiological processes within the body. They can be somewhat broader, as with "specific external exposures" like chemical inputs or dietary choices. Or they can be "general external exposures," the most expansive category, which focuses on socioeconomic determinants of health (2015:226). Such a framework holds some promise for including environmental factors. But in practice, Shostak and Moinester suggest, attempts to incorporate such elements take place in a framework of biomedicalization. "The environment in exposome research," they write, "is defined as a characteristic of individuals and measured as a discrete biomarker inside the human body" (2015:226). As long as we have this orientation to individuals, the origin of the identified factors – genes, environment or both – is of secondary importance. The individualizing impulse pushes us toward a framework that is conceptually along the lines of genetic explanations.

This is not necessarily a bad thing – or not always so. For one thing, the questions we wish to ask are often about individuals; this is particularly true when it comes to medicine. And biomedical interventions have evident promise as well as peril. Perhaps the idea of "regimes of perceptibility" – which the authors import from the historian Michelle Murphy – is most useful in this context as a means to help change the cultural understanding of the gene, clarifying what genomics can and cannot do for us (Shostak and Moinester 2015). Genes can provide a kind of information which can be fairly readily measured and seen – by experts, at least. And questions about identity, politics and health must rest, in part, on biological foundations. But to make sure that they rest there firmly and equitably, we must learn to understand genomics as an essential but only partial way of seeing the natural and social worlds around us. And the authors conclude by describing attempts, some currently in practice, to do just that.

In the conclusion to her chapter, Benjamin writes that "in the context of new biopolitical regimes, biological race is not so much destiny, as it is dexterous" (2015:211). There is much truth to this sentiment, and all three chapters in Part III contribute to our understanding of the dexterity of genes. But there is something paradoxical in this notion as well. Genes work as a rhetorical resource – in politics, in identity formation, in business models – only to the degree that people think of them as having more substance than mere rhetoric. In other words, a concept can be dexterous only to the extent that people do not think of it as such. This raises the counterintuitive but intriguing point that in order to come to terms with the dexterity of the gene, we must come to terms first with its apparent solidity. Why have genes come to hold a cultural place "as a secular equivalent of the Christian soul?" (Nelkin and Lindee 2004[1995]:2). This view is not shared by everyone, but aptly characterizes the enthusiasm for genetic explanations that has occurred at a number of moments in recent history. And one need not elevate genes to quasi-religious status in order to see them as having something substantial to offer. Consider, for instance, the example alluded to at the outset of this commentary: gay rights activism and the benefits it has derived from the supposition that sexual orientation is inborn. There is no reason why a genetic phenomenon needs to be considered good or bad, normal or abnormal, desirable or undesirable. Genetic explanations for homosexuality might lead to calls for eradication, rather than acceptance. That they have generally not done so – in other words, that the rhetoric of heredity has done more for the gay rights movement than the rhetoric of choice has – is but one of many indications of the cultural power of genetic stories.

As a complement to the studies in this section, therefore, I would suggest attention to the history of images: why do genes hold the power that they do? It may be that there are some timeless reasons for this – for example, that the simplicity they offer makes them inherently easier for human brains to process than the more complicated stories that do justice to intricate environmental interactions. But I am skeptical that such decontextualized explanations can be sufficient. Instead, we must look to particular features of the historical moments that reify genetic explanations. We might ask, for example, about the social norms of scientific practice. We might investigate the funding patterns and priorities that shape which kinds of studies can be performed – and can later get the necessary hearings in policy and public venues. We can explore the pathways by which audiences get exposed to scientific information. And, perhaps most promisingly, we can examine the assumptions that those audiences carry with them and the ways that such preconceived notions affect how they approach genetics and genetic information. It seems no accident, for example, that the current enthusiasm for biomedicalization has emerged alongside neoliberal visions of expansive markets and limited states. Since the nineteenth century, evolutionary biology has been associated – frequently if not universally – with the maintenance of the status quo (Claeys 2000). Genetics was born in this intellectual context, and, as the chapters in Part III illustrate, has yet to fully shake those origins. The way to do so – if and when societies wish – lies in the imagination of new sorts of political arrangements. Genes can be a part of such visions, but they will never drive them.

References

Baldwin, James. 1963. *The Fire Next Time*. New York: Dial Press.

Benjamin, Ruha. 2015. "Racial Destiny or Dexterity?: The Global Circulation of Genomics as an Empowerment Idiom." Pp. 197–215 in *Reimagining (Bio)Medicalization, Pharmaceuticals and Genetics: Old Critiques and New Engagements*, edited by Susan E. Bell and Anne E. Figert. New York: Routledge.

Bliss, Catherine. 2015. "Biomedicalization and the New Science of Race." Pp. 175–96 in *Reimagining (Bio)Medicalization, Pharmaceuticals and Genetics: Old Critiques and New Engagements*, edited by Susan E. Bell and Anne E. Figert. New York: Routledge.

Claeys, Gregory. 2000. "The 'Survival of the Fittest' and the Origins of Social Darwinism." *Journal of the History of Ideas* 61:223–40.

Kahn, Jonathan. 2007. "Race in a Bottle." *Scientific American* August:40–5.

Kevles, Daniel J. 1995[1985]. *In the Name of Eugenics: Genetics and the Uses of Human Heredity*, 1st edn. New York: Alfred A. Knopf.

Lombardo, Paul A., ed. 2011. *A Century of Eugenics: From the Indiana Experiment to the Human Genome Era*. Bloomington, IN: Indiana University Press.

Nelkin, Dorothy and M. Susan Lindee. 2004[1995]. *The DNA Mystique: The Gene as a Cultural Icon*, 1st edn. New York: W. H. Freeman & Co.

Shostak, Sara and Margot Moinester. 2015. "Beyond Geneticization: Regimes of Perceptibility and the Social Determinants of Health." Pp. 216–38 in *Reimagining (Bio)Medicalization, Pharmaceuticals and Genetics: Old Critiques and New Engagements*, edited by Susan E. Bell and Anne E. Figert. New York: Routledge.

Epilogue
Mapping the Biomedicalized World for Justice

SUSAN M. REVERBY

Power, Politics and Profits

In 1970 when the politically left health think-tank Health/PAC (Policy Advisory Center) published its book *The American Health Empire*, the map of power and analysis of what was wrong with the American healthcare system seemed knowable (Health/PAC 1970). The book's alliterative subtitle "Power, Politics and Profits" linked the growing hospital/medical empires to the for-profit medical industrial complex through various nefarious political deals, an underfunded public sector and a growing insurance system all bathed in class warfare, colonialism, racism and sexism (Chowkwanyun 2011).[1] The obvious solution that flowed from this critique was a naïve belief in local primary care reprioritized away from narrow and fragmented research interests, growth of alliances between communities and health professionals/workers, removal of the profit motive and support for struggles against medical paternalism, sexism, racism and colonialism.

Nearly half a century later, a seemingly baffling array of political, economic and cultural powers, beliefs and institutions shape what is broadly thought of as health systems, medical care or public and global health around the world. Terms like biomedical, technoscience, post-genomic, geneticization and pharmaceuticalization are not just academic jargon; they are necessary analytic concepts that describe this landscape. Concerns that Health/PAC never considered have come to the fore and its US focus is completely dated. As Rebecca Herzig argues in her commentary for this volume, the old forms of domination have been complicated and the embodied nature of control and resistance has to be explored in light of this complication (Herzig 2015, Chapter 4, this volume). Yet the simple mantra by Health/PAC remains true: it is still about "power, politics, and profits." How those forces operate, however, and how they might be challenged and changed is another matter. Health/PAC's contribution was to map the institutional priorities and political alliances aligned against equitable care in the 1960s–1990s and to encourage activism to overthrow them. Although much has changed since then, we still need that map.

Mapping the Biopolitical World

All of the scholars in this volume are making a contribution to that cartography project. As always with maps, the nature of what is measured depends on scale, direction, legend and destination. Now the microscopic/unseeable-but-knowable tied to cultural assumptions about race, class, gender, sexuality and disability from what used to be thought of as the unknown edges shape the interactions among the body, the state, the medical empires and Big Pharma at the very center. The map we need has grown, but how we understand its contours really does depend on what we draw.

The authors of this volume use differing analytic approaches, theoretical frames and narrative analysis to both *reimagine* how we might understand what is happening and to *re-image* the forces that need to be held at bay. Editors Susan Bell and Anne Figert chose a focus on three arenas of crucial knowledge/power in the contemporary medical/health world: critiques of technoscience/biomedicine, the influence of pharmaceuticals as an industry and a process, and the limitations of the search for genetic/genomic/epigenetic understandings of our bodies, ancestry, behaviors and illnesses. The old critiques that focused on the social construction of disease, the rapacious power of medicine and one-sided genetic/individualist reductionism in a "zero-sum relationship" between the "genetic" and "environmental" are being abandoned (Shostak and Moinester 2015:220, Chapter 11, this volume).

The flat maps may have been replaced by networked images that move across time and space; yet sometimes they just seem flat in the end, because the same old assumptions about gender, class, race, disability and sexuality and their interactions are still there (Clarke et al. 2009; Richardson 2015). To obtain the fulsome mapping needed, this volume's authors join other scholars who have begun to search for new terms for biomedical reality, even if the linguistic use of "-ization" seems both awkward and wordy, at least to this historian used to more narrative analysis than theorizing. It is, as fellow historian Jeremy Greene notes, hard to wrap your brain around a term like "pharmaceuticalization," even if it does explain that drugs are sold as the answers to medical and public health problems that really do not begin in an individual body, or that through biomedicalization we are seeing the re-scientizing of social phenomena in new ways (Greene 2015, Chapter 5, this volume; Bliss 2015, Chapter 9, this volume).

We do need new concepts. As the editors argue, at the very least we need new interpretations of old theories to explore the world where 99 percent of us are genetically the same, and yet differences are made of the remaining 1 percent in the name of personalized medicine and behavioral genetics, or where big pharmaceutical company executives can really think they are saving the world as they make everyone into "drug swallowers" (Lewontin 1995; Morning 2011; Kahn 2013; Samsky 2015, Chapter 6, this volume).

We can read the key points in these chapters with "dexterity and agility" as we explore the "historical ontology, that is, an examination of the history of things – such as 'genes,' 'the environment,' . . . to specific epistemological traditions and practices" (Benjamin 2015:197, Chapter 10, this volume; Shostak and Moinester 2015:217). Ultimately all the volume's authors are trying to map these "things" in a 3-D manner that does not reduce individuals into populations, environments into bodies and bodies into fragments (Benjamin 2015; Annandale and Hammarström 2015, Chapter 2, this volume). This book focuses us to consider the financial and human costs of making decisions to implement strategies that depend on drugs or technical fixes while ignoring what is really happening on the ground (Birn 2005; Rosenberg 2014).

The authors seek to explain how multiple understandings of environment, gender and race operate together and separately within various scientific communities, even when the scientists do not think they are doing more than explaining "what is out there." They remind us what geneticist Richard Lewontin has argued: that scientists "isolate objects as discrete entities with clear boundaries while we relegate the rest to a background in which the objects exist" (Lewontin 2011:381). In differing ways, the volume's authors are making visible this obliviousness to the limitation of what Lewontin calls "perception" and its significance. They also ask us to consider whether this unawareness is merely a consequence of the nature of doing science, the drawbacks of particular science fields and their specialized vocabularies, a refusal to see political implications, or more nefarious motives.

In the Health/PAC era, the map was easier to read because it translated into a critique of genetic reductionism without any environment, or an assumption that many diseases were socially constructed, or that gender and race should never matter in the search for more equity in healthcare and science. Our scholarship has moved us away from such simplicities toward a focus on conceptualizations of gene/environment interaction (writ large), critiques of "determinism and mechanical reductionism" or positing of how race and gender both have "to matter and not matter" at the same moment in time (Reverby 2009; Richardson 2015).[2] As scholars traverse this landscape there might be points when we can think the intellectual fights are resolved: that everyone understands that drugs cannot cure everything, or that everyone knows that genes alone do not determine behaviors or that everyone agrees that ancestry informative markers (AIMS) should not somehow fall out into the same categories of human races that were posited in the 1790s (Painter 2010).[3] We often are not working, however, from the same map as others.

We thus keep fighting the same battles over and over (Fox Keller 2010). Former *New York Times* science writer Nicholas Wade's most recent screed, for example, is called *A Troublesome Inheritance: Genes, Race and Human History* and attempts to explain that there is genetic evidence to prove there are human *races* that determine behaviors and population success (Wade 2014a). While the book has received almost unanimous negative reviews in both social and biological science journals (even in his old home newspaper) for its suppositions and lack of real evidence, it demonstrates how hard it is to kill off this kind of thinking (Dobbs 2014). It is difficult to know right now if Wade's book is just a throwback, or represents the continued re-emergence of racialized and even racist ideas that serve political purposes (Murray 2014). Its publication is a reminder, as many of the authors in this volume note in other ways, of how persistent these older and highly politicized ways of thinking are as they become dressed up in newer language that insists its evidence just reflects what is out there in nature. The overwhelmingly negative reviews of Wade's imagined analysis, however, suggest that today these older views are having more difficulty appearing in such simplistic and speculative forms. Yet, as historians Evelynn Hammonds and Rebecca Herzig have often argued, the "logic of difference" persists, and is seemingly always available as an appeal to what appears knowable and there (Hammonds and Herzig 2008).

This volume's contribution is to give us new ways to think critically about what is happening in a more sophisticated manner, and to use new forms of evidence to counter the kind of "analysis" that claims it is fighting a "political correctness" that fears what is somehow supposed to really be out there in "nature" (Wade 2014b). Many of the chapters are warnings that the older ideas can be redressed up to appear new and more reflective of the natural world, even when they are not new, as Wade's book attests. Some authors provide us with guides to what kind of "genomic scientists" are being tasked "to interpret inequality and the social environment" (Bliss 2015:191). Others still are focused on how the actual measurement takes place, ending with warnings, that "the recognition of the importance of environmental factors does not always translate to measuring it successfully" (Hecht 2015:244, Chapter 12, this volume). Thus many of the authors take us away from the kind of analysis economists often offer when they say, "x is true, all other things being equal" when of course all other things are never equal or even examined.

In the global world of disease and medicines, "all other things" are never equal. In the summer of 2014 when the Ebola epidemic spread through Sierra Leone, Guinea, Nigeria and Liberia, for example, the necessity of understanding the social context of disease that can go global was clearly demonstrated. The American victims of the epidemic were flown home, covered in virus-containing mufti, by their nongovernmental organization (NGO) to be treated with an experimental, and unproven, serum at a hospital adjacent to the Centers for Disease Control. Many in the rural areas of the African countries affected continued to distrust Western/colonial medical ideas and practices while needing local healers and community health workers to explain prevention and transmittal (Patterson 2014). A disease that was once containable in the plains or rainforests quickly became the subject of xenophobic worries half a world away (Maloy 2014).

The maps that we need to create to explain this are now much harder to read. There is no know-it-all voice coming out of the GPS telling us it is "recalculating" along the way yet still providing a predetermined map. And sometimes we all know this recalculation can lead literally to the precipice rather than the right way to turn. We still are searching for the proper legend on the maps that make it knowable, or subject to clear "regimes of perceptibility" to those who want to arrive at justice (Shostak and Moinester 2015:217). The mapping has to be the one that social scientists/humanities scholars do together with groups of physicians and scientists as we try and explain ourselves to one another (Reardon 2013).

Scale, Legend, Symbols and Direction

There has to be consideration of scale, legend, symbols and direction to map our way toward justice in a biomedical world. When it comes to scale, it is clear it must be global. Historians have demonstrated how practices developed to contain colonial subjects also come back to the metropole (Anderson 2006). We must note how, as historian Nancy Tomes has argued, "the 'imperial periphery' worked to produce 'metropolitan transformations'" (Tomes 2009:274). That is, ideas, personnel and administrative ways of handling public health first tested in settler expansionism, then in the far-flung colonies, often came back to change practices in the home country throughout the expansion of imperial power. How these practices and ideas travel now in a neoliberal postcolonial time still need to be understood in very specific terms.

In the context of globalization where the diseases contained in one country can easily be in another a few hours later, and where policies developed in one place have consequences for another, we must also realize that more than just germs make this kind of far-flung travel back and forth. As Kathy Davis has shown in her book on the history of the Boston Women's Health Book Collective's *Our Bodies, Ourselves* volumes, these "translations" are more readily described as adaptations that develop in other countries, and then can return to the USA, or other home countries, in new forms (Davis 2007). If we see the investment in science and research as part of a worldwide form of attempts to gain biosecurity, we need to look home, or as long-time HIV/AIDS researchers Ida Susser and Zena Stein argue, "within the context of the [creation of] local bio-insecurity ... of poor populations, ... especially of women" or our efforts will fail (Susser and Stein 2014:1).

The map's scale in a post-genomic time has to be vaster than ever before, but much of it has to still focus on what is defined by researchers as "the environment." As Shostak and Moinester note in this volume, "how the environment is conceptualized, operationalized and made knowable and actionable" is crucial to explain (Shostak and Moinester 2015:220). "The environment" as part of the map, then, can move inward to determine a human organism's future, or outward to explain the possibility of social structural transformations. Even when, for example, another gene to explain the incidence of breast cancer is discovered, frequently there is little attention given to what causes the gene to activate, or why some people who carry it do not develop the disease (Antoniou et al. 2014). As biologist Robert Pollack and social critic/lawyer

Patricia Williams argue: "It is habit to think of 'inheritance,' for example, as the definition of a person's inalterable genetic fate. But the vulnerability of transcriptional activity and cellular differentiation to environment renders that accounting intrinsically incomplete and therefore simply wrong" (Pollack and Williams 2014). It depends, in the end, on the scale of our map and the directions the mapmaker wants to make visible.

The legend on a map explains: "the symbols used ... and what they depict" (Department of Geography, University of Colorado 2005). The symbols, or elements of this biopolitical map, need to integrate race, gender, class, disability and sexuality together in ways that lead to what feminist/race scholars have labeled "intersectionality" for the last three decades (Crenshaw 1991). That is, we cannot imagine that race operates separately from assumptions and cultural structures of gender or sexuality or class or ability. How that process works, however, needs to be constantly explained and interrogated. Too often scholars seem to deal with only one concern, but not the others, or they do not consider how they are related in the making of essentialist categories. The insight that historian Nancy Stepan had decades ago, that links how scientists connect race and gender as forms of categorical thinking in the making of science and citizenship, is in desperate need of updating and reconsidering (Stepan 1998; Herzig 2015).

The symbols/terms on the map's legend we use may be familiar to one discipline, as Bell and Figert note, and unfamiliar to others. The move sideways they call for cannot easily be made unless we learn to read and understand the symbols/terms in differing disciplines and make them useful. Understanding the depth of the unanalyzed symbolic language, its lexicon or rhetoric, is essential to any reading of a biomedical map. The necessity to educate social scientists in the rhetoric/thinking of particular scientific sub-disciplines, and the willingness of scientists to understand the limits of their own assumed "just out there thinking," were never more profoundly needed.

And finally, we need to consider to what destination we want this map to take us. The authors of many of the chapters here make clear that those who would tell you they are seeking equality and justice in healthcare have led many of the projects analyzed in false directions and the re-inscription of older ideas. Trying to get to the right direction does not always mean that the map we have provides us with tools for getting us there. Instead, as sociologist Jenny Reardon has argued, getting to a public good and justice requires understanding that there are multiple situated understandings of a "justice frame" that can be hidden if we only speak of "universals" (Reardon 2013). To do this we need to learn to read one another's maps. This is not, however, just a plea for a *Kumbaya* moment that assumes everyone has good will and similar aims. There is too much power, profit and politics at stake here for that to be possible. There will often be divisions over what gets us to justice (Smith 2014). As Shim and her colleagues argue, we have to test our categories (or maps in my words here) against real world applications to see how they are used in practice (Shim et al. 2015, Chapter 3, this volume). At our best, we need to write and then read maps developed from multiple perspectives that allow activists and those whose lives and existence are at stake to always question where we are going and who is leading us.

The Power of Biological and Pharmaceutical Citizenship

Underlying all of these chapters is a worry about what it means to create "biological citizenship," a term first coined by anthropologist Adriana Petryna, to explain how much health needs become the basis for claims made by individuals and populations on the state and global governance for assistance (Petryna 2002; Cuthbertson 2015, Chapter 7, this volume; Benjamin 2015). Other scholars are worried more about how this kind of citizenship actually undermines collective demands by making "individuals ... express their concerns in terms of problems in biological processes that are interpreted as illnesses" (Cuthbertson 2015:141).

It is, then, this tension between analyzing the ways power under neoliberal and global regimes becomes biologized or pharmaceuticalized, and when these circumstances allow the underserved to make demands to which the state and drug companies must respond. Generations of scholars have made us aware as well that biologizing is not merely accepted by the powerless, but is also continually challenged, reabsorbed and reapplied (Metzl and Herzig 2007; Nelson 2008). Those *left out* often make the demand to be *let in* as one response to the biomedical world (Epstein 2007). Our focus on the need to accept treatments as individuals can demonstrate how being let in aids the underserved in the short term, but then it obscures our ability to see how "technoscientific interventions" can create "passive biological citizenship" (Cuthbertson 2015:155).

It is worth considering that passivity is not always the outcome of these "technoscientific interventions." Such demands to be let in can become, however, essentializing practices. They can be turned into the arguments for medical care only for women when it is not only women who need it, or drugs only for African Americans. Such essentializing still misunderstands our experiences as both individuals and populations, and reifies and freezes the effects of class discrimination, racism and sexism on the human response to disease (Reverby 2008; Kahn 2013; Annandale and Hammarström 2011, 2015).

Or, as a group of bioethicists argued in 2009, if we think of biomedical research as a "public good," then "participation in research is a critical way to support an important public good. Consequently, all have a duty to participate" (Schaefer, Emanuel and Wertheimer 2009:67). This kind of argument assumes that "all" benefit equally or that "all" will fulfill this duty. As drafts for military service have shown over and over, not everyone serves even when they are called and those with money can find ways to buy their way out of the service

(Chambers 1987). The recruitment of the homeless as the guinea pigs in clinical trials is just one demonstration of the ways inequalities invade biomedical research (Elliott 2014). Such a sense of duty and obligation in the fantasy of these bioethicists, in a world of unequal public and private goods, only serves to reinforce a false notion of the ways required participation in the world of biomedicine could become a part of citizenship.

Lack of equality and the pressures to "participate" in geneticized research is not an issue just between the global North and South. In the postindustrial/mill town of Kannapolis, North Carolina, the unemployed mill workers are now given something else: a chance to be part of the genetics revolution. The Murdock Foundation has built a biomedical colossus that will employ skilled technicians and professionals. The former workers are being offered a chance to participate in genetic studies that will "connect family histories to genetics sequences in the pursuit of personalized medicine." They are given a "$10 gift card to WalMart," while the purposes of the studies are left completely open-ended. As one critic has noted, "once blood and urine is taken, the material and information is out of their control. Participants are informed that they can make no claims to the benefits of the commercial products that may be made possible by the biological materials and information they provide" (Massie 2014). No longer the producers of goods, these former mill workers are becoming the goods themselves.[4]

In analyzing the limitations of the demands for more pharmaceutical and genetic approaches, we also need to be aware of why such demands are made in the name of justice, not just inclusion. Debates within the HIV/AIDS treatment/patient/survivor communities offer a good case in point. In the early part of the twenty-first century, it appeared as if there would be a divide between expensive drug treatments available to save lives of those with HIV in the global North and only messages about prevention for those in the global South. When activists took on the global pharmaceutical agreements backed by governmental protection of intellectual property and argued in the parliaments and in the streets for equity, increasingly generic drugs were allowed into or produced in global South countries (Smith and Siplon 2006; Biehl 2007; Nguyen 2010; Forbath et al. 2011). Do we label this negatively as "pharmaceuticalization?"

Even if we realize that the solution to the AIDS epidemic lies more in equitable resource allocation, sexuality freedoms, community health programs and gender equality than in access to pharmaceuticals, does this necessarily mean not making demands for funding research on the possibility of a vaccine or better distribution that makes possible a lifetime on drugs? Or do we need more fine-grained analyses to explain their limitations so that activists can focus on a different arena for struggle? (Belluz 2014).

Furthermore, we continue to need scholars to explore how states, NGOs, global health organizations, foundations and pharmaceutical companies work together not just to create a biopolitics, but also to help us identify the conditions under which, as philosopher Achille Mbembe argues, biopolitics becomes "necropolitics" (2003). Mbembe uses this term as an expansion of Foucault's biopower to explore the neoliberal, neo-colonialist state's "power and … capacity to dictate who may live and who must die … What place is given to life, death and the human body … how are they inscribed in the order of power? (Mbembe 2003:14). By this he is trying to understand the effects of pre-identifying populations as already expected to die, even while still alive, and to explain attacks on bodies in these populations, or as treatment naïve fodder for pharmaceutical trials for drugs they will never use. We can use such analytic concepts to further map and understand what is at stake, how to resist these forms of power and routes for escaping states of expected dying. The contributions in this volume are a reminder that it is not merely the state, or even forms of global governance, that create populations destined to die as soon as they are born, or to be constantly available to science.

"Power, profits and politics" are still the major symbols that are needed to understand biomedicine and all its elements and effects in a neoliberal world. Health/PAC's sense of what this meant nearly half a century ago, however, no longer can be our guide. Power is distributed in multiple ways, what counts as profits cannot be just measured in dollars, and politics has to be understand as beyond the governmental. This volume, with its focus on technoscience, genetics and pharmaceuticals, is an excellent start on the way to map the global transformations in medicine, health and science before us. Justice still beckons in the distance.

Acknowledgments

I am very grateful to Susan E. Bell and Anne E. Figert for their comments and edits in the various drafts of this epilogue. They are consummate editors/ colleagues who made me think and write more clearly, especially as I traversed the history/social science line.

Notes

1 Health/PAC coined the terms medical empire and medical industrial complex (a play on Dwight Eisenhower's label in the mid-1950s of the military industrial complex). While many on the Health/PAC staff contributed to the book, the major editing was done by John and Barbara Ehrenreich.
2 Nancy Cott, in *The Grounding of Modern Feminism* (1989), uses the phrase that the problem for feminism has been to make "gender matter and not matter at the same moment in time." I have borrowed that phrase here.
3 Johann Friedrich Blumenbach was a German physiologist/anatomist (1752–1840) who is known for measuring brains to divide the human race into five races: Caucasian (white), Mongolian (yellow), Malayan (brown), Ethiopian (black) and American (red). He believed that Adam and Eve were originally white and that the other races "devolved." Since the eighteenth century, his terms have appeared and reappeared, especially the use of the word "Caucasian" to mean white. This term was first coined by German philosopher Christoph Meiners and referred to peoples from the Caucasus regions of southern Europe and where Noah's Ark was supposed to have come to rest in mountains of Ararat in what is now Turkey.
4 I am grateful to anthropologist Karen-Sue Taussig for alerting me to this.

References

Anderson, Warwick. 2006. *Colonial Pathologies: American Tropical Medicine, Race, and Hygiene in the Philippines*. Durham, NC: Duke University Press.

Annandale, Ellen and Anne Hammarström. 2011. "Constructing the 'Gender-specific Body': A Critical Discourse Analysis of Publications in the Field of Gender-Specific Medicine." *Health* 15:571–87.

Annandale, Ellen and Anne Hammarström. 2015. "A New Biopolitics of Gender and Health? 'Gender-specific Medicine' and Pharmaceuticalization in the Twenty-First Century." Pp. 41–55 in *Reimagining (Bio)Medicalization, Pharmaceuticals and Genetics: Old Critiques and New Engagements*, edited by Susan E. Bell and Anne E. Figert. New York: Routledge.

Antoniou, Antonis C., Silvia Casadei, Tuomas Heikkinen et al. 2014. "Breast-Cancer Risk in Families with Mutations in *PALB2*." *New England Journal of Medicine* 371:497–506.

Belluz, Julia. 2014. "The Truvada Wars." *British Medical Journal* 348:3811–13.

Benjamin, Ruha. 2015. "Racial Destiny or Dexterity?: The Global Circulation of Genomics as an Empowerment Idiom." Pp. 197–215 in *Reimagining (Bio)Medicalization, Pharmaceuticals and Genetics: Old Critiques and New Engagements*, edited by Susan E. Bell and Anne E. Figert. New York: Routledge.

Biehl, João. 2007. *Will to Live: AIDS Therapies and the Politics of Survival*. Princeton, NJ: Princeton University Press.

Birn, Anne-Emanuelle. 2005. "Gates's Grandest Challenge: Transcending Technology as Public Health Ideology." *The Lancet* 366:514–19.

Bliss, Catherine. 2015. "Biomedicalization and the New Science of Race." Pp. 175–96 in *Reimagining (Bio)Medicalization, Pharmaceuticals and Genetics: Old Critiques and New Engagements*, edited by Susan E. Bell and Anne E. Figert. New York: Routledge.

Chambers, John Whiteclay. 1987. *To Raise an Army: The Draft Comes to Modern America*. New York: Free Press.

Chowkwanyun, Merlin. 2011. "The New Left and Public Health: The Health Policy Advisory Center, Community Organizing, and the Big Business of Health, 1967–1975." *American Journal of Public Health* 101:238–49.

Clarke, Adele, Sara Shostak, Janet Shim and Alondra Nelson. 2009. "Biomedicalizing Genetic Health, Diseases and Identities." Pp. 21–41 in *Handbook of Genetics and Society: Mapping the New Genomic Era*, edited by Paul Atkinson, Peter Glasner and Margaret Lock. London: Routledge.

Cott, Nancy. 1989. *The Grounding of Modern Feminism*. New Haven, CT: Yale University Press.

Crenshaw, Kimberlé W. 1991. "Mapping the Margins: Intersectionality, Identity Politics, and Violence against Women of Color." *Stanford Law Review* 43:1241–99.

Cuthbertson, Courtney A. 2015. "Pharmaceutical Technologies and the Management of Biological Citizens in Chile." Pp. 137–59 in *Reimagining (Bio)Medicalization, Pharmaceuticals and Genetics: Old Critiques and New Engagements*, edited by Susan E. Bell and Anne E. Figert. New York: Routledge.

Davis, Kathy. 2007. *The Making of Our Bodies, Ourselves: How Feminism Travels Across Borders*. Durham, NC: Duke University Press.

Department of Geography, University of Colorado. 2005. "Elements That are Found on Virtually All Maps." Accessed July 12, 2014 (www.colorado.edu/geography/gcraft/notes/cartocom/elements.html).

Dobbs, David. 2014. "The Fault in Our DNA: 'A Troublesome Inheritance' and 'Inheritance.'" *The New York Times* July 10:BR11.

Elliott, Carl. 2014. "The Best-Selling, Billion-Dollar Pills Tested on Homeless People." *Matter* July 28. Accessed July 29, 2014 (https://medium.com/matter/did-big-pharma-test-your-meds-on-homeless-people-a6d8d3fc7dfe).

Epstein, Steven. 2007. *Inclusion: The Politics of Difference in Medical Research*. Chicago, IL: University of Chicago Press.

Forbath, William, with assistance from Zackie Achmat, Geoff Budlender and Mark Heywood. 2011. "Cultural Transformation, Deep Institutional Reform, and ESR Practice: South Africa's Treatment Action Campaign." Pp. 51–90 in *Stones of Hope*, edited by Lucie White and Jeremy Perelman. Palo Alto, CA: Stanford University Press.

Fox Keller, Evelyn. 2010. *The Mirage of a Space between Nature and Nurture*. Durham, NC: Duke University Press.

Greene, Jeremy A. 2015. "Vital Objects: Essential Drugs and Their Critical Legacies." Pp. 89–111 in *Reimagining (Bio)Medicalization, Pharmaceuticals and Genetics: Old Critiques and New Engagements*, edited by Susan E. Bell and Anne E. Figert. New York: Routledge.

Hammonds, Evelynn M. and Rebecca Herzig, eds. 2008. *The Nature of Difference*. Cambridge, MA: MIT Press.

Health/PAC. 1970. *The American Health Empire: Power, Politics and Profits*. New York: Random House.

Hecht, David K. 2015. "Commentary and Reflections: The Lure of the Gene." Pp. 239–47 in *Reimagining (Bio)Medicalization, Pharmaceuticals and Genetics: Old Critiques and New Engagements*, edited by Susan E. Bell and Anne E. Figert. New York: Routledge.

Herzig, Rebecca M. 2015. "Commentary and Reflections: On Stratification and Complexity." Pp. 79–86 in *Reimagining (Bio)Medicalization, Pharmaceuticals and Genetics: Old Critiques and New Engagements*, edited by Susan E. Bell and Anne E. Figert. New York: Routledge.

Kahn, Jonathan. 2013. *Race in a Bottle: The Story of BiDil and Racialized Medicine in a Post-Genomic Era*. New York: Columbia University Press.

Lewontin, Richard C. 1995. "The Apportionment of Human Diversity." *Evolutionary Biology* 6: 381–98.

Lewontin, Richard C. 2011. "It's Even Less in Your Genes." *The New York Review of Books* 58:9.

Maloy, Simon. 2014. "Conservative Media Hysteria Explodes: Muslims! Ebola! A Xenophobic Fiasco." *Salon* July 17. Accessed July 28, 2014 (www.salon.com/2014/07/17/conservative_media_hysteria_explodes_muslims_ebola_a_xenophobic_fiasco/).

Massie, Victoria. 2014. "North Carolina and Genetics: From Sterilization to Research Subjects." *Biopolitical Times*. Accessed October 6, 2014 (www.biopoliticaltimes.org/article.php?id=7976).

Mbembe, Achille. 2003. "Necropolitics." *Public Culture* 15:11–40.

Metzl, Jonathan and Rebecca M. Herzig. 2007. "Medicalisation in the 21st Century: Introduction." *The Lancet* 369:697.

Morning, Ann. 2011. *The Nature of Race: How Scientists Think and Teach about Human Difference*. Berkeley, CA: University of California Press.

Murray, Charles. 2014. "Book Review: 'A Troublesome Inheritance' by Nicholas Wade." *Wall Street Journal* May 2. Accessed July 14, 2014 (http://online.wsj.com/news/articles/SB100014240527023033800045795214822478698 74).

Nelson, Alondra. 2008. "Genetic Genealogy, Testing and the Pursuit of African Ancestry." *Social Studies of Science* 38:759–83.

Nguyen, Vinh-Kim. 2010. *The Republic of Therapy: Triage and Sovereignty in West Africa's Time of AIDS*. Durham, NC: Duke University Press.

Painter, Nell. 2010. *The History of White People*. New York: W. W. Norton & Co.

Patterson, Donna. 2014. "Better Public Education Programs Could Help Stop the Spread of Ebola." *Huffington Post* August 6. Accessed August 6, 2014 (www.huffingtonpost.com/donna-a-patterson/better-public-education-p_b_5655087.html?1407343497).

Petryna, Adriana. 2002. *Life Exposed: Biological Citizens after Chernobyl*. Princeton, NJ: Princeton University Press.

Pollack, Robert and Patricia Williams. 2014. "Who You Really Are." *GeneWatch* 27:529. Accessed July 16, 2014 (www.councilforresponsiblegenetics.org/GeneWatch/GeneWatchPage.aspx?pageId=529).

Reardon, Jenny. 2013. "On the Emergence of Science and Justice." *Science Technology and Human Values* 38:176–200.

Reverby, Susan M. 2008. "Inclusion and Exclusion: The Politics of History, Difference and Medical Research," *Journal of the History of Medicine* 63:103–13.

Reverby, Susan M. 2009. *Examining Tuskegee: The Infamous Syphilis Study and Its Legacy*. Chapel Hill, NC: University of North Carolina Press.

Richardson, Sarah S. 2015. "Maternal Bodies in the Postgenomic Order: Gender and the Explanatory Landscape of Epigenetics." In *Postgenomics*, edited by Sarah S. Richardson and Hallam Stevens. Durham, NC: Duke University Press (in press).

Rosenberg, Tina. 2014. "On AIDS: Three Lessons from Africa." *The New York Times* July 21. Accessed August 4, 2014 (http://opinionator.blogs.nytimes.com/2014/07/31/on-aids-three-lessons-from-africa/).

Samsky, Ari. 2015. "The Drug Swallowers: Scientific Sovereignty and Pharmaceuticalization in Two International Drug Donation Programs." Pp. 112–36 in *Reimagining (Bio)Medicalization, Pharmaceuticals and Genetics: Old Critiques and New Engagements*, edited by Susan E. Bell and Anne E. Figert. New York: Routledge.

Schaefer, G. Owen, Ezekiel J. Emanuel and Alan Wertheimer. 2009. "The Obligation to Participate in Biomedical Research." *Journal of the American Medical Association* 302:67–72.

Shim, Janet K., Katherine Weatherford Darling, Sara L. Ackerman, Sandra Soo-Jin Lee and Robert A. Hiatt. 2015. "Reimagining Race and Ancestry: Biomedicalizing Difference in Post-Genomic Subjects." Pp. 56–78 in *Reimagining (Bio)Medicalization, Pharmaceuticals and Genetics: Old Critiques and New Engagements*, edited by Susan E. Bell and Anne E. Figert. New York: Routledge.

Shostak, Sara and Margot Moinester. 2015. "Beyond Geneticization: Regimes of Perceptibility and the Social Determinants of Health." Pp. 216–39 in *Reimagining (Bio)Medicalization, Pharmaceuticals and Genetics: Old Critiques and New Engagements*, edited by Susan E. Bell and Anne E. Figert. New York: Routledge.

Smith, Leslie L. 2014. "The Missing Link in the HIV Debate: Post-Exposure Prophylaxis?" *HIV Plus Magazine* July 9. Accessed July 18, 2014 (hwww.hivplusmag.com/opinion/2014/07/09/missing-link-hiv-debate-post-exposure-prophylaxis).

Smith, Raymond A. and Patricia D. Siplon. 2006. *Drugs into Bodies*. New York: Praeger Press.

Stepan, Nancy Leys. 1998. "Race, Gender, Science and Citizenship." *Gender & History* 10:26–52.

Susser, Ida and Zena Stein. 2014. "Bio-insecurity and HIV/AIDS." *Open Democracy* 50.50 July 20. Accessed July 21, 2014 (www.opendemocracy.net/5050/ida-susser-zena-stein/bioinsecurity-and-hivaids).

Tomes, Nancy. 2009. "Introduction: Imperial Medicine and Public Health, Bodies as Subjects." Pp. 273–76 in *Colonial Crucible: Empire in the Making of the Modern American State*, edited by Alfred W. McCoy and Francisco A. Scarano. Madison, WI: University of Wisconsin Press.

Wade, Nicholas. 2014a. *A Troublesome Inheritance: Genes, Race and Human History*. New York: The Penguin Press.

Wade, Nicholas. 2014b. "Race Has a Biological Basis: Racism Does Not." *Wall Street Journal* June 22. Accessed July 16, 2014 (http://online.wsj.com/articles/nicholas-wade-race-has-a-biological-basis-racism-does-not-1403476865).

Contributor Biographies

Sara L. Ackerman is a medical anthropologist and Assistant Adjunct Professor in the Department of Social and Behavioral Sciences at the University of California, San Francisco. Her research interests include the uptake and sociocultural implications of new medical technologies, including genomic testing in research and clinical settings.

Ellen Annandale is Professor and Head of Department of Sociology at the University of York, UK. Her recent publications include *The Sociology of Health and Medicine* (2nd edition, Polity Press, 2014), *Women's Health and Social Change* (Routledge, 2009) and the *Palgrave Handbook of Gender and Healthcare*, co-edited with Ellen Kuhlmann (Palgrave, 2012).

Matthew E. Archibald is Assistant Professor of Sociology at Colby College. He studies the delivery of healthcare in the field of behavioral health. His book, *The Evolution of Self-Help* (Palgrave, 2007), centered on informal delivery mechanisms provided by self-help support groups. Currently, he focuses on more formal healthcare provision by examining institutional routines of a hospital psychiatric unit.

Susan E. Bell is A. Myrick Freeman Professor of Social Sciences/Professor of Sociology and Chair of the Department of Sociology and Anthropology, Bowdoin College. She is the author of *DES Daughters: Embodied Knowledge and the Transformation of Women's Health Politics* (Temple University Press, 2009) and the guest editor with Alan Radley of a special issue of *health*, "Another Way of Knowing: Art, Disease, and Illness Experience" (2011).

Ruha Benjamin is Assistant Professor of African American Studies at Princeton University and an honorary international affiliate faculty member at the University of the Witwatersrand Centre for Indian Studies in Africa (CISA). She is author of *People's Science: Bodies and Rights on the Stem Cell Frontier* (Stanford University Press, 2013) and the recipient of numerous grants and awards including the American Council of Learned Societies faculty fellowship.

Catherine Bliss is Assistant Professor of Sociology at the University of California, San Francisco, and author of *Race Decoded: The Genomic Fight for*

Social Justice (Stanford University Press, 2012). Her research explores the sociology of race, gender and sexuality in medicine, with a focus on scientific controversies in genetics.

Peter Conrad is the Harry Coplan Professor of Social Sciences at Brandeis University. He has written widely on medicalization including *Deviance and Medicalization: From Badness to Sickness* (with Joseph W. Schneider; Mosby, 1980) and *The Medicalization of Society: On the Transformation of Human Conditions into Treatable Disorders* (Johns Hopkins University Press, 2007).

Courtney A. Cuthbertson is a postdoctoral fellow at Michigan State University. She received a PhD in sociology from the University of Illinois in 2014. Her research interests include global mental health, biomedicine, sociology of science and sociology of knowledge.

Katherine Weatherford Darling is a doctoral candidate in sociology and a graduate student researcher at University of California, San Francisco. Her dissertation is an ethnography tracing the uses of health information technologies within clinical and policy strategies for managing HIV as a chronic illness in US healthcare.

Anne E. Figert is Associate Professor of Sociology at Loyola University Chicago. She is the author of *Women and the Ownership of PMS: The Structuring of a Psychiatric Disorder* (Aldine de Gruyter, 1996) and the co-editor of two volumes: *Building Community: Social Science in Action* (Pine Forge Press, 1997) and *Current Research on Occupations and Professions*, Vol. 9 (JAI Press, 1996).

Jeremy A. Greene is a historian of medicine with training in medical anthropology and an active clinical practice in a community health center in East Baltimore. His research focuses on the mediation of health and disease through medical technologies, with particular interest in pharmaceuticals, diagnostic technologies and communications media. Greene received his MD and PhD in the history of science from Harvard in 2005, completed a residency in Internal Medicine at the Brigham & Women's Hospital in 2008 and is board certified in Internal Medicine.

Anne Hammarström is Professor of Public Health, focusing on gender research at Umeå University in Sweden. She has published more than 100 articles in international peer-reviewed journals, among them: Hammarström, A., Johansson, K., Annandale, E., Ahlgren, C., Aléx, L., Christianson, M., Elwér, S., Eriksson, C., Fjellman-Wiklund, A. C., Gilenstam, K., Gustafsson, P. E., Harryson, L., Lehti, A., Stenberg, G., Verdonk, P. 2014. "Central Gender Theoretical

Concepts in Health Research – The State of the Art." *Journal of Epidemiology and Community Health* 68(2):185–90.

David K. Hecht is an Assistant Professor of History at Bowdoin College, specializing in the History of Science. His work focuses on public images of science, with a particular focus on nuclear history and environmental history.

Rebecca M. Herzig is Christian A. Johnson Professor of Interdisciplinary Studies and Chair of the Program in Women and Gender Studies at Bates College. Her most recent book is *Plucked: A History of Hair Removal* (New York University Press, 2015).

Robert A. Hiatt is Professor and Chair of the Department of Epidemiology and Biostatistics at the University of California, San Francisco, and the Associate Director for Population Science of the UCSF Comprehensive Cancer Center. His research interests include cancer epidemiology, health services and outcomes research and the social determinants of cancer.

Sandra Soo-Jin Lee is a medical anthropologist at the Stanford Center for Biomedical Ethics and faculty in the Program in Science, Technology and Society at Stanford University. Dr Lee's research interests are in the sociocultural and ethical dimensions of emerging genomic technologies and their translation into biomedical practice.

Margot Moinester is a PhD student in sociology and a doctoral fellow in the Multidisciplinary Program in Inequality and Social Policy at Harvard University. Her research interests include health inequalities, immigration policy and enforcement, and crime and punishment.

Susan M. Reverby is the Marion Butler McLean Professor in the History of Ideas and Professor of Women's and Gender Studies at Wellesley College. Her most recent book was *Examining Tuskegee: The Infamous Syphilis Study and its Legacy* (University of North Carolina Press, 2009). Her current project involves a biography of an American radical doctor who served time as a political prisoner of the USA and went on to be a world-admired HIV/AIDS researcher and global health physician.

Ari Samsky is a cultural anthropologist specializing in medical anthropology and social studies of science. He received a PhD from Princeton University in 2009. His current research investigates the history of yellow fever control in Brazil in the 1930s.

Janet K. Shim is Associate Professor of Sociology at the University of California, San Francisco. Her current research focuses on analyzing the science of health disparities and the production of healthcare inequalities. She is the author of *Heart-Sick: The Politics of Risk, Inequality, and Heart Disease* (New York University Press, 2014).

Sara Shostak is Associate Professor of Sociology and Chair of the Health: Science, Society, and Policy Program at Brandeis University. Her research and teaching interests include the sociology of health and illness, science and technology studies, and environmental sociology. Across these domains, she focuses on how to understand – and address – inequalities in health. Her first book, *Exposed Science: Genes, the Environment, and the Politics of Population Health* (University of California Press, 2013), received the Robert K. Merton Book Award and the Eliot Freidson Outstanding Publication Award.

Index

264